EMOTIONS IN EUROPE 1517–1914

EMOTIONS IN EUROPE 1517–1914

Volume III

Revolutions, 1715–1789

Edited by
Katie Barclay and François Soyer

First published 2021
by Routledge
2 Park Square, Milton Park, Abingdon, Oxon OX14 4RN

and by Routledge
605 Third Avenue, New York, NY 10158

Routledge is an imprint of the Taylor & Francis Group, an informa business

© 2021 selection and editorial matter, Katie Barclay and François Soyer; individual owners retain copyright in their own material.

The right of Katie Barclay and François Soyer to be identified as the author of the editorial material, and of the authors for their individual chapters, has been asserted in accordance with sections 77 and 78 of the Copyright, Designs and Patents Act 1988.

All rights reserved. No part of this book may be reprinted or reproduced or utilised in any form or by any electronic, mechanical, or other means, now known or hereafter invented, including photocopying and recording, or in any information storage or retrieval system, without permission in writing from the publishers.

Trademark notice: Product or corporate names may be trademarks or registered trademarks, and are used only for identification and explanation without intent to infringe.

British Library Cataloguing-in-Publication Data
A catalogue record for this book is available from the British Library

Library of Congress Cataloging-in-Publication Data
A catalog record for this book has been requested

ISBN: 978-0-367-21095-3 (set)
eISBN: 978-0-429-26546-4 (set)
ISBN: 978-1-032-00764-9 (volume III)
eISBN: 978-1-003-17551-3 (volume III)

Typeset in Times New Roman
by Apex CoVantage, LLC

CONTENTS

Acknowledgements	x
List of figures	xi

General introduction	1
Introduction to Volume III	21

PART 1
The self   **27**

1 Charles Johnson, *A General History of the Pyrates, from their Rise and Settlement in the Island of Providence, to the present time* . . .   31

2 Anne-Thérèse de Marguenat de Courcelles (1647–1733), *The Philosophy of Love, or New Reflections on the Fair Sex*   37

3 John Cleland (1709–1789), *Memoirs of a Coxcomb*   43

4 Jean-Jacques Rousseau (1712–1778), *Emilius and Sophia: or, a New System of Education*   49

5 Confession of James Duncan, theft, 1770   55

6 Johannes Ewald (1743–1781), *Life and Opinions (Levnet og Meninger)*   61

7 Sophie von la Roche (1730–1807), *Sophie in London, 1786: being the Diary of Sophie v. la Roche*   69

CONTENTS

8   Olaudah Equiano (1745–1797), *The Life of Olaudah Equiano: or Gustavus Vassa, the African*   75

PART 2
Family and community   **81**

9   Selection of letters from Philip Doddridge (1702–1751) to his wife Mercy Doddridge (1709–1790)   85

10   Series of porcelains   91

11   Criminal indictment of David Young for assaulting his father and mother, 1738   97

12   *The Royal African: or, Memoirs of the Young Prince of Annamaboe*   103

13   David Zeisberger (1721–1808), *Diary of David Zeisberger: a Moravian Missionary among the Indians of Ohio*   109

14   Caroline–Stéphanie–Félicité, Madame de Genlis (1846–1830), *Adelaide and Theodore; or Letters on Education, containing all the Principles relative to Three Different Plans of Education; to that of Princes, and to those of Young Persons of both Sexes*   116

PART 3
Religion   **125**

15   Selection of children's samplers with religious aphorisms   129

16   Erik Pontoppidan (1698–1764), *Truth unto Godliness (Sandhed til Gudfrygtighed)*   135

17   George Brown (c.1715–1779), *Diary of George Brown, Merchant in Glasgow, 1745–53*   146

18   Nicolaus Ludwig von Zizendorf und Pottendorf (1700–1760), *Hymns composed for the Use of the Brethren* (1749), a selection   153

CONTENTS

19 Edward Synge (1659–1741), *Sober Thoughts for the Cure of Melancholy, especially that which is Religious*   160

20 José María Genovese (1681–1757), *The Sacred Heart of the Most Holy Patriarch saint Joseph, venerated for every day of the week* (*El Sagrado Corazon del Santissimo Patriarcha, Sr San Joseph, Venerado por todos los dias de la semana*)   167

21 Elizabeth Cairns (1685–1741), *Memoirs of Elizabeth Cairns*   175

22 Pehr Stenberg (1758–1824), *Diary of Pehr Stenberg: 1758–1784*   181

PART 4
Politics and law   **187**

23 Reuben Thwaites, ed. (1853–1913), *The Jesuit Relations and Allied Documents: Travels and Explorations of the Jesuit Missionaries in New France, 1610–1791: vol. 67 Lower Canada, Abenakis, Louisiana 1716–1727*   191

24 Cesare Bonesana di Beccaria (1738–1794), *An Essay on Crimes and Punishments*   197

25 Adam Ferguson (1723–1816), *An Essay on the History of Civil Society*   204

26 Catherine II (1729–1796), *The Grand Instructions to the Commissioners appointed to frame a New Code of Laws for the Russian Empire*   211

27 Patrick Henry (1736–1799), *Shall Liberty or Empire be Sought?* A speech given on 5 June 1788 at the Virginia Convention to ratify the Constitution of the United States   218

28 Andrew Greenfield (1750–1788), *The Cause and Cure of National Distress: a Sermon*   223

29 John Hawkesworth (1715–1773), *An Account of the Voyages undertaken by the Order of his Present . . .*   230

CONTENTS

PART 5
Science and philosophy   **237**

30   James Blondel (1666–1734), *The Power of the Mother's Imagination over the Foetus*   241

31   Jewish love potion, from a medical recipe book, Italy, 18–19th C   247

32   Martin Engelbrecht (1685–1756), after C. le Brun, collection of etchings of emotions   248

33   Johann Georg Zimmerman (1728–1795), *Solitude*   256

34   Adam Smith (1723–1790), *The Theory of Moral Sentiments*   263

35   John Leake (1729–1792), *Practical Observations towards the Prevention and Cure of Chronic Diseases Peculiar to Women*   270

36   Johann Herder (1744–1803), *Outlines of a Philosophy of a History of Man*   277

37   Louise Florence Pétronille Tardieu d'Esclavelles d'Epigny (1726–1783), *The Conversations of Emily*   283

PART 6
Art and culture   **293**

38   Scottish broadside ballads (c.1720)   297

39   Voltaire [François-Marie Arouet] (1694–1778), 'Poem on the Lisbon Disaster; or an Examination of the Axiom, "All Is Well"'   303

40   Julia Mandeville [Frances Brooke] (1724–1789), *The History of Emily Montague*   310

41   Henry McKenzie (1745–1831), *The Man of Feeling: a Novel*   317

42   Johann Wolfgang von Goethe (1749–1832), *The Sorrows of Werter: a German Story*   324

CONTENTS

43 Charles Avison (1709–1770), *An Essay on Musical Expression*   331

44 Vittorio Alfieri (1749–1803), 'Myrrha', (1786), in *The Tragedies of Vittorio Alfieri: Complete*, ed. Edgar Bowrig   337

45 Series of paintings/prints on theme of 'the love letter'   348

ACKNOWLEDGEMENTS

This project was inspired by our time working together at the Adelaide node of the ARC Centre of Excellence in the History of Emotions, and the collegial and intellectual networks gained from that experience. We would like to thank many of our colleagues in the centre and beyond for the research that highlighted the importance of particular sources, for offering us source material for this collection, for checking translations, and more. We are particularly grateful to: Susan Broomhall; Kirk Essary; Nina Koefoed; Ina Lindblom; Dolly MacKinnon, Una McIlvenna; Dana Rehn; Yann Rodier; Deborah Simonton; Raisa Toivo; Kaarle Wirta; and Ghil'ad Zuckermann. Thanks also to the various archives and collections that have made their materials available for this collection. We also thank our families for their support and patience, particularly during 2020 – a trying year for everyone.

FIGURES

10.1 *Lady and Cavalier*, known as 'The Handkiss', Meissener Porzellan Manufaktur, 1737, porcelain, courtesy of Rijksmuseum, Amsterdam   92

10.2 *Group with a Pedlar* (Herzdosenkauf), Meissener Porzellan Manufaktur, c. 1738, porcelain, courtesy of Rijksmuseum, Amsterdam   92

10.3 *Shepherd Group*, Porzellanmanufaktur Frankenthal, c. 1760, porcelain, courtesy of Rijksmuseum, Amsterdam   93

10.4 *Lovers with a Birdcage*, Meissener Porzellan Manufaktur, 1737, porcelain, The Metropolitan Museum of Art, New York, The Jack and Belle Linsky Collection, 1982   94

10.5 *Couple Drinking Chocolate*, Meissener Porzellan Manufaktur, c. 1744, porcelain, The Metropolitan Museum of Art, New York, The Jack and Belle Linsky Collection, 1982   95

10.6 *The Thrown Kiss*, Meissener Porzellan Manufaktur, ca. 1736, porcelain, The Metropolitan Museum of Art, New York, The Jack and Belle Linsky Collection, 1982   96

15.1 Eighteenth-century British sampler, cotton on linen, The Metropolitan Museum of Art, New York, From the Collection of Mrs. Lathrop Colgate Harper, Bequest of Mabel Herbert Harper, 1957   130

15.2 Martha Wright, British sampler 1719, silk on linen, The Metropolitan Museum of Art, New York, From the Collection of Mrs. Lathrop Colgate Harper, Bequest of Mabel Herbert Harper, 1957   131

15.3 Rebekah Rowe Sampler, charity school, 1731, silk on linen, The Metropolitan Museum of Art, New York, From the Collection of Mrs. Lathrop Colgate Harper, Bequest of Mabel Herbert Harper, 1957   132

15.4 Sarah Pelling, Eighteenth-century British sampler, cotton on linen, The Metropolitan Museum of Art, New York, From the Collection of Mrs. Lathrop Colgate Harper, Bequest of Mabel Herbert Harper, 1957   133

FIGURES

15.5 Eighteenth-century British sampler, wool, The Metropolitan Museum of Art, New York, From the Collection of Mrs. Lathrop Colgate Harper, Bequest of Mabel Herbert Harper, 1957   134

32.1 M. Engelbrecht (1685–1756), Augsburg, after C. Le Brun, *A Bearded Man expressing Scorn*, engraving, 1732, Wellcome Collection. CC BY   249

32.2 M. Engelbrecht (1685–1756), Augsburg, after C. Le Brun, *A Female Face expressing Admiration Tinged with Astonishment*, engraving, 1732, Wellcome Collection. CC BY   250

32.3 M. Engelbrecht (1685–1756), Augsburg, after C. Le Brun, *A Laughing Face,* engraving, 1732, Wellcome Collection. CC BY   251

32.4 M. Engelbrecht (1685–1756), Augsburg, after C. Le Brun, *Head of a Man with Hair Raised, expressing Despair*, engraving, 1732, Wellcome Collection. CC BY   252

32.5 M. Engelbrecht (1685–1756), Augsburg, after C. Le Brun, *The Face of a Man expressing Horror*, engraving, 1732, Wellcome Collection. CC BY   253

32.6 M. Engelbrecht (1685–1756), Augsburg, after C. Le Brun, *A Man Glowering, expressing Hatred or Jealousy*, engraving, 1732, Wellcome Collection. CC BY   254

32.7 M. Engelbrecht (1685–1756), Augsburg, after C. Le Brun, *Face of a Bearded Man expressing Anger*, engraving, 1732, Wellcome Collection. CC BY   255

45.1 Jean-Honoré Fragonar (1732–1806), French, *The Love Letter*, oil on canvas, 1770s, The Metropolitan Museum of Art, New York, The Jules Bache Collection, 1949   349

45.2 François Boucher (1703–1770), French, *The Love Letter*, oil on canvas, 1750, Courtesy National Gallery of Art, Washington   350

45.3 Nicolas Delaunay (1739–92), Swedish, after Nicolas Lavreince, *Le Billet doux*, etching and engraving, 1778, Courtesy National Gallery of Art, Washington   351

45.4 E. J. Dumée (active 1790), British, after George Morland (1763–1804), *The Discovery*, engraving, published by John Raphael Smith, 1788, Yale Centre for British Art   352

45.5 Thomas Rowlandson (1756–1827), *The Love Letter*, watercolour, c.1790, Yale Centre for British Art   353

GENERAL INTRODUCTION

Katie Barclay and François Soyer

The history of emotions is a flourishing field that seeks to understand how emotions, and things that resemble them in historic societies, are defined and categorised in different times and places, and what difference that makes to human experience. Scholars working in this area have come from a range of disciplines – history, art history, music, film studies, theatre, philosophy, literary studies, linguistics, anthropology, sociology, and more – producing an array of studies that deploy a wide variety of sources and methodological approaches. As with other historical topics, there is no single type of source useful for uncovering emotions. Rather emotions, or something like them, can be found in most areas of life and so can be found in all sorts of source materials. This four-volume collection of sources for the history of emotions provides a diverse range of sources that survive for Europe and its empires between 1517 and 1914.

Given the scope of the topic, it cannot hope to capture every type of source, or indeed represent every group. Rather the collection collates a range of sources where emotions, passions, affections and similar experiences were explored or used by individuals and groups, with the goal of providing a resource that acts as a starting point for conducting research in the history of emotions. The sources, grouped into thematic sections, are intended to highlight how emotions might be identified in sources of different periods, and the themes and issues to which emotions scholarship offers insight. There are now several resources that provide methodologies and approaches to working with emotions in historical sources and this collection is designed to be used alongside them, for those seeking to expand their skills and knowledge in this area.[1] This general introduction to the volumes complements this work by offering a brief overview of what the history of emotions is, the way scholarship has developed in the field (especially in relation to the thematic sections that order the collection), some methodologies and approaches that are helpful when working with sources, and finally some insight into the scope and logic of the four volumes. Each volume, divided by historical period, contains its own separate introduction that places its sources in their specific contexts.

GENERAL INTRODUCTION

What is the history of emotions?

What is an emotion? The answer may appear simple: emotions are feelings like love, joy, anger or fear but an emotion has been defined by psychological research variously as a feeling in the body, a mental state that results in a specific physiological reaction and behaviour, or a cognitive judgment caused by a stimulus resulting in an emotion. Emotions have been divided into two categories by contemporary science: 'basic' emotions associated with facial and gestural displays of emotions such as joy, sadness and anger, for example, and 'complex' emotions such as surprise, hate, shame and contempt. Mixed or even seemingly conflicting emotional states have also been identified, for instance fear and awe, or horror and fascination.[2] Nevertheless, there still remains much to learn about emotions and scientists continue to seek to understand their origins and how they relate to the body. A comprehensive review of the existing scientific data produced by neuroscientists recently concluded that there exists little concrete evidence proving that emotion categories originate in a particular section or area of the brain, but how they are produced through the body is still a topic of exploration.[3] Whilst historians of emotions are interested in emotions as such and how they have been understood at different historical moments, their focus extends further to consider another question: how have emotions shaped individuals, societies and cultures in the past?

Compared to other historical methodologies, the history of emotions is a relatively recent development. In the first half of the twentieth century, a number of eminent scholars pointed to the significance of emotions as drivers of historical change. Seeking to account for the rise of Nazism, the French historian Lucien Febvre encouraged his fellow historians to study emotions and the 'irrational', what he termed the history of 'sensibility' (*sensibilité*). Febvre passionately argued in 1941 that 'the emotional life [is] always ready to overflow into the intellectual life . . . [; people might say:] The history of hate, the history of fear, the history of cruelty, the history of love; stop bothering us with this unexciting literature! But that unexciting literature [. . .] will tomorrow have turned the universe into a fetid charnel house'.[4] Even before Febvre, Johan Huizinga and Nobert Elias were influenced by Freudian psychoanalysis to assign a major role to emotions in a perceived shift from the medieval to the modern period. Elias, in particular, perceived the change from a Middle Ages characterised by anger and violence to a more genteel modern period as part of a 'civilising process' driven by the emotion of shame.[5]

Whilst such early theories about the role of emotions in historical change are now subject to considerable critique among historians, the history of emotions continues to thrive as a historical methodology. Research monographs, edited collections of chapters and peer-reviewed articles on topics related to the emotions in history are appearing in seemingly ever-increasing numbers.[6] Research institutes devoted to the history of emotions have appeared in Europe and Australia. Historians have increasingly engaged in interdisciplinary collaboration with

GENERAL INTRODUCTION

neuroscientists and psychologists to further our understanding of emotions or mental states as part of a broader biocultural historicism.

Since the 1980s, the historians Peter and Carol Stearns, Barbara Rosenwein and William Reddy have authored influential studies and elaborated concepts that have helped to shape the History of Emotions. The Stearnses coined the term 'emotionology' to define 'the attitudes or standards that a society, or a definable group within society, maintains towards basic emotions, and their appropriate expression; ways that institutions reflect and encourage these attitudes in human conduct'.[7] Their published work on the emotionology of anger in the history of the United States has provided scholars with an exemplar and provoked debate about the possible class bias in that work's use of primary sources.[8] Barbara Rosenwein, on the other hand, has critiqued the emphasis on standards in emotionology and focused instead on the concept of 'emotional communities', groups of individuals bound together by 'systems of feeling' where emotions are understood and valued, or not, in the same way.[9] Such emotional communities, Rosenwein contends, can be identified through a careful analysis of written texts. Finally, Reddy pioneered the concept of 'emotional regimes', which he defined as a set of normative emotions as well as the official rituals, practices and emotional expressions that are used to express and inculcate them.[10]

Historians of emotions are confronted by, and seek to come to grips with, important and challenging questions about the nature of emotions. Are emotions universal mental states, which is to say biological and identical among all humans? Are they socially and culturally constructed, and therefore shaped by an individual's specific cultural and/or social background? In her work on the emotion of fear, the historian Joanna Bourke has noted the complexity of this issue.

> Fear is *felt*, and although the emotion of fear cannot be reduced to the sensation of fear, nevertheless, it is not present without sensation. In noting that the body is not simply a shell through which emotions are expressed, the social contructivists are correct. Discourse shapes bodies. However, bodies also shape discourse: people are 'weak or pale with fright', 'paralysed by fear' and 'chilled by terror.' The feeling of fear may be independent of social construction, a one-sided process. [. . .] Nevertheless, emotions are fundamentally constituted.[11]

To the thorny issue of nature versus nurture can be added even more questions. Are emotions shaped by time and place? Did a sixteenth-century European experience love, anger or fear differently from a twentieth-century European? Did the words used in past centuries to convey mental states have the same meanings when compared to those used today, even when those words are the same ones? How did the meanings attached to words shape the experience of emotion and vice versa? Finally, to what extent are emotions really drivers of political, religious, cultural and social change?

3

GENERAL INTRODUCTION

To answer these questions, or at least to formulate theories that could help us answer them and challenge many assumptions about emotions in the past, historians of emotions work with a wide variety of source evidence: words (texts/poetry), pictures (paintings, movies, posters), sound (effect of music on people). They search for, and analyse 'emotives' (expressions that produce emotions), 'emotional habitus' (the embodied, partly unconscious emotional disposition of a group) and 'emotional practices' (the things that we do to produce emotion, involving the self (as body and mind), language, material artefacts, the environment and other people). It is perhaps unsurprising that, given the diverse range of sources used, the history of emotions gathers together historians with a remarkable variety of approaches. Some historians analyse 'emotion words' and how they changed.[12] Other scholars have explored the history of medicine and ideas for evidence of changes in the way that people understood emotions and body to be related or how people practiced emotions in everyday life in a variety of different contexts (for instance in religious and political rituals, in private writings or in courtrooms). Some historians of the emotions have focused their research on a historical analysis of emotional norms and rules. More recently, the methodological spectrum of the history of emotions has expanded to include performative, constructivist and practice theory approaches.[13]

Whilst the history of emotions seeks to study the emotions of individuals in the past, it also seeks to foster a better understanding of what can be termed 'collective emotions' in history. This is a particularly problematic subject. 'Mental structuralists' such as Sigmund Freud (1856–1939) and Carl Jung (1875–1961) accepted the existence of a collective unconscious and they thus contended that collective mental states could influence individuals. For these early psychologists, there existed 'universals' and 'archetypes' of the human mind that, like instincts, could trigger such collective mental states. Examples of such 'collective mental states' were 'war fever' or the collective love for the leader that seems to power personality cults.[14] More recently, some psychologists have interpreted collective emotional states as a form of mass sociogenic illness: a medical condition similarly affecting numerous individuals within a wider group.[15] Yet the concept of a collective mental state is problematic for historians since it is difficult to obtain conclusive primary source evidence supporting the notion that individuals who appear to be involved in a 'collective mental state' actually experience the same emotion.[16]

Even though it is difficult to establish the existence of collective mental states using historical primary source evidence, there can be no doubt that those who exercise power in human societies have believed in their existence and sought to foster or enforce such collective emotional states. Historians of emotions have elaborated upon this concept by examining the role that emotions have played in the formation of communal identities or 'emotional communities'. In his work on the emotions, the historian and anthropologist Reddy has coined the phrase 'emotional regimes' to describe such a situation, in which 'any enduring political *regime* must establish as an essential element a normative order for *emotions*'.[17] This is particularly significant for historians studying Europe in the period covered by these four volumes, which witnessed the rise of national states and national identities against the context of the Reformation, imperial expansion, Absolutism, the Enlightenment and the Industrial Revolution. Between 1517 and 1914, secular and religious authorities invested considerable resources and efforts into attempts to shape the emotions of their subjects to bring about (or alternatively to prevent) social, religious or political change.

The centuries covered in the first and second volumes of this sourcebook witnessed the growth of the modern European state system and what historians have described as the process of 'confessionalisation'.[18] Across both Catholic and Protestant Europe, rulers sought to secure the unity and loyalty of their subjects, and therefore their hold on power, by promoting among them a homogeneity of religious belief. By way of illustration, the Jesuit theologian and political theorist Juan de Mariana argued in his 1599 Latin treatise on royal government that a shared faith was the only 'social bond' (*societatis vinculum*) that could maintain social order in a kingdom and that lack of religious unity was a path that would inevitably lead to anarchy.[19] Emotions such as love, fear, hatred and disgust were (and are) crucial to defining who belongs within a religious community and who does not, and so played a significant role in how this 'social bond' of faith was understood. Moreover, the period covered by the third and fourth volumes saw the rise of national identities and nation-states. In 1983, Benedict Anderson published *Imagined Communities: Reflections on the Origin and Spread of Nationalism*, arguing that the origins of modern nationalism are to be found in mass vernacular literacy, the movement to abolish the ideas of rule by divine right and hereditary monarchy and the emergence of printing press capitalism.[20] Historians of emotion will add to this that it is impossible to understand national identities as anything but emotional communities sustained by ritual practices and supposed cultural and/or ethnic affinities. Indeed, what are national communities if not emotional communities? As this example suggests, collective emotions are important, not only because they move emotion from the personal to the social, but because they are therefore central to explaining historical change. In this sense, emotions are not just interesting experiences that provide insight into the intersection between the biological and the cultural but key to a broad range of historical subfields and themes.

Historical emotions

A scholarship on the history of emotions is growing rapidly across time and increasingly around the globe. Doing justice to such a diversity of work and the sources they deploy is beyond the scope of a single source compilation, and so this collection settled on Europe and its empire between 1517 and 1914. This in part reflects that this period has now a rich and established secondary literature on the topic, that has in many ways led the field, marked now in a range of general introductions and surveys to this topic.[21] This is particularly the case when we turn to the themes used to organise the collection: the self, family and community, religion, politics and law, science and philosophy, and art and culture. Viewed through these lenses, the role of emotion in biological and personal experience is significant, but as central is how the study of emotions brings insight into the operations of groups and societies, to the exercise of power, to systems of belief and values, to the production of knowledge and ideas, and to human expression in its diverse forms.

Both emotions and the 'self' are relatively novel concepts used to explore the human as a sensate and self-reflective creature. Yet if such labels have emerged only in the last few centuries, nonetheless Europeans have attended to what makes the person, including explorations of mind and body, emotions, passions and affections, motivation and will, intention, and many other similar concepts that seek to locate what makes the human. The history of emotions has contributed to a broader conversation about the nature of the self in different historical moments, whilst drawing attention to the important role that emotions have played in shaping concepts like will, motivation, morality, judgements, imagination and the capacity of the body to interpret information.[22] Mental health and illness has been significant to discussions here, where 'disordered' emotions have not only caused people distressing symptoms but also been used as mechanisms of control and exclusion of those whose emotional world is seen as disruptive or disorderly.[23] Over 400 years and the various language groups that distinguish Europe, historians have drawn attention to the various words associated the self and emotion, explaining what they mean in context, and how they have developed over time. Significant here has been a history of passions, affections and later emotions themselves, all concepts with distinct meanings in different times and places, as well as the history of how people experience individual emotions like melancholy, jealousy, love or compassion.

As well as exploring ideas about the self, historians have also sought to explore how they were applied in everyday life or in specific contexts, like the practice of the faith, or by people of different genders, races or even ages. Words and ideas change over time, and so has how these knowledges shaped individual behaviours. Emotions are also things that people have sought to manage in various ways, using a range of tools to train the self to feel and so behave in different ways. An interest in emotion management has placed significant attention on the history of prescriptive and self-help literature, a form that existed across this period if changing in style and the nature of advice given.[24] However, perhaps the predominant source to which a history of the self and emotion has drawn attention has been what are called 'narratives of self', the diaries, letters, oral histories and other forms of personal testimony where people offered an accounting of the self. If prescriptive literature sees some significant continuities, narratives of self can vary enormously over time. Diaries are rare in the sixteenth century, but expand dramatically in the following centuries. Letters are an ancient form, but survival rates for different groups vary enormously, limiting whose voices are heard, and their uses evolve. Oral histories and similar data are a product of new scientific collecting activities from the late nineteenth century onwards. Such technologies, and how they were produced, shape the selves that could be narrated and so a rich vein of scholarship explores how such accounts relate to the embodied experience of emotion by individuals.[25]

Personal experiences of emotions, as this might suggest, are closely associated with ideas about what emotions are and how they work. Prescriptive literature provided a useful source of information about how such ideas were communicated to ordinary people, as does a history of religious teachings. But to understand how knowledge about emotion was developed and changed over time, historians have tended to turn to a formal body of religious, philosophic and scientific writings. Much of this work was produced in formal 'academic' contexts, such as the theological writings of monks, the philosophical texts of academics, or the experiments produced by scientists in laboratories, and so reflects the ideas of those who had access to education, time to write and think, and means of publishing their ideas. When these ideas are compared, however, it is possible to chart a trajectory of changing ideas about the mind, body and emotion, as the emotions moved from the sphere of religious life to a secular philosophy and eventually to the laboratory. Here historians have emphasised both changes from passions and affections to modern categories of emotion, and new ideas of the body as the humoural model declined in favour of vitalities, nerves, senses and so forth.[26]

For all of the period 1517 to 1914, a focus on formal scholarship gave especial authority to the ideas of men, and typically elite and highly educated men, about emotion, with implications for the knowledge produced. As a number of scholars have shown, ideas about emotion were often used to delimitate women as especially emotional or irrational, and so to limit their role in public life. Increasingly, especially with imperial expansion, similar stereotypical beliefs were applied to other racial groups, where emotional expression was often used to categorise people as 'civilised' or otherwise. This picture should not be overstated. In all periods, a small number of elite women or ethnic minorities –a group that grew with every century – tried to intervene in such conversations, not least to counter their own oppression. In some areas, like education and child development, they even became particularly influential.[27]

Historians seeking to widen this conversation on what emotion is in particular contexts have therefore sought to expand definitions of what counts as formal knowledge about emotion. This has included looking at branches of knowledge that were influential at the time, but later discredited and therefore underplayed in formal histories of science and medicine. An important example here is the nineteenth-century practice of phrenology, a quack science but extremely popular during the period.[28] Folk knowledges and practices also offer suggestive potential, although remaining an understudied area of research for emotions.[29] The knowledges and beliefs of minority groups provide insight into subcultures or alternative systems of information. Significantly, such histories often bring a broader range of voices – those of women, minority groups, different cultures – into sight, not only democratising scholarship but highlighting how ideas that we later, in hindsight, recognise as important competed with a rich diversity of others during particular historical periods.

As this might suggest, ideas about emotions are produced by groups and societies. This idea has been especially critical for historians of emotion who have understood the experience of emotion to be shaped not only by formal knowledges of how the body works but by socially agreed ideas and norms about how, when and by whom emotion should be expressed, what that looks like on the body, whether such emotion is moral or immoral, 'negative' or 'positive', how others should respond to such emotional expression, and so forth. The practice or performance of emotion for most historians is understood as socially-constituted and so therefore informed by the culture and society in which it is experienced. Emotion is also an experience that mediates the relationship within the group. Family is here perhaps a central unit, which for all of the period of this study in Europe was expected to be a site of emotion. Family members were expected to love one another, and show associated emotions that might include loyalty, obedience, trust, compassion and care; family members, ideally at least, should conversely not experience anger or hate towards one another. In practice, as a range of historians show, family was a location where people felt and expressed the full gamut of emotional experience available in any given period, and where the expression and experience of such emotion was informed by cultural ideas about what was appropriate or otherwise, as well as what an emotion – say love – meant.[30] Familial emotions were also influenced by changing ideas about the role of family within philosophical and scientific writings, where parental love became a critical emotion that ensured the survival of the species and where child-rearing practices produced the emotionally mature adult.[31]

A key idea in the scholarship of emotions is that some emotions are especially 'social' and so designed to mediate group relationships, through providing an emotional connection between individuals. Significant emotions here include love, especially *caritas* or neighbourly love, compassion, pity, sympathy and later empathy. Different terms held different resonances at particular historic moments, but they share the quality of allowing, to greater or lesser degree, for people to commiserate with another and so to encourage people to act together to relieve suffering or reduce harm.[32] For contemporary scientists, such feeling has biological value in ensuring human survival, but other periods too prized such feeling as especially moral or ethical. If this is the case, emotion could also be anti-social, with selfish and competitive feelings placing people in competition, sometimes encouraging violence or conflict.[33] Following the lead of these variously sociable emotions, historians, then, have been especially interested in exploring the role of emotion in different group activities, as well as how these were informed by specific contexts.

In many respects, a scholarship on religious emotion and another on law and politics are a subset of these larger questions around group feeling. Emotion has long been significant to religion in Europe, where the experience of the divine, or of moral rectitude, was understood as an embodied experience. As a result, people engaged in a range of activities to try and produce certain feelings associated with the divine, such as joy or peace, or to avoid those that were associated with sin, like anger or lust. These might include personal devotional practices, including prayer, worship, keeping a spiritual diary, acts of charity, reading and many others. They also included group events and rituals, such as attending religious services, group singing and worship, listening to a sermon, reading or teaching, prayer, religious processions and engaging in ritual practices.[34] Some environments, like churches, were designed to promote religious devotion, through their architecture, but also by including moving paintings of religious scenes designed to direct the emotions of their audiences.[35] Religious rituals have often been of special interest to historians because they were designed to shape emotional experience, not simply through imagination or ideas, but through embodied practices, such as moving the body, eating or fasting, mortifications of the flesh or similar visceral experiences.[36] Thus, a history of religious ritual has provided important insight not only into a key part of the lives of most people during the period 1517 to 1914 and how that changed over time, but also to how people imagined emotions to operate in general.

Religious rituals and experiences were also critical to group dynamics. Not only did religious identities fragment and reform repeatedly in the centuries under study here, but they were key to the formation of communities and their boundaries. Thus religious practices were often designed to consolidate the group – inducing feeling as part of a group activity was designed to consolidate affective connections within the community and to reinforce a sense of cohesiveness. In this sense, religious practice often overlapped significantly with political identities, and indeed many states and their monarch co-opted religious rituals to consolidate their own power. For example, a king might hold public baptisms of converts to reinforce his own authority. As this suggests, many rulers across this period were acutely aware of the importance of deploying rituals to produce political and group identities, including that of the nation itself.[37] Increasingly these activities were designed to bring together diverse communities, whether that was people of various religions, of different languages and regions, or – and especially as Europeans moved aggressively into the rest of the globe – people of different races and cultures. Yet, these were not the only political tools available. Propaganda, political writings, speeches and other forms of rhetoric were all designed to persuade individuals and groups of the nature of authority and its appropriate seat.[38]

More broadly, and following Reddy's lead, the polity itself could be defined by the experience and valuation of emotion, where emotions viewed as wrong or antisocial could be prohibited in law or discouraged through less formal mechanisms, like shunning. Thus a history of emotions has attended to how the management and control of emotion has been used to produce power relationships, and their role in acts of resistance and negotiation.[39] The role of emotions in the law is a growing field, not least in Anglophone contexts where the law was seen to be the rational counterpart to feeling.[40] Who could experience particular emotions, or indeed control their emotions, has also been explored as a site of contest for social groups limited from power due to their supposed emotionality. Thus women used claims to their rationality to gain access to political power, and enslaved people highlighted their sensibility to argue for human rights. Emotions have played an important role in the history of rights-making, with social emotions like empathy seen to be deployed to persuade people to expand rights.[41] Conversely, such humanitarian emotions have also vested power in some groups, like the middle class or imperial authorities, over those who they are seen to 'help' or 'care for', like the poor or indigenous communities.[42]

If emotions are implicated in the production of power and the oppression of individuals and groups, their significance to communication meant they could also be critical to art and culture, where people sought to describe, imagine, reinvent and encourage humanity, including their feelings. In European culture, the efficacy of most formal art forms, not unlike religious belief, has been related to its capacity to move an audience. Some types of art were expressly designed with this purpose, while by the nineteenth century, philosophers were exploring art as emotion itself. Instrumental music was considered a special form of art, situated outside of language; for some eighteenth-century philosophers, music was the original mechanism for communicating before the invention of language – here people used the capacity of music to move people as a form of communication.[43]

Across the period covered in these volumes, people explored how to effectively represent human emotions in different art forms – whether on the body in paintings or in ways that 'felt' real to readers of novels. Art could also provide a pedagogic function, whether in encouraging religious devotion and so godly feeling, or in providing examples of emotional behaviour that people could use to expand their emotional range.[44] As a result, art and culture has been used by historians of emotions not only to further our understanding of emotion in the realm of creative life but also for its insights into how communities imagined emotions to work in a range of contexts. Paintings of emotional expression on faces and bodies provide evidence of emotional gestures and expressions; instructions for expressive dance or the stage highlight how people should move or gesture to display emotion; the elaborate scenes described in novels provide insight into how people imagined emotions to work in particular contexts, such as courtship or during a riot. If art and literature requires to be explored sensitively – like fiction today, not all art was meant to reflect 'real' life – it nonetheless can provide access to a range of human experiences that often don't survive elsewhere.

Art and culture are an area where significant variations and inventions in genre can be traced over time. Thus, styles in portraiture evolve significantly, sometimes for technical reasons (e.g., new paints are invented) and sometimes because artistic fashions change; expressive writing adapts, with poetry and drama moving aside for an increase in prose works. The expansion of some art forms, like drama or music, reflect that these practices moved outside the field of religious practice into more everyday cultural expressions. Explorations of art and culture therefore raise particularly interesting questions for historians as to the role of genre in shaping the expression of emotion, and where the historian has to ask whether a change in a description of emotion reflected changing social practice or simply the evolution of artistic style and its associated emotional expression. Yet, if art and culture perhaps highlight such questions, such issues are pertinent for all sources. Thus, if a wide secondary literature in this field highlights the exciting range of directions that research can take in this field, new historians also want to ensure they approach their sources with appropriate concepts, methods and theories.

Sources and methods

As a form of historical research, the history of emotions shares many methodological concerns with the rest of the field, where primary sources – the data that survives from a period which we wish to understand – are the critical building blocks for our debates and arguments. Therefore, like all historians, we attend to the conditions in which a source was produced and survived. This means asking who made it, for what purpose, and why did it survive, and then using these insights to inform our analysis of it as a piece of evidence. Yet, the history of emotions also raises novel issues – what does it mean to look for emotion in historical material, what counts as evidence of emotion, and how do we know when we have found it? Emotion, perhaps especially as something ephemeral, has therefore required the development of a range of concepts, methodologies and approaches to aid source interpretation.[45]

Perhaps the earliest approaches to the history of emotion focused on what might be called the history of science and medicine – of the development of the modern concept of emotion and its history. Where texts used this language and largely reflected ideas that the modern reader is used to today, this was a relatively straightforward exercise – scholars looked for the words and ideas that we recognised as related to emotion and explored how thinkers developed them. Moving backwards in time to the predecessors of such concepts was more fraught. How does a historian decide what to place in the 'category' of 'emotion'? Passions and affections seem to describe similar concepts to emotions – they are embodied experiences – but they arise from a very different model of biology and contain elements that we would not recognise as part of emotion today. The decision to include passion and affection in the category of emotion was therefore a choice made by scholars today and one that another scholar might dispute or argue about. We might feel comfortable with that choice, but such decisions raise important questions about categorisation, especially across time and culture. At some level, we make connections between ideas or words because we think the overlap is close enough, not because it is perfect.

In the history of emotions, this has led to one of our most significant debates – can we truly compare emotions? On the one hand, most historians accept that if we are to be a 'field' – a group of people engaged in a conversation on the same topic – then we're going to have to be happy with a capacious category called emotion. However, we are less happy that it is useful to compare, say, anger with *ire* or *choler*. Some historians, rather, emphasise that cultural concepts associated with emotion should be interpreted strictly in context and comparisons kept to a minimum. Others, especially those interested in change over time, argue that if we are to create a *history* of emotion that such comparisons are required, even if we recognise their flexibility.[46] For scholars who ultimately believe the body is universal across cultures, they also see such comparisons as helpful at capturing shared experiences across human cultures. One of the first things a historian of emotion has to decide, therefore, is what they are studying in the past and how that relates to contemporary concepts, and so the study of emotion often begins with defining the categories of research quite closely.

Often the first place to begin an exploration of emotion is by identifying emotion words in sources and then building up a 'corpus' or body of emotion words. Today, with the availability of academic dictionaries, a scholar starting out has a significant advantage in identifying such words. If the vocabulary might be different from today's, nonetheless the process of looking for the words would be similar to now. The historian closely reads their material, looking for emotional words, where they appear, why, and their impacts, and from that begins to understand what they mean. Importantly, not all emotion words relate to an emotional concept – like love or hate; rather, sometimes emotion words are words that have emotional effects in particular cultures. An example today might be child or terrorist, where the usage of such a term brings with it rich affective connotations that 'move' the reader or produce emotion. If these might be less obvious to a new historian, nonetheless the principle of identifying them through a close reading of the material and trying to understand their rhetorical impact remains the same.

Such an approach is particularly useful for identifying and understanding particular emotional concepts, like love or hate. But historians might also be interested in why such words are being used in that particular source material and the intended effect of such writing. Here we might ask ourselves why a person was writing and what they wanted to achieve by doing so. Was this a personal spiritual diary designed for them to reflect on their relationship with God and therefore bring themselves closer to the divine? Or was this a political pamphlet designed to persuade a reader to a revolutionary action? Understanding the relationship between emotion words and their uses for particular purposes can help us better understand how emotions are meant to work in a particular culture. For example, if a spiritual diary described grief at personal sin at considerable length, then we might learn about the importance of the emotions of contrition to becoming closer to God. Similarly, if a political pamphlet used the word love repeatedly to persuade people to a cause, we might better understand how people were meant to feel about the revolutionary cause in which they engaged. Sometimes we find unexpected emotions in such places, challenging our own modern ideas about the role of emotions in everyday life, or indeed see how emotions that no longer exist were used in historical context.

This sort of exploration can be especially important for historians of emotion who are less interested in tracing meanings and ideas about particular emotions than in understanding what role emotion played in social, economic, political, and intimate life. Here the historian might be less interested in the exact emotion being produced than in how emotions are engaged in social action. Thus a historian might read a source with the goal of understanding its intended impact on an audience, and look for the emotional effects of a source. Doing so might mean exploring the place of emotion in texts that contain very few 'emotion words' (like love and hate) but still have rhetorical impact. It also opens up a history of source materials that do not contain writing – material goods, buildings, landscapes. Historians may, for example, study a cathedral to explore how its design and features were intended to produce particular feelings in a person; similarly, they might consider how goods were exchanged in courtship or where clothing was worn to mark that a person was grieving. Here the physical and material world might become part of how people 'do' emotion and so useful for helping us access such experiences.

Not all emotional experiences are immediately apparent in source material, especially when we are looking at societies very different from our own. And so historians have also developed a set of tools or concepts to help us identify emotions in source material. Such tools might be understood as a set of lenses that help us see things we might otherwise not have noticed, or ways of defining emotions that lets us recognise them in very different cultures. As noted above, these include 'emotional communities', 'emotional regimes' and 'emotional practices', alongside others like 'emotional economies', 'affective atmospheres' and 'emotional arenas'.[47] Each of these concepts has been defined by emotions theorists for use when approaching our sources, and they are helpful because they allow us to see where emotions might be operating between individuals or within groups. For example, 'affective atmospheres' describes the way that environments can shape human behaviour and emotion to produce collective feelings or group connectedness. A historian might therefore have a source where people at a pop concert all become overwhelmed by the experience, and can identify this experience as 'emotional' because it is explained by the idea of affective atmospheres. Another historian might find 'emotional economies' useful for highlighting how emotions, like hate, stick to people or things, and so inform how they are treated by others. An example here might be hatred towards migrants that 'sticks' to them so they are abused or assaulted in the street. A historian seeing a description of such an event might recognise that emotions were in operation in such an experience because the idea of 'emotional economies' helps them interpret what they have encountered.

There are many such tools available and other resources that explain them and how they might be used with historical sources. Some more traditional historical tools – like the lenses of gender, race and class – might also be helpful in aiding analyses. Were emotions expected to, or indeed did they, vary across social groups? The sources chosen for these volumes have been selected for those coming to the study of emotions with no prior learning. However, it may be that further reading on emotions concepts might enable new or different readings of the sources in this volume, and readers may wish to experiment and explore how applying such ideas enriches understanding of the material.

GENERAL INTRODUCTION

Emotions in Europe 1517–1914

The editors have chosen to separate this sourcebook into four volumes. Volume 1 spans the period between 1517 and 1602; Volume 2 between 1603 and 1714; Volume 3 between 1715 and 1789; Volume 4 between 1790 and 1914. Historical periodisation is always subjective and the editors recognise the choice of dates to divide these volumes might appear to be arbitrary to some readers. It is impossible to pinpoint precise dates in early modern history as marking 'turning-points' in the history of emotions. Martin Luther's publication of his *Ninety-Five Theses* in 1517, the establishment of the Dutch East Indies Company (1602), the end of the War of the Spanish Succession (1714), the start of the French Revolution (1789) and the start of the First World War (1914) are all watersheds in European history. These events caused political, religious, social and cultural upheavals and developments in the early modern and modern periods that also affected the way that Europeans thought and wrote about emotions. As such, it is more profitable to consider that these four volumes correspond roughly to the sixteenth, seventeenth, eighteenth and nineteenth centuries.

In the sixteenth century, the impact of the reclamation of Greco-Roman culture and art as a result of the Renaissance can be seen in the influence of ancient authors on texts written about the emotions. Yet the Protestant Reformation, and the Catholic response to it in the decades that followed it, also had a major influence on the way that emotions were discussed in relation to faith and presented in texts and artworks produced in Europe. Emotions were understood to be central to a heartfelt religious experience. Moreover, the propaganda produced by both sides sought to exploit emotions and emotional reactions through ridiculous caricatures of the beliefs of others, narratives of victimhood and scenes of horrifying violence.

Religious and political conflicts continued to plague Europe during the 'General Crisis' of the seventeenth century, but it was nonetheless also a century of intellectual exploration and discovery. The works of 'natural philosophers' (scientists) led to major breakthroughs in the way that Europeans understood the human body, the universe and the natural world. Some writers challenged ancient theories that linked emotions and the 'bodily humours' to contend instead that the 'passions' were the direct result of mechanical processes within the brain. Moreover, philosophers like Thomas Hobbes, Baruch Spinoza, René Descartes and many others laid the foundations of the Enlightenment. They examined 'the human passions' as types of emotion that are internal to the body and connected to the will as well as seeking to understand their effects on human society.

In the eighteenth century, European attitudes towards emotions were increasingly affected by what can be described as a 'cult' of emotion, the 'culture of sensibility', originating in the idea that the body gained knowledge through the senses. The shift from humoural explanations of emotions in scientific texts, which had begun in the previous century, rapidly gathered pace as writers now increasingly favoured explanations that presented the body as mechanical and sensate. Influenced by philosophical and scientific writings, the culture of 'sensibility' had a

14

lasting impact among the literary classes as well as across the whole of society. It is probably best known through the way that the culture of sensibility developed an English-language literary movement, especially in the emerging genre of the novel.

Finally, in the nineteenth century, the way that Europeans understood emotions was also being changed by new sciences of the body, including evolutionary theories, with particular importance being given to 'nature' as a cause of emotional behaviour. At the same time, however, psychologists were also seeking to explain human emotions as the result of cultural influences as well as biological drivers. The rise of nation-states and nationalism led to the search for emotional communities marked by a 'love' of the country/nation, anger and hatred directed at other national groups and sorrow and melancholy over real as well as perceived national slights and grievances. Rituals, artworks, songs and symbols – such as national anthems, flags or patriotic songs – were created to support these emerging national emotional communities.

The editors hope that the readers – both students and scholars – will come to appreciate how the variety of sources in these volumes illustrate the complex history of emotions in Europe across the four centuries that separate 1517 and 1914. Readers should note that, with the exception of those sources translated into English, the texts contained in these volumes are offered with the original non-standardised spellings and some abbreviations. Where words and quotations are italicized, bold or underlined in the original documents, these have been carried over here. When we have varied from the original, this has been indicated at the appropriate point in the text. Inevitably, when comparing sources over the centuries, there is both continuity and change; continuity, for example, in terms of how emotions were deployed to incite love and hate, anger and sorrow but also considerable change in the way that Europeans explained the existence of emotions and sought to understand their significance. Today questions and debates about the nature of emotions continue to be relevant and exercise the minds of neurologists, psychologists, sociologists and historians. The texts contained in these volumes serve as a reminder that we need to consider such questions about emotions within a wider historical context than just the late twentieth or early twenty-first century.

Notes

1 Katie Barclay, *A History of Emotions: A Guide to Sources and Methods* (Basingstoke: Palgrave Macmillan, 2020); Katie Barclay, Sharon Crozier-De Rosa, and Peter Stearns, eds, *Sources for the History of Emotions: A Guide* (London: Routledge, 2020); Jan Plamper, *The History of Emotions: An Introduction* (Oxford: Oxford University Press, 2015); Rob Boddice, *The History of Emotions* (Manchester: Manchester University Press, 2018); Barbara H. Rosenwein and Riccardo Cristiani, *What Is the History of Emotions* (London: Wiley, 2017).

2 Bradley Irish, 'A Strategic Compromise: Universality, Interdisciplinarity, and the Case for Modal Emotions in History of Emotion Research', *Emotions: History, Culture, Society* 4, no. 1 (2020): 231–251.

GENERAL INTRODUCTION

3 Kristen A. Lindquist, Tor D. Wager, Hedy Kober, Eliza Bliss-Moreau and Lisa Feldman Barrett, 'The Brain Basis of Emotion: A Meta-analytic Review', *Behavioral and Brain Sciences* 35 (2012): 121–202.

4 Lucien Febvre, 'La sensibilité et l'histoire: Comment reconstituer la vie affective d'autrefois?', *Annales d'histoire sociale* 3 (1941): 5–20

5 Norbert Elias, *The Civilizing Process* (Oxford: Blackwell, 1994).

6 An excellent bibliography for the history of emotions can be found at the ARC Centre of Excellence in the History of Emotions website: www.zotero.org/groups/300219/che_bibliography_history_of_emotions, accessed 22 November 2020.

7 Peter N. Stearns and Carol Z. Stearns, 'Emotionology: Clarifying the History of the Emotions and Emotional Standards', *American Historical Review* 90, no. 4 (1985): 813–836.

8 Carol Z. Stearns and Peter N. Stearns, *Anger: The Struggle for Emotional Control in America's History* (Chicago: University of Chicago Press, 1989).

9 Barbara Rosenwein, *Emotional Communities in the Early Middle Ages* (Ithaca: Cornell University Press, 2011).

10 William Reddy, *The Navigation of Feeling: A Framework for the History of Emotions* (Cambridge: Cambridge University Press, 2001); for discussion, see Anna Green and Kathleen Troup, *The House of History: A Critical Reader in History and Theory* (Manchester: Manchester University Press, 2016), 403–15.

11 Joanna Bourke, *Fear: A Cultural History* (London: Virago, 2005), 8.

12 Ute Frevert, 'Defining Emotions: Concepts and Debates Over Three Centuries', in *Emotional Lexicons: Continuity & Change in the Vocabulary of Feeling 1700–2000*, ed. Ute Frevert et al (Oxford: Oxford University Press, 2014), 1–31.

13 Monique Scheer, 'Are Emotions a Kind of Practice (and Is That What Makes Them Have a History)? A Bourdieuian Approach to Understanding Emotion', *History and Theory* 51. No. 2 (2012): 190–220; Katie Barclay, *Men on Trial: Performing Emotion, Embodiment and Identity in Ireland, 1800–1845* (Manchester: Manchester University Press, 2019).

14 C. Jung, 'Wotan', *Neue Schweizer Rundschau*, III (Zurich, 1936): 657–669; Sigmund Freud, *Massenpsychologie und Ich-Analyse* (Leipzig: Internationaler Psychoanalytischer Verlag, 1921).

15 Robert E. Bartholomew and Simon Wessely, 'Protean Nature of Mass Sociogenic Illness: From Possessed Nuns to Chemical and Biological Terrorism Fears', *The British Journal of Psychiatry* 180 (2002): 300–306.

16 Christian von Scheve, 'Collective Emotions in Rituals: Elicitations, Transmission, and a "Mathew-effect"', in *Emotions in Rituals and Performances*, ed. A. Michaels and C. Wulf (London, Routledge, 2011), 55–77.

17 Reddy, *The Navigation of Feeling*, 124 and 129

18 See H. Schilling, *Konfessionskonflict und Staatsbildung* (Gütersloh: Gütersloher Verlagshaus Gerd Mohn, 1981); W. Reinhard, 'Reformation, Counter-Reformation and the Early Modern State: A Reassessment', *Catholic Historical Review* 75 (1989): 385–403; W. Reinnard and H. Schilling, eds, *Die Katholische Konfessionalisierung* (Gütersloh and Münster: Gütersloher Verlagshaus, 1995); and R. Po-chia Hsia, *Social Discipline in the Reformation: Central Europe 1550–1750* (London: Routledge, 1989).

19 Juan de Mariana, *De rege et regis institutione* (Toledo: Pedro Rodriguez, 1599), vol. 3, 421–426.

20 Benedict Anderson, *Imagined Communities: Reflections on the Origin and Spread of Nationalism* (London: Verso, 1983).

21 Susan Broomhall, ed., *Early Modern Emotions: An Introduction* (London: Routledge, 2017); Susan Broomhall, Jane W. Davidson, Andrew Lynch, eds, *A Cultural History of Emotions*, 6 vols (London: Bloomsbury, 2019); Michael Champion and Juanita Feros Reyes, eds, *Understanding Emotions in Early Europe* (Turnhout: Brepols, 2015); Susan

Broomhall and Andrew Lynch, eds, *Routledge Companion to Emotions in Europe: 1100–1700* (London: Routledge, 2019).

22 Thomas Dixon, *From Passions to Emotions: The Creation of a Secular Psychological Category* (Cambridge: Cambridge University Press, 2003); Katie Barclay, *Caritas: Neighbourly Love and the Early Modern Self* (Oxford: Oxford University Press, 2021); Clare Langhamer, 'Love, Selfhood and Authenticity in Post-War Britain', *Cultural and Social History* 9, no. 2 (2012): 277–297; Laura Kounine, *Imagining the Witch: Emotions, Gender, and Selfhood in Early Modern Germany* (Oxford: Oxford University Press, 2018).

23 Fay Alberti, ed, *Medicine, Emotion and Disease, 1700–1950* (Basingstoke: Palgrave Macmillan, 2006); Allan Ingram et al, *Melancholy Experience in Literature of the Long Eighteenth Century: Before Depression, 1660–1800* (Basingstoke: Palgrave, 2011); Jeremy Schmidt, *Melancholy and the Care of the Soul: Religion, Moral Philosophy and Madness in Early Modern England* (Aldershot: Ashgate, 2007); Katie Barclay and Bronwyn Reddan, eds, *The Feeling Heart in Medieval and Early Modern Europe: Meaning, Embodiment and Making* (Berlin: De Gruyter/Medieval Imprint Press, 2019).

24 Ute Frevert, Pascal Eitler, Stephanie Olsen, Uffa Jensen et al, *Learning How to Feel: Children's Literature and Emotional Socialization, 1870–1970* (Oxford: Oxford University Press, 2014); Peter Stearns, 'Girls, Boys and Emotions: Redefinitions and Historical Change', *Journal of American History* 80 (1993): 36–74.

25 Diana G. Barnes, 'Emotional Debris in Early Modern Letters', in *Feeling Things: Objects and Emotions through History*, ed. Stephanie Downes, Sally Holloway and Sarah Randles (Oxford: Oxford University Press, 2018), 114–132; Katie Barclay, *Love, Intimacy and Power: Marriage and Patriarchy in Scotland, 1650–1850* (Manchester: Manchester University Press, 2011); Joanna Bornat, 'Remembering and Reworking Emotions: The Reanalysis of Emotion in an Interview', *Oral History* 38, no. 2 (2010): 43–52; Alison Twells, '"Went into Raptures": Reading Emotion in the Ordinary Wartime Diary, 1941–1946'. *Women's History Review* 25, no. 1 (2016): 143–160.

26 Dixon, *From Passions to Emotions*; Robb Boddice, *The Science of Sympathy: Morality, Evolution, and Victorian Civilization* (Urbana: University of Illinois Press, 2016); Stephen Pender, 'Rhetoric, Grief and the Imagination in Early Modern England', *Philosophy and Rhetoric* 43, no. 1 (2010): 54–85; Lisa Hill, '"The Poor Man's Son" and the Corruption of Our Moral Sentiments: Commerce, Virtue and Happiness in Adam Smith', *Journal of Scottish Philosophy* 15, no. 1 (2017): 9–25; Elizabeth Radcliffe, 'Love and Benevolence in Hutcheson's and Hume's "Theories of the Passions"', *British Journal for the History of Philosophy* 12 (2004): 631–653; Kirk Essary, *Erasmus and Calvin on the Foolishness of God: Reason and Emotion in the Christian Philosophy* (Toronto: University of Toronto Press, 2017).

27 Matej Blazek, 'Emotions as Practice: Anna Freud's Child Psychoanalysis and Thinking – Doing Children's Emotional Geographies', *Emotion, Space and Society* 9 (2013): 24–32.

28 Thomas Dixon, 'The Psychology of the Emotions in Britain and America in the Nineteenth Century: The Role of Religious and Antireligious Commitments', *Osiris* 16 (2001): 288–320.

29 Jeffrey Watt, 'Love Magic and the Inquisition: A Case from Seventeenth-Century Italy', *Sixteenth Century Journal* 41, no. 3 (2010): 675–689.

30 Joanne Bailey [Begiato], *Parenting in England, 1760–1830: Emotion, Identity and Generation* (Oxford: Oxford University Press, 2012); Susan Broomhall and Jacqueline van Gent, 'Corresponding Affections: Emotional Exchange Among Siblings in the Nassau Family', *Journal of Family History* 34, no. 2 (2009): 143–165; Susan Broomhall, ed., *Emotions in the Household, 1200–1900* (Basingstoke: Palgrave Macmillan, 2008); Joanne McEwan, '"At My Mother's House": Community and Household Spaces in Early Eighteenth-Century Scottish Infanticide Narratives', in *Spaces for Feeling:*

Emotions and Sociabilities in Britain, 1650–1850, ed. Susan Broomhall (London: Routledge, 2015), 12–34.

31 Katie Barclay, 'Natural Affection, the Patriarchal Family and the "Strict Settlement" Debate: A Response from the History of Emotions', *Eighteenth Century: Theory and Interpretation* 58, no. 3 (2018): 309–320.

32 Katherine Ibbett, *Compassion's Edge: Fellow-Feeling and Its Limits in Early Modern France* (Philadelphia: University of Pennsylvania Press, 2017); Margrit Pernau, 'Love and Compassion for the Community: Emotions and Practices among North Indian Muslims, c. 1870–1930', *The Indian Economic and Social History Review* 54, no. 1 (2017): 21–42; Lynn Hunt, *Inventing Human Rights: A History* (New York: W. W. Norton, 2008); Jane Lydon, *Imperial Emotions: The Politics of Empathy across the British Empire* (Cambridge: Cambridge University Press, 2019); Richard Ashby Wilson and Richard D. Brown, eds, *Humanitarianism and Suffering: The Mobilization of Empathy* (Cambridge: Cambridge University Press, 2009).

33 Nicole Eustace, *1812: War and the Passion of Patriotism* (University Park: University of Pennsylvania Press, 2015); Stephanie Downes, Andrew Lynch and Katrina O'Loughlin, eds, *Emotions and War: Medieval to Romantic Literature* (Basingstoke: Palgrave, 2015); Thomas J. Scheff, *Bloody Revenge: Emotions, Nationalism, and War* (Boulder: Westview Press, 1994).

34 Yasmin Haskell and Raphaële Garrod, eds, *Changing Hearts: Performing Jesuit Emotions Between Europe, Asia and the Americas* (Leiden: Brill, 2019); Susan Karant-Nunn, *The Reformation of Feeling: Shaping the Religious Emotions in Early Modern Germany* (Oxford: Oxford University Press, 2010). Phyllis Mack, *Heart Religion in the British Enlightenment: Gender and Emotion in Early Methodism* (Cambridge: Cambridge University Press, 200); Claire Walker, 'Governing Bodies, Family and Society: The Rhetoric of the Passions in the Sermons of Samuel Wesley', *English Studies* 98, no. 7 (2017): 733–746.

35 Sarah Randles, 'Labours of Love: Gender, Work and Devotion in Medieval Chartres', *Emotions: History, Culture, Society* 4 (2020): 374–397; Charles Zika, 'The Transformation of Sabbath Rituals by Jean Crépy and Laurent Bordelon: Redirecting Emotion through Ridicule', in *Emotion, Ritual and Power in Europe, 1200–1920*, ed. Merridee L. Bailey and Katie Barclay (Basingstoke: Palgrave Macmillan, 2017), 261–284.

36 Bailey and Barclay, eds, *Emotion, Ritual and Power in Europe*; Kiril Petkov, *The Kiss of Peace: Ritual, Self and Society in the High and Late Medieval Peace West* (Leiden: Brill, 2003).

37 Francois Soyer, 'The Public Baptism of Muslims in Early Modern Spain and Portugal: Forging Communal Identity through Collective Emotional Display', *Journal of Religious History* 39, no. 4 (2015): 506–523; Alejandro Caneque, 'The Emotions of Power: Love, Anger and Fear, or How to Rule the Spanish Empire', in *Emotions and Daily Life in Colonial Mexico*, ed. Javier Villa-Flores and Sonya Lipsett-Rivera (Albuquerque: University of New Mexico Press, 2014), 89–121.

38 Amy Milka and David Lemmings, 'Narratives of Feeling and Majesty: Mediated Emotions in the Eighteenth-Century Criminal Courtroom', *Journal of Legal History* 38, no. 2 (2017): 155–178; Robert Cockcroft, *Rhetorical Affect in Early Modern Writing: Renaissance Passions Reconsidered* (Houndmills: Palgrave Macmillan, 2003); Jonas Liliequist, 'The Political Rhetoric of Tears in Early Modern Sweden', in *A History of Emotions, 1200–1800*, ed. Jonas Liliequist (London: Pickering and Chatto, 2012), 181–205; Wadda C. Ríos-Font, '"How Do I Love Thee": The Rhetoric of Patriotic Love in Early Puerto Rican Political Discourse', in *Engaging the Emotions in Spanish Culture and History*, ed. Luisa Elena Delgado, Pura Fernández and Jo Labanyi (Nashville: Vanderbilt University Press, 2016), 39–55.

39 Mary Fairclough, *The Romantic Crowd: Sympathy, Controversy and Print Culture* (Cambridge: Cambridge University Press, 2013); Deborah Gould, *Moving Politics:*

Emotion and ACT UP's Fight Against AIDS (Chicago: University of Chicago Press, 2009); Emma Hutchison, *Affective Communities in World Politics: Collective Emotions after Trauma* (Cambridge: Cambridge University Press, 2018).

40 Merridee Bailey and Kimberley-Joy Knight, 'Writing Histories of Law and Emotion', *Journal of Legal History* 38, no. 2 (2017): 117–129; Kathryn Temple, *Loving Justice: Legal Emotions in William Blackstone's England* (New York: NYU Press, 2019).

41 Margaret Abruzzo, *Polemical Pain: Slavery, Cruelty and the Rise of Humanitarianism* (Baltimore: Johns Hopkins University Press, 2011); Christine Levecq, *Slavery and Sentiment: The Politics of Feeling in Black Atlantic Antislavery Writing, 1770–1850* (Hanover: University Press of New England, 2008).

42 Lydon, *Imperial Emotions*.

43 Katie Barclay, 'Sounds of Sedition: Music and Emotion in Ireland, 1780–1845', *Cultural History* 3, no. 1 (2014): 54–80; Jane W. Davidson and Sandra Garrido, eds, *Music and Mourning* (Abingdon: Routledge, 2016).

44 Katharine Ann Jensen, *Writing Love: Letters, Women and the Novel in France, 1605–1776* (Carbondale and Edwardsville: Southern Illinois University Press, 1995); Eleonora Rai, 'Spotless Mirror, Martyred Heart: The Heart of Mary in Jesuit Devotions (Seventeeth – Eighteenth Centuries)', in Barclay and Reddan, eds, *The Feeling Heart*, 184–202; Sarah Blick, *Push Me, Pull You: Imaginative, Emotional, Physical, and Spatial Interaction in Late Medieval and Renaissance Art* (Leiden: Brill, 2011); Stephanie Dickey and Herman Roodenburg, eds, *Passion in the Arts of the Early Modern Netherlands* (Leiden: Brill, 2010); Bradley Irish, *Emotion in the Tudor Court: Literature, History, and Early Modern Feeling* (Evanston: Northwestern University Press, 2018).

45 For an overview see Barclay, *A History of Emotions*. For a guide to analysing sources for emotion see Barclay, Crozier-De Rosa, and Stearns, eds, *Sources for the History of Emotions*.

46 Thomas Dixon, 'What Is the History of Anger a History Of', *Emotions: History, Culture, Society* 4, no. 1 (2020): 1–34.

47 Sara Ahmed, *The Cultural Politics of Emotion* (Edinburgh: Edinburgh University Press, 2004); Ben Anderson, 'Affective Atmospheres', *Emotion, Space and Society* 2 (2009): 77–81; Mark Seymour, 'Emotional Arenas: From Provincial Circus to National Courtroom in Late Nineteenth-Century Italy', *Rethinking History* 16, no. 2 (2012): 177–197.

INTRODUCTION TO
VOLUME III: REVOLUTIONS

Katie Barclay and François Soyer

The eighteenth century was a significant period of change in the ideas and practices of emotions for Europeans across the globe. Ideas about emotion were central to the science and philosophies of Enlightenment thinkers, while the culture of sensibility shaped not only art and literature but also personal practices of emotion. As the title of this volume suggests, the eighteenth century was a time of revolution, of change and transformation, events that were caused by and in turn shaped people's emotional lives and practices. The introduction to Volume III highlights some key themes, placing them in a wider context of eighteenth-century emotions scholarship. It then highlights future directions and some tips for working with this volume.

Historians of eighteenth-century emotion, like those of other periods, seek to locate the experience, understanding and practice of emotions within their social, economic and political contexts. In any period this brings into play a wide range of different social groups and forms of knowledge. Eighteenth-century Europe is perhaps distinctive, however, in being associated with a particular 'cult' of emotion: the culture of sensibility. It had a widespread hold on the cultural imagination of the literate classes, and, evidence increasingly suggests, those further down the social ladder. The culture of sensibility prized the expression of emotion, particularly in delicate or complex forms. While they recognised the power of the sublime – where one was overwhelmed by emotion, especially in relation to natural scenery or other remarkable sights – equally important for the culture of sensibility was that emotion operated as a form of information and decision-making. The capacity to feel delicate emotions, and to accurately interpret feeling, was a form of literacy, and one that marked a person's sophistication and civilisation. Art and literature produced during this period therefore often emphasised their role in providing audiences with the opportunity to explore and experience different emotions (safely in the realm of the imagination) and to enhance emotional literacy.

The culture of sensibility was underpinned by transformations in the medical sciences and philosophy that had begun in the previous century. Slowly scientists were moving from humoural explanations to those that emphasised the body as mechanical and sensate. The idea that the body gained knowledge through the senses was not new to the eighteenth century, but this became increasingly important to explanations of human action and activity. The imagination was critical, both in helping translate information gained through the senses and due to its creative capacity in offering people knowledges outside of their direct experience. Nerves, too, were significant, as the mechanism through which sensate knowledge was translated in the body, and in shaping corporeal emotional experiences. That the human was 'sensible' – gaining knowledge through things like touch and sight, experiencing that knowledge as corporeal feeling and using such feeling to direct moral behaviour – underpinned a culture of sensibility where emotions were central to human life and expression.

If new biologies provided a physical underpinning for the sensate body, they were developed not simply through anatomical experiment but also through global encounters with diverse peoples. Eighteenth-century European explorers increasingly approached those they met through an anthropological lens, viewing their engagements with other cultures – both in terms of geography and across the social ladder in their own nations – as opportunities for education in human nature. Drawing on older ideas about societies progressing through stages – hunting; pasturage; agriculture; commerce – they sought to evaluate those they met by locating them in particular points of development, where Europeans were the peak of civilisation. Drawing on observations of other cultures' emotions – or at least, what the Europeans thought they observed as emotion – how people responded to events became part of a narrative of human emotion and its evolution. This anthropological approach also drove a concern with close observation of the body for emotional gesture and expression, where physiognomy offered a truth to the internal person.

These ideas intersected with those of scholars in political economy, which sought to explain forms of human governance and to produce new models to reflect new imaginings of the human, debates that often explicitly tied into the political events of the day, such as a decline in absolute monarchy and the rise of patriotic feeling. Seeking to situate the organisation of human life in natural processes, rather than Scripture or other philosophical interventions, scholars explored the boundary between the selfish or self-interested individual and the sociability required for social co-operation and success. Here they turned not only to other societies but to children, arguing that babies – fundamentally selfish – learned to be sociable as they came to recognise the importance of care-givers in their survival. Education came to be seen as critical to producing sociable human beings, and eighteenth-century thinkers placed particular emphasis on the malleability of children and on providing space for them to develop as well-adjusted humans. Education in emotion was critical here for a people who saw the capacity to feel as a mark of civilisation and success.

Partly these ideas were shaped by the concept of sympathy, something that was to be increasingly important in the second half of the century, where one of the skills of the sensible human was to be able to convey their feeling to others and to interpret others' feeling in turn. Sympathy was a central mode of communication, and vital to the success of not only the experience of forms of art but to speech-making, persuasive rhetoric and governance. The capacity to convey emotions through sympathetic exchanges shaped experience in a wide array of domains, from parliaments to churches to political rallies to courtrooms. Sympathy was also important in the everyday, mediating encounters between people and ide-ally ensuring compassionate action as people learned to feel as others felt. It was feeling that could overwhelm the other, if the latter could not exercise reason to manage emotional excess. Thus, sympathy was related to debates about the rela-tionship between the individual and society, where people had to balance self-love with sociability for the good of society. If too much self-interest was bad for soci-ety, losing oneself could have equal risks. Different groups were better at main-taining emotional distance than others; women, in particular, were often imagined as especially susceptible to others' feelings due to a heightened humanity.

The sympathy of the sociable world was given moral force through love, not least Christian *caritas* – the neighbourly love of the Bible, sometimes rendered into a language of benevolence and pity. Rooting the emotions in nature may have provided secular explanations of human action, but humanity's nature was determined by God, who ordered society, and thus religion remained a central moral force. Love pervaded a wide range of social domains, from religious prac-tice, to marriage and family life, to the political affections between a monarch and the people. Like sympathy, love could also justify benevolence and pity, and discourage people from violence or anti-social action. The cultural significance of love also ensured that even if many of the ideas associated with the culture of sensibility were restricted to a social elite, emotion and especially sociable action remained critical to social and political relationships for all groups.

If ideas about emotion and how it operated were central to scientific, philo-sophical and cultural discourse during the eighteenth century, emotions were also things experienced by ordinary people and practiced in everyday life. As many sources in this volume suggest, the ideas explored above were not just theoretical but played a significant role in shaping ordinary modes of expression and com-munication. Writers across the social ladder often deployed flowery descriptions of emotion – by twentieth-century standards – in ordinary communication and in a wide range of social relationships. Expressions of heartfelt love, weeping and corporeal accounts of emotion were routinely exchanged not just between lovers, but parents and children, and same-sex friends. A particular form of sentimental masculinity was especially prominent in eighteenth-century Europe, although not always with resistance or critique. A 'cool' letter might be evidence of a formal business relationship, but even there some courtesy – perhaps through a concern about health or family – was polite and smoothed an engagement. Too little emo-tion might suggest hostility or distrust. People, taught to interpret the self in emo-tional terms, also described their personal experiences in emotional terms; it was how someone felt and responded that marked, for example, effective religious practice or an enjoyable walk with friends. Feeling was part of how experience was interpreted, but also how it was explained to oneself and to others.

Emotions can also be encountered in contexts where less-emotive language is used. Court records and descriptions of the poor, for example, often used a less effusive emotional vocabulary but nonetheless captured the operation of emotion in everyday life. The use of physical space and material goods, the exchange of gifts, and displays of hospitality or violence provide insight into the emotional worlds that underpinned such actions. Notably, many of these behaviours show similar emotional logics to elite groups, suggestive of the breadth of sensibility as a cultural ideal. If this is the case, the historian perhaps should also look for resistances to social norms, and sites of alternative cultures, emotional ideals and even refuges from dominant norms, and some examples of these appear across this volume.

The eighteenth century is also a moment of 'revolution', and this volume ends with the French Revolution that was such a fundamental moment in the political and cultural imagination of the period. Preceding this was the American Revolution, *Patriottentijd* (the Time of the Patriots) in the Dutch Republic and a number of smaller rebellions and revolts across the European empires, but perhaps more significantly this was a period where people developed an emotional readiness for revolution, both in learning to love a set of symbols beyond the monarch (a patriotism built on laws, constitutions and liberties) and in a growing sense of injustice that led to demands for social and political change, and for toleration of a broader range of ideas, values and feelings. It was perhaps also a moment of revolution in Europe's relation to the rest of the world. European empires, not least the Spanish in South and Central America, and the Dutch in Indonesia, long proceeded the eighteenth century. But new sciences of humanity hardened attitudes towards people who the Europeans classed as lower on the ladder of evolutionary development, and were used to justify not only invasion and seizure of land but genocide and enslavement. The boundaries of sympathy were increasingly in evidence, informing how bodies were read by white observers. Thus, if this sourcebook provides opportunity to witness the emotions of encounter and invasion, this is a history of what white women and men saw, not indigenous experience, and such sources need to be read carefully as evidence of non-European cultures.

By the eighteenth century in Europe, a broad range of sources survive that provide evidence of people's emotional worlds. The print revolution of earlier centuries was continuing to expand the range of written genres, not least promoting works like the novel that were explicitly designed to provide an emotional education through descriptions of people's lives and experience. Older forms persisted. Prescriptive literature, that provided advice on how to behave, remained an important form, and offered advice on emotional education for children and adults, often underpinned by new scientific writings. Scientists and philosophers were now printing their works, and translators and popularists transformed their writings for audiences with different languages and levels of expertise. There was also a broad range of ephemeral print that survives in significant numbers, including political pamphlets, sermons, newspapers, bawdy songs and jokes. Alongside print culture, the eighteenth century developed new forms of art. Developments in painting style and technique produced scenes and portraits that can be analysed for gesture, behaviour and expression (alongside the manuals that taught artists how to depict particular emotions); musical forms advanced, not least with the popularisation of the opera and musical performances in newly built auditoriums. These accompanied a continuing tradition of hymn-singing and domestic music at all social levels, as well as a growing numbers of theatres and theatrical styles. Cultural forms are significant sources for emotion as they were often designed to produce emotions in their audiences, as well as offering observations and educations in appropriate emotional expression in a range of contexts. Moreover, they sometimes give insight into experiences which are not well recorded in other types of sources, especially as they pertain to ordinary and everyday life.

Sources written by individuals about their own emotional experiences also survive in significant numbers for this period. The letter was an important genre of the century not only as a mode of communication but represented in art and literature. Diaries, autobiographies, memoirs, family books and similar sources of the self offer insight into feeling. Emotions can be found through imaginative engagements with more ephemeral or everyday records too – the account books, receipts, advertisements and similar papers that survive for family life. Material culture – from clothes and jewellery to household furniture to ritual and religious objects – offers clues to things people valued, as well as how they used them as part of emotional practices, both in the everyday and on special occasions. Increasingly historians are also interested in the emotions of institutions, and look for how emotions shape the production of business records and correspondence, the funding and uses of charitable organisations and the operation of parliaments, schools and courtrooms. Legal records have long provided important insights into the internal world of ordinary people, not least as they often capture people during traumatic incidents where emotions are very evident. As several examples in this volume suggest, emotions are also part of social structures, such as law and governance, directing how feeling was practiced by groups.

As this suggests, the eighteenth-century scholar has ample opportunity to explore and evaluate emotions. Yet, some cautions should be acknowledged. Some forms of source – not least letters and family papers – are much more likely to survive for the elite than those further down the ladder. They can be exceptionally rare for groups like enslaved peoples or vagrants. Art and cultural forms are important but not all social groups had equal access to them, and especially to producing them, and so we have to be cautious when we use them to understand the diversity of eighteenth-century communities. Those with more limited formal literacy are often viewed through the lens of institutions, like the court or a workhouse, or in the writings of an anthropological explorer. These can provide invaluable evidence of the lives of groups that are otherwise hard to access, but they have to be read cautiously with attention to the values and assumptions of the author. As with all sources, the conditions under which they are made are central to what they can tell us.

In selecting sources for this volume, we have emphasised those that offer insights into some of the more mainstream ideas about emotional life, and also those where emotions are more easily accessible to the non-expert reader. That has meant choosing sources that use emotion words (love, hate, anger), use persuasive rhetoric or describe events where the emotional worlds of those involved are more easily identified. For a sourcebook this seemed appropriate, but we would encourage readers to reflect on how this shapes the evidence provided. A focus on emotion words relies on the historian's capacity to identify them, and so perhaps disguises emotions that are less familiar to the modern reader. It also encourages us to consider emotions as discrete entities (love, hate), rather than complex experiences that involve social practices, behaviours, gestures and mixed feelings. As traces of human investment, most historical sources tell us something of emotion, and readers are encouraged to look for emotions in less obvious places, as well as those that are more familiar.

No sourcebook can cover everything, but we particularly note that there is considerable space for more work on marginal cultures and ideas – especially those that resisted the big trends of the culture of sensibility. The smooth narrative of the culture of sensibility provided above, if reflective of general trends, belies that each of these ideas and developments were the product of debate, revision and resistance. In hoping to give some geographical range across Europe and its empires, there has been limited opportunity to explore multiple perspectives from within particular cultures or societies, and especially to include the wide range of minorities that lived in Europe and its domains. We have hoped to give some range of voice in offering perspectives across social class, gender and race, and also the life course – children are central in the eighteenth-century imagination and feature here in several places – but there is significant scope to extend these perspectives and room for future research. An issue that is common to the four volumes is the question of translation, not least for emotion words that do not easily transfer across cultures. For many sources, we have used eighteenth-century translations with the goal of providing insight not only to the source culture but how such texts were interpreted by other people during the period. Modern translators may make different choices, but this is part of the history of emotions too. A final note of warning is that a volume that engages with Europeans' encounters in empire reflects the attitudes and values of the period; some eighteenth-century people spoke very positively of those they encountered, whilst others were patronising and racist. The emotions of historic people reflected their prejudices and beliefs, but also their aspirations and ethics. This volume provides some opening insights into eighteenth-century feelings.

Part 1

THE SELF

Part 1

The self

The emotions were central to the construction of the eighteenth-century self in Europe. The cult of sensibility posited the body as a sensate organism, where the human interpreted the world through its senses, and transformed them into emotions that they used to guide moral action. If all humans were emotional, eighteenth-century writers encouraged humankind to exercise reason over the passions, and the ability to do so marked 'civilised' Europeans from other groups, including women, the poor and different races (or so they claimed). Managing emotion required education, and this resulted in the production of a variety of texts where people sought to both develop emotional range and master such feeling. These ideas were featured in a range of sources, from genres that had long histories like prescriptive literature to newer forms designed for the eighteenth century, like the novel. This section provides a number of examples where eighteenth-century people seek to explore how sensibility and emotions shape how they think about themselves as selves, and about their social relationships with others. Self-love and sociability are key themes, as they provided a critical tension in the imagination of the period between the interests of individuals and groups. Love, and especially romantic love, was particularly important as feeling that increasingly was situated as a form of resistance to stifling social order and unnecessary hierarchy. Childhood was considered especially important for eighteenth-century writers, because of their emphasis on education and culture as what made different groups human and distinct from each other. The sources in this section explore how a variety of eighteenth-century people articulated the self as a product of sensibility, how it was produced through education, and how sensibility was used to claim authority for groups that were often excluded from social power.

1

CHARLES JOHNSON, *A GENERAL HISTORY OF THE PYRATES, FROM THEIR RISE AND SETTLEMENT IN THE ISLAND OF PROVIDENCE, TO THE PRESENT TIME . . .*

(London: T. Warner, 1724), pp. 157–65

Mary Read (1685–1721), known as the pirate Mark Read, was brought to historical attention in *A General History of the Pyrates*, published in 1724 by Charles Johnson – apparently a pseudonym. The account provides the fullest known version of her life; records for her criminal conviction and death support her existence. Cross-dressing women, often found amongst soldiers and sailors, were a common motif of the eighteenth century, fascinating the public for their capacity to pass as men and to exceed the limitations imagined for their sex. The account given places the decision to cross-dress as less a choice of gender identity, than pragmatic survival in challenging conditions. Indeed, at many points, the author wishes to affirm her femininity, both through the emphasis placed on her irrational behaviour while in love and in her commitment to chastity. Such authorial decisions both affirm Read's moral character while highlighting the admirable contradiction of such a woman performing so effectively in a masculine role. As a source for the history of emotions, this account highlights how emotions, like love and courage, are used to enforce gender norms and differences between the sexes, and the ways that some individuals, like Read, challenged these ideas, to public fascination.

***

The life of Mary Read

NOW we are to begin a History full of surprizing Turns and Adventures; I mean, that of *Mary Read* and *Anne Bonny*, alias *Bonn*, which were the true Names of these two Pyrates; the odd Incidents of their rambling Lives are such, that some may be tempted to think the whole Story no better than a Novel or Romance; but since it is supported by many thousand Witnesses, I mean the People of *Jamaica*, who were present at their Tryals, and heard the Story of their Lives, upon the first discovery of their Sex; the Truth of it can be no more contested, than that there were such Men in the World, as *Roberts* and *Black-beard*, who were Pyrates.

Mary Read was born in *England*, her Mother was married young, to a Man who used the Sea, who going a Voyage soon after their Marriage, left her with Child, which Child proved to be a Boy. As to the Husband, whether he was cast away, or died in the Voyage, *Mary Read* could not tell; but however, he never returned more; nevertheless, the Mother, who was young and airy, met with an Accident, which has often happened to Women who are young, and do not take a great deal of Care; which was, she soon proved with Child again, without a Husband to Father it, but how, or by whom, none but her self could tell, for she carried a pretty good Reputation among her Neighbours. Finding her Burthen grow, in order to conceal her Shame, she takes a formal Leave of her Husband's Relations, giving out, that she went to live with some Friends of her own, in the Country: Accordingly she went away, and carried with her her young Son, at this Time, not a Year old: Soon after her Departure her Son died, but Providence in Return, was pleased to give her a Girl in his Room, of which she was safely delivered, in her Retreat, and this was our *Mary Read*.

Here the Mother liv'd three or four Years, till what Money she had was almost gone; then she thought of returning to *London*, and considering that her Husband's Mother was in some Circumstances, she did not doubt but to prevail upon her, to provide for the Child, if she could but pass it upon her for the same, but the changing a Girl into a Boy, seem'd a difficult Piece of Work, and how to deceive an experienced old Woman, in such a Point, was altogether as impossible; however, she ventured to dress it up as a Boy, brought it to Town, and presented it to her Mother in Law, as her Husband's Son; the old Woman would have taken it, to have bred it up, but the Mother pretended it would break her Heart, to part with it; so it was agreed betwixt them, that the Child should live with the Mother, and the supposed Grandmother should allow a Crown a Week for it's Maintainance.

Thus the Mother gained her Point, she bred up her Daughter as a Boy, and when she grew up to some Sense, she thought proper to let her into the Secret of her Birth, to induce her to conceal her Sex. It happen'd that the Grandmother died, by which Means the Subsistance that came from that Quarter, ceased, and they were more and more reduced in their Circumstances; wherefore she was obliged to put her Daughter out, to wait on a *French* Lady, as a Foot-boy, being now thirteen Years of Age: Here she did not live long, for growing bold and strong, and having also a roving Mind, she entered her self on Board a Man of War, where she served some Time, then quitted it, went over into *Flanders*, and carried Arms in a Regiment of Foot, as a *Cadet*; and tho' upon all Actions, she behaved herself with a great deal of Bravery, yet she could not get a Commission, they being generally bought and sold; therefore she quitted the Service, and took on in a Regiment of Horse; she behaved so well in several Engagements, that she got the Esteem of all her Officers; but her Comrade who was a *Fleming*, happening to be a handsome young Fellow, she falls in Love with him, and from that Time, grew a little more negligent in her Duty, so that, it seems, *Mars* and *Venus* could not be served at the same Time; her Arms and Accoutrements which were always kept in the best Order, were quite neglected: 'tis true, when her Comrade was ordered out upon a Party, she used to go without being commanded, and frequently run herself into Danger, where she had no Business, only to be near him; the rest of the Troopers little suspecting the secret Cause which moved her to this Behaviour, fancied her to be mad, and her Comrade himself could not account for this strange Alteration in her, but Love is ingenious, and as they lay in the same Tent, and were constantly together, she found a Way of letting him discover her Sex, without appearing that it was done with Design.

He was much surprized at what he found out, and not a little pleased, taking it for granted, that he should have a Mistress solely to himself, which is an unusual Thing in a Camp, since there is scarce one of those Campaign Ladies, that is ever true to a Troop or Company; so that he thought of nothing but gratifying his Passions with very little Ceremony; but he found himself strangely mistaken, for she proved very reserved and modest, and resisted all his Temptations, and at the same Time was so obliging and insinuating in her Carriage, that she quite changed his Purpose, so far from thinking of making her his Mistress, he now courted her for a Wife.

This was the utmost Wish of her Heart, in short, they exchanged Promises, and when the Campaign was over, and the Regiment marched into Winter Quarters, they bought Woman's Apparel for her, with such Money as they could make up betwixt them, and were publickly married.

The Story of two Troopers marrying each other, made a great Noise, so that several Officers were drawn by Curiosity to assist at the Ceremony, and they agreed among themselves that every one of them should make a small Present to the Bride, towards House-keeping, in Consideration of her having been their fellow Soldier. Thus being set up, they seemed to have a Desire of quitting the Service, and settling in the World; the Adventure of their Love and Marriage had gained them so much Favour, that they easily obtained their Discharge, and they immediately set up an Eating House or Ordinary, which was the Sign of the *Three Horse-Shoes*, near the Castle of *Breda*, where they soon run into a good Trade, a great many Officers eating with them constantly.

But this Happiness lasted not long, for the Husband soon died, and the Peace of *Reswick* being concluded, there was no Resort of Officers to *Breda*, as usual; so that the Widow having little or no Trade, was forced to give up House-keeping, and her Substance being by Degrees quite spent, she again assumes her Man's Apparel, and going into *Holland*, there takes on in a Regiment of Foot, quarter'd in one of the Frontier Towns: Here she did not remain long, there was no likelihood of Preferment in Time of Peace, therefore she took a Resolution of seeking her Fortune another Way; and withdrawing from the Regiment, ships herself on Board of a Vessel bound for the *West-Indies*.

It happen'd this Ship was taken by *English* Pyrates, and *Mary Read* was the only *English* Person on Board, they kept her amongst them, and having plundered the Ship, let it go again; after following this Trade for some Time, the King's

THE SELF

Proclamation came out, and was publish'd in all Parts of the *West-Indies*, for pardoning such Pyrates, who should voluntarily surrender themselves by a certain Day therein mentioned. The Crew of *Mary Read* took the Benefit of this Proclamation, and having surrender'd, liv'd quietly on Shore; but Money beginning to grow short, and hearing that Captain *Woods Rogers*, Governor of the Island of *Providence*, was fitting out some Privateers to cruise against the *Spaniards*, she with several others embark'd for that Island, in order to go upon the privateering Account, being resolved to make her Fortune one way or other.

These Privateers were no sooner sail'd out, but the Crews of some of them, who had been pardoned, rose against their Commanders, and turned themselves to their old Trade: In this Number was *Mary Read*. It is true, she often declared, that the Life of a Pyrate was what she always abhor'd, and went into it only upon Compulsion, both this Time, and before, intending to quit it, whenever a fair Opportunity should offer it self; yet some of the Evidence against her, upon her Tryal, who were forced Men, and had sailed with her, deposed upon Oath, that in Times of Action, no Person amongst them were more resolute, or ready to Board or undertake any Thing that was hazardous, as she and *Anne Bonny*; and particularly at the Time they were attack'd and taken, when they came to close Quarters, none kept the Deck except *Mary Read* and *Anne Bonny*, and one more; upon which, she, *Mary Read*, called to those under Deck, to come up and fight like Men, and finding they did not stir, fired her Arms down the Hold amongst them, killing one, and wounding others.

This was part of the Evidence against her, which she denied; which, whether true or no, thus much is certain, that she did not want Bravery, nor indeed was she less remarkable for her Modesty, according to her Notions of Virtue: Her Sex was not so much as suspected by any Person on Board, till *Anne Bonny*, who was not altogether so reserved in point of Chastity, took a particular liking to her; in short, *Anne Bonny* took her for a handsome young Fellow, and for some Reasons best known to herself, first discovered her Sex to *Mary Read; Mary Read* knowing what she would be at, and being very sensible of her own Incapacity that Way, was forced to come to a right Understanding with her, and so to the great Disappointment of *Anne Bonny*, she let her know she was a Woman also; but this Intimacy so disturb'd Captain *Rackam*, who was the Lover and Gallant of *Anne Bonny*, that he grew furiously jealous, so that he told *Anne Bonny*, he would cut her new Lover's Throat, therefore, to quiet him, she let him into the Secret also.

Captain *Rackam*, (as he was enjoined,) kept the Thing a Secret from all the Ship's Company, yet, notwithstanding all her Cunning and Reserve, Love found her out in this Disguise, and hinder'd her from forgetting her Sex. In their Cruize they took a great Number of Ships belonging to *Jamaica*, and other Parts of the *West-Indies*, bound to and from *England*; and when ever they meet any good Artist, or other Person that might be of any great Use to their Company, if he was not willing to enter, it was their Custom to keep him by Force. Among these was a young Fellow of a most engageing Behaviour, or, at least, he was so in the Eyes of *Mary Read*, who became so smitten with his Person and Address, that she could

34

JOHNSON, *A GENERAL HISTORY OF THE PYRATES*

neither rest, Night or Day; but as there is nothing more ingenious than Love, it was no hard Matter for her, who had before been practiced in these Wiles, to find a Way to let him discover her Sex: She first insinuated her self into his liking, by talking against the Life of a Pyrate, which he was altogether averse to, so they became Mess-Mates and strict Companions: When she found he had a Friendship for her, as a Man, she suffered the Discovery to be made, by carelesly shewing her Breasts, which were very White.

The young Fellow, who was made of Flesh and Blood, had his Curiosity and Desire so rais'd by this Sight, that he never ceased importuning her, till she confessed what she was. Now begins the Scene of Love; as he had a Liking and Esteem for her, under her supposed Character, it was now turn'd into Fondness and Desire; her Passion was no less violent than his, and perhaps she express'd it, by one of the most generous Actions that ever Love inspired. It happened this young Fellow had a Quarrel with one of the Pyrates, and their Ship then lying at an Anchor, near one of the Islands, they had appointed to go ashore and fight, according to the Custom of the Pyrates: *Mary Read*, was to the last Degree uneasy and anxious, for the Fate of her Lover; she would not have had him refuse the Challenge, because, she could not bear the Thoughts of his being branded with Cowardise; on the other Side, she dreaded the Event, and apprehended the Fellow might be too hard for him: When Love once enters into the Breast of one who has any Sparks of Generosity, it stirs the Heart up to the most noble Actions; in this Dilemma, she shew'd, that she fear'd more for his Life than she did for her own; for she took a Resolution of quarreling with this Fellow her self, and having challenged him ashore, she appointed the Time two Hours sooner than that when he was to meet her Lover, where she fought him at Sword and Pistol, and killed him upon the Spot.

It is true, she had fought before, when she had been insulted by some of those Fellows, but now it was altogether in her Lover's Cause, she stood as it were betwixt him and Death, as if she could not live without him. If he had no regard for her before, this Action would have bound him to her for ever; but there was no Occasion for Ties or Obligations, his Inclination towards her was sufficient; in fine, they applied their Troth to each other, which *Mary Read* said, she look'd upon to be as good a Marriage, in Conscience, as if it had been done by a Minister in Church; and to this was owing her great Belly, which she pleaded to save her Life.

She declared she had never committed Adultery or Fornication with any Man, she commended the Justice of the Court, before which she was tried, for distinguishing the Nature of their Crimes; her Husband, as she call'd him, with several others, being acquitted; and being ask'd, who he was? she would not tell, but, said he was an honest Man, and had no Inclination to such Practices, and that they had both resolved to leave the Pyrates the first Opportunity, and apply themselves to some honest Livelyhood.

It is no doubt, but many had Compassion for her, yet the Court could not avoid finding her Guilty; for among other Things, one of the Evidences against her,

35

deposed, that being taken by *Rackam*, and detain'd some Time on Board, he fell accidentally into Discourse with *Mary Read*, whom he taking for a young Man, ask'd her, what Pleasure she could have in being concerned in such Enterprizes, where her Life was continually in Danger, by Fire or Sword; and not only so, but she must be sure of dying an ignominious Death, if she should be taken alive? – She answer'd, that as to hanging, she thought it no great Hardship, for, were it not for that, every cowardly Fellow would turn Pyrate, and so infest the Seas, that Men of Courage must starve: – That if it was put to the Choice of the Pyrates, they would not have the punishment less than Death, the Fear of which, kept some dastardly Rogues honest; that many of those who are now cheating the Widows and Orphans, and oppressing their poor Neighbours, who have no Money to obtain Justice, would then rob at Sea, and the Ocean would be crowded with Rogues, like the Land, and no Merchant would venture out; so that the Trade, in a little Time, would not be worth following.

Being found quick with Child, as has been observed, her Execution was respited, and it is possible she would have found Favour, but she was seiz'd with a violent Fever, soon after her Tryal, of which she died in Prison.

2

ANNE-THÉRÈSE DE MARGUENAT DE COURCELLES (1647–1733), *THE PHILOSOPHY OF LOVE, OR NEW REFLECTIONS ON THE FAIR SEX*

Trans. John Lockman (London: J. Hawkins, 1729 and 1737), pp. 22–48

Anne-Thérèse de Marguenat de Courcelles, known as Madame de Lambert, was a French writer and salon hostess, bringing together key members of the French social elite for intellectual and social exchanges. She was especially interested in female education, and her advice writings aimed at women and girls contributed to a broader Enlightenment discussion on human nature and how sex shaped the nature of the self. Her ideas here – of an underlying universal human nature – that was improved by education was a central strand of Enlightenment thinking during this period; that women 'improve' men through their humanity was also a very popular idea. In advocating for education for women, Lambert's text explores how key moments of sociability between men and women, and especially romantic relationships, would be enhanced and contribute to virtue and the greater good of society. Love is a key emotion here, as it is for so many writers of the period, as human relationships in all forms were envisioned through its lens; sensibility was also an important idea, as a type of self that was open to emotion and to sympathetic exchanges with other people. Her philosophy of love is in a tradition of similar reflections by female French writers in the seventeenth century.

Prescriptive writing such as this text provided a guide on how to feel – an ideal model for behaviour, and was frequently, as here, contrasted with imperfect behaviours that were to be avoided. Such texts were designed to shape a particular type of self and related behaviours. They have been especially useful for historians of emotion who are interested in exploring emotional norms, and because they highlight some of the rich vocabulary of emotion used by particular historic communities. This text was originally written in French but translated into English; this translation is from the early eighteenth century and so reflects how eighteenth-century English-speaking audiences translated French emotion words and concepts into their own vocabulary.

. . .

SENSIBILITY is a disposition of the soul, which it is advantageous to meet with in others; without this quality, the soul is dead to humanity or generosity. A bare sensation or impulse, a single emotion of the heart, has more power over the soul, than all the maxims of the philosophers; Sensibility assists the mind, and is subservient to virtue. "Tis allow'd, that persons of that character possess numberless charms; those sprightly, those swift-darting graces, which *Plutarch* mentions, are indulged to them only. A lady who was so finish'd a woman, that that she might have sat for the *Graces*, is a proof of my assertion. A man of wit, a friend of her's, being one day asked what were her employments, what her thoughts, in her recess; he answered, her life was never a life of thought, but of pure sensation. All those who knew her, are agreed, that nature never formed so inchanting a creature; and that tastes, or rather passions, prevail'd over her imagination and her reason, in so happy a manner; that her tastes were ever justified by her reason, and respected by her friends. None of her acquaintance ever presumed to censure her, but in her absence; for the moment she appeared,[1] she was no longer in fault. This is a proof that nothing triumphs in so absolute a manner, as that superiority of mind which flows from sensibility, and a strength of imagination; and that, because it is ever attended with persuasion.

WOMEN generally owe nothing to art. Wherefore then should any one be displeased, because nature has freely indulged them a perfection of mind? we deprave all those dispositions which nature has bestowed on them: we begin by neglecting their education; we don't imploy their minds in things of a solid turn, and this the heart takes advantage of; we form them purely to please; and they give pleasure only from their graces or their vices; they seem to be made merely to delight the eye. In consequence of this, they devote their whole study to the improvement of their exterior charms, and are easily carried away by the propension of nature; they give into pleasures, which they are persuaded they never received from nature, in order to combat them.

BUT an odd circumstance, is, that at the same time we form their minds for love, we prohibit them the use of that passion. But a resolution should be taken in this case: if we design them merely to please, let us not forbid them the use of their charms; if we would have them witty and rational, don't abandon them, when they possess that kind of merit only; but we require in them such a mixture, such a discreet use of these qualities, as is difficult to hit upon, and to reduce to a just proportion. We are for having them witty, but then 'tis purely to conceal, to check their wit, and keep it from displaying itself; and no sooner is it upon the wing, than 'tis immediately called back, by what the world calls Decorum. Fame and glory, the soul and support of all witty productions, are denied them. Their mind is robbed of every object, every hope; 'tis humbled, and if I may be allowed to borrow an expression from *Plato*, its wings are cut. We may justly wonder, they have one grain of sense left.

THE PHILOSOPHY OF LOVE

WOMEN have a great authority on their side, 'tis no less than that of *St. Evre-mont*. In laying down a model of perfection, he is far from ascribing it to men. *I believe*, says he, *we shall sooner find the solid judgment of men in the fair sex; than the sprightly graces of women, in men.* Let me, in the name of my whole sex, put these questions to the men. What is it you require in us? you all are desirous of seeing yourselves happily united in the society of women of character, of an amiable turn of mind, and an upright heart: allow them therefore the use of such things, as contribute to the improvement of reason. But are you for such graces only as are subservient to pleasure? don't therefore murmur, if women devote some few moments, to the improvement of their outward charms.

BUT in order to give every thing its due place, and just value; let us make a proper distinction between such qualities as are of an estimable, and such as are of an agreeable nature. The estimable, are real and intrinsically in things; and by the laws of justice, have a natural claim to our esteem. But agreeable qualities; qualities that move the soul, and administer the softest impressions, are neither real, or suited to the object; they result from the dispositions of our organs, and the strength of our imaginations. This is so true, that the same object does not make the same impressions on all men; and that we frequently vary in opinion, though the object has not suffered the least change.

'TIS impossible for exterior qualities to be lovely in themselves; they are so only by the dispositions they meet with in us. Love is not obtained by merit; it refuses itself to the greatest qualities. Would it therefore be possible for the heart to be independant on the laws of justice, and subject to those of pleasure only? Men may, whenever they please, obtain an happy assemblage of all these qualities; and then they will meet with women equally lovely and awful. In degrading them, they substract from their own happiness and pleasure. But in the present conduct of women, virtue and good manners have been very great losers, and not so much as the least advantage has accrued to pleasures.

THE world is universally agreed, that 'tis necessary for women to procure esteem; but when this is obtained, shall we not want still something more? Reason will dictate to us, that this ought to suffice; but we easily give up the rights and privileges of reason, for those of the heart. We are to take nature as we find her; estimable qualities please only in proportion to the advantage we may draw from them; but amiable qualities are likewise of service to us, to employ and busy the heart; for to love, is as necessary to us, as to esteem; we even grow tired with admiring, if the object of our admiration is not at the same time formed to please. Nay, 'tis not even enough for men to please, they seem indispensably obliged to move and affect us; merit was never at enmity with the Graces; 'tis that alone has a privilege of fixing them; without it they are fickle and fleeting. Besides, virtue never made any person ugly, and this is so true, that beauty devoid of merit and good sense is insipid; whereas merit atones for deformity.

I don't place the lovely quality among the external ones, but extend it much farther. The *Spaniards* say that beauty is like fragrant odours, the effect of which is very short and transient; when we are once used to them, they affect us no more.

THE SELF

But virtue and good manners, a just and penetrating mind, an upright and tender heart, are so many ravishing beauties, and ever new. But now our pleasures are less delicate and refined, because our manners are more corrupt and less pure. Let us see who we are to thank for it.

THE conduct of women has long been the object of reproach; 'tis pretended they were never so disorderly as in this age; that they have banished purity from their hearts, and decency from their conduct; I don't know whether there may not be some grounds for this accusation, however, I might answer, that the same thing has been long complained of; that one age may be justified by another; and to excuse the present, I need only refer to the last. There is a great similitude between the inward dispositions in all ages, and they only exhibit themselves under various shapes; but as the power of custom extends itself only on outward things, and has no authority over thought, 'tis far from rectifying nature; it does not remove the cravings of the heart, and the passions are the same in all ages. But are the manners of men so pure and uncorrupted, as may authorize them to censure those of women? Certainly, neither sex has a right to reproach the other, but equally contribute to the depravity and corruption of the age they live in. However it must be owned, that the manners have suffered a change. Gallantry is banished, and no one has been a gainer by it: men have withdrawn from the society of the other sex; and have lost all politeness, sweetness, and that exquisite delicacy which is acquired only in their company; and on the other side, women having less converse with men, have lost the desire of pleasing, by those modest and engaging arts, they before made use of; and yet this was the real source of all their charms and graces.

Notwithstanding that the *French* are fallen from their antient gallantry, it must nevertheless be owned, that no other nation had ever carried it to a greater height, or had more refined upon it. Men have changed it into an art of pleasing; and such of them as have exercised themselves there in, and have got a thorough acquaintance with it, have formed to themselves fixed and infallible rules, whenever they are to address the weaker part of the female sex. Women, on the other side, have laid down several rules to resist them: as they are allowed a great liberty in *France*, and are restrained by no other checks than their own innate modesty, and the laws of decorum; they have learnt to oppose the impressions of love, with such maxims as duty inspires. 'Tis from the desires and designs of men, from the shyness and modesty of women, that results the delicate commerce which polishes the mind, and purifies the heart; for love improves a virtuous foul. It must be confessed that the *French* are the only nation that have refined love into a delicate art.

THE *Spaniards* and *Italians* are utter strangers to it; as most of their women are immured, as it were, in their houses; the men bend their whole application to the surmounting of exterior obstacles; and when once these are removed, they meet with none in the object beloved: but love so easily obtain'd, has very few charms; and it seems to be the work of nature, not that of the lover. In *France*, a much better use is made of time; as the heart bears a part in these engagements; and that frequently among virtuous persons, the correspondence is carried on with that only, it is looked upon as the source of all pleasures. To those delicate sensations of the soul, we likewise owe all those beautiful and witty romances, which the above-mentioned nations are wholly unacquainted with. A *Spaniard* reading the conversations of *Clelia*,[2] cried out; *How much wit is employed here to little purpose!* The moment we have but one employment for love, the romance is soon at an end; if we take away gallantry, we at once pass over all the delicacy of wit and sentiments. The *Spanish* women are sprightly and warm; they resign themselves up to the dominion of the senses, not the soft impulses of the heart; 'tis by resistance that the intellectual sensations gain strength, and acquire fresh-delicacy. The moment a passion is satisfied, it dies away; take away fear and desires from love, and you rob it of its very soul.

LOVE is the chief pleasure; the most soft, the most delightful of all illusions, that paint themselves in the fancy. Since then this affection is so essential to the happiness of mankind, we ought not to banish it from society; we must only learn to direct it aright, and carry it to a greater degree of perfection. Since we have so many schools for improving the mind, why have we none for cultivating the heart? This is an art that has been very much neglected. However, the passions are so many strings, which require the touch of the most excellent finger. Is it possible to secure one's self against those, who have the secret to move the springs of the soul, by the most strong, the most forcible impressions?

LOVE was not had in so, much contempt among the ancients, as in our age. Wherefore do we degrade it? why do we not rather maintain it in all its dignity? *Plato* pays the highest deference to this affection: he no sooner touches upon it, than, his imagination grows warm, his wit brightens, and his style rises in beauty; whenever he speaks of a man whose soul yields to the soft impressions of love; *that lover*, says he, *whose person is sacred*, &c.[3] The title he bestows on lovers, is that of divine friends, and persons inspired by the Gods.

PLEASURE, according to the ancients, ought not to be the chief object of love: they were persuaded that virtue must be the basis of it. But we have banished virtue and good manners from it, and this is the source of all our misfortunes. Most men now-a-days are of opinion, that such oaths as love dictates, are no ways binding. Morality and gratitude, are too weak to defend the senses against the pleasing allurements of novelty. Most people love out of mere whim, and change from complexion.

THE torments which love often makes us suffer, so far from engaging us not to give into that passion, teach only to deplore it. Let us see what we can do in this case, by examining how women behave in love, and their different characters.

THESE are of various kinds. Some women make the pleasures of love their whole search, and the sole object of their desire. Others unite love to pleasure; and others again will admit of love only, and reject every kind of pleasure. I shall touch but very lightly on the first character. Those seek only the gratification of the senses, in love; no other pleasure than of being violently agitated, and hurried away by their transports, and that of being lov'd. In a word, they love the passion, and not the lover; persons of this complexion give themselves a prey to the most raging passions. You shall see them devote themselves to gaming, to feasting; in short, they bid welcome to every thing that assumes the appearance of pleasure.

I have ever wondred how it could be possible for us to associate other passions to love; that the least void should be left in the heart; and that after one has given up all, the object beloved should not be the sole employment of the mind. It commonly happens, that when persons of this character lose their innocence, the whole train of virtues disappear at the same instant; and when once their glory and reputation is fallen a sacrifice, they lay aside every regard. When Madam ***** was reproach'd for violating all the laws of decency and good manners; she answered, *I am resolved to enjoy the loss of my reputation.* Women who follow such maxims, reject all the virtues of their sex. They consider them in no other light than as a political custom, which they are resolv'd to elude. Some women fancy that if they can but fill up the duties of life by a specious show, and screen their frailties from the world, 'tis sufficient: but to believe, that to be ignorant, is to be innocent, is a very dangerous tenet. They reject all sound principles, in order to shift off remorse, and for this appeal from the decision of all men in general. Their whole life is one continual succession of frailties, and they are quite lost to reflection.

THE moment a woman has banished from her heart, that tender and delicate punctilio, that honour which ought to be the guide of all her actions, all the rest of the virtues are threatned with ruin. What privilege will they have to command respect? Do we owe more to them, than to our own honour? Such characters are never amiable. In these women, you find neither modesty or delicacy; they make gallantry habitual to them, and are unable to unite the quality of friend, to that of a lover. As pleasure, not the union of hearts, is all they seek after, they are wanting in every duty of friendship. Such is the practice of women, with regard to love, in this age; and this is wholly owing to the trifling and inconsiderate life they lead.

Notes

1 If to her share some female errors fall, Look on her face, and you forget them all. Pope's *Rape of the Lock*. [*In original*]
2 This is a reference to Madeleine de Scudéry's ten-volume work, *Clélie, histoire romaine* (1654–1660).
3 Plato's main reflections on love are in his *Symposium* and *Phaedrus*.

3

JOHN CLELAND (1709–1789),
MEMOIRS OF A COXCOMB

(London: R. Griffiths, 1751),
pp. 16–23, 74–76, 356–360

John Cleland was born into a wealthy English family and well connected in artistic and literary circles. After working for the British East India Company in his youth, he began writing to pay off his debts in the 1740s. His first and best known work was *Fanny Hill: or the Memoirs of a Woman of Pleasure* (1748), which was banned due to its pornographic content. *Memoirs of a Coxcomb* was a subsequent novel that did not have the same commercial success, but had some admirers. Early in the text, the story's protagonist Sir William Delamore meets a young woman, 'Lydia', who is visiting his neighbour and with whom he falls in love. Once she leaves, he cannot find her again but she haunts his memory. The story follows Delamore's adventures as he looks for her, finally learning she hid her name on their first meeting. The text is considered an important exploration of eighteenth-century masculinity, particularly in providing a male narrator who, far from ideally, places himself into the 'feminine' role of seeking to please and charm a lover.

Cleland's work is considered to be an important contribution in the development of the prose novel, a genre that in the eighteenth century was designed to help readers imagine what it was like to live as another, and especially how to 'feel'. This education in emotion was designed to improve a person's sensibility, offering them emotional opportunities that they might not encounter on their own. Historians of emotion have found them useful not only for their emotional language, but as a guide to how people imagined emotional encounters to operate, as well as the moral valance of such behaviour.

. . .

I staid then as long as was consistent with the advance of the evening, and the measures of respect, which the little I knew of the world, and the fear of displeasing, suggested to me the propriety of. But in all that time, Lydia, or Miss Liddy, which was the name of the youngest, had scarce opened her mouth, and that only in monosyllables; but with such a grace of modesty, such a sweetness of sound, as made every string of my heart vibrate again with the most delicious impression. I

THE SELF

could not easily decide within myself which I wished for most ardently, to be all eye, to see her beauty, or all ear, to hear the music of her voice.

Forced then to take my leave, I did myself that violence, but not before I had obtained the permission Mrs. Bernard could not very politely refuse me, and which I protested I should not abuse, to visit them during their stay in that part. But as I had observed that there was not a soul in the house except the poor old woman, I could, without any affectation, or obtrusion, order the boy, her grandchild, to stay behind, to be at hand for any service they might want; in which too I had a second view, of knowing from him all that should pass in my absence: an employ he was admirably fitted for by nature, who had bestowed upon him one of those simple, harmless, unmeaning faces, which are, invaluable, when joined to wit enough to make the most of the little guard one is on against them.

I was scarce got half way down the little sort of lane, which led to the cottage, before the wishful regret, of what I left behind me, made me stop, and look back, Then, then I perceived, all: the magic of love. I saw now every thing with other eyes. That little, rustic mansion, had assumed a palace-air, Turrets, colonades, jet-d'eaus, gates, gardens, temples, no magnificence, no delicacy of architecture was wanting to my imagination, in virtue of its fairy-power, of transforming real objects into whatever most flatters, or exalts that passion. I should now have looked on every earthly paradise with indifference or contempt, that was not dignified and embellished with the presence of this new sovereign of all the world, to me.

Nor was the transformation I experienced within myself one jot less miraculous. All the desires I had hitherto felt the pungency off, were perfectly constitutional: the suggestions of nature beginning to feel itself. But the desire I was now given up to, had something so distinct, so chaste, and so correct, that its impressions carried too much of virtue in it, for my reason to refuse it possession of me. All my native fierceness was now utterly melted away into diffidence and gentleness. A voluptuous langour stole its softness into me. And for the first time in my life, I found I had a heart, and that heart susceptible of a tenderness, which endeared and ennobled me to myself, and made me place my whole happiness in the hopes of inspiring a return of it to the sweet authoress of this revolution.

I naturally hate reflexions. They are generally placed as rescues to a reader, to point out to him, what it would be more respectful to suppose would not escape him, Besides they often disagreeably interrupt him, in his impatience of coming to the conclusion, which facts alone lead to. Yet, I cannot here refrain from observing, that, not without reason, are the romance, and novel writers in general, despised by persons of sense and taste, for their unnatural, and unaffecting descriptions of the love-passion. In vain do they endeavour to warm the head, with what never came from the heart. Those who have really been in love, who have themselves experienced the emotions and symptoms of that passion, indignantly remark, that so far from exaggerating its power, and effects, those triflers do not even do it justice. A forced cookery of imaginary beauties, a series of mighty marvellous facts, which spreading an air of fiction through the whole all in course weaken that interest and regard never paid to truth, or the appearances of truth,

JOHN CLELAND, *MEMOIRS OF A COXCOMB*

and are only fit to give a false and unadulterated taste of a passion, in which a simple sentiment, is superior to all their forced productions of artificial flowers. Their works in short give one the idea of a frigid withered eunuch, representing an Alexander making love to Statira.[1]

Let me not lengthen this digression by asking pardon for it. It may be more, agreeable to promise as few more of them as possible. I resume then the thread of my narrative.

Returned to my aunt's: it was easy for me to give what colour. I pleased to the having left the boy at his grandmother's; but it was not so easy, for one of my age and inexperience, to conceal the change of my temper and manners, which betrayed itself in every look and gesture, My aunt was surprized at the gentleness and softness which now breathed in all I said or did. Unacquainted with what had happened, she could not account for a novelty that so much delighted her. At supper too, I forced a gaiety, very inconsistent with the state of my heart, which was not without those fears and alarms inseparable from the beginnings of so violent a passion; but I made the pains of it, as much as I could, give way, at least in appearance, to the pleasure of my recent adventure.

The day had hardly broke before I was up, and disposing every thing for the renewal of my visits. And as I well knew it would be impossible for me to pay them so often as I fully proposed to myself, with out the motives being, presently-known and published: I resolved, so far at least wisely, to disappoint the discovery, by determinately braving it. I ordered then, without any air of mystery, or reserve, my servants to carry to the old woman's every thing I could think of, such as tea, chocolate, coffee, fruits, and whatever might not probably be come at in such a country-habitation, in that delicacy, and perfection, as we abounded in at this seat of my aunt's. The worst of which conduct was, and here is the place to set it down, that my aunt was soon informed, that I had a little mistress there, that I kept to divert myself with. And though the falsity of it shocked the delicacy of my sentiments, I preferred it however as a less dangerous disturbance, than if my aunt had been alarmed so as to view my resort there in a more serious light. She once however ventured to touch upon it to me, in a taste of remonstrance, but I gave it such a reception, and she was so thoroughly subdued by the superiority I had managed myself with her, that she was not tempted to renew in haste the attack. Perhaps too she comforted herself with thinking it was the least of two evils, that I should carry the war abroad, rather than make it at home, amongst her maids; one of whom by the by, in spite of all the caution used to prevent it, I was on the point of consummating an impure treaty with, when chance threw this new passion in my way, which erazed every thought of any but the object of it out of my head and heart.

At ten in the morning then, the hour I guest, might be my charmer's breakfast time, I set out, in my chariot, drest in the richest suit I was master of, with my hair trimmed and curled, in all the perfection it was capable of; in all which my intense wish to please had even a greater share than my vanity. Thus equipped for conquest, I landed at the bottom of the lane, and walked up to the house, where I was immediately admitted, to the ladies, who were just set down to their tea.

45

THE SELF

The eldest had not in the least changed her clothes: but Lydia was, if possible, yet more modestly and undesignedly drest than the day before. A white frock and a glimpse of a cap, lost in the hair that curled every where over it, and eclipsed it, whilst a plain cambrick hankerchief covered a bosom easily imagined to be of the whiteness of snow, from what it did not hide of her neck, and which in the gentlest rise and fall seemed to repeat to me the palpitations of my heart: such was her morning dishabille, in which simplicity and neatness clearly triumphed over all the powers of dress and parade.

. . .

Returned to my aunt's, I told her, according to my plan of secrecy, no more than the ladies were gone, which indeed she might have read plain enough, in the change of my air, and countenance. Seeing then how seriously I was affected, she openly said every thing she could think of to lessen my affliction, and hugged herself no doubt, at what an escape I had.

My sense of Lydia's absence was not however soon, nor indeed ever, thoroughly got over. For some time I remained melancholy, stupefied, and feeling severely the want of something essential to the enjoyment of my life. It had been, during her stay, deliciously indeed filled, and taken up with the pleasures, of seeing and attending on her. But her desertion of me had made such a sensible gap, so inseparable a void, that I had no longer a relish for my existence. All the women I saw, and who had once inspired my desires, were now nothing to me. I looked just enough at them, to satisfy myself they were not Lydia, and I fought no more. Hunting country sports, conversation, studies, all grew insipid to me, every thing put me in mind of Lydia, but nothing could supply her place with me.

By degrees however the violence of my grief subsidised and softened into a certain languor and melancholy, which was not even without its pleasure. Lydia, present to my memory, always engrossed my heart: but time, that great comforter in ordinary, introduced intervals of insensibility, which other objects, other passions, seized the advantage of. I still did not love Lydia less, but now I did not think of her so often, or with that continuity as at first. The number of things that made impression on me, augmented in proportion as that of my grief grew fainter and fainter. I was of a constitution too which began to interfere powerfully with that system of constancy, and Platonics, which a world rather spoilt than refined, has agreed to banish into the corner of those old musty romances that went out of fashion with ruffs and high-crowned hats, and which is most certainly exploded out of the present practice: perhaps with less profit to true pleasure, than is generally imagined.

I pined now for the term fixed for our going to London; still in the hopes of hearing from, or tracing Lydia out. But in the mean time I felt more than ever the insipidity, and wearisomness of a country life, in which, generally, one day is the dull duplicate of another. What, in short I now found most wanting to me, was amusement: whilst the promptership of nature, and the sollicitations of a curiosity which began to resume its rights, left me no room to doubt about the sort of it.

JOHN CLELAND, *MEMOIRS OF A COXCOMB*

I had besides soon an opportunity to ascertain, and indeed realize, all my wants and desires.

. . .

Everything being now soon ready for my proceeding to Deal, where I proposed embarking for Flanders, I had only left myself to pay a few visits of duty or business. And on the foot of the latter it was, that I could not help calling at lady Shellgrove's, from whom I was to take letters of recommendation to a brother of her's, then residing at Brussels. Mervile was in the chariot, and engaged for the rest of the evening, with me. We found she was at home by a coach being at the door, and were immediately let up to the drawing-room, in which she was in company with two ladies, who were then upon a visit to her. We advanced towards them. They had got up at our entrance into the room, and as I was sliding my bow, my heart yet more than my eyes, discerned that one of them was – who? even the Lydia so long lost to me; and in pursuit of whom I was preparing to range the universe, and to seek for her every where but where, she was not to be. Yes! I shudder yet to think how near I was to wandering from the center of all my wishes, all my happiness. At this dear and unexpected sight then, I stood in, a trance of surprize and joy, unable to-command any motion, or exert one power of free agency, under the oppression of such sudden sensations acting unitedly upon me, and keeping every other faculty of my soul suspended. I gazed, I devoured her with eyes insufficient to all the raptures, and avidity of my heart. But the vivacity of my ideas kept down the burst of expressions with which it heaved, and choaked my utterance. I was even too much engrossed by all I felt, to attend to, or distinguish, what impressions the sight of me made upon her: but the instant of my recovering my natural liberty of motion, I precipitated myself at her feet, I seized her hand before she could draw it away from my grasp, and could not but disconcert her with an impetuosity, of which I was not in these moments of transport, the master. I tried in vain to speak, but my emotions still overpowered me. And when at length my sentiments forced a passage, it was only in an exclamation of the name of Lydia, in inarticulate breaks, and heart-fetched sighs. Lydia herself appeared to me as soon as I was capable of remarking her situation, if less surprized, not less confounded, or agitated than myself: yet the quickness of discernment so peculiar to the love-passion, that it may be called its instinct, made me feel a some what, if not dry or reserved in her reception of me, at least, wanting much of that warmth of welcome, which I should have wished in such a re-meeting. But even that remark could not materially dash my draught of delight. The violence of my sentiments expunged all memory or reflexion on every thing but the present object. I saw Lydia, and that was enough.

The lady, however, who was with Lydia, did not leave me time to recover myself, before taking her by the hand with an air of authority, and an unexpected suddenness, which cut off all explanation, led her out of the room, whilst I represented the figure of one petrified alive, without the sense or courage to follow, or oppose them. I heard too the oldest lady murmur as she passed me, that "I should not make a bad actor."

I looked wildly round me, expending from Mervile some succour or consolation. But he too was vanished: so that deserted at once by my mistress and friend, I remained in a state of stupor, and desolation, till unable to support myself under all this distraction of distress, the severer for so quick a shift, I sunk down under my weight upon a chair, Lydia still swimming before my eyes, Lydia so happily found, and so unaccountably lost in one and the same instant.

Lady Snellgrove, who was herself astonished at this scene, approached, and asked me, what I had done to affront or drive away lady Gertrude Sunly and her mother in that manner.

Lady Gertrude Sunly! I cryed out. Is the whole earth combined to perplex and torture me? what lady Gertrude! what relation has she to Lydia? to this Lydia, who has just left me in this cruel manner?

I do not know what you mean by Lydia, replied lady Snellgrove, coolly enough, but surely you jest; you cannot but know that these ladies, were the countess of M– and her daughter lady Gertrude.

Note

1 The Roman historian Curtius suggests that Alexander had little passion for his wife Statira, but rather held 'paternal feelings'.

4

JEAN-JACQUES ROUSSEAU (1712–1778), *EMILIUS AND SOPHIA: OR, A NEW SYSTEM OF EDUCATION*

2 vols (Émile, ou De l'éducation) (London: R. Griffiths, 1762), vol. 2, pp. 135–146, 150–153

Jean-Jacques Rousseau was a Genevan philosopher, who produced some of the most influential writings of the eighteenth century. He wrote in French, but his works were widely translated across Europe; this excerpt was from an English translation. *Emilius and Sophia* was a philosophical treatise on the nature of man and education, particularly providing a model for child-rearing to produce the 'enlightened' subject. It has a novelistic quality in providing a history of Emilius, the imagined youth educated according to Rousseau's model, and his future love, Sophia. While it was initially burnt in Geneva upon publication due to Rousseau's philosophy of religion, it was remarkably popular and widely referenced, as several other sources in this volume suggest (see especially sources 5, 14, and 36). He provides an account influenced both by his Calvinist heritage, and natural law theorists of the previous century, where man has an innate self-love that has to be moderated by reason and directed into sociable relations with others. Like others of the period, much of the evidence for his claims arises less in experiment than in examples from the classical tradition and from anthropological observations of other societies and races.

Rousseau's work has been useful for historians of emotions as a piece of philosophical literature that provides an account of how eighteenth-century thinkers understood the role of emotion in child development, and as highly influential piece of prescriptive literature that offered people a model for understanding and performing emotion, not least in the context of childhood.

. . .

Our passions are the principal instruments of our preservation; therefore to endeavour to destroy them is equally vain and absurd; it is to find fault with nature, to attempt to reform the works of God. Should the almighty require man to annihilate those passions which he had given him, he would not know his own mind, he would contradict himself; but the Almighty never gave such a ridiculous command; the heart of man has received no such injunction; and whatever is required of him, is not made known to him by the mouth of another; God himself imprints it on his heart.

To suppress the passions, in my opinion, is almost as absurd as intirely to destroy them; whoever imagines this to have been my intention, has grosly mistaken my meaning.

But because it is in the nature of man to have passions, is it therefore rational to conclude, that all the passions which we feel within ourselves, and which we perceive in others are natural? Their source indeed is natural, but that source is increased by a thousand adventitious streams; it is a great river continually augmenting, in which it would be very difficult to find one drop of the original spring. Our natural passions are extremely limited; they are however the instruments of our liberty, and tend to our preservation. Such passions as are prejudicial, and by which our reason is subdued, spring from some other source; nature does not give them to us, we adopt them to the prejudice of nature.

The source of our passions, the origin and chief of every other, that which alone is born with man, and never leaves him while he lives, is SELF-LOVE: this is the original passion prior to every other, and of which, in one sense, all the rest are only modifications. In this sense they may be considered as natural. The greater part of these modifications proceed from adventitious causes, without which they would not exist; but these modifications are of no advantage to us; on the contrary, they are extremely detrimental; they change and counteract their first and principal object: in this case men become unnatural, and act in contradiction to themselves.

True self-love is always right, and always consistent. Every Individual being especially charged with his own preservation, his first and greatest anxiety is, and ought to be, to watch over it continually; and how can he do this if he does not make it his principal concern?

We must therefore love ourselves for our own preservation; consequently we love that which contributes towards it. Children are particularly attached to their nurses. Thus Romulus ought to have been attached to the wolf that gave him suck; for this attachment is at first merely physical. Whatever contributes to the welfare of an individual engages his affection, whatever is likely to destroy it, he will repel. This is merely instinct; but what transforms instinct into sentiment, attachment into love, aversion into hatred, is a manifest intention either to injure or to serve us. We are not indeed over-solicitous concerning those inanimate beings, which are only capable of acting as they are influenced by others: but those from whose disposition and will we may expect good or evil, those in whom we perceive a power to serve us, inspire the same sentiments in us, with regard to themselves which they discover towards us. We seek those who are able to be of use to us, but we love those who are actually willing to be so: we fly from those who have the power to injure us, but those who seem disposed to offend us, we hate.

The first sentiment of a child is to love himself, and the second, which may be deduced from the former, is to love those who are employed about him; for in his present helpless state his knowledge of persons is founded on the assistance which he receives from them. His attachment to his nurse or his governess is merely habitual. He looks for them because they are necessary, and he finds them convenient; but this is rather acquaintance than affection. It requires a much longer time to make him sensible that they are not only useful, but desirous of serving him; as he grows sensible this, he begins to love them.

A child, therefore, is naturally inclined to benevolence because he sees everybody round him ready to give him assistance; and from this constant observation he learns to think favourably of his species; but in proportion as he extends his connexions, his necessities, his active and passive dependencies, the idea of his relation to others, awakens and produces sentiments of duty and preference. The child then becomes imperious, jealous and vindictive. If you educate him to be submissive and obedient, not perceiving the use of your commands, he attributes them to a capricious design to torment him, and becomes mutinous. If, on the contrary, you generally comply with his humours, as soon as ever he meets with opposition he conceives a species of rebellion in every intention to oppose him, and revenges himself even upon the chairs and tables for disobeying his commands. Self-love, which regard our own personal good only, is contented when our real wants are supplied; but self-interest, or that self-love which stands in competition with the good of others, cannot possibly be contented, because as it prefers ourselves to others, it expects that others should likewise give us the preference; which is impossible. Thus we see how the soft and affectionate passions arise from self-love, and the hateful and irascible ones from self-interest. That which renders man essentially good, is to have few wants, and seldom to compare himself with others; that which renders him essentially wicked, is to have many wants, and to be frequently governed by opinion. Upon this principle it is easy to perceive that all the passions of men or children, may be so directed, as to produce good or evil. True it is, as we cannot always live in solitude, it will be difficult for us to continue uniformly good: this difficulty must necessarily increase in proportion to our connections; and therefore the dangers of society render our care more indispensable, to prevent in the human heart the depravation which proceeds from increasing necessities.

The proper study of man is that of his connexions and dependencies. During his mere physical existence, he should study only his relation to things. This is the employment of his infancy; when he begins to be sensible of his moral existence, his relation to mankind should then be the object of his contemplation; this is the proper employment of his whole life, beginning at the period to which we are now arrived.

As soon as man has need of a companion, he is no longer an unsocial being: his heart is no longer single. All his connexions with his species, all the affections of his soul are born with this sensation. His first passion soon ferments the other into being.

THE SELF

The peculiar tendency of instinct is indeterminate. One sex attracts the other; so far it is the operation of nature. Choice, preference, personal attachment; these are the produce of knowledge, prejudice, and custom. Time and experience are necessary to render us capable of affection: we love only after having judged, and there can be no preference without comparison. This judgment is formed unknown to ourselves, nevertheless it is real. True love, let men say what they please, will always be honoured by mankind; for however its extravagance may lead us astray, tho' it does not exclude every vicious quality from the heart, it supposes some estimable ones, without which it could not exist. That choice which we put in competition with reason is, in fact, the effect of reason. We have made love blind, because he has better eyes than ourselves, and sees things which are to us imperceptible. To one who has no idea of merit and beauty, every woman must be alike, and the first he beholds will be the most amiable. Love is so far from being the child of nature, that he restrains and regulates her inclinations: under his influence, if we except the beloved object, each sex becomes indifferent to the other. The preference which we bestow we expect should be returned; love ought to be reciprocal. In order to be beloved we must render ourselves amiable, to be preferred we must render ourselves more amiable than another, more amiable than every other person; at least in the eyes of the beloved object. Hence we first regard our fellow-creatures, hence we first compare them with ourselves, and hence proceeds emulation, rivalship and jealousy. A heart overflowing with a new sensation, is glad to diffuse itself to its utmost extent; the want of a mistress soon produces the want of a friend; having experienced the pleasure of being beloved, we wish to be beloved by all the world, and this universal desire of preference must necessarily be productive of much discontent.

From the love of friendships proceed dissensions, envy and hatred. On the foundation of these various passions, I see opinion erect its immoveable throne; and senseless mortals, submitting to its empire, found their own existence on the judgement of each other.

Extend these ideas, and we shall see whence self-interest acquires that form which we suppose to be natural; and how self-love, ceasing to be a natural sentiment, becomes pride in great souls, in little souls vanity, and in all, is continually cherished at the expense of society. The seeds of these passions not having existence in the heart of an infant, they cannot grow spontaneously; we plant them there ourselves, and they never take root but by our own fault. In the heart of a youth, of a certain age, the case is very different; there they will take root in spite of us. It is time therefore to change our method.

Let us begin by making some important reflections, on that critical state of which we are now speaking. The step from childhood to the age of puberty is not so positively determined, as not to vary according to the temperament of individuals, and with regard to people according to climate. Every one knows the difference observable is this particular, between the hot and cold countries, and it is generally allowed, the warm constitutions arrive at the age of maturity soonest; but we-may be deceived as to the cause; and may frequently attribute to a physical, what ought to be ascribed to a moral source, which is one of the most common mistakes in the philosophy of the present age. The instructions of nature are late and tedious, those of man are almost always premature. In the first case, the sense rouse the imagination, in the second the imagination awakens the senses, and gives them a too early activity which cannot fail to enervate individuals, and in time the species. That the age of puberty in both sexes is always more forward in a polished and enlightened people, than amongst the ignorant and savage, is a more general and certain observation.[1] Children have a singular sagacity in seeing, through the affectation of decorum, the vices which it is intended to conceal. The refined language which we are pleased to dictate, our lectures on decency, the mysterious veil formally held before their eyes, are so many spurs to their curiosity. 'Tis evident from the effects, that by endeavouring to keep children in ignorance we really instruct them, and that of all the instructions they receive, this makes the greatest impression.

. . .

I see but one certain method of preserving the innocence of children; namely, that it be cherished and respected by those who surround them: otherwise the artifice and reserve with which they are treated will, sooner or later, infallibly be discovered. A smile, a glance, or a single gesture, is sufficient to discover to them all we intended to conceal, and effectually to betray our design of deceiving them. The delicacy of expression used by polite people in the presence of children, supposing a kind of knowledge which they should not have is extremely injudicious; but in conversing with them if you pay a proper regard to their innocence, you will naturally use those terms which are most proper. There is a certain simplicity of expression which is suitable and pleasing to innocence, and this I take to be the best method of diverting the dangerous curiosity of children. By speaking to them plainly of every thing, you leave them no room to suspect that there is any thing more to say. By uniting to indelicate words the disgusting ideas which they excite, you suppress the first fire of the imagination: you do not hinder them from pronouncing these words, and having these ideas; but you extinguish, unknown to themselves, the desire of recollecting them. And what a world of embarrassment do you avoid by thus expressing your ideas with circumlocution or disguise!

How are children made? This, though an embarrassing question, may naturally be asked by a child, whose conduct and health, during his whole life, may possibly depend, in a great measure, on the answer. The shortest method which a mother can devise to extricate herself, without deceiving her son, is to impose silence: this might do well enough, if he had been, for some time, accustomed to it, in questions about indifferent things and that he suspected no mystery from this new command. But a mother seldom stops here. *This*, says she, *is the secret of married people; little boys should not be so curious.* In this manner she many indeed extricate herself; but let me tell her, the little boy piqued at the appearance of contempt in her reply, rests not a moment till he learns the secret of married people, and he will not long remain in ignorance.

THE SELF

Permit me to relate a very different answer which I remember to have heard given to the same question, and which struck me the more as it proceeded from a woman as modest in her discourse as in her behaviour, but who was wise enough, for the advantage of her son, and for the sake of virtue, to disregard the pleasantry of fools. It happended, a little while before, that the child had voided a small stone, which tore the passage; but the pain being over was soon forgotten. *Mamma*, says the boy, *How are children made? Child*, replied the mother, without hesitation, *women make them in their water, as you did the stone, with such terrible pain that it sometimes costs them their lives.* – Let fools laugh and blockheads be offended; but let the wise recollect whether they have ever heard a more judicious and pertinent answer.

Instantly the idea of any thing mysterious is absorbed in that of a natural necessity already known to the child. The accessory ideas of pain and death case a veil of sadness over the imagination and stifle curiosity: his thoughts center, not upon the cause, but the consequence of childbirth. The infirmities of human nature, images of disgust and horror, such will naturally arise from the explanation of this answer, if he has any inclination to be farther inquisitive. How can the inquietude of desire be produced by such a conversation? Nevertheless we have not deviated from the truth, nor have we instead of instructing, deceived our pupil.

Note

1 In great towns, says Mr. de Buffon, and amongst people in affluence, children accustomed to eat plentifully and upon succulent food, arrive soon at maturity; in the country and amongst poor people, their food being less nourishing, they require at least three years more. Hist. Nat. T.4 .p. 238. I admit the justice of the observation, but of the cause assigned for it; for in countries where the inhabitants live extremely well, and eat a vast deal, as in the Valais and even in some of the mountainous provinces of Italy, the age of puberty in both sexes come as late as in great cities, where to indulge their pride, they frequently eat sparingly. One is surprized to see amidst these mountains, boys as robust as men, with female voices and beardless chins; and to find girls tall and perfectly formed, who have not the periodical distinction of their sex. This difference I am of opinion is owing to the simplicity of manners; the imagination remaining longer in tranquillity, is later before it ferments the blood, and accelerates the circulation. [*In original*]

5

CONFESSION OF JAMES DUNCAN, THEFT, 1770

National Records of Scotland, Edinburgh
JC26/191

Confessions or declarations were statements given by those accused of crime to the authorities in Scotland (as elsewhere). They were often used as part of the criminal process to enable a prosecution. This example is found amongst the surviving records of the Justiciary Court, the highest criminal court in Scotland, and was part of the prosecution case against the teenager James Duncan, accused of theft in 1770. Personal narratives for very poor and illiterate people are often hard to find for the eighteenth century and court records provide a useful access point to their lives and voices. As can be seen below, such accounts tend not to use a lot of 'emotion words' as traditionally understood, but they nonetheless can provide some insight into the emotional worlds of these communities. In Duncan's confession, we are provided with a rich account of his relationships with other men and local communities as he travelled across the country. Despite not having the best reputation, many people provided him with hospitality, sometimes food and drink. On the road, he also met people with whom he formed friendships of sorts, sometimes sleeping with them for company. Such an account might be used to explore concepts of neighbourly love, trust and security amongst the Scottish poor.

While his story is written in the third person by a Sherriff clerk, nonetheless this particular confession has a strong narrative structure, that is suggestive that it closely aligned to the speech of the defendant. There are indications that Duncan is trying to build sympathy from his audience, both through his emphasis on his youth and his childhood experiences, and by his disarming honesty, laying out his crimes in detail. That this presentation might not be quite truthful is suggested in the later questioning where some of his story did not conform to the evidence of other parts of the investigation. We might suggest that his first confession contained rhetoric designed to sway the emotions of the listener/reader, and this in turn can be used as evidence of the sorts of stories and events that shaped the feelings of audiences at this time. Thus, while sources like this are perhaps less straightforward to analyse than

THE SELF

many others, they nonetheless can provide clues to the emotional world of this community.

. . .

At Stonehaven the Twenty-Fifth day of May in the year one thousand seven hundred and seventy in the present of James McDonald, Esquire, Sheriff Substitute of Kincardineshire.

There was brought before the sheriff a young lad who says that his name is James Duncan, and that he is the son of James Duncan a Stockingwasher and Dresser in Aberdeen. That he is only about sixteen years of age, and that he has been about Four years in the seafaring way. And the last vessel he was aboard of, was one Captain Beatson of Leith, from whom about a Fourthnight agoe he got some money to buy Cloaths, with which he ran off from the Ship, which was lying at Queensferry and staid some days in Leith, and from there upon Saturday last week, he sett off for the North by himself, and as long as his money lasted, which was Twenty five shillings in all & held out till he was near Stonehaven, he did not think of doing any thing wrong. That on last Tuesday night he slept in the publick house at Kirk of Benholm, and was in company with one Robert Strachan, a young butcher of the town of Aberdeen whom he accidentally met with, And a boy who was helping Strachan to drive his sheep. That on the Wednesday Morning what with drinking at their Quarters and on the road towards Stonehaven they got themselves drunk, but the Declarant was more so than Strachan for he went on his Road, but the Declarant when near Stonehaven between five and six o'clock at night lay down to sleep on the Road side, and was found sleeping by Magnus Erskine Stonehaven carrier who awaked him, and desired him to go to Michael Davidsons a publick house at Bridgeend of Invercarron which accordingly he did, and there he got a Bed, and about Ten o'clock next morning he sett off from Michael Davidsons. But here he corrects himself And Declares that it was on Monday night he came to Benholm on Tuesday night he came to Michael Davidsons and on Wednesday morning he left it. That he had a Bundle with him consisting of only one shirt and a White Linen Napkin. That from Michael Davidsons he travelled towards Aberdeen only about a mile to the head of the hill of Corvie and there he was so sick with his former days drinking That he lay down & sleept & sauntered off the whole day, till about five or six o'clock of the Evening. That he returned again towards Stonehaven and in a publick house at the north end of the Bridge of Cowrie he got a Bottle of Ale & some Meat & staid about an hour & then sett back again towards Aberdeen & after travelling about a Mile he mett the Post, with whom the Declarant was acquainted & whose name is Robert Cassie and he invited the Declarant to return back to Stonehaven. That the Declarant accordingly returned after him and found him in his Quarters where they drunk some Strong beer together. That it seems Cassie had advised the people of the house to refuse Lodging to the Declarant, but as he was no Stranger in the Town, he imagined he would easily find quarters to himself. However as he found, that the Towns people were gone to bed he accidentally discovered an open Byre and there he lay down among the Straw tying his Linnen

CONFESSION OF JAMES DUNCAN, THEFT, 1770

Napkin about his Neck and wraping his spare shirt about his feet. Declares that about this time he bethought himself, that his money was nearly gone for he had only about Twenty pence or Two shillings remaining, and as he thought shame to go into Aberdeen with little money about him, he resolved to make shift for more. And with this intention about Three o'clock of yesterday being Thursday morning, he went down the Town of Stonehaven to the house of Lieutenant Meldrum but he did not know it to be his house, and there he jumped in over the Dike of an butter Court, & drew the Bolt of the Gate of the Court and then he went to a low Window and lifted up the Sash, and by that Window he entered the house and found himself in a Room and people sleeping in a Bed and a Woman called out as to her husband and said "are you getting up so earlye my dear". That as the declarant did not make answere the Woman seemed as if getting out of Bed, and being thus scared and detected, he tumbled himself directly out at the Window again which he had been keept up with an Iron pin for the purpose of his Escape, and then he went clean off, but having thus failed in getting what he wanted he then went to another house on the street in Stonehaven, & which he afterwards found was the house of one John Charles. That that house he entered in the same way he did Mr Meldrum's, only it was naked in the inside, which he drew off, by putting his hand in at one of the Losens[1] which he found broken. That the Declarant finding nothing fitt for his purpose in the Lower Room, went up stairs to another Room, where the people were Sleeping, & there he saw a Watch on the Brass of the Chimney which the declarant took & put into his pocket. That the Mans Coat was lying before the Bed. That the Declarant searched the pocketts of it for money, but found none however he took the Mans pockett book and two silk Napkins one Black, and the other Yellow and Red, the one lying on the mans Cloaths and the other he unpined from the Womans Cloaths. All which with a snuff box which he also took, he made off with upon hearing the Woman call to her husband but in the hurry running away he flung the pockett book and snuff box from him on the Stair within the house and got clear out of it having his shoes in his hand which he had put off when he went up stairs. That his spare shirt he lost in running away, and his shoes he flung over a Dyke, with an Intention to have jumped after them but he found that the sea was below it. And upon that discovery he run out at the head of the Town, with a Resolution to procure Shoes for himself and directly went to a house on the Brae of Courie, which he since has been told belongs to one William Taylor and there he broke the lozen of a Window & took off the Snacke[2] on the Inside & opened it, & thereby entered the house, & went to an Inner Room where people were sleping, & there he picked a Womans pocket of a penny & a Snuff box which was all that the pockett Contained, and he took a pair of men Shoes with Brass buckles in them, a pair of black stockings & a pair of Garters, and with this booty he made off undiscovered at the same window by which he entered. That then he went to a Brae on the sea side and lay down to sleep and when he awaked he saw people looking and running about upon which he hid his watch, but he could not get quit of the other things for he was wearing the Shoes & Buckles, Stockings & Garters, & one of the Napkins & the other napkin with the snuff box were in his pocket. And the Declarant went & hid himself below a Rock, but was soon discovered and taken. Upon which he directly acknowledged himself the theif. And after getting pretty severe usage to force him to discover the watch he still denied her till at last he got a promise that they would let him go if he would do it. And then he took them to where the Watch lay. And being instantly shown a silver Watch, a pair of Men's shoes & brass buckles, a pair of black stockings, a pair of Garters and a snuff box and two silk napkins. He Declares and Acknowledges that they are the same things which he stole in manner above mentioned. Declares that till now he was always innocent of any bad things, but he was once accused of being concerned with others in breaking a house near Aberdeen and he was a Night in preson in Aberdeen on that Account but Next day he was letten goe. And this was in the Month of March one thousand Seven Hundred & Sixty Nine And that time he was also questioned about some things which had been stole out of a ship in the harbour of Aberdeen, but the Declarant knew nothing about it. And the Declarant being show a Bundle of Linnen being two pieces of Sheets and questioned about it He Declares it is not the bundle he had in Michael Davidsons and that he never saw it before. And he Declares also that no body was concerned with him in any part of the before mentioned adventures, and that the scheme was entirely formed & executed by himself. And all this he Declares is truth In testimony whereof These presents being Written by Patrick Cushrie, Writer in Stonehaven are Subscribed upon this & the six preceeding pages by the said James Duncan & the Sherriff Before & in presence of the said Patrick Custimie John Charles Merchant Taylor in Stonehaven & James Clark keeper of the Tolbooth of Stonehaven Witnesses also to the said James Duncan Emission of the premises & to his approbation thereof when it was read over to him. But he Declared he did not hide himself below the Rock but when he saw that the people had discovered him he sett himself down upon a Rock and waited til they came up to him.

At Aberdeen the Twenty Eighth day of June One Thousand Seven Hundred and Seventy years In presence of Robert Burnes, esq, sheriff substitute of Aberdeenshire.

Which day James Duncan son to James Duncan, sometimes residenter in Aberdeen, being brought before the sheriff and examined Declares and acknowledges That in spring One Thousand Seven hundred and sixty nine he was brought to Tryall before the Sheriff of Aberdeen being accused of theft and at that time gave in a Petition to the Sherriff craving to be banished from the Shire of Aberdeen and was Banished accordingly with the Consent of the Prosecutor. Declares that he has been in the Tolbooth of Stonehaven for five weeks past and until the morning of Tuesday last the Twenty sixth current when he made his escape thereupon by setting fire to the Prison Door that he was Confined on an Accusation of theft. Declares that before he was apprehended at Stonehaven he was possessed of Twenty four pound sterling which consisted of Twenty shillings notes partly Aberdeen and partly Glasgow and partly Dundee and two or three Edinburgh Notes Eleven guineas in gold and some silver all which he wrapt up in a piece of paper and concealed in a green bank at the seaside near to Cowrie in the neighbourhood of Stonehaven. Declares that he gott out of the Prison at Stonehaven about two or three o'clock in the morning. That he went up through the country but called at no house and gott no victuals the whole of that Day. Declares that on Tuesday night he went into a mans barn a good way up the country where he slept for some time until he could see to Travell. That he left the said Barn when day Light appeared and came to Aberdeen where he arrived about Ten o'clock Declares that after he left Aberdeen upon being banished as formerly mentioned he went to London and went to sea and Continued at sea about ten months at the rate of eighteen shillings of monthly wages. That he had no other way of Earning any money than by the wages he so received part of which money he Expended in buying cloaths and being Interrogate from whom he received the foresaid sum of Thirty four pound sterling which he says he concealed as formerly mentioned refuses to give any account from whom he received it or how he came by it but declares that when he went to London from Aberdeen he had no money but Eighteen shillings which he received from his father. Declares that he was at Fettereso on Tuesday after he left the Prison at Stonehaven. And that he was at Jillybrand or the neighbourhood thereof any part of the day or night of the said Tuesday. Declares that the bonnet which he presently has was bought by him upon Tuesday last from a man who was Casting Peats,[3] in a moss, whose name he does not know. Declares that he bought the three watches which were found in his custody yesterday when he was apprehended from people in this Town but will not condescend upon the persons names from whom he bought them or what price he paid for them as which he Declares to be Truth and Declares he cannot Write. In testimony of which this declaration is wrote upon this and the preceeding page by George Forbes writer in the Sherriff Clerk's Office of Aberdeen was emitted by the Declarant and subscribed by the Sherriff Substitute before these witnesses the said George Forbes and William Forbes William Robson and Patrick Mackie sheriff officers in Aberdeen.

Aberdeen Sixth July 1770. In presence of Robert Turner, esq, Sheriff Substitute of Aberdeen.

Compeared the said James Duncan who being again Examined, Declares and acknowledges That on the night between the twenty sixth and twenty seventh of June last He entered the house of the said George Mason by a window, and took out a small locked Chest and Carried the said chest out of the house with him, By opening the door of the house with the Key which he found in the Inside. Declares and acknowledges That he forced upon the Chest with a piece of Crooked iron and took out of the same, about Thirty eight pounds sterling in Gold Silver & Bank notes, which he carried off with him. That among the Silver then was some Crown pieces. That he also too out of said house a Bonnet which he found in the room where the Chest was. Declares that he brought said Money to Aberdeen, and upon Wednesday the Twenty seventh being the day on which he entered there. He brought two Silver Watches from a Mason or Quarrier in the house of John Bunyan stabler in the Gallowgate. In presence of a flesher & a mason and Youngson's Servant Maid. That he paid Four pound Fourteen shillings Sterling for said two watches out of the foursaid money which he brought with him. Declares That he bought another silver watch from a man in Old Aberdeen, and paid for said watch and for a coat which he also bought Four pound eleven shillings Sterling being likeways paid of the said money. Declares that when he was apprehended the remainder of the money which he took out of George Mason's Chest, the bonnet formerly mentioned & the foresaid three watches were found about him and taken from him. And being further Interrogate Declares That there was no person in consort with him, or assisted him in making his escape from the prison of Stonehaven, having effected his escape himself by setting fire to the prison door. That after he got out of Prison he Broke his Irons & threw them into water. All which he Declares to be truth in Testimony whereof this declaration so wrote upon this and the preceeding page by James Clerk writer in Aberdeen and subscribed by the Declarant & Sherriffs Substitute before these witnesses William Gray Merchant in Aberdeen and he said James Clerk.

Notes

1 A losen or lozen was a glass windowpane.
2 A 'sneck' is a latch on a door or window.
3 Casting the peat involves cutting slices of peat out of the ground and building them into a wall to allow them to dry in the wind.

6

JOHANNES EWALD (1743–1781), *LIFE AND OPINIONS* (*LEVNET OG MENINGER*)

(Copenhagen, [written 1774–1778, published 1804–1808] 1856)[1]

Johannes Ewald was a Danish dramatist and poet, the son of a Lutheran pietist minister, who became a writer following a short-lived military career and period spent studying theology. Writing as a Danish sentimentalist, his style was influenced by European writers, including Jean-Jacques Rousseau, Lawrence Sterne and Edward Young. The excerpt below is taken from his 'Life and Opinions', a stylised autobiography, one of his few pieces of prose writings. The work was unfinished and published after his death. Written in the first person, it is a compelling narrative account of his life, and reflects both a tradition in Protestant self-writing, and their fictional counterparts in the novel. Ewald's influences are particularly evident in this excerpt, which both follows Rousseau's account of love in childhood (see source 4), and which references characters in Samuel Richardson, Lawrence Sterne and classical literature. As a source for the history of emotions, it provides a compelling account of the highs and lows of youthful love. That he recounts his life through fictional motifs offers an interesting example of how people use popular literature to make sense of feelings and events that are otherwise intensely personal. His artistry, wordplay, and engagement with his audience destabilise any sense that this is a private text, asking us to reflect on the authenticity of his text and why a description of feeling plays such a critical role in the production of the eighteenth-century self for the reader.

. . .

Arendse

Did I then also have an Arendse? Or was it a Dulcinea, which my Imagination alone created because it needed it? No, by Cupid, I had one, or rather I was had by a lovely, a fine and perceptive, a noble, a majestic Arendse – one of these shadowy beauties, whose smile is like the sun through a rainy sky – her wave penetrates like an irresistible ray of melancholy virtue – one of those insistent, charismatic, bewitching brunettes that one cannot see without awe and hardly love without adoration – An Arendse, with large dark brown, radiant eyes, with a small crooked nose, a mouth on which the Graces seemed to play, thick chestnut-brown curls, which shaded a snow-white neck, two round, expanding, swelling – O Heaven! – I forget myself! The most important thing! An Arendse, with a virtuous, a witty, a sedate and a high Soul. An Arendse, with the tenderest heart, that has ever beaten behind a stay! – I had her – O Heaven! O mine Readers! O you, who Pain has made sensitive and tender, you who abused, abandoned by the world, sit in your lonely cabins and read this book, so to slay your sorrow – let a single compassionate tear drop on it! I had my Arendse – and now another has her! Once nagging and tormenting, now insidious and murderous poison![2] Remembering my Loss! Consuming, destroying Thought! Source of my Despair, My Disorders and My Misfortunes! Source of my daily sorrows, and my tears! When will you evaporate?

In as far as I know myself, I believe I would have gotten over my loss if my Arendse had been happy. She is not, far from it. Gladly more than gladly, I think, would I have wished for her one who better than I could have appreciated her, could have rewarded and maintained her Perfections. O God! O Pity! Sorrow, nagging sorrow has emaciated my blooming Arendse. Now she is the imprint of grief, the image of death. Now a terrible disease, Horror's Daughter and Mother, brings her daily to the grave side.

Arendse

It is scarcely two years since my Arendse came to me, while I lay in my lonely cabin without other Company than my sorrow and my pain. Pale and sunken were her lovely cheeks and only a dull spark of the fire so familiar to me still shone in her eyes. She seemed to me like the suffering Virtue; like Arria, when she, with Death on her lips, with the deep deadly wound in her chest, passed Paetus' the dagger – and said – it does not hurt my Poete! With a Clementina's[3] melancholic, sedate and measured walk, with venerable grief in each feature, with struggling and undefeated dignity, she went to my bed and laid the outer tips of three fingers on my trembling hand. "Past times are gone, Ewald", she said, and hurried away, as if she feared having said too much. "Yes, they are lost", I replied, and looked fixedly at that place where she had stood. Not a single kind tear would soothe my troubled heart – O my Arendse! My Arendse!

Love

Early my heart found a smoldering spark of thee thou Remnant of Paradise, you Heavenly Love. Formed as it was by its Creator for all tender and strong feelings, it opened up easily to the sweetest and most penetrating of all, without either knowing its dangers, or itself. I loved before I knew what it was to love, before I was aware of any differences between the sexes than the one that daily confronts the eye. Those who wish to know mankind will not lose thereby if they carefully attend to this paragraph of my biography. They will find in it the partly uplifting, partly dispiriting degrees of a childish, a true and virtuous, a romantic, an abundant but delicate and pleasing, and in essence wild and brutal Love. But I must arm myself with a better humour before I can write thereon – lend me therefore a glimpse of that spirit, My Yorick, that taught you to flee from Death to the banks of the Garonne![4] Lend me that, so that I can flee this deadly thought, which pursues me – from this murderous recollection of times that have disappeared!

I cannot – I cannot think of anything but the part of my bliss which they took with them into their abyss. Away! Away!

The merry, healthy, brave Youth, the innocent, immaculate Conscience, the sensitive, warm, happy, hopeful Heart, the bold, creative Imagination, float by me in a long host, like the many pale ghosts of deceased friends. Away! Away! Miserable Shadows! I want to cover my eyes with my hands and not see them –

Do I not know that God loves me? And will not forsake me? Besides, have I not sincere true friends? Have I not an income to support myself for more than a year? Am I not sitting in a good armchair with a good glass of red wine standing by my side? – Why then do I cry as if indifferent to them?

I was at most only thirteen years old when I felt the first glimmer of love. Not that I knew at that time what it was I felt. But I have since found that it could not be otherwise. Hardly any child could be more ignorant and innocent in such things than I was then, and a good part of the year thereafter. I was then receiving board and education from SI Rector Licht in Schleswig, who lived in the long street, and a middle-aged Regimental Quartermaster-lady was the one who first threw her grappling hook into my Heart. Love is like all our other Passions – it forms itself carefully according to the things we knew, according to the notions we have. That is why a Professor of Philosophy loves like a Platonist, or at least like one of the Heroes of the Birth of Christ, a courtier like a deceiver, and a farmer like a bull. I was a Child, and loved, as a Child. That is to say, I regarded the one I though ignorantly worshiped as a Mother, but, as the most gracious of all Mothers, against whom I would not only without coercion, but even wished, burned to show the most unrestricted obedience, the deepest submission. I wish that once I could come into company with her, and she would command me something, said my little swollen heart. How I would fly! I wished she in a rage, without me having deserved it, punished me – Beat me! How would I not then with tears in my eyes kiss her hands! Her Feet! Then she would repent when she saw that she had done me wrong, express sorrow, and perhaps call me her Ewald. These were reliably the most arousing images with which Cupid at the time tempted me. Every moment I could steal from my books, I spent ordinarily and most of the time mechanically, unintentionally, in the window or in the street door. I stroked my hair back, pulled out my half-sleeves and calf-cross, and when I then discovered my Beloved, stared at her expectantly, until I was made happy when her eyes met mine. Then I would bow with my nose to the ground, and if fate was with me, she would accompany the curtsy with which she thanked me with a little smile. O then I wished her away, just so that I could enjoy this smile in private. I am curious to know if this good lady noticed anything in my audacious folly. I have never spoken to her in my life, but it is evident that she was a great deal more experienced than I was, and that without doubt it would only have been her contempt for my Childhood that would have led her to misunderstand all my deep Compliments.

This Fire was soon extinguished – whether it was because it had consumed all the Curtsies and Smiles, by which it was nourished and consequently had no more material with which to burn, or because my Regimental Quartermaster-Lady had moved away, I no longer remember. And now my heart was still, until a Flensburg girl, after half a year, again lit it on fire. This girl, who served us, had as far as I remember one of the ordinary faces, which gladly lets one go in peace, who would otherwise take care of themselves.[5] Her upper lip was also, from the nose down, always tightly covered with used and unused tobacco, which Circumstance is not of the most alluring. But like I said, I loved, like a child. A pair of snow-white bulging beauties, which she to abundance exposed, so much as she well could, and which immediately reminded me of the sweetness I had tasted in my most tender infancy, stole my attention and my heart in a moment. In a few words, if I loved the Regimental Quartermaster-Lady as my mother, then I loved the little Flensburger, like my nurse. Who there may touch them – kiss them! – I said! Who there was still a child, and could stroke, hug, suck them! One sees that here was already more substance, more truth in this Love, than in the previous. How many of the desired Freedoms she granted me I do not recall and I will not remember. I do know that I played my romance so far that on a good market day, for the last of my pocket money, I bought a pair of two-foot straw-coloured silk ribbons, which I gave her as a gift, and that she rewarded my gallantry with one or more powerful kisses, at which I, in view of what I have said above, probably sneezed.[6] Yet I remember that some years later, on my trip abroad, I met this girl by accident on Flensburg Street; the beauties once so beloved seemed to me like a pair of dandelions, and notwithstanding I am by nature both kind-hearted and polite to the fair sex, it felt to me almost oppressive to answer all the courtesies with which she addressed me with two friendly words. But this is the end of all these wild entombed passions – And besides, my heart was full of Arendse at that time.

Another little flame, in the shape of a pretty, narrow-waisted, white-skinned, freckled Chancellor's daughter, that lit up in my young breast when I was studying for Confirmation with the Rev. Mr. Cramer, would hardly be worth talking about was it not for how it kindled. I was, as I have recounted and as one can easily believe, then so innocent that I really did not know what love was, and I, simple-minded enough, thought that one did not love any other but the person one married. Since the latter was not in my plans, it is quite evident that at that time I never thought to love my Regimental Quartermaster-lady, or my Flensburg girl, or my freckled maiden. It may then be this last one, which I had made so serious an attack on, but I do not recall. For as far as the first two are concerned, novels themselves, which at that time had already corrupted my Imagination, could not teach me what I should do with them. But now that I look back with more experience to this period, I find not only love in my then behaviour, but even all the motives, if only in miniature, that have since driven me, and that so often have driven others to the fiercest Passions. What drove me to love the Regimental Quartermaster-lady was truly a Glimpse of Heavenly Sympathy, like I know not what, but immediately births Reverence or Awe, and as united with it compels us to love, to honour, to worship not only the Person of our Conqueror, not only her smallest actions, but her breath, the place where she has stood, her failings, the injustice she does to us – compels us to wish her well above all things, and to promote her wellbeing to the best of our ability, with no underlying agenda of our own. My desire for the Flensburg girl was, in respect to its motivations, of an entirely opposite nature. I can believe that some bodily Beauty could set the aforementioned *je ne sçai qvoi*[7] in motion, just as the Wind brings a Warship to sail, or an ignited firelighter a gunpowder magazine to blow up – but to produce it, the most perfect beauty in my mind is far from sufficient. The two seductive beauties which my Flensburg girl had to show did not imprint me with either Reverence or any wonderous desire for her well-being. It was really only my Self, my Pleasure, of which I thought. I could on this occasion write as skilfully as Vinetti, and maybe even as well as Aretin himself,[8] a Dissertation on the Nudities[9] and their effects, which would be of considerable benefit both to naturalists and to moralists; but I fear to leave behind me a word, a letter, which can, even by accident, force from a young face a blush, from a blameless heart, an unworthy flutter. Indeed, I almost fear that already I have said too much on this matter. The kind of love I felt for my little freckled maiden had an origin that was quite different again from the two above.

Vanity was, as I now understand, the snare in which my heart was then caught – actually captured. For it would have been unsurprising that, having always kept my desires close, I was regarded as loved. But unobtrusively my desire changed from wanting to be considered so to wanting to be so. And this I think is a rarity. For often one who likes to have someone who is highly esteemed only for the purpose of adorning oneself has an incompatible prejudice against it. My biography would be infinite if I on all occasions extensively detailed my reflections, and this subject, as said, is moreover too tender. I will therefore spare the many beautiful Things I had to say in this case; write my History as it is and let everyone conclude from it what he can. I was the top among the Boys who went to Reading class, just as my Beloved was among the Girls. This circumstance alone moved us straightaway and without agreement to give each other our preference, by distinguishing ourselves in a recognizable manner from the crowd, and to greet each other both before, and more often, and more deeply than anyone else. But never did my body bend so deeply that my soul, in proportion, did not tower the higher, and I think that in this we shared a similar character. "From experience", communicated my Compliment roughly, "of Self-Consciousness, I know, my maiden, that you would not enjoy this rank unless birth and merits justified it. I therefore grant you, according to my duty, the reverence which undeniably belongs to the people of your and my kind." "It's your just place, my lord," she thus answered with her curtsy, "It is precisely your place that makes you more worthy of my attention than any of the others." This Distinction grew, like everything, gradually. Our regard

THE SELF

for others declined, from coldness, to indifference, and thence to contempt – and rose in relation to ourselves from politeness to reverence, and thence to an almost real esteem. At least she gradually turned more and more, so that at last, when she nodded to me, she almost turned her back to her companion sisters, where she had in the beginning stood in a straight line with them, and I who at first deigned one and then another with a rather confidential Greeting, finally dismissed them all together with a quick flourish of my hat. On the other hand, we never forgot, when we recited our lesson to the priest, to affect the closest attention to each other's least word, to the movement of our lips, just as we always, when it was over, gave each other, whether we had done it right or wrong, our applause through an admiring smile. When the others were interrogated, on the other hand, we affected carelessness, and vanity drove me unworthy to such an extent that at that time I begged her applause for several small tricks, that when they, upon desire, were rewarded, encouraged me to more and greater, until I thereby finally attracted the attention of everyone and especially the pastor. In this we already began to distinguish ourselves from each other, just as I am convinced that it was me alone whose heart fell into the snare I had myself established. I could clearly see in our little company that each assumed a kind of understanding between me and my heroine, and it became my ambition thereof to maintain this presumption. I spared nothing for this purpose, without words, of which I reliably do not believe to have exchanged twenty in my Lifetime, with my then Beloved. But I exerted all the powers of my soul to refine, to strengthen, and to expand the language of the pantomime, which nature itself had taught me, I do not know how, and it could not other than put all the tenderest, most sensitive fibres of my heart in motion. As a good Actor, in the heat of his role, often forgets himself, and truly becomes the one he should only imagine, thus it went for me. I wished, though only gradually and unnoticed more and more reality in my glamour. I began to feel a kind of tormenting cold in my heart when I went from the pastor, and I longed more to come there again than I should have done if I had not supposed my freckled girl there. This went so far that I, even after the connection in which we had stood was terminated, for a few weeks wasted many a walk past her windows just to beg by my deep greetings a nod from her. The circumstances forbade me at that time to come further and then this curtsey, as significant as even it sometimes could be, was too little nourishment for my heart; it soon hibernated and the whole thing disappeared by itself. I repeat, before I end this paragraph, that I then, as far as I remember, notwithstanding all these listed Emotions, did not trust myself able to Love or really knew what it was. If I loved the first two as my mother and as my nurse, I loved the latter as a sister or a friend, and my highest desire rose only to be esteemed and favored more than others by her. Two prejudices that were ingrained in me at the time prevented me from having a bigger impact: that one could not love except whom one married, and that one could only marry when one had a livelihood. The novels that I read taught me no more. That is they said more than they should say to young readers, of which, to my happiness, I did not understand a word. But my destiny willed that I soon, all too soon, should be better informed.

Yet I may recall that I so early not only felt, but even, without praising myself, aroused a Kind of Love. A short, fat, copper-faced girl, in her middle age – when one reckons 90 years for the outermost point of human life – a girl, who had spent roughly the last thirty years of her life in my Rector's House, not only waiting on his boarders, but considering herself justified in exercising some kind of authority over them. A grumpy, if not snarling beauty, to whose hair I was really drawn the first evening I had the honor of her acquaintance, and who – as I since and only with coercion have been able to reconcile – must, as I can now conclude, at some point have discovered something in me that pleased her. Some caresses by her fashion, a growing and otherwise incomprehensible docility, and especially some liberties, which she on certain occasions afforded herself, convince me now of that, as I have enough experience to understand them. Had I then been three or four years older, I have no doubt that I would have become a new proof of the very well-founded sentence that a young man is in the greatest danger of losing his innocence in the arms of a middle-aged woman. A cause of this, on which I have already stated some, and which I almost doubt that anyone before me has explicitly observed, is this – that love, as well as the one we love, exactly converts in our heart, according to the notions we have, and that we, accordingly, as children, may sooner fall in love with them who resemble our mother, and our nurse, than those who resemble our sisters. For the sake of those who perhaps will say that this paragraph of my biography is immoral, I will just point to those lessons that those without all careful reflection might skim straight over. Thus, without a doubt, the regimental quartermaster-wives will, at first glance, learn to address their kindnesses and their greetings to young boys with vigilance, prudence, and even with strictness, the girls of Flensburg will learn to cover their breasts a degree more thoroughly, the priests will, as I hope, hereafter take care not to provide the least fuel for vanity in their young congregations, and those who have fourteen year old boarders will not let their unmarried servants, though old, get too close to them.

When, in my fifteenth year, I came to Copenhagen and became a student, my heart was as unstained by Love as a tablet on which nothing is written. But here Vanity soon laid me a new snare. I came to lodge in a chamber with my oldest brother and two other young students, the youngest of whom was at least two years older than me. I do not know if generally all young people, when they become what is called men, place so great a price on their manhood as we put on it. But it seems that we regarded this new rank we had attained both as our highest and our most tender *Point d'honneur*,[10] and that I especially at that time, would rather have been scolded a thousand times as a rogue, than as a child or a boy. I now understand that my bad conscience alone was the cause of this – for I found myself more offended by an accusation which the most excessive pride could not imagine as entirely unfounded, than by others where my Heart immediately acquitted me. I had however, if I would otherwise vindicate my position, many more difficulties to overcome than any of the others. I was both the youngest and the smallest, and as I earlier believe I have remarked, even for my age was very little. Since now, as is well known, in all or at least most domestic societies prevails a lawful custom, which has its origin in a desire for pleasure – that one, as they say, must keep the Light for all the others – so it was no wonder that my three comrades-in-arms immediately saw me as a person that was best suited for this use. I brought all my jokes and all my reluctant courage to avert this misfortune. Yet, in spite of all my efforts, I could not bring myself to be taken seriously. It seems that there are four signs in particular by which a newly-made man can indisputably prove his manliness, and without which his academic achievements, and even his sword only little will help him. None of these four evidences did my three Contubernales[11] lack, and I alone unluckily could not exhibit a single one of them. The first, which is to smoke tobacco, produced in me a then invincible Disgust, the second, to go the pub, I was still at that time too bashful and timid to try. The third was to shave, and I unhappily was then as smooth on my chin, as I am now on the palm of my hand; the fourth was to have a sweetheart. This seemed the most likely for me to attain, and I resolved that I would have one and the sooner the better, so that if at that time pious Magdalene, or the Cumaean Sibyl, or the Witch of Endor, with a single friendly face, had made me bold enough to offer myself, I should then, without the slightest hesitation, have thrown myself into her arms.

Notes

1 Translated by Katie Barclay, with thanks to Nina Koefoed for her advice.
2 Ewald uses the Danish word 'gift' here, which means both marriage and poison. That it has this double meaning is the root of many Danish jokes and he seems to be being playful here too.
3 Clementina is a character in Samuel Richardson's *Sir Charles Grandison* (1753), who becomes melancholic after a failed courtship.
4 Yorick is a character of Lawrence Sterne and this references a scene in *The Life and Opinions of Tristram Shandy, Gentleman* (1759–67).
5 The meaning here implies the woman is uninteresting.
6 Here Ewald uses the word 'nyse', which has a double meaning of sneeze and a childish/sexless kiss, and he appears to intend this double reading.
7 French for 'I know not what', an expression used to mean something that is hard to define or give words to.
8 Nicolas Venette (1633–1698) wrote *Conjugal Love, or, The Pleasures of the Marriage Bed*; Pietro Aretin (1492–1556) was a prolific writer.
9 By which he means her breasts.
10 Point of honour.
11 The smallest organised unit of soldiers in the Roman Army.

7

SOPHIE VON LA ROCHE (1730–1807), *SOPHIE IN LONDON, 1786: BEING THE DIARY OF SOPHIE V. LA ROCHE*

Trans. Clare Williams
(London: Jonathan Cape, 1933), pp. 293–300

Sophie von la Roche was a German novelist, and mother of eight children. After her husband's death, she supported herself through her writings, a mark of her economic success. La Roche mainly wrote novels, designed to instruct young women in how to live morally. This excerpt is taken from a travel diary she kept whilst on a 'Grand Tour' of England in 1786. The diary was written in German for her children, offering them an educational account of what she saw, customs and manners, those she met, and what she read; it may have been intended to also have been published in her periodical for young women, *Pomona*. It was translated in 1930 for an English audience. The text is didactic, both in the nature of its observations – largely interesting accounts of geography, conversations or ideas – and in offering a model of polite, Enlightenment femininity for others to emulate. The excerpt below explores her last few days in England. Like the confession in 5, this is less an account of emotion than a source that allows us to see everyday life is threaded with emotional experiences (including boredom), and the way that descriptions of emotion are used to help explain and describe our encounters with the world. This is particularly important in the eighteenth century, where the enlightenment self is meant to demonstrate its sensibility, a characteristic evidenced through our sensitivity and emotional engagement with our environment. La Roche models this sensible self for her reader, as well as assessing the sensibility of various people she observes.

. . .

Oct. 11 [1786]

This afternoon I was vividly reminded of Miss Burney,[1] as there was some talk in the paper of good Lavater,[2] and somebody, on hearing that his mind had become fuddled, said, 'It was a good thing for humanity, as this example would cure many

THE SELF

of the exaggerated enthusiasm to which he had brought them.' Charming Miss Burney would almost certainly have made as pointed a remark as she did over the Cook incident.[3] During a discussion on physiognomy Mr. Hurter expressed the idea that it was nothing more than a game of chance. It was only a matter of drawing some fine figure or other, and then either contracting the said features a little or expanding them, so that three different physiognomies of the same person would excite a similar number of different versions of their moral character. With reference to the above, I expressed the hope that I should find Lavater in good health on arrival, and should like to hear him talk with the author, as due to inclement weather we had to stay about here quite a long while, and the sight might have dispelled the tedium; but it gave us the advantage of a rest, and we were thus able to select our ship from amongst the packet-boats lying at anchor.

I should very much like to sketch the schoolmaster, who has a school opposite my window in the room of a really miserable abode; a large, powerful man, strong enough to strangle four youths at a time, and who, in addition, has his square head bound up in a large cloth which, plus his dark brown overcoat, gives him a disagreeable look which must frighten the children. Nor can anything more joyful than the faces and capers of those little ones when school is over be imagined. During those dreary days in Dover, these boys of six to fourteen years, in that fine flower and with the splendid stature peculiar to the English, cheered me somewhat. Youthful spirits, sensation of freedom, companionship and mischief; some of them having a sense of justice and protection towards the oppressed, others aggressive and offensive, then beating a cowardly retreat, showing malice or sympathy, all these characteristics could be discerned amongst the fifteen or sixteen boys, and just as I am writing this, they are gathering for school again. Five of them still have some important task to perform, and are investigating their tiny pipes and squirts made of elm-wood, smiling kindly at them before putting them away in their pockets, and then they troop into school together. There are very fine boys amongst them, but those with the little pipes seemed to me gentler, while the owners of the squirts were more violent and more decided in their gestures, which was the natural outcome of their characters, as perhaps they fashioned the soft, simple pipe from the wood of some shrub to give themselves and others pleasure, while the squirts were cut for teasing purposes or perhaps for revenge. They did not put their books down, and I regret not having asked them to show me their school-books. May they grow into honest citizens supporting their old parents, and become good husbands to the pretty lasses with whom Dover abounds.

I remember to have heard from Mr. le Bret that in the inn at which he stopped during his trip with the Duke of Wiirtemberg in Dover, there was a library for foreigners where several languages might be had, so that the period of waiting for a favourable wind should be pleasantly whiled away. I made inquiries at our lodgings, too, and saw a cupboard opened which contained besides a supply of tumblers and bottles a few copies of very good English sermons.

One volume of Plutarch translated into English in 1686. A copy of a Paris newspaper, which some traveller must have left behind, and one book, with the

BEING THE DIARY OF SOPHIE V. LA ROCHE

title-page missing, from Louis XIV's time, describing a *fête galante* held by the latter at Marly.[4]

The rain cleared up a little, so I went to buy a travellingbonnet, and visited a book-shop as well, and asked for Brath's charming tale, *Emma Corbet* from which Angelika borrowed the subject for a stirring picture representing Virtue bending over Emma's urn, and mourning her death.[5] But the man did not have this tale in stock. I was tempted to buy a delightful little engraving, however, showing a lovely peasant girl holding ears of corn in her hand in pious rural manner, and her eyes lifted to heaven. The inscription reads, 'Lord, Thou who tookest away my parents and madest me poor, grant me work and protect my innocence, and I shall never bemoan my fate.'

I bought the September and October numbers of the *Lady's Magazine*, and was sorry I had not procured them all, as they contained very nice essays, most useful for the information of my sex, as, for example, An idea of true philosophy and wisdom; On the spirit of contradiction; Educational institutes; Medical notes for women; Blind delusions of love; A fine picture of the value of a loyal stepmother; charming poems on various subjects, and a number of riddles, some made up especially from the names of boy and girl pupils in different counties, some requiring a thorough knowledge of the language, others observation in natural and racial history, art and other branches. I was informed too late of the publication of a handbook for ladies dealing with feminine interests and amusements, and directions as to how to become prosperous with honour. Further, dedicated to men of small means, advice showing how families can live on £750 to £130 a year. As such sums are often the lot of eminent persons at home, and as now the state revenues and expenditures of kings and princes are becoming known, it seems to me a useful piece of work might be done using this material as a companion study to our estimable Professor Crome's catalogue of European products, entitled, *Europe and her Expenditure*. But this useful English book cannot be very well known, even in its own country, as in the latest papers I saw a number of estates up for sale; it seems to me as long as paint *á la* Ninon Enclos, soap-bubbles of Venus, hair-oil of Athens, and exaggerated fashions are sought by the 'ladies,' as this paper reports, and as long as there are men who dodge the ban upon the coming fashion of tying shoes with laces, which threatens to ruin buckle-makers, by wearing a buckle on one foot and a shoe-lace on the other, so as not to cause too precipitate a change – so long there will be family estates on the market, and this booklet will need to go through more than five editions, especially if ministers be returned again of the type rebuked for spending untold millions, for the nation cannot always count on a William Pitt to succeed with virtuous precepts in counteracting this irresponsible squandering.

I was very glad to have this reminder of the great man while still on the shores of his own country, just as the last drop of a rare elixir from the chalice of human joy is quaffed rapturously. I derived great pleasure from reading the invitations to four different winter clubs – for philosophers, doctors, politicians and economists – where practical problems are dealt with. There is also one announced for fools and idiots, in which the maddest member acts as president. I do hope the economic club will encourage Mr. Watson's excellent suggestions for teaching young people of rank and means the principles of agriculture, commerce and manufacture,[6] so that they may one day be of real service to their country in important matters in parliament by their understanding, and on their estates become models and leaders in a sound land policy and be assured against the tedium of which gay, wealthy noblemen complain in the country. Further, this excellent man strikes chords, the sound of which excites my grief; for instance, he suggests that this would cause a sound increase in agriculture and the good, honest, peasant population, as millions of acres are lying there fallow; and let me add that it would remove the reproof that highway robbery is a native English characteristic. Secondly, Mr. Watson continues that parents leave their children at the university too short a time, as they take them away at the age of seventeen, give them a horse and money at random to pursue gaieties galore, teach them to drink at table like their elders, and then send them to France or to Italy – so that Great Britain overflowed with babblers on good taste, literature, art and religion.

Millions of untilled acres, and so many young people ruined by the senseless kindness of their parents – this was a double crime, and grieved me extremely. Swarms of young Englishmen in Gottingen, Geneva and Lausanne came to my mind, confirming such complaints. I am indeed sorry that parents are accused of this, thereby throwing a great moral shadow over the fair isle.

My children must allow me one more extract from this last paper read on English soil, for so many desires with regard to my own country are entailed; and I openly confess that I am sorry to find in this extract the faults of the teachers in the English academies I have praised so highly.

Mr. Digby wants to found an academy for fifteen scholars, who are to learn Latin and French, and a perfect knowledge of their English mother tongue, with pleasant, harmonious pronunciation and every fine turn of phrase, to enable them to pursue their studies or travel worthily and with enjoyment. They are supposed to be made familiar with the classical authors of these three languages, and mathematics. Besides which, they must be trained to show a fine candid spirit and a pleasant demeanour; nor will any punishment be inflicted which might harm the mentality of a sensitive, honourable youngster, as happens in so many academies amongst disagreeable, stupid teachers, often for quite minor youthful offences caused by thoughtlessness, making learning a torture for them, and suppressing all noble ambition.

He guarantees large, clean rooms in addition; simple, nourishing food; boasts that his dwelling is situated far away from any disturbing racket and has an exit into the park for open air and walks, so that good parents might rest assured regarding their sons' health. I only wish as many academies were provided in our German Fatherland, and that the scholars were given English frock coats, hats, boots and cravats to wear, and that something of Mr. Digby's programme were adopted in their general training, and that their intellect were polished by social intercourse and modern languages, while avoiding the glaring mistakes in teaching which he reproves.

The apparently vainglorious tone assumed in praising the pretty, spacious rooms and the cleanliness and his position near a good walk is no small matter – I have heard good parents complain of the incredible dirt prevailing in educational establishments at home, ruining the health, orderliness and good habits of the pupils, so that they were taken away before they had received half their instruction.

I should have liked to write some excerpts from the history of Dover, but found nothing but the fact that the castle had been constructed on the foundations of the great Roman castle which Caesar had built, and that once the town had seven parishes, only two of which remain; that Dover had once been rich enough to equip twenty-one battleships, but was not so prosperous now. So the good city is, in fact, only meant for transit and a passage through, for fortune and affluence do not settle here. We too assert that had we only known we should have to stay some days in Dover, we could have remained in London a little longer. Some few more days there would have meant so much to me. One more amongst the finest in my life at Windsor, which some high mercy had decreed for me; another little trip with friends and Carl. . . . Oh, I feel in these and other joys, I experienced the sensations of an artist scheming an ideal for a painting or a statue, with a mental picture of the glorious creation in its supreme perfection before him, striving to give it form, using every effort in his power, and then discovering that the image he had planned was quite different from the one confronting him. But a peculiar, rare specimen of genius is required to hew Apollo from out a block of stone, or with the brush present immortal masterpieces. The spirit in question, combined with happy hours, would have to cast and mould circumstances in such a way that the image of a happy moment would grow as we had fancied it. Very ably drawn was the picture of my enjoyment, both mental and emotional, during this tour contour, blend of colours, all in finest perspective; perhaps, however, I have forgotten the shadows which overcast all earthly phenomena.

I owe my *Pomona* one very real pleasure in winning Mme. W– for a generous friend, for she gave me the amount of the remaining hundred copies, enabling me to let my son make the return journey with Mr. Hurter via Paris, and so give the dear boy yet another pleasure which will last him the rest of his life – that of seeing one of the world's most remarkable cities in the company of his parents' trusty friend, who loves him too, and at the same time of visiting with him physicists and mechanics there. This prospect for your brother crowns the pleasure of my tour to England, and of my work with the friendly pages of *Pomona*.

Notes

1 Frances Burney (1752–1840).
2 Johan Kaspar Lavater (1741–1801) was a well-known physiognomist who thought that a person's character could be read through their face and head.
3 Previous to this diary entry, Burney and la Roche had been part of a discussion about the death of Captain James Cook (1728–1779), and Burney had made some witty remarks.
4 There follow pages of translated extract from *L'Ennui san sujet* (tedium without cause) describing the pasttimes of the age, building of Marly, a *fête galante* held there at the

time of Louis XIV which are omitted as irrelevant. [*This note was added by the original translator of the diary*].

5 *Emma Corbett: or the Miseries of the Civil War* (1780) was written by Samuel Jackson Pratt under the name of Courtney Melmouth; it is unclear if this error is in the original or was made by the translator (perhaps misreading the hand-writing). A scene from the book was the subject of a painting by Angelica Kauffman (1741–1807).

6 Richard Watson (1737–1816) was a chemist and minister who advocated for universities to offer vocational learning in agriculture, commerce and manufacture.

8

OLAUDAH EQUIANO
(1745–1797), *THE LIFE OF OLAUDAH EQUIANO: OR GUSTAVUS VASSA, THE AFRICAN*

2 vols (Boston: Isaac Knapp, [1789] 1837), pp. 53–62

Olaudah Equiano was a writer and slavery abolitionist from Eboe in Benin (today southern Nigeria), who was sold into slavery as a child, but who purchased his freedom in 1766. Living in Britain as an adult, he was a member of the *Sons of Africa*, an abolitionist group, and published his autobiography to draw attention to the humanity of Africans and the horrors of slavery. It was remarkably popular, running to nine editions in his lifetime. He travelled across the United Kingdom, offering lectures on his experiences and promoting the abolitionist cause. Here, Equiano, like many other black abolitionist writers, sought to highlight his sensibility, that prized Enlightenment disposition, which marked civilisation and readiness for self-governance. Like other eighteenth-century writings, Equiano's autobiography is marked not only by a chronological account of events, but scenes which enable him to display a variety of emotional reactions, from horror to pain and suffering to love and loyalty. Like in the novel, such accounts were designed to enable the sensible reader to vicariously experience the emotions described. In the excerpt below, in an account of his recent removal from Africa, Equiano uses his naiveté in encountering American and British behaviours to draw attention to immoral and harsh practices. If many eighteenth-century writers used descriptions of 'savage' nations to explore human nature, Equiano's text is designed to suggest that European practices are no better and indeed may be more cruel than the 'savage' nations to which they routinely compare themselves.

. . .

I now totally lost the small remains of comfort I had enjoyed in conversing with my countrymen; the women too, who used to wash and take care of me were all gone different ways, and I never saw one of them afterwards.

THE SELF

I stayed in this island for a few days; I believe it could not be above a fortnight; when I, and some few more slaves, that were not saleable amongst the rest, from very much fretting, were shipped off in a sloop for North-America. On the passage we were better treated than when we were coming from Africa, and we had plenty of rice and fat pork. We were landed up a river a good way from the sea, about Virginia county, where we saw few or none of our native Africans, and not one soul who could talk to me. I was a few weeks weeding grass, and gathering stones in a plantation; and at last all my companions were distributed different ways, and only myself was left. I was now exceedingly miserable, and thought myself worse off than any of the rest of my companions; for they could talk to each other, but I had no person to speak to that I could understand. In this state, I was constantly grieving and pining, and wishing for death rather than any thing else. While I was in this plantation, the gentleman, to whom I suppose the estate belonged, being unwell, I was one day sent for to his dwelling-house to fan him; when I came into the room where he was I was very much affrighted at some things I saw, and the more so as I had seen a black woman slave as I came through the house, who was cooking the dinner, and the poor creature was cruelly loaded with various kinds of iron machines; she had one particularly on her head, which locked her mouth so fast that she could scarcely speak; and could not eat nor drink. I was much astonished and shocked at this contrivance, which I afterwards learned was called the iron muzzle. Soon after I had a fan put in my hand, to fan the gentleman while he slept; and so I did indeed with great fear. While he was fast asleep I indulged myself a great deal in looking about the room, which to me appeared very fine and curious. The first object that engaged my attention was a watch which hung on the chimney, and was going. I was quite surprised at the noise it made, and was afraid it would tell the gentleman any thing I might do amiss; and when I immediately after observed a picture hanging in the room, which appeared constantly to look at me, I was still more affrighted, having never seen such things as these before. At one time I thought it was something relative to magic; and not seeing it move, I thought it might be some way the whites had to keep their great men when they died, and offer them libations as we used to do our friendly spirits. In this state of anxiety I remained till my master awoke, when I was dismissed out of the room, to my no small satisfaction and relief; for I thought that these people were all made up of wonders. In this place I was called Jacob; but on board the African Snow, I was called Michael. I had been some time in this miserable forlorn, and much dejected state, without having any one to talk to, which made my life a burden, when the kind and unknown hand of the Creator (who in very deed leads the blind in a way they know not) now began to appear, to my comfort; for one day the captain of a merchant ship, called the Industrious Bee, came on some business to my master's house. This gentleman, whose name was Michael Henry Pascal, was a lieutenant in the royal navy, but now commanded this trading ship, which was somewhere in the confines of the county many miles off. While he was at my master's house, it happened that he saw me, and liked me so well that he made a purchase of me. I think I have often heard him say he gave thirty or forty pounds sterling for me; but I do not remember which. However, he meant me for a present to some of his friends in England: and as I was sent accordingly from the house of my then master, (one Mr. Campbell,) to the place where the ship lay; I was conducted on horseback by an elderly black man, (a mode of travelling which appeared very odd to me). When I arrived I was carried on board a fine large ship, loaded with tobacco, &c. and just ready to sail for England. I now thought my condition much mended; I had sails to lie on, and plenty of good victuals to eat; and every body on board used me very kindly, quite contrary to what I had seen of any white people before; I therefore began to think that they were not all of the same disposition. A few days after I was on board we sailed for England. I was still at a loss to conjecture my destiny. By this time, however, I could smatter a little imperfect English; and I wanted to know as well as I could where we were going. Some of the people of the ship used to tell me they were going to carry me back to my own country, and this made me very happy. I was quite rejoiced at the idea of going back; and thought if I could get home what wonders I should have to tell. But I was reserved for another fate, and was soon undeceived when we came within sight of the English coast. While I was on board this ship, my captain and master named me Gustavus Vassa. I at that time began to understand him a little, and refused to be called so, and told him as well as I could that I would be called Jacob; but he said I should not, and still called me Gustavus: and when I refused to answer to my new name, which I at first did, it gained me many a cuff; so at length I submitted, and by which I have been known ever since. The ship had a very long passage; and on that account we had very short allowance of provisions. Towards the last, we had only one pound and a half of bread per week, and about the same quantity of meat, and one quart of water a day. We spoke with only one vessel the whole time we were at sea, and but once we caught a few fishes. In our extremities the captain and people told me in jest they would kill and eat me; but I thought them in earnest, and was depressed beyond measure, expecting every moment to be my last. While I was in this situation, one evening they caught, with a good deal of trouble, a large shark, and got it on board. This gladdened my poor heart exceedingly, as I thought it would serve the people to eat instead of their eating me; but very soon, to my astonishment, they cut off a small part of the tail, and tossed the rest over the side. This renewed my consternation; and I did not know what to think of these white people, though I very much feared they would kill and eat me. There was on board the ship a young lad who had never been at sea before, about four or five years older than myself: his name was Richard Baker. He was a native of America, had received an excellent education, and was of a most amiable temper. Soon after I went on board, he showed me a great deal of partiality and attention, and in return I grew extremely fond of him. We at length became inseparable; and, for the space of two years, he was of very great use to me, and was my constant companion and instructor. Although this dear youth had many slaves of his own, yet he and I have gone through many sufferings together on shipboard; and we have many nights lain in each other's bosoms when we were in great distress. Thus such a friendship was cemented between us as we cherished till his death, which, to my very great sorrow, happened in the year 1759, when he was up the Archipelago, on board his Majesty's ship the Preston: an event which I have never ceased to regret, as I lost at once a kind interpreter, an agreeable companion, and a faithful friend; who, at the age of fifteen, discovered a mind superior to prejudice; and who was not ashamed to notice, to associate with, and to be the friend and instructor of one who was ignorant, a stranger, of a different complexion, and a slave! My master had lodged in his mother's house in America; he respected him very much, and made him always eat with him in the cabin. He used often to tell him jocularly that he would kill and eat me. Sometimes he would say to me – the black people were not good to eat, and would ask me if we did not eat people in my country. I said, no: then he said he would kill Dick (as he always called him) first, and afterwards me. Though this hearing relieved my mind a little as to myself, I was alarmed for Dick, and whenever he was called I used to be very much afraid he was to be killed; and I would peep and watch to see if they were going to kill him; nor was I free from this consternation till we made the land. One night we lost a man overboard; and the cries and noise were so great and confused, in stopping the ship, that I, who did not know what was the matter, began, as usual, to be very much afraid, and to think they were going to make an offering with me, and perform some magic; which I still believed they dealt in. As the waves were very high, I thought the Ruler of the seas was angry, and I expected to be offered up to appease him. This filled my mind with agony, and I could not any more, that night, close my eyes again to rest. However, when daylight appeared, I was a little eased in my mind; but still, every time I was called, I used to think it was to be killed. Some time after this, we saw some very large fish, which I afterwards found were called grampusses. They looked to me exceedingly terrible, and made their appearance just at dusk, and were so near as to blow the water on the ship's deck. I believed them to be the rulers of the sea; and as the white people did not make any offerings at any time, I thought they were angry with them; and, at last, what confirmed my belief was, the wind just then died away, and a calm ensued, and in consequence of it the ship stopped going. I supposed that the fish had performed this, and I hid myself in the fore part of the ship, through fear of being offered up to appease them, every minute peeping and quaking; but my good friend Dick came shortly towards me, and I took an opportunity to ask him, as well as I could, what these fish were. Not being able to talk much English, I could but just make him understand my question; and not at all, when I asked him if any offerings were to be made to them; however, he told me these fish would swallow any body which sufficiently alarmed me. Here he was called away by the captain, who was leaning over the quarter-deck railing, and looking at the fish; and most of the people were busied in getting a barrel of pitch to light for them to play with. The captain now called me to him, having learned some of my apprehensions from Dick; and having diverted himself and others for some time with my fears, which appeared ludicrous enough in my crying and trembling, he dismissed me. The barrel of pitch was now lighted and put over the side into the water. By this time it was just dark, and the fish went after it; and, to my great joy, I saw them no more.

THE LIFE OF OLAUDAH EQUIANO

However, all my alarms began to subside when we got sight of land; and at last the ship arrived at Falmouth, after a passage of thirteen weeks. Every heart on board seemed gladdened on our reaching the shore, and none more than mine. The captain immediately went on shore, and sent on board some fresh provisions, which we wanted very much. We made good use of them, and our famine was soon turned into feasting, almost without ending. It was about the beginning of the spring 1757, when I arrived in England, and I was near twelve years of age at that time. I was very much struck with the buildings and the pavement of the streets in Falmouth; and, indeed, every object I saw, filled me with new surprise. One morning, when I got upon deck, I saw it covered all over with the snow that fell over night. As I had never seen anything of the kind before, I thought it was salt: so I immediately ran down to the mate, and desired him, as well as I could, to come and see how somebody in the night had thrown salt all over the deck. He, knowing what it was, desired me to bring some of it down to him. Accordingly I took up a handful of it, which I found very cold indeed; and when I brought it to him he desired me to taste it. I did so, and I was surprised beyond measure. I then asked him what it was; he told me it was snow, but I could not in anywise understand him. He asked me, if we had no such thing in my country; I told him, No. I then asked him the use of it, and who made it; he told me a great man in the heavens, called God. But here again I was to all intents and purposes at a loss to understand him: and the more so, when a little after I saw the air filled with it, in a heavy shower, which fell down on the same day. After this I went to church; and having never been at such a place before, I was again amazed at seeing and hearing the service. I asked all I could about it, and they gave me to understand it was worshipping God, who made us and all things. I was still at a great loss, and soon got into an endless field of inquiries, as well as I was able to speak and ask about things. However, my little friend Dick used to be my best interpreter; for I could make free with him, and he always instructed me with pleasure. And from what I could understand by him of this God, and in seeing these white people did not sell one another as we did, I was much pleased; and in this I thought they were much happier than we Africans. I was astonished at the wisdom of the white people in all things I saw; but was amazed at their not sacrificing, or making any offerings, and eating with unwashed hands, and touching the dead. I likewise could not help remarking the particular slenderness of their women, which I did not at first like; and I thought they were not so modest and shame-faced as the African women.

Part 2

FAMILY AND COMMUNITY

Part 2

Family and community

Emotions are experienced by individuals, but they are also informed by families and groups. Most, but not all, children are socialised in emotional practices and cultures within families. Society and culture produce norms for emotional behaviour and feelings, and emotions are critical to group relationships and engagements. The sources in this selection reflect key emotional engagements for Enlightenment Europeans as they moved across the globe. The rise of the culture of sensibility can be seen in the language of letters between spouses, while new philosophies of self and emotion inform child-rearing practices. Growing consumption and trade practices enable new emotions, new connections and new anxieties, whilst other groups are still working together, and sometimes failing, to support basic needs. A critical issue of the period is how to interpret the emotions of those from very different cultures, who are encountered through exploration, invasion and colonisation. Letters, diaries, popular writings, criminal indictments and even art evidence not only the range of emotions available to eighteenth-century Europeans but also how emotions were a product of shared norms, cultural rules and group experiences.

9

SELECTION OF LETTERS FROM PHILIP DODDRIDGE (1702–1751) TO HIS WIFE MERCY DODDRIDGE (1709–1790)

Dr Williams's Library, London

Philip Doddridge was a non–conformist minister, teacher and writer of popular religious texts in England. He married Mercy Maris in 1730; the couple had nine children. These letters arise from early in their marriage, while Doddridge travelled to preach across England, or later when Mercy made visits to friends and family. The correspondence is a typical example of love letters between spouses of the period, demonstrating a command of affectionate language and expression, but also using stories of friends and family as both a source of news and to build intimacy between the couple. Health and wellbeing is a key feature of such writing, where demonstrating care of yourself, as well as others, was an evidence of a commitment to returning to a loved one, in an era where people often died young due to disease or accident. Letters like these have been an especially popular source for the history of emotions as they tend to display a broad range of emotional vocabulary as it was used in everyday written language, and in the negotiation of personal relationships. The types of emotional rhetoric and functions of letters varied depending on the relationship between the writer and reader, and the reason for writing.

. . .

16 July 1734, Hackney

My Dearest Creature can hardly imagine the Pleasure with which I receiv'd hers for which indeed I had waited with some Impatience I am very much oblig'd to you for the great Care & Tenderness which you express on my Account & assure you my Love, I will be so just to you as to take all possible Care of my self. My Friend here & especially those of Mr Waters's Family treat me in the most engaging Manner I can truly say I never met with greater Kindness in any Journey I ever made. As for Hurry & Fatigue tho some Degree of it be unavoidable yet I make it as moderate as possible by allowing my self all proper Assistances from Water men & Hackney Coaches. Yesterday I dined with Mrs Cooke & to Day I wait upon My Lady Russell who was to be in Town on Thursday. And the beginning of next Week I propose going to Ongar. Abundant friends enquire after you & send Service to you especially those of this family whose remarkable & most endearing goodness to me I desire you would take some Notice of in your next. Mr Waters who is undoubtedly one of the best of Men seldom fails to pray very particularly for you when he officiates in the Family & his pretty Daughter tells me that a Thousand kind things she does for me are for your sake. In short my Dear I know not when I shall have an Opportunity of making you a greater Compliment or rather of giving you a greater proof of my sincere & tender Affection than when I tell you that you are so dear to me that your Absence is a very sensible Affliction to me even here. I have the pleasure to think that I shall have you in my Arms in less than a Fortnight and in the Mean Time would never forget her at the Throne of Grace who has so great an Interest there & so constantly employs it for me. My hearty Service attends all Friends assure Mrs Wright that I don't forget her & hope amongst all my Friends some thing may be done towards obtaining her a Comfortable Settlement where the Necessity of our Affairs must oblige us to resign the pleasure of her Company & Assistance. As for the House do as you please. I hear at present of no more Pupils. I depend upon it that Mr Hawtyn & Mr Wilkinson will take Care of Jacky of yr ingenious Mr Hextall. Assure Jacky that I shall be greatly disappointed if he be not very perfect in all the Greek Vers both Active & Passive Barytones & Circumflexes. I don't trouble him with more particular Directions knowing under whose Direction he is. Mr Waters & his Lady, Mr J Waters & his Sister join their Services to you. As is for the Fair Lady I mentioned last she is so fast asleep that I do not apprehend her at present capable of servicing you which however she will certainly do before night in entertaining me. Yet after all my Dear there is no Entertainment so delightful to me as that which you Letters give me which there fore I hope you will be so good as to continue & frequently my Dearest Self yours most obliged faithful & affect. servt Doddridge.

I have a key in my pocket which I suspect to be that of your Chest of Drawers preay forgive my stealing it thro' the Goodness of God

Since I wrote I've rece'd Mr Hawtyns & heartily thank him for the Care he has taken of my people & of you I desire he would continue his Lectures in the parlour. Now I mention Mr Hawtyn desire him to give my hearty service to Miss Roppit & with it what else he pleases in my Name. I hope the Elbow will be kept down.

London July 13 1734

My Dearest Creature

Tho it be but a few hours since I sent you a letter by the Post yet as Mr Aitchinsons return gives me another Opportunity of sending I could not omit it The Letter I rec'd from you since the Date of my last gave me abundance of pleasures, but tho you are pleas'd to give so agreeable a Turb to some little mistakes in Writing yet I will be so just to you as not to judge of your Tenderness for me by the very small Number of them. Were that to be the Rule I should think it my great Misfortune that your Letter was generally so well spelt. I hear you are now alone as Mrs Wright is gone to Welford but I hope Mr Wilkinson is careful to let you have as much of his Company as he conveniently can & I am especially pleas'd to reflect that so much good Sense & Piety can never want Entertainment at Home.

Tomorrow I set out for Ongar from whence I propose to return to Hackney on Fryday & promise my self the pleasure of your good Company toward the End of next week. Nothing in life is so delightful to me. In the mean time I have the pleasure of telling you that Mr Saunder's Troublesome Affairs is coming as we hope to a speedy [torn]ppy Issue for his Antagonist terrified with Apprehension of the Pillory in all its most dismal Circumstances offer all the Demands & sues for peace on any terms.[1] Give my hearty service to my friends at Northampton Assure them I long to see them & never was so impatient of any Journey as of this & that I never met with so agreeable Entertainment in Town. Farewell my Dear Life. I am yours most obliged faithful & Affectionate Servant Doddridge,

I continue perfectly well I saw Mr Hawtyn & Mr Archer today.

30 Jul 1735 London

My Dearest, I could not forbear sending you one Line for a verbal message would not satisfy me. You may depend on my being with you on Saturday even tho I should walk it. Perhaps on Fryday if there be any coach. I will tell you another secret & that is that in all these married years I never long'd to see you more than I now do. I would travel many miles in the Dark this night to have the pleasure of meeting you at the end of my Journey. I know I have been very stupid correspondent this journey for Love has swallowed up all my lot & indeed has found it but a very small morsel. However Mr Cooke is not so consumed. He desires me to make hast home & to tell you what ever he means by it that the Turks have a proverb amongst them which says that the Barn is never so full but there is a room to thresh. I cant enlarge but my heart is so much with my dear dear Girl that I'm afraid my Friends find a poor insipid Creature but I am please to think you will not think me so & very tender sentiments fixed on so excellent a person seems to have something in it almost sacred & above reproof or Restraint assure yourself my dearest life that I love you beyond all power of language to express that hours are days til I see you I hope to be with you at Fosgeus[?] in 3 months in the mean time think of me & pray for me & will me in your Arms & prepare to receive me as cheerfully as your disorders will admit remembering with how much fondeness & Indearment I am my best love your own P Doddridge.

I hope to find you on two legs

I have bought china & I have walked near 10 miles today yet feel me weariness while I am writing to you & I could feel none if I was conversing with you why should that be is continually in my Heart be so often separated from my arms.

Duty to Mrs Maries Service to all friends especially the girls I have brought them some Macaroons.

Woodbridge Suffolk Jul 7 1737

As this is a letter I send by this post you will excuse me of the Length of it be not proportionate to the affection which dictates it. Indeed if it were a Ream of Elephant paper would hardly be sufficient to contain it & I should spend much more time in writing that I hope to imply in all the Remainder of my journey.

If you consult the Map you will see by comparing the Date of my last that like the Sun which is still in the Tropick of Cancer or like the Crabs which I yesterday caught I am now in a kind of Retrograde Motion at least go sideways. I could not refuse the importunity of my Friends here (happy for me that I was not a woman) but came back in a chaise which they sent for me on Sunday Night & preached (wicked worm that I was) an Evening Lecture after my other work but thers being a singular instance you will I hope excuse it especially as I was well enough to use at a[?unclear] yesterday morning & to make a voyage down the River which is 16 miles to the sea, where I had the pleasure of meeting 35 sail of ships & of catching a great number of soals, plaise flounders & crabs & two lobsters & a fair maid who immediately threw her self upon her back frisked about with a very strange kind of motion & so far as I could judge by the strong motion of muscles in her face & especially of her mouth made a very pathetic oration to us in a Language I did not understand but the name she had the honour to bear & her resemblance to your very agreeable sex impress'd me so far that had not my Companions been less compassionate than my self I believe she had still been sporting with the river Nymphs & perhaps celebrating with them the Courtesy of that gallant knight to whom she became a Captive. But I must assure you my dear that tho we were detained on the vessel nothing pass'd between us that give you any reasonable umbrage & fair as she was these Lips have not yet touch'd her nay for unsensible is my heart to the Charms of her whole species that give it you under my hand I had rather have a single shrimp then as many of these fair creatures as would stock a Turkishe Seraglio.

But to be serious it was a very pleasant day & I concluded it in the Company of one of the finest women I ever saw who tho she has seven children grown up to marriageable years or very near it is her self still almost a beauty & a person of sense, good breeding & piety which might promise one who had not the happiness of being intimately acquainted with you.

I am just returning in the vehicle in which I came for [illegible] providence has there also strangely cast my lot in one of the most friendly & agreeable families I have met with as absolutely as I am informed of Captain in of whole town tho not that where I intended to have lodged at. Mr Wood is extreamly obliging. Every thing is done that can be to make me if possible forget you & yet every circumstance serves a contrary purpose The more agreeable & more pleasurable scenes I pass thro the more do I wish to share with you & by sharing to double them. But I forget that a young Lady has done me the honour to invite me to breakfast with her & pardon my vanity when I tell you it was one who was pleased to say she would have gone a Thousand Mile for such a interview with me as she enjoy'd last week. She is I see Mistress of a very handsome House & independent Fortune but believe me that should such things as these happen to me every day I should still rejoice, I am my dearest Love securely & intirely yours P Doddridge.

24 Aug 1740 Northampton

My Dearest

I thought it incumbent upon me to let you know by good Mr Hutton Count Zinzindorff's[2] particular friend that dear Calia is still living tho she was so bad when I wrote last that I fear'd she would have been dead before the Post had set out. She seems considerably better & I am not without some cheerful hope that God will rise her up. Her Looseness is stopped her convulsions gone off & her fever much abated. A Few days will to be sure determine the case perhaps a few hours thro the great goodness of God my Mind kept in perfect peace as I hope yours will also be. If we love God & are beloved by him all things shall work together for our good & this trying Dispensation among the rest. May God support you & the consolations of his good Spirit & prepare us for all his will. I expect to see you in a few days Mrs Collier who behaves more like a Mother than a stranger sends her most affectionate service & thinks every day a walk til you come. I need not tell you how welcome you will be to My dearest Creature your ever affectionate & faithful PD

Dec 17[?] 1741

My best Dear,

As you grow in every Respect continually more & more agreeable it is no wonder that your letters yield me an increasing Pleasure, your last in particular I did rejoice in I hope that it is the last I shall receive from you a long Time. It does indeed grieve me to think how soon we must lose the small but very precious Remainder of our dear Delepree Friends & how that Favourite Place will be as empty to us as formerly. But the hope of your Return to Northampton of thro the Divine Goodness it may be safe as I trust it will gives me a very sendle[?] Support. I can hardly bear this little Delay but think what a kind of extacy of that happy Hour that is to restore you to my longing Arms. My venturing to get out as I purpose to do on Monday Morning will I hope be esteemed as Proof of this as it will more evidently appear when you come to hear all of the Circumstances of the Story. . . . I am so heartily weary with the Hurries of this tedious day that I have very little Spirits to inlarge if I had ever so much time. I hope my Dearest to go to Bed & dream of you & the Scene which I long for so eagerly that I hardly allow my self time to tell you how affectionately intirely & constantly I am your man P Doddridge

2 Aug 1742 London

If it were possible my dearest & most delightful creature that every line & word of this letter should express more Tenderness than all my former epistles put together I am sure I should not say all that you deserve or all that my heart means. I feel no to[?] easiness after days of Labour when at night I am sitting down to pour out a little of the fulness of my soul to you & I could go on till Day Light appeared if Reason did not tell me that a proper Regard to my necessary Repose to be more acceptable Expression of my affection to you. My Post nights are the joy of my life & seems that I love Letters chiefly for you & Northampton itself chiefly on your account. I almost forget that I have there friends & children there that I may remember what a wife I can call my own & do really think that where any of them have one thought you my dear Charmer have a thousand. It seems to me tho I did not once think it that a Man must live forty years before he knows how much love his heart can contain & how vigorously it can beat & that he must have been married between eleven & twelve years before he knows how to get a just value on a person of your various Excellencies. I care not to forbade evils but I assure you that the ardour & eagerness with which I long to fold you in my impatient arms makes me almost tremble less something should happen to prevent or retard it.

Tuesday Morning

Thus far my Dearest I wrote last night in a kind of Transport into which your endearing very delightful Letter threw me & then having pray'd for you very heartily & much more largely than for my self I went to Bed with my Head & Heart so full of you that amidst the fond assemblage of Lively Ideas which presented it self on that occasion I could not go to sleep till the morning was pretty far advanced the further consequence of which is that I am but presently wakened at a time when by appointment I should have been the ready to get on horseback . . . I am perfectly pleased with the Method you took about the Bill that I hope Sammy's appointment will turn out well & shall not scruple when we have concerted it together to advance of it be necessary ten or twenty pounds more for her service because he had honor of being related to the best of sisters of wives & of women that I dind not one word of nonsense in any of your letters so that all your stock of that seems still intire & that I do really apprehend that Love is so odd a kind of treasure that the more it draws out of mine the faster it grows. Go on therefore my dearest that to nourish it on yourself & me & fear not that poor Mr Evan's Lunacy should be thought to have any part in that high approvals & esteem as well as affection which I have as you prettily express of the unalterable happiness off being intirely yours P Doddridge

Notes

1 The pillory was a form of public shaming used as punishment for minor crimes.
2 Zinzindorff was a Moravian minister; his hymns feature as a source in section 18.

10

SERIES OF PORCELAINS

Meissen porcelain began being produced in Meissen, near Dresden, Germany, in 1710, inspired by popular and expensive imports from China and Japan. Within a decade, the factory was producing dishes and ornaments, with elaborate paintings of flowers, animals, landscape, chinoseries, and courtly scenes for upper and wealthy middle–class homes. Other porcelain factories followed, including the Frankenthal Porcelain Factory that was established in 1755. From the 1730s onwards, European porcelain factories produced a range of ornaments representing sentimental scenes in an ornate rococo style, reflective of the growing culture of sensibility during the period. Sometimes symbolising scenes from plays or literature, they attempted to capture and romanticise particularly interesting moments, allowing the viewer to imagine themselves in these contexts; this was not dissimilar to the novel of the period, which was designed to enable people to explore a range of emotions and experiences through allowing them to envision particular experiences. As a source for the history of emotions, the scenes can be read for their emotional encounter. Some, such as the lovers with the birdcage in figure 10.4 or the 'thrown kiss' in figure 10.6, might appear relatively straightforward as evidence of courtship practices. Others open up a world of the emotions of wealthy consumption and the sensate body, such as the chocolate drink thrust under the nose of the gentleman in figure 10.5, or the wealthy couple exploring the wares of the peasant in figure 10.2. Here we have the opportunity to reflect on how the body language of the figures might be read as emotional gestures and practices, highlighting how such emotion was thought to look, or perhaps how people wished to look when having such experiences. We may also reflect on whether these scenes act as moral commentary on such behaviour, and what that might suggest of the emotions on display. The ornaments themselves can be used as evidence of emotional practices, fashionable items, often coveted and placed on display in the home.

FAMILY AND COMMUNITY

Figure 10.1 Lady and Cavalier, known as 'The Handkiss', Meissener Porzellan Manufaktur, 1737, porcelain, courtesy of Rijksmuseum, Amsterdam.

Note: for more information see: http://hdl.handle.net/10934/RM0001.COLLECT.315452.

Figure 10.2 Group with a Pedlar (Herzdosenkauf), Meissener Porzellan Manufaktur, c. 1738, porcelain, courtesy of Rijksmuseum, Amsterdam.

Note: for more information see: http://hdl.handle.net/10934/RM0001.COLLECT.315461.

92

MEISSENER PORCELAIN MANUFACTURER

Figure 10.3 Shepherd Group, Porzellanmanufaktur Frankenthal, c. 1760, porcelain, courtesy of Rijksmuseum, Amsterdam.

Note: for more information see: http://hdl.handle.net/10934/RM0001.COLLECT.61003.

FAMILY AND COMMUNITY

Figure 10.4 Lovers with a Birdcage, Meissener Porzellan Manufaktur, 1737, porcelain, The Metropolitan Museum of Art, New York, The Jack and Belle Linsky Collection, 1982.

Note: for more information see: www.metmuseum.org/art/collection/search/207179.

Figure 10.5 Couple Drinking Chocolate, Meissener Porzellan Manufaktur, c. 1744, porcelain, The Metropolitan Museum of Art, New York, The Jack and Belle Linsky Collection, 1982.

Note: for more information see: www.metmuseum.org/art/collection/search/207203.

Figure 10.6 *The Thrown Kiss*, Meissener Porzellan Manufaktur, ca. 1736, porcelain, The Metropolitan Museum of Art, New York, The Jack and Belle Linsky Collection, 1982.

Note: for more information see: www.metmuseum.org/art/collection/search/207191.

11

CRIMINAL INDICTMENT OF DAVID YOUNG FOR ASSAULTING HIS FATHER AND MOTHER, 1738

National Records of Scotland, Edinburgh
JC26/128/d2059

The criminal 'letters', as the indictment was referred to in the Scottish legal system, was the document that authorised the prosecution of an individual for an alleged crime. It allowed the court agents to gather witnesses and proceed with the trial. As an important legal document, it was required to contain certain types of information – the nature of the crime, the location, the name of the accused – as well as particular legal phrases, e.g. 'are guilty Actor Art and Part'. These ensured that indictments often closely resembled each other in their construction. Despite this, they were important emotional documents, often read aloud at the beginning of a trial and so designed with an emotional language to heighten the wrongdoing of the accused and to drive home the criminality of the accused's actions. This means such texts can be read for their rhetorical effects on their audience, and so provide useful information on how lawyers tried to persuade and move the emotions of their listeners. As documents that also detail crime, we can also learn significant information about community relationships and emotions. In the example below, David Young was arrested after a series of disputes, both within his own family and with his neighbours. The events provide insight into expectations around the parent–child relationship in adulthood, as well as appropriate neighbourly relations. For many ordinary people, legal documents like these are one of the few sources that we have on everyday family and community life.

. . .

David Young, portioner in Gilmeadowland within the Parish of Muiravonside and Shire of Stirling now Prisoner within the Tolbooth of Edinburgh You are indicted and accused at the instance of Charles Areskine of Tinwald Esq his Majestys Advocates for his Highness Interest and Alexander Mitchell of Mitchell writer to the signet one of his Majestys Justices of the Peace for the shire of Stirling with

Concourse of his Majestys said Advocate. That where By the Laws of God the Laws of this and all other well Governed Realms the injurious and unnatural beating and cursing of parents by their own children the cruell and malicious attempting to bereave any of his majestys Lieges of their lives and for that purpose lying in wait for them with swords or other offensive mortal weapons As also the Breaking of Prisons, beating and deforcing of messengers jailors and other officers of the law. Likeas the villainous cruell and desperate attempting to Destroy any of his Majestys Leidges by fire and the willful and malicious setting fire to and Burning any of his Majestys Leidges their houses Corn-stacks Barns office-houses are all and each of them Crimes of an abominable nature Highly criminall and severely Punishable by Law Yet True it is and of Verity that you have presumed to commit and are guilty Actor Art and Part of all and each or one or other of the above specified enormous Crimes. In So Far as you having Thrown off all fear of God and abandoned yourself to your own Cruell and Revengefull Temper which you had suffered to Break out in many instances by Assaulting Beating and Cursing your own father and mother in a most Injurious and unnatural manner to the Terror of the Whole Neighbourhood who had occasion to see you repeat the said detestable action you going on in your wicked courses did on the Eighth day of Aprile One Thousand Seven hundred and thirty seven or one or other of the Days of that month or one or other of the Days of March preceeding or May following come to that part of the Lands of Gilmeadowland lying in the Parish of Muiravonside and Sheriffdom of Stirling and possessed by Isobell Haddoway your Mother as her Jointure where finding Alexander and Robert Youngs your Brethren employed at the plough assisting their and your mother in Labouring the said Lands which you had neglected to do tho' specially bound and oblidged thereto you having thrown off all Ties of Blood and Relation and having Meditated and designed the Death of your said Brothers drew from under your Coat a small sword or other offensive mortal weapon which you have concealed there for perpetrating your murderous purpose and with the said sword you assaulted and attacked in a fierce and cruell manner your said Brothers and most certainly had bereaved them of their Lives unless they had defended themselves with the Plough-goad and other instruments which Providence put in their hands till you was disarmed and So Deep was your Revenge and Resentment Rooted in your minde against your said Brothers that on the sixth or one or other Days of August last or one or other of the Days of the months of July preceeding or September following your said Mother Isobell Haddoway having come to your house in Gilmeadowloand and having expostulate with you about the treatment you had given your Brothers and the Enmity you Kept up against them your Regairdless of your filial Duty did in a most impious Barbarous and unnaturall manner Curse your said Mother by saying God Damn you for an old Bitch and God Damn you for a Liar or words to that purpose at the same time your violently seized upon your said mother and endeavoured by force to thrust her out of your house which you certainly would have accomplished unless prevented by the Interposition of your Wife Servants and Neighbours, who gave their assistance for the Defence and Protection of your Mother And Further

CRIMINAL INDICTMENT OF DAVID YOUNG

you having conceived a groundless grudge enmity and hatred and malice against Andrew Dick of Compston your neighbour with whom you was engaged in a Law–Suit before the Lords of Council and Session or who had Diligence against you you most feloniously formed a Design to Murder and destroy the said Andrew Dick and for that purpose upon the eighteenth of February being Sunday or one or other Days of the said month one thousand seven hundred and thirty three you in a most treacherous manner lay in wait for the said Andrew Dick armed with a sword or other mortal offensive weapon which you kept concealed under your great Coat upon the way that Leads from the Parish Kirk of Muiravonside to the said Andrew Dick his house of Compston and as the said Andrew Dick was returning from attending Divine worship at the said Kirk you in a Cruell and barbarous manner after Exchanging a few words on a sudden Drew the sword which was hid under your Coat and made several furious Passes at the said Andrew Dick which he pary'd and set aside with his Cane till he made his Retreat to a Dyke where with stones in his hands he stood upon his defence until he was Relieved and his Life saved by the Timely Intervention and coming in of some persons then near Likeas you having been Incarcerate by Legal Diligence at the Instance of Andrew Dick of Compston within the Tolbooth of Linlithgow as John Clarkson one of the toune officers of Linlithgow then jailor and Keeper of the said Prison house was upon the twentieth day or one or other of the Dayes of Aprile on thousand seven hundred and thirty four or one or other of the Dayes of March preceeding or subsequent May bringing in Victuals to you within the said Tolbooth you having taken advantage of the said John Clarkson did violently Rush upon him and assault him and forcibly threw him over the stairs of the said Prison house by Which Desperate Fall he was so Bruised and Crushed that he was Confined to his bed and in imminent Hazard of his Life and you by that violence and Deforcement Broke his Majestys Prison and Made your Escape As Also the said Andrew Dick of Comptson having procured Caption and other Legall Diligence against you Did Employ John Wilson messenger in Falkirk to put the same in Execution against you and accordingly on the tenth or one or others Days of the Month of January one thousand seven hundred and thirty five the said Messenger and his assistants having found you in the House of Mr Thomas Young schoolmaster in the Parish of Muiravonside and sheriffdom of Stirling and there and then by virtue of the said Diligence after Displaying his Blazon Batton and other Ensigns of his office The said Messenger having seized and apprehended you his prisoner nevertheless after you Continued some short space in the custody of the said messenger you in Contempt of the Laws did with some Desperate persons your associates invade assault Beat and Bruise the said Messenger and his assistants and by force and violence Deforce the said Messinger and Rescue yourself Att Least at the times or the places and in the manner above condescended on the abovenamed facts were done perpetuate and committed and you are Guilty Actor Art and Part of all and each or one or other of the above specified crimes And further you having Conceived a Mortall Hatred and Enmity against the said Alexander Mitchell without just cause or provocation did on the night Intervening betwixt the fourteenth and fifteenth

99

Days of March Last one thousand seven hundred and thirty eight or upon one or other of the nights of the said month of March in a most Hellish and Malicious Manner attempt to destroy the said Alexander Mitchell his house and his whole family willfully under the Cloud and Silence of night when he and his whole Family and neighbourhood were gone to bed and Rest by setting fire with Kindled Peats Turf Torch or other Combustible stuff and Matter to his Barn adjoining to that part of his Mansionhouse of Parkhall in the Parish of Muiravonside and sheriffdom of Stirling where the said Alexander Mitchell and his family usually Lay at four or at least at several Different parts of the thatch on the outside by which the said Barn the Granaries Grain victual and others therein Contained and two Rooms of the said mansion house wherein the Family for ordinary Resided with the furniture and other valuable Contents as Likewise a byre joined to the Barn on the other end were totally consumed As Also you sett Fire to a stack of victual standing in the Barnyeard at some distance from the Barn which stack was Likewise destroyed by the said fire As Also to a haystack by putting a Kindled Peat in the same which happily Extinguished all the Property of the said Alexander Mitchell Complainer and had not the Timely Assistance of Neighbours prevented the Whole Mansion house of Parkhall and office houses would have been wholly burnt down to the ground At Least at the Time above mentioned the house barn office–houses and stack at Parkhall were willfully maliciously and Premeditatly set on fire and Burnt and you was accessory art and Part to the said wilful Fire–raising and Burning At Least you having conceived Hatred and ill–will against the said Alexander Mitchell without any Just Cause did in several publick Companys and before famous Witnesses declare you bore a Hatred and Ill–will against the said Alexander Mitchell and that you had Envy and Resentment against him and Expressed your self much to the disadvantage of his Character and Rumouring and Reporting that the said Alexander Mitchell was a bankrupt and at the same time you Declared that you had good Reason for your Implacable Rage and Malice against the said Alexander Mitchell because you alledged that he as an agent had assisted Andrew Dick of Compston in a Law–Suit he had against you and that he had taught Compston to swear an oath by which you Lost your Cause for which you at Several times and upon Several Occasions with Horrid Oaths and Imprecations swore Revenge and Vengeance against the said Alexander Mitchell and after emitting these menaces and threats of the [illegible] and deepest malice against the said Alexander Mitchell and his family you was observed to be three nights before the said Burning Lurking in the Twilight, about the Entry Inclosures and Parks of Parkhall and Particularly on one of the three nights immediately preceeding the Burning about Sunsett you Came to the house of John Boag weaver which is situate at the East Entry Parkhall where you had an opertunity to observe what was doing at the House although you had no manner of Business in the said John Boags House and was not in use to frequent the same and while in that house upon the said Alexander Mitchell his passing by the Door thereof and Calling who was within you Conscious of your own Hellish Design said that's Craigend and Desired the maid of the house to go out and tell him that there was no person within and having the said night gone home from Boag's house to your own wife you Expressed to your wife in Presence of your servant severall Bad Words and Threatenings against the said Alexander Mitchell upon account of a Conversation That Happened Betwixt your about one Robert Buchanan And having Tarried in your own house till towards Bed–time of the very night on which the said willful fire and Burning was Raised you then took a Peat and put it into your fire and after the same was thoroughly kindled you took it in your hand and went to the Door saying you were going to see how your Pidgeons were although the night was far advanced and Extremely Tempestuous and then you put the same into an Earthen Pitcher or Can which had served for bringing home water to your house and you Continued abroad all the Remainder that night untill the Dawn or Gray of the Morning That upon your Return you whispered something to your wife and seemed to be in great Confusion and upon hearing the news of the Disastrous Burning at Parkhall you and your wife appeared to be struck with great Remorse and unneasyness and so conscious was you of your Guilt that although upon the Report and News of the Burning at Parkhall all the neighbours Either went personally or sent messages to Condole the distressed Family yet you though the nearest neighbours Conscious of your guilt forebore and avoided and on the contrary you left your own house for severall Days and upon your Return you kept yourself always Concealed That upon the news of the burning you was by your servant maid and the Comon Bruit and Open Fame of the whole Country pointed out as the Malefactor and Burner at which Your Wife Expressed her Concern saying "That rather than you should be Brought before the Justices of Peace she would Rather see you in the Kirk–yeard on a Bier" And Further when your house was surrounded by the Constables in order to apprehend you by a warrant from the Justices of Peace you Refused to give them access and from a Consciousness of Your Guilt and before the saids Constable had so much as mentioned the Crime on which the warrant proceeded you told them without being asked that it was upon the account of the Burning of Parkhall they were sent and that in Case they persisted in Endeavouring to make their way into your house more Corpses than one should go to the Kirk–yeard and that you would give them warm Lugs or Words to that purpose and being self Convict of your Guilt you Broke a hole through the Roof of your Byre which joins your house and saved yourself by flight As Also when the Pitcher or Can in which the Kindled Peat was Carried which Can had been for some days amissing was Brought Back to your house the same when observed by Your servant who Complained for missing it was found standing Dry in its Ordinary place and Smelling Exceeding Strong of Burnt Peats and During the Time of the Burning when the neighbourhood was Employed in Endeavouring to Extinguish the fire the Tread of a man was heard Running very fast by the said John Boag's house upon the way Leading Directly from Parkhall to Gilmeadowland where you Reside and Further before Sundrie famous witnesses you Declared that you thought Mr Mitchell would not be unreasonable in blaming you as Guilty of the said Burning in Respect that you said he behoved to be Conscious that the Deserved as much at your hands or words to that purpose and whoever set fire to the said house Certainly meant to Destroy him and his whole family And you always expressed great Fear and appeared to be much Troubled and confused in the several house where you sought shelter and was Lurking and when told in Company That you was blamed by the whole Country as the Person guilty of Setting fire to the said Compainer his house you without Denying the fact said that Mr Mitchell had got one whip and that if he himself came in somebodys gate he would get another or words to that purpose Besides since your last Incarceration in the Tolbooth of Edinburgh you threatned that in Case Mr Mitchelll would not Consent to your Liberation it would be worse for him and for the house of Parkhall before twelve months past And Moreover you acknowledged that you knew or could tell of the person who set fire to and burnet the said house Barns and stack and would Reveal the same to Mrs Mitchell of her husband would consent to your getting out of Prison and that Craigend had wrought well for Compston wherefore should he not get his wages from which Facts and Circumstances it is plan you are guilty actor art and part of all and each of the atrocious crimes above specified and particularly of the said abominable and Horrible destructive Crime of wilfull Fire–raising Which Crimes Facts and Circumstances on your being guilty actor art and part of all or one or other of the foresaid crimes being found proven by the verdict of an assize before the Lord Justice Generall Lord Justice Clerk and Lords Commissioners of Justiciary you ought and should be Exemplarly punished with the pains of Law to the Terror of others to Commit the Like in times coming and also Decerned to make payment to the said Alexander Mitchell Complainer of the sum of [blank] nominee Domni William Grant AD

12

THE ROYAL AFRICAN: OR, MEMOIRS OF THE YOUNG PRINCE OF ANNAMABOE

(London: W. Reeve, [1750]), pp. 35–45

This popular pamphlet purported to give an account of the life of Prince William Ansah Sessarakoo, a noble from present day Ghana, sold into slavery between 1744 and 1748. The anonymous account is not considered accurate, but rather reflects the celebrity potential of Sessarakoo to sell products after he arrived in Britain in 1748. The story draws on a number of popular tropes of the period found in novels, newspapers and similar writings. As can be seen in the account below, Sessarakoo is located as a youthful victim of an unscrupulous sea captain, exploiting the desires of a family to promote the well-being of their child and success of their family. If the text explicitly notes Sessarakoo's father's polygamous household, his ambition and tenderness for his children is that of a middling British patriarch. In this respect, it is not dissimilar to the moral tales of the period that cautioned parents about the dangers of city life for unsuspecting youth. Rather than the tale warning the reader of the dangers of urban life however, the account reflects on whether Africa's interest is better served by England or France, with England eventually securing the safety of both the African monarch's sons. As a text for the history of emotions, it provides insight into the idealised and expected emotions of the parent–child relationship, as well as that of Sessarakoo in response to his enslaved condition. The bombast and patriotism that frames the account is also useful evidence of political emotions. If this is a text that provides a history of race and the British empire, that the author chose to universalise (elite) African and British feeling was a significant authorial choice, designed to undermine discourses of racial difference during the period.

. . .

It was to this Captain particularly, that the Caboceiro of *Annamaboe* opened himself frequently upon the Head of his Son's Voyage to *France*, and the Sense he had of the great Honours that were done him during his Residence in that Country; asking at the same Time, what Difference there was between *France* and *England?* whether the latter was as good a Country, the King as powerful, or his Subjects as rich? to which the Captain gave such Answers as he judged convenient, not

FAMILY AND COMMUNITY

apprehending perhaps at first, to what these Inquiries tended. When Opportunities offered, the Caboceiro, proposed the same Question to such of the Company's Servants as he had Occasion to transact Business with, from whom he received more clear and explicit Answers, and who told him plainly that the *French* were a Nation that delighted in Pomp and Splendour; but that the *English* were much superior to them in Naval Power, and in the Extent of their Trade; of which the Negroe was easily convinced, on comparing the Number of Ships sent by the two Nations on the Coast of *Guinea*. From these Conversations, he picked up Hints that were very serviceable to him in many Respects, and enabled him to sift even out of the *French* Traders themselves Matters of Fact, that left him no Room to doubt of the Truth of what the *Englishmen* had told him.

This dwelt very much upon his Mind, and finding how useful the Knowledge which one of his Sons had acquired by Travel was, by his serving as an Interpreter with one Set of People, he had a Mind to procure the like Advantages, by employing another Son to enter as thoroughly into the Affairs of another Nation; which from their Superiority in Trade, and much greater Variety of Commodities and Manufactures in which they dealt, promised still greater Advantages. Several Accidents concurred to fortify him in this Opinion, but particularly his observing that the *English* separate Traders were much keener, and more expert in the Management of their Business than the *French;* that they frequently formed Schemes of outwitting them in their Commerce, and, generally speaking, succeeded in it; and in respect to this, he was the more confirmed by conferring with the most experienced of his own Nation, whose Observations concurred in this Particular, as likewise did those of the Inland Merchants, whose Demands were chiefly for *British* Goods and Manufactures.

The Son he intended to send to *England*, and who is actually here at present, was his greatest Favourite; his Mother was not only a free Woman and his chief Wife, but also the Daughter of one of the principal Persons in the Country. The Youth had been always distinguished by the quickness of his Parts, and the Affability of his Behaviour, as well as by a graceful Deportment, and a very agreeable Person. He had lived for a Time, when a perfect Child, in the Fort with one of the *African* Company's principal Officers, where he had learned to speak *English*, and had acquired a great Confidence in as well as a sincere Affection for the Nation. The old Caboceiro encouraged this Disposition in him all he could, told him frequently that himself was an *Englishman*, and that he ought to think himself so too; that the *English* were their best Friends, and treated them with the most Kindness, that they were a great and powerful Nation, as appeared from the Number of Ships that arrived annually in the Road of *Annamaboe*, and their rich Cargoes; that their Dominions in other Parts must be very large and productive of vast Riches, since they bought yearly such a Number of Blacks, who were employed in their Tillage and Cultivation, and that therefore he could not do better than to improve that Kindness and Esteem they had for him, by endeavouring every Day to merit more and more their Favour and Friendship.

As these Rules suited exactly with his Inclination, the Lad pursued them with all the Spirit and Diligence imaginable, attached himself entirely to the *English* who frequented the Port, and from thence was taken Notice of and caressed by them in a very extraordinary Manner. The *French* Traders easily perceiving how much this Son was beloved of his Father and respected in the Family, as well as pleased with the Modesty of his Carriage, and his superior Abilities, were not wanting in their Applications, which however had very little Effect; for tho' he was never deficient in Civility, yet his Humour of piquing himself upon being an *Englishman*, and the strong Impressions he had received in the Fort, gave him a Distaste to that Nation, which it was not possible for him to conceal. He was besides very little struck with Finery, and had accustomed himself to a frank and open Manner of expressing his Sentiments, without the Gloss of Compliments or any dark Reserves.

Amongst all the People that had Business with the Caboceiro of *Annamaboe*, the Captain before–mentioned had not only the greatest Credit with him, but was the freest and most intimate with his Family; and seeing his Father's Affection for him, professed always a peculiar Regard and a singular Tenderness for this Youth; who on his Part loved him with the Sincerity natural to his Years, and testified as much Duty towards him as if he had been his Father. When therefore the old Caboceiro expressed in general Terms his Wish, that some Opportunity might offer of sending him to *England* that he might be educated there, and acquire that Knowledge which rendered white Men so much superior to themselves, and to the rest of the Negroe Nations; it was very agreeable News both to the Lad and to the Captain.

The former, to whom the *English* had given the Name of CUPID, as most expressive of his sweet and amiable Temper, shewed the greatest Willingness imaginable to enter into his Father's Scheme, and to make a Voyage to *Europe;* as on the other Hand the Captain seemed to be ravish'd with the Proposal, which at once shewed the Confidence of the old Man, and afforded him an Opportunity of adding to the Marks of Kindness and Good-will, that he had formerly given to his Son. Their Voyage to *England* was thenceforward the sole Topick of their Conversation; the Father was settled in his Resolution, the Boy was delighted with it, and the Captain spoke to him in a Language that was perfectly paternal. He was continually forecasting what Advantages he might draw from this Adventure, and without knowing it, was a very true Prophet of the Respect and Esteem which the young Man would certainly attract by his good Qualities, when in *England.* In a Word, this Project was the great Topick of Discourse in the Family, and they all delighted themselves with the Expectation of seeing with what mighty Improvements their young *Englishman* would return to *Annamaboe.*

As the Season was at a Distance in which the Captain proposed to depart, all Parties had sufficient Leisure to contemplate their respective Schemes in every Light, of which they were capable, and to flatter their Imaginations with any Circumstances that might set off and adorn them.

105

The *Caboceiro* might probably propose the preserving in his Family that Post of Honour, tho' in its Nature elective, by rendering his Children so much superior in Knowledge to his Countrymen; and at the same time qualifying them to serve the Community with such extraordinary Advantages. His darling Son ran over in his Mind all the strange Things he had heard in the *English* Fort, or among the Traders and Sailors of that Nation: He pleased himself with the Hopes of seeing these, and of comprehending perfectly a Multitude of Subjects, of which in spite of all his Inquiries he had only dark and confused Ideas. In respect to the Captain, it may be presumed from his future Conduct, that he looked upon his young Pupil as an Acquisition of so much Wealth as he would sell for, and applied himself besides to make all the Uses in his Power of the *Caboceiro*'s Interest and Influence, while he remained in the Country.

Indeed this had been all along of very great Benefit to him, and tho' the *Caboceiro* did not enter in every Respect into his Views, he had made him subservient to his carrying into Execution most of his Projects, by which himself and his Associates had gained the Reputation of being among the Number of the most clear–sighted and adroit Traders that ever visited the Coast of *Guinea*. What Returns both the old *Cabocier* and his Son have met with for their Friendships, Hospitality and Favours, the World is not unacquainted with; and what Right they have to treat with the most ignominious and contemptible Language the Negroes in general, Mankind will likewise judge. But supposing them as low and mean as those who hate and despise them most can represent them; this can afford no Justification for deceiving or maltreating them. There is certainly no Credit to be acquired by outwitting the Ignorant, nor will it prove a Recommendation in any Country under the Cope of Heaven, for Men who have had a good Education, to compass their own Ends by imposing false Colours upon such as they look upon as beneath them in every Respect. What Grounds there is for this Opinion, or how Man can differ from Man, but by the superior Virtues of the Mind, the best Judges will find it hard to distinguish, since as to all other Advantages they are meerly accidental, and he who makes the best use of them is the best Man, let his Complexion be *black* or *white*.

At length the Time came that the Captain had finish'd his Affairs upon the Coast, and was to leave it, which gave great Pleasure to all Parties; the old Man was desirous that his Son should go speedily, that he might have the better Chance of living to see him return Home. The sprightly Youth, full of the fond Hopes of seeing the World, was impatient to depart; the Captain gave not the least Check to their Hopes, but on the contrary, continued to inspire his Pupil with a passionate Desire of viewing all the Beauties of an Island the most celebrated in the known World. His Conduct was in every respect as kind as it had ever been; and indeed the noble Youth does him even now the Justice to acknowledge, that he had no Hardships to complain of in the Passage, and that on the contrary, he treated him with all the Tenderness, all the Attention of a Father.

This no doubt confirmed him entirely in those Sentiments of Respect and Veneration, which he had been so long accustomed to have for his Father's Friend, and kept even the slightest Suspicion from entering into his Thoughts. Under this happy Delusion he compleated his Voyage from the Road of *Annamaboe*, to *Bridge-Town* in *Barbadoes;* nor was he undeceived even there. The very same Behaviour was kept up to the last, and the unfortunate Youth had not the least Foresight of the impending Evil, till like a Torrent it came pouring upon him all at once; and but for the Interposition of Providence, had irretrievably buried him in Misery and Despair.

When the Captain had sold him, and he was put into a Boat to be carried to his Master, he thought he was going on board the Ship that was to carry him to *England*. But what Language can express his Surprize, when from the rough Usage that he met with from two Slaves that were in the Boat, he had no Room left him to doubt that his Condition was the same with theirs? It must be left to the Reader's Imagination to frame a Notion of his Distress, which will be so much the harder, as the Freedom and Happiness of our Situation hinders us from ever beholding a Sight that any way resembles it. It must assuredly have struck him with a Horror, for white Men in general; have filled his Mind at once with as black Thoughts of them, and with better Foundation than some of these, affect to have for those of his Country with very little Cause.

But whatever his Thoughts, whatever his Reflections might be, they left him scarce a glimmering of Hope, distant from Home, far from Father, Family, or Friends, betrayed and a [torn page] doned by him whom he had always esteemed [torn page] Protector; and this in the very Dawn of Life. He had before him a Prospect so gloomy, that he stood in need of superior Greatness of Mind to bear the Shock without sinking under it, or taking some desperate Method to remove the Load. It was some Relief to him that he fell into the Hands of a Gentleman of distinguished Character, where he was treated with much Humanity, which abated somewhat of the Bitterness of that sudden and undeserved Reverse of Fortune, revived him a little, and encouraged him to breathe and live. This by Degrees gave him Leisure to look round him, to compare his past and present Condition, and to furnish himself with the best Helps that Reflection and Experience could suggest towards his Amusement and Relief.

He saw numbers in the like Condition, from a Variety of Accidents, but none of them in any Degree comparable to that which had brought this heavy Lot upon him. He was ashamed however to shew less Courage than the rest, or not to oppose Misfortune with equal Steadiness of Mind; he resolved therefore to bear, tho' he could not be reconciled to his Fate, and to sustain without complaining a Calamity it was out of his Power to remove. In this sad State his Innocence afforded him the only Consolation; it was a Satisfaction that he had not drawn this upon himself, and by Degrees the Fairness and Mildness of his Behaviour, procured other Alleviations of that galling Yoke. But neither Time nor these transient Comforts, could so far dissipate the Sense of his Condition, as to remove that Melancholy which followed his first Consternation; but as this was not attended with any Tincture of Sullenness or Obstinacy, it rather heightened than abated his other good Qualities, which gained him universal Esteem, while in the low State of a Slave.

The Captain, to cover this Matter in the best Manner possible, either about the Time, or soon after his selling his Pupil, transmitted to the Caboceiro of *Annamaboe*, an Account current, upon the Foot of which he was considerably in his Debt; the Justice of this however he has since controverted. But be the Matter how it will, it seems very clear, that both Parties knew one another well enough to give Credit at other Times; so that there could be no Cause for proceeding with that amazing Severity at this Juncture: it is also apparent, that if procuring Satisfaction for his Debt was all the Captain had in View, he might as well have obtained it by keeping the young Man in his Custody, till the Father had satisfied his Agents; but to proceed in so abrupt, so strange, and so clandestine a Manner, affords sufficient Light for the World to judge of the Nature of this Transaction. However, not long after this the Captain died, and left the young *African* in Cicumstances as miserable, and at desperate as could be imagined; for he was not only a Slave, but a Slave at such a Distance from his Country, Father, and Friends, and so totally deprived of the Means of communicating to them his Condition, that if his Relief had in any degree depended upon his own Abilities to promote it, there is no doubt that he had lived and died in that deplorable Condition.

Yet if the Author of his Misfortune had been so pleased, he might have prevented this, by giving the old Caboceiro such Lights as would have put it in his Power to have redeemed his Son; or it may be, if he had acted ingenuously with the Gentleman to whom he sold him at *Barbadoes*, the same might have been brought to pass; but by doing neither, he plainly shewed, that, in his Opinion, all Blacks were destined to be Slaves; and this therefore satisfied him, that he had only left the Youth, for whom he professed so much Friendship, in his proper Situation. But it is now Time to leave the young Man for the present, and return to *Africa*, in order to observe by what strange and secret Steps divine Providence provided for the extricating out of his Misfortunes an innocent Youth, unable to help himself.

13

DAVID ZEISBERGER (1721–1808), *DIARY OF DAVID ZEISBERGER: A MORAVIAN MISSIONARY AMONG THE INDIANS OF OHIO*

Trans. Eugene F. Bliss, 2 vols
(Cincinnati: Robert Clarke 1885),
vol. 1, pp. 51–57, 68–70, 71–72

This excerpt is taken from the diary of David Zeisberger, a German Moravian missionary who moved to North America to establish a religious community and to bring his faith to the American Indian peoples. The Moravians were a Protestant sect, formed in central Germany, but with a wide reach due to their missionising efforts across the globe. They are marked, especially in the eighteenth century, by communal forms of living, devotion to the wounds of Christ, and practice of spiritual diary-keeping, that left a rich resource for historians (see also source 18 for some of their hymns). The passages given here reflect the tense political situation in, what is now, Pittsburgh, Pennsylvania, during a period where British and French vied for power with each other, and local communities – the Wyandots, Delawares, and Shawanese. Allegiances could be short-lasting and anxious. The diary, translated into English in the late–nineteenth–century, provides insight into the everyday workings of the faith, where we see accounts of religious practice, community discipline, and the emotions such activities engendered, but it also highlights how these practices were underpinned by the underlying tensions produced by the political environment. Moravian relationships with the people they missionised are especially interesting, not least as they attempt to reconcile assumptions about natural white superiority with the physical resources and military power that Indian Christians brought to the Moravian community. If it is important to read this text as the work of a German missionary, and with reflection on how emotional languages are changed in translations, nonetheless it can provide useful insights into the emotions of ongoing community relationships during this period of conflict.

. . .

109

FAMILY AND COMMUNITY

[1781]

Sunday, 23 [Dec]. Br. David preached upon the Epistle: Rejoice in the Lord alway, about the joy of the children of God in the Saviour's incarnation, sufferings, and death. Sensemann held the children's service and Edwards the congregation meeting over the Scripture-verse. The brothers Samuel, John Martin, and Isaac, came back from the Shawanese, where they had good success, and their petition was very well received. They had then forthwith, for one hundred string, brought together corn for our town, and promised them, so soon as their people should be at home, for only a few men were there, since they were all off hunting or otherwise scattered, that they would collect it all and then send us word to come and get it. The chief, who was at home, received them in a very friendly way, and said to them they had long waited for us to ask them for help, and if we had not done it they would yet have thought of us and helped us, but that it was so much the more agreeable to them that we had come to them. They well knew that neither we nor our laziness was the cause of our coming to such want; they also were not the cause of it, but we were torn away from our towns by force where we had the means of life in overabundance, therefore were they willing to help us. [The Mingoes who live there said the same.] They pitied us much for our losses and for what we had endured, and now, especially, that we lived near the Wyandots in such a wretched district of land, which was quite unsuitable for us, that we could not plant enough for ourselves, as we had been used to do; they said we could seek out a better place which no one could prevent; they looked only to our good, and if they should see that we supported ourselves and wished to move to a better place, they wished to come to our aid at once with as many horses as they could get together. It troubled them, as it did also the Delawares in the same neighborhood, that Pipe[1] herewith grew and boasted that he had taken prisoners the believing Indians and their teachers, and they were therefore his prisoners and slaves, and they say, "Are not the believing Indians his friends? It was a shame to regard his own friends as slaves." The chief and some others who were at home talked almost all night with the brethren, and asked them, among other things, this also, where their teachers and ministers came from and got here, for all white people, English, French, Spanish, and so many as they had seen, had their ministers and their worship of God, but they all went to war, but we not. The brethren answered: They were originally from over the sea, and finally came to us and brought us the word of God, and we have received it, since we found and felt in our hearts that it is truth, eternal life, and glory, among all white people there are indeed ministers, all have their worship of God, have the Scriptures, and can read them, but since they are unbelievers, they become no better therefrom; they are thus unbelievers, as are the Indians, and so no better. The chief bade them greet, us, their teachers, and said he would like, to see us, perhaps he would come sometime to visit us.

This afternoon the Half-King[2] came with his interpreter, partly on business, partly for a visit. The brethren took occasion to speak with him about the two who had gone to the Fort, of whom we have already heard so much from other places, and told him as much as we knew about them. But we soon heard that he had more news of them than we, for they sent word to him by Indians, and let him know what they intended, so that it can cause us no prejudice or harm.

Monday, 24. We begin Christmas week with praise and thanks that God, our Creator, himself became man, and, that we, through him, have peace with God, since he has blotted out our sins through his blood. We asked him also forgiveness of all our transgressions, not to be mindful of them, and to be merciful to us, again to bless us, to be with us in this place, and to recognize us as his peculiar people, and to send us his peace, which he also did, and we had comfort and assurance therefrom. Love-feasts[3] we could not have, for we were too poor and could not afford so much. The history was read, and over the Scripture-text was a discourse. The chapel was quite filled.

Tuesday, 25. The morning sermon by Br. Heckewelder, the children's service by David. These rejoiced, and sang: The Infant Jesus in his manger lies, right prettily, and all who were present let tears of joy run down their cheeks. Br. Jungmann held the congregation meeting over the Scripture–verse. The brethren encouraged one another, and rejoiced together in God, our Saviour, who in all circumstances had shown himself gracious to them, and filled their hearts with comfort and joy.

Wednesday, 26. Br. Edwards held early service; there upon we had a conference with the assistants. A woman, a widow, obtained, upon her request and prayer, permission to dwell with the church. Nicodemus, who in the spring, from fear, allowed himself to be moved and went from the church, and now came again, was likewise received. Israel was told we could not yet allow him to be in the church. It was told to the church that we could not suffer Jacob's family to be in the church, seeing the manner they had conducted themselves in Gnadenhütten and up to the present time, on account of the children, and other reasons too. At last also Nathaniel and A. Salome were earnestly spoken with about their daughter, and they were advised what they had to do.

Friday, 28. There was a conference with the assistants about maintaining order among the people and putting disorder out. of the way. Many of our brethren suffer hunger, and as no corn can be had, they must subsist upon wild potatoes (Ipomcea Pandurata), which they have to dig up laboriously and bring from a distance.

. . .

Monday, 31. Jungmann held the morning service, and exhorted the brethren for Jesus sake to bury every thing in his death, and to take nothing over into the new year. In the afternoon was the burial of Br. Nathaniel, who died yesterday in blessedness. He was baptized in Bethlehem, Aug. 30, 1749, by Br. Nathaniel Seidel, and July 8, 1775, in Gnadenhütten, on the Muskingum, was admitted to the enjoyment of the Lords supper. He remained steadfast by the Saviour whom he loved and by the church, and had a lovely and blessed intercourse with the Saviour. By

FAMILY AND COMMUNITY

nature he was somewhat simple, but if he spoke with his laborers from his heart, it could be seen that he well knew what he wanted, and what he had from the Saviour, for this he had understanding enough, and he was not wanting to him, but for other matters, especially bad things, he was indiscreet, yet it was never observed that he frequented and gave himself up to bad company. That his mother, who died in peace in Lichtenau, told him, shortly before her death, he should abide by the Saviour and the church his life long, that forgot he not, and he repeated it often. The occasion of his death was a broken leg, and thereupon gangrene, so that in a few days he departed with the blessing of the church. He was forty-two years old. To–day was the conference of assistants: they investigated the old matters about the children of Jacob and Philippa.

At the usual time we assembled at the end of the year, thanked the Saviour for all the mercy and kindness he had shown us, but confessed to him also our faults and shortcomings, and begged the forgiveness of all our transgressions and the consolation of his grace, to be merciful to us, and to acknowledge himself to us as our Helper and Saviour.

[1782]

Tuesday, Jan. 1. Br. Edwards preached from the Gospel about Jesus name, who is our Saviour and Redeemer. The baptized brethren renewed their covenant with him, to be and to remain his own. They were exhorted to give their hearts entirely to him; to desire nothing in the world except to live for him. Sensemann held the congregation meeting from the Scripture-verse: I will not contend for ever, neither will I be always wroth. Meekness, humility, and love Through all thy conduct shine. We took the texts from last year for use, since we have now indeed no hope left of getting any. In regard to other matters, we had to hear from without many bad and unpleasant stories over the fact that two of our Indians had secretly gone to the Fort,[4] without our knowledge, on which account many lies were spread around that we had sent letters by them, and they said we should again be made prisoners and altogether brought away from the Indians. Satan rages and it is as if we were, given over to devils to plague us utterly, to torment us and to make trial of fortune with us, while we are here, more than ever before, not only from without, but also from within. For in the church there were people who upheld them in their false dispositions and applauded them, who wished to establish by force that wicked life of his and heathenism. If we oppose them they become angry and set on the wild Indians against us, wish to stop our mouths, bearing witness thereagainst, and to bind our hands, so that we may do nothing to dispense the powers of darkness and root them out from among us. But we did not let ourselves be turned aside, but courageously bore witness against them. Such a change has now come in the Indian church that the bad, wicked people can not be cast out, but they wish to be there and to cause harm in the church, for they in the wild towns have occasion enough therefor and no one would say any thing to them about their sinful life. If we discipline them, therefore, or only say

DIARY OF DAVID ZEISBERGER

it were better if they remained away from us, they go into the towns and accuse us of sending people away, urge on the savages against us, who then tell them they should not regard us, that we are prisoners, and that it is their business to command us.

We are not, however, cast down nor disheartened, but oppose with might and with all our strength, to destroy and cast out of the church the works of Satan.

· · ·

Friday, March 1, through a messenger, were summoned to Pomoacan, who sent word he had something to tell us. Br. David, who was especially summoned, went there Saturday, the 2d, with Br. Heckewelder and two Indian brethren, where also a council of Wyandots and Delawares was assembled; there it was told us by the Half-King that a letter had come from the commandant in Detroit, which a white man, Simon Girty by name, had given him to read, and indeed it was not written to us, but to him, and to our great amazement it contained the following sentence regarding us missionaries

> "You will please present the strings I send you to the Half-King and tell him I have listened to his demand. I therefore hope he will give you such assistance as you may think necessary to enable you to bring the teachers and their families to this place. I will by no means allow you to suffer them to be plundered or any way ill-treated."

So far his order. It is easy to conjecture what heartrending news this was to us, and here nothing was to be done but to resign ourselves willingly to our fate, for the most common objections we could have made would have been utterly useless, and only have given the Wyandots opportunity to take us in hand, and misuse their power by treating us; this we could conjecture from the order, though it may not have been so intended. We gave then to the Englishman a written acknowledgment that we had received the commandant's order, would conduct ourselves accordingly, and obey his command, that in fifteen days we would be in Lower Sandusky, when we begged that we might be brought over the lake by water, for our sisters, with the little children, could not possibly make the toilsome journey by land; and this also was granted us.

In the evening we came back home to our brethren, who at this news were with ourselves amazed and saddened, and all the Indian brethren who heard it passed a sleepless night. Yes, we could not contentedly resign ourselves to leaving our Indian church, and thought it impossible that the Saviour could permit it. If we were all destroyed, then once for all we were freed from all need; thus, however, were we upheld to endure more deaths. But so it was, and we saw no other plan wherever we cast our thoughts, and meanwhile we had to comfort ourselves with to-day's Scripture-verse, which read: My thoughts are not your thoughts, neither are your ways my ways, saith the Lord, and with the collect therein say to the Saviour: We will put our trust in thee.

FAMILY AND COMMUNITY

Sunday, 3. To–day we sent at once a messenger to the Shawanese towns, where some of our brethren were, likewise an express to the Muskingum, to call in some brethren with horses, to take us to Lower Sandusky, and also once more to take counsel with them. The brethren in the neighborhood, who were making sugar in the bush, of whom there were only a few, all came home at this sad news, and to them, in a meeting, a discourse was delivered over to–day's Scripture–verse: Since thou wast precious in my sight, thou hast been honorable, and I have loved thee. Jesus! thou art all compassion – Pure, unbounded love thou art. It was told them that in a short time we should be taken away from them, and they were exhorted to cling the closer to the Saviour, to keep together in love and unity, and not to give Satan the satisfaction of seeing the church destroyed. They could now perceive clearly and plainly enough that from the outset it had been their object and aim to hinder the Saviour's work and to destroy it utterly. There was such weeping in the room that our hearts broke. A stone might feel pity to see and hear the distress of the brethren; should not God feel pity for his elect, who wept and cried aloud to him? All the brethren who came home wept their fill with us, and we comforted them the best we could, though we ourselves needed comfort. Advice we could not and dared not give them, save a little, for good reasons, but only say to them to look to their old, sensible brethren, to obey them and do as they did.

. . .

Monday, 4. Few as are the brethren now at home, we spent the whole day in listening to them, comforting them, encouraging them, and exhorting them to stay fast by the Saviour and his death on the cross. We heard and saw now the condition of our brethren's hearts and minds, how disinclined they are to the heathen's life, and how dead to those friends who have brought them to such want and wretchedness. They are prepared and hardened for these circumstances, and their eyes have been opened. These events have conduced more to bring them to a proper state than we have been able to accomplish the whole time we have been with them; for they always inclined towards their friends, who did them harm. Many now said to us: "I care nothing for outward loss; that I am stripped of every thing I had, and am become poor; that I have to suffer hunger and want; that all my cattle have perished: all this will I cheerfully endure and not be concerned, but that they at last rob us of our teachers and wish to destroy our souls' weal and food, that cuts me deep to the heart, and is above every thing. They shall not see, however, that I associate with them, and take up again their heathenish life; rather will I go into the bush, separate myself from all human society, and pass the rest of my life piteously. They shall not get me into their power nor force me to any thing for which I have no pleasure or inclination." [Others again had other plans, many of them, however, to go to Pittsburg.] Some said this from whom we had not expected it, and it was to us a great comfort to see them in such disposition of soul, but as often as they thought that in a short time they would see us no more, the tears immediately ran down their cheeks.

DIARY OF DAVID ZEISBERGER

Notes

1 Captain Pipe, whose Indian name was Kogiesch quanoheel, a Delaware captain of the Wolf (Monsey) tribe.
2 The Half-King was Wyandot (Pomoacan).
3 Communal meals shared by Moravians to promote harmony and love within the community.
4 Fort Pitt, near modern day Pittsburgh, Pennsylvania.

14

CAROLINE–STÉPHANIE–FÉLICITÉ, MADAME DE GENLIS (1846–1830), *ADELAIDE AND THEODORE; OR LETTERS ON EDUCATION, CONTAINING ALL THE PRINCIPLES RELATIVE TO THREE DIFFERENT PLANS OF EDUCATION; TO THAT OF PRINCES, AND TO THOSE OF YOUNG PERSONS OF BOTH SEXES*

3 vols (London: C. Bathurst, 1783), vol. 1,
pp. 5–8, 10–18, 62–66

Madame de Genlis was a French writer and minor aristocrat, who was known for her educational writings and children's books (and in subsequent centuries for her love letters and diaries). Often compared to Rousseau (see source 4), whose work she explicitly engages with, de Genlis provided a similar model of childhood as a time to be nurtured and gently guided. Her work was considered to be especially useful as it combined philosophy with practical child–rearing and educational tips, and so offered insight into everyday life for the elite. Her most famous work, *Adelaide and Theodore*, offers advice in epistolary form – a series of letters between female friends – about raising children, with the Baroness d'Almane situated as the source of wisdom. It is an important example of a form of writing where women could be situated with an authoritative voice in the public sphere. The epistolary form was remarkably popular in the eighteenth century, where the format allowed for advice to be asked and answered, and as a writerly mode that could be used in everyday life. In the first few letters, de Genlis explores how women wishing to pursue this form of education might extricate themselves from fashionable society, whilst later essays largely account for the education of Adelaide and Theodore, contrasted with that of her friend's children. As a source for the history of emotions, the text not only evidences ideas about the socialisation of childhood emotions, but the emotional tensions and dynamics of female friendship, and interesting reflections on subjects such as cruelty to animals. This version was translated into English from French in the eighteenth century.

...

LETTER II

Baroness d'Almane to the Viscountess d'Limours.

Feb 2.

We arrived at B–, my dear friend, all in good health. My boy and girl, at six and seven years old, bore their journey perfectly well; and as they slept as easy in the carriage, as in their beds, are infinitely less fatigued than I was so myself.

This country is charming, though I am not yet acquainted with its environs; yet the delightful views which may be seen from the castle, are sufficient to give me an idea of them. Every thing here puts on a plain and humble appearance; I have left pomp and magnificence behind me at Paris, in that large and disagreeable house we lived, and which was always so displeasing to me. I at length find myself lodged according to my taste and my wishes. My little *Adelaide* too is charmed with this country, and our habitation. She says she likes instructive pictures much better than damask hangings, and that "the Sun of Languedoc is brighter than that of Paris." As I conclude my dear friend is at this time a little displeased with me, I shall reserve my more particular accounts and descriptions for the happy moment of reconciliation. When you have read my heart, I dare believe, far from condemning me, you will approve every step I have taken. Consider, though you may be permitted to quarrel with your friend, when in the space of five minutes you can ask her pardon, you have no longer that privilege when she is at the distance of two hundred leagues. Besides, what crime have I been guilty of more than concealing a secret from you, which was not my own to divulge? Mons. D'Almane positively forbid my trusting you with it. But do you not remember the last time we supped together? In truth, you might have guessed from my melancholy, from my tenderness, what it was impossible to acquaint you with! Adieu, my dear friend! I shall expect you answer with the utmost impatience, for I cannot be happy, whilst I think you are displeased with me. I embrace Flora, and the sweet little Constantia with all my heart; and I entreat the former will sometimes talk to you about the best friend you have in the world.

...

LETTER III

The Countess d'Ostalis, to the Baroness d'Almane.

THE day of your departure, my dear aunt, I went as you desired to Madame *d'Limours*. In the morning she was denied to me; but in the evening she gave me admittance. I found her a little angry, but more grieved. She wept on seeing me, and then gave a loose to complaints against you; and treated me with a coolness, the cause of which I easily penetrated, and which was nothing more than an impulse of jealousy, occasioned by the idea of my having been entrusted with the secret, you had so carefully concealed from her. I could have said to her, "How, my dear Madam, was it possible that my aunt, my benefactress, my mother, that she, to whom I owe my education, my establishment, almost my existence, could have any reserves with her child, or could fear from me, either the objections or the oppositions she dreaded from you?" But I happily recalled to my mind one of your maxims, which forbids our making use of reason to oppose ill humour, and I remained silent. I dined yesterday at her house, and found her nearly in the same temper. She had many people with her; and I perceived several of her visitors endeavoured to irritate her against you, my dear aunt, by repeating with ill nature, how "incredible and inconceivable it was, that you should not have imparted your secret to her:" this has given such a wound to her self–love, that at this moment you must not expect your letters will have that effect on her which you hope for. But her heart is so good, she loves you so tenderly, and has so much frankness and vivacity, in her disposition, that it is impossible she should long retain these disagreeable impressions.

Mons. *d'Ostalis* does not go to his regiment till the first of June: and I shall set out the same day for Languedoc. How happy, my dear aunt, shall I be to find myself in your arms, after an absence of upwards of four months! To see my uncle again; the amiable *Theodore*, and the charming little *Adelaide*! And, ah, how cruel will it be to be separated again from these objects so dear to my heart! Adieu, my dear aunt; do not forget your eldest, your adopted child, who every moment of her life thinks of you, and loves you as much as she admires and respects you. My little twins are perfectly well; they begin to pronounce some words both of French and English: and they already afford me the greatest pleasure I am able to enjoy in your absence.

LETTER V

Baroness d'Almane to the Viscountess d'Limours.

HOW much do I owe to that "melancholy idea," which presented me four such tender and sweet lines! Although you have at present forgiven me, with so much kindness and generosity, I am still apprehensive we may have more disputes; but, however, attend to all that may serve to justify me. I never was fond of the bustle and amusements of the gay world, and you know with what ardour and anxiety I wished for children, and how much of my time has been employed during my whole life, in whatever concerned their education. Married at seventeen years of age, and not being a mother till I was twenty-one, I was apprehensive I shou'd never enjoy that happiness for which I had so ardently wished, and to make myself as much amends as I possibly could for this disappointment, I adopted Madame *d'Ostalis*; she was at that time ten years old, and was of an excellent disposition. I educated her with all the care of which I was then capable; and every body was pleased with the method I had pursued. My scholar at sixteen, was the most distinguished young person of her age, for her talents, knowledge, and disposition. I alone was sensible by the experience I had acquired, that I could do much better in future. *J. J. Rousseau* says, "Most people chuse Governors for their children who have been accustomed to that employment. But this is too much to expect; the same man can never compleat more than the education of one." Experience has proved to me that *Rousseau* opposes an opinion well sounded: the deepest study of the human heart, with every talent united, which is so essentially necessary in a Tutor, will avail nothing, without that experience which alone can be acquired by long practice. It was with great concern I made this discovery, yet it increased the extreme desire I always had for children; certain, that the greatest pleasure of my life would be to dedicate my time to their improvement. I cannot express what I felt at being disappointed of such happiness. Heaven at length heard my prayer: the birth of *Theodore*, and that of *Adelaide* a twelvemonth after, made me the happiest creature in the world. I had already finished some Works on Education. I laboured at it again with such earnestness, that it affected my health; I then found I could not follow my plan in the extent I wished, without breaking those bonds of society to which custom subjects us: in short, I saw it was necessary either to quit the world, or to renounce for ever the project I had formed, and which was so dear to my heart. Mons. *d'Almane* was entirely of my opinion, and he declared himself determined to leave Paris, as soon as Theodore had reached his seventh year. The difficulty was, what retreat to fix upon? We were desirous of inspiring our children with a taste for humble pleasures, and of removing them far from the pomp and magnificence of the metropolis. Could we therefore have been contented to go to a villa we had at only six leagues from Paris? Would it have been possible to prevent our acquaintance from following us thither? Would not *Adelaide* and *Theodore* have heard every day of Operas, Comedies, &c. And how could we have prevented their regretting these amusements, which they would have heard mentioned with so much pleasure? The result of these reflections, and many others, determined our preference of an estate of Mons. *d'Almane's* in the province of Languedoc; where we should meet with freedom and retirement. From that moment Mons. *d'Almane* began to arrange every thing at the castle for our reception. If you wish to know in what manner we have furnished our apartments, I will give you an exact description of it in my next letter. And now, my dear friend, I must intreat you for one moment to put yourself in my place; do not judge me by yourself, formed as you are for society, and to give and receive pleasure in the high stile of life which you have been used to; but represent me in the way you have always found me, fond of study and attention to my domestic duties, unable to bear restraint, where no rational aim was in view; and indifferent to the last degree to those trifling matters, which employ so many people in the world; I find myself interested in things only which are useful; not conceiving it possible to have any desire to please those we do not love, and detesting grand entertainments, dress, and cards; in short, expecting and looking for happiness only in my children, have I not followed the course most suitable to my disposition? And can you after this accuse me of "caprice?" It is very true, as you observe, my children can have no masters in Languedoc; but Mons. *d'Almane* and I shall be able to supply their places, at least during their infancy. Besides, I have with me two persons well qualified to instruct children, who will remain here till their education is compleated. When four years are elapsed, I mean to spend all my winters at Paris, and then I shall procure all the masters we shall think necessary to finish their improvements. Now confess, my dear friend; had I communicated this scheme to you two years ago, would you have thought yourself much obliged to me? No persons love to have secrets entrusted to them, but when you communicate them by way of asking advice. Our resolution was not to be shaken so that in trusting the secret to you, we should have only exposed ourselves to oppositions and to arguments which could only have vexed both parties, and perhaps have produced a mutual coolness. Here, my dear friend, is a part of my justification. When you know the plan of education we have formed, you will be more convinced how indispensably necessary it was for us to leave Paris. Let the world censure me as it pleases, the testimony of my own conscience will easily console me for their injustice, provided I can but attain the approbation of my friend. Those who make a sacrifice of their pleasures to their duty, may be sure the publick will turn to ridicule actions which are influenced by such laudable motives; and will find out imaginary causes to take away all their merit. This unjust way of judging is not always the effect of envy, but frequently takes place without any ill intention; for in effect the greater part of mankind are unable well to believe motives of which they themselves do not see the propriety, in which case their incredulity is more flattering than their approbation. In short, my dear friend, if you approve my conduct, and will always love me, I shall be satisfied, and perfectly happy.

LETTER VI

Viscountess d'Limours to the Baroness

OUR disputes always end in the same manner. I find you in the right, and I am obliged to confess my faults; and I perceive this will ever be the case between us. Yes, my dear friend, you are still right, when the motives of your conduct are explained, however I may find fault with you on the first appearance, in which I constantly see irregularity. Your plans always succeed well in the end. This is at present as much as I can allow you. But I cannot answer for its being my last word upon this subject. You have acted in every respect according to your disposition and sentiments. And though your scheme should not succeed so well as I suppose, you are setting an example, which in these days must have great merit; therefore it is impossible for me to disapprove your conduct any longer. Nothing can be more like than the picture you draw of yourself. At each word I read, I cried out, "how true that is!" And I then said to myself, but how can I love a person so tenderly, who bears so little resemblance to myself! You, who have so much knowledge, must explain this to me. Friendship has its caprices as well as love. All you have told me concerning the education of Madame *d'Ostalis*, has struck me in the most lively manner. I sincerely think, there can be no mother who would not be proud of such a daughter; yet from your sentiments I apprehend, if Adelaide has as good a disposition, she will infinitely surpass her. This, however, is a melancholy consideration for eldest daughters, since it is the youngest only who can be compleatly educated. How then is this inconvenience to be remedied? There must be some method, and you ought to employ yourself in finding it out. Think about it, I intreat you. I am this day thirty–one years old. I have a daughter in her sixteenth year. It is time I should renounce some of the follies of the world, which I have hitherto been engaged in; and, perhaps, it may be even now too late for me to repair the faults I have committed in *Flora's* education. Her sister, you know, is only five years old. Inform me of the plan you have laid out for *Adelaide*, and I will pursue it with as much steadiness as I possibly can in my situation. I have the greatest desire to render her worthy of being one day your daughter–in–law. Instruct me, guide me, my dear friend! How delightful will it be for me to be indebted to you for new virtues, and consequently for new sources of happiness! You have known me very gay and dissipated; but indeed my faults are more to be attributed to the neglected education I received, than to my natural disposition. When I first entered into the world, having just left the convent, one single idea had possession of my mind, which was that of making myself amends for a long and painful slavery, by entering into all the pleasures and amusements of life. All the instructions I received at that time was how to dress myself to advantage, and to dance well. I never missed an assembly; and the consequence was, that towards the end of the winter, I had an inflammation in my lungs, which I thought would have been fatal, and I was in debt to my mantuamaker, sixteen thousand livres! You see how tractable I was, and how strictly I followed the advice you gave me. Nevertheless, I can assure you with the greatest truth, that dissipation never charmed me but in idea, and I always returned from those noisy and tumultuous scenes, with a weariness and disgust, which ought to have convinced me, that they were not designed for me, at least not in the degree I had imagined. Yet I suffered myself to be led to them again by custom and complaisance. And thus it is I have passed my life; giving myself up to the pleasures of the world without loving them, and committing follies which my reflection condemned. And what is the consequence of all this? I enjoy not one agreeable recollection; my health is impaired; and now, when it is too late, I regret the time past. My vivacity is much talked of. I myself do not think it is natural to me; though I am praised for the appearance of it, you, who seem so serious in your

FAMILY AND COMMUNITY

manner, are in reality much more chearful than I am. I never saw you entertain "gloomy ideas," you know not what they mean. But as to myself, I am sometimes seized on a sudden with the most melancholy thoughts, and they present themselves to my imagination at the most unseasonable times, and even when I have been in the gayest humour. For instance, I find myself at this moment so sad and so peevish, that I will not lengthen my letter. Adieu, my dear friend! Send me the description of your castle, and all the other accounts you have promised me. I received a letter yesterday from my brother; he appears charmed with his young Prince, and every day congratulates himself on having undertaken his education. There is certainly much honour to be acquired, in well educating a Prince born to sovereignty. But it will cost my brother dear; for is it not a cruel sacrifice to be banished from one's own country for twelve years? He desires me to tell you, that the plan you have formed adds still more to the high esteem and attachment with which you have always inspired him, and that he will himself write to the Baron, to express to him the admiration he has conceived for you both. You most certainly set excellent examples, but such are not always the most useful; for if it be difficult to avoid praising you, it is still more difficult to imitate you.

LETTER XV

The same to the same. [Baroness d'Almane to the Viscountess d'Limours]

WE had yesterday a charming ride. We carried to *Nicole* the young peasant I mentioned to you, all the furniture, clothes, &c. we intended them; *Adelaide* was loaded with a bundle of childrens' cloathing; which, notwithstanding the extreme heat of the weather, she kept holding on her lap, the whole time we were in the carriage. She arrived at the cottage in a violent perspiration, her little heart beating, so that you could see its motion. Her cheeks flushed, and the purest and most lively joy sparkling in her eyes! Delightful, happy age, when every gesture, every action, presents an innocent and faithful picture of the sentiments of the heart! By degrees, as we lose this amiable simplicity, the silent, but interesting language of the eyes, becomes less intelligible; but they cannot quite deceive till the heart is wholly corrupted; for it is much more criminal to deceive by looks, than even by words. For he who cannot tell a falsehood without blushing, is not yet a complete liar, and whilst we preserve any traces of this sincerity, we are not arrived at the highest pitch of this odious vice. But to return to *Adelaide*. On getting out of the coach, she ran from us, dragging after her, in the dirt, the heavy parcel she had not strength to carry; and when we entered the cottage, we found, her already employed in undressing one of the little girls, to put on a new gown, repeating every moment, "It was I that made this hem;" "I sewed on this ribbon," "and fastened on this clasp," &c. &c. If this little picture affects you, how much more pleasure would you have felt, on seeing the satisfaction of the young peasant and her family. I have never till now found in this class of people any thing more than that kind of gratitude, which does honour to human nature. Hearts uncorrupted as

MADAME DE GENLIS, *ADELAIDE AND THEODORE*

theirs are, are affected with the benefit we confer on them, but are not surprised at it; while the extreme astonishment we shew at a good action, is a silent confession that we are incapable of doing it! Adieu, my dear friend! I quit you to go and read with *Adelaide*, who at this moment is leaning on my chair, and begging me to give her a lesson.

My sweet *Adelaide* has done so pretty an action, I cannot help telling it to you. And I have opened my letter again on purpose. After our reading, we went to take a walk, and amongst the chestnut trees, found a little bird just ready to fly; we took it up, and *Adelaide*, transported with joy, carried it to my chamber, and put it into a cage, every moment taking it out, and stifling it with caresses, and then crying over it as if it was dead. Here begins our dialogue word for word:

ADELAIDE. Mamma, my bird is hungry. I (writing at my desk) replied, "give it something to eat then; you have got what is necessary."

ADELAIDE. But he will not eat.

ANSWER. It is because he is sad.

ADELAIDE. Why is he sad?

ANSWER. Because he is unhappy.

ADELAIDE. Unhappy! Oh Heaven, why is my sweet little bird unhappy?

ANSWER. Because you do not know how to take care of him, and feed him, and because he is in prison.

ADELAIDE. In prison!

ANSWER. Yes, certainly he is; attend to me, *Adelaide*. If I was to shut you up in a little room, and not permit you to go out of it, would you be happy?

ADELAIDE. (Her heart full) Oh my poor little bird!

ANSWER. You make him unhappy.

ADELAIDE. (Frighten'd) I make him unhappy!

ANSWER. This little bird was in the fields, at his liberty, and you shut him up in a little cage, where he is not able to fly: see how he beats against it; if he could cry, I am sure he would.

ADELAIDE. (Taking him out of the cage) Mamma, I am going to set him at liberty; the window is open, is it not?

ANSWER. As you please, my dear child; for my part, I never would keep birds; for I would have every thing about me, and all that comes near me, happy!

ADELAIDE. I would be as good as my dear mamma. I am going to put it on the balcony, shall I?

ANSWER. (I still writing) If you please, my little dear.

ADELAIDE. But first I will feed him. Oh, my dear mamma, he eats!

ANSWER. I am very glad of it, if it gives you pleasure.

ADELAIDE. He eats. I know how to feed him. Sweet bird! Charming little creature! (she kisses him) How pretty he is. Ah, he kisses me. How I love him. (She puts him into the cage again, then is thoughtful, and sighs. After some silence, the bird begins to beat himself again) I (looking compassionately at him) say, "Poor little unfortunate!"

123

ADELAIDE. (With tears in her eyes) Oh, mamma! (taking him again out of the cage) I will give him his liberty; shall I?

ANSWER. (Without looking at her) As you please, *Adelaide.*

ADELAIDE (Going to the window) Dear little one! (she returns, crying) "Mamma, I cannot!"

ANSWER. Well, my dear, keep it then; this bird, like other animals, has not reason enough to reflect on the species of cruely you have, in depriving him of his happiness, to procure yourself a trifling amusement. He will not hate you, but he will suffer; and he would be happy, if he was at liberty. I would not hurt the smallest insect, at least not maliciously.

ADELAIDE. Come, then, I am going to put it on the window.

ANSWER. You are at liberty to do as you please, my dear, but do not interrupt me any more; let me write.

ADELAIDE. (Kissing me, then going to the cage) Dear, dear bird! (She weeps, and after a little reflection, she goes to the window, and returns with precipitation, her cheeks glowing, but with tears in her eyes) says, "Mamma, it is done; I have set him at liberty!"

ANSWER. I (taking her in my arms) say, my charming Adelaide, you have done a "good action," and I love you a thousand times more than ever.

ADELAIDE. Oh then I am well rewarded!

ANSWER. You always will be, every time you have courage to make a real sacrifice. Besides, sacrifices of this kind are only painful in idea. They are no sooner done, but they render us so amiable, that they leave nothing but joy and satisfaction in our hearts: for example, you wept at the thoughts of setting your bird at liberty; but do you regret it now?

ADELAIDE. Oh, no mamma; on the contrary, I am charmed at having made him happy, and at having performed a "good action."

ANSWER. Well, my dear child, never forget that, and if you are under any difficulty, in determining "to do right," remember your little bird, and say to yourself, There are no sacrifices, for which the esteem and tenderness for those we love cannot make useful amends.

Part 3

RELIGION

Part 3

Religion

Christianity was only one of the major religions practiced in eighteenth-century Europe, but it provided a significant body of emotional writings and ideas. Eighteenth-century Christians, from a wide range of denominations, experienced their faith as something felt and marked by a broad range of emotional responses. Spiritual life and teaching educated Christians to interpret their emotions through a moral framework. As a result, a wide range of texts provided guidance on how to manage or entrain the emotion to enable a Christian life, sometimes offering readers spiritual and practical exercises as part of emotion management. Spiritual writing could be important here as a tool with which people could explore how they felt, account for their sins and seek to better themselves. Some forms of spiritual writing were also written with an audience in mind, designed to offer lives that could be reflected on and emulated. Given the longevity of Christian teaching in this area, many of the ideas found here were not dissimilar to those in previous generations. But they could also be shaped by local context and conditions, not least the moral power given to emotion by the culture of sensibility, and the growth of rationalism that sought to better account for the differences between the spiritual and temporal domains of life.

15

SELECTION OF CHILDREN'S SAMPLERS WITH RELIGIOUS APHORISMS

European Christian children were educated in the practices and doctrine of the faith from a young age. These samplers, made by young girls across the eighteenth century, display how religion was integrated into other forms of education. Here the girls are practicing sewing, their alphabet and spelling, their religious knowledge and in some cases foreign languages. The use of symbols – like crowns or royal emblems – also suggests an education in political systems and royal authority. Girls from a wide range of social backgrounds made these samplers, and they often survive with little contextual evidence, other than the child's name or a date. However, we can guess something of class, from the nature of their education, like learning a language, or the quality of material used. As sources for the history of emotion, we can see how children are socialised in moral emotions, framed through bible verses, prayers and religious metaphor. Such sources provide insight into how religious belief was imagined to shape how people felt, as well as the emotions involved in praise and worship, and the role of repetitive activities like sewing to reinforcing a moral education. If we imagine that students selected their bible texts themselves, then we might also learn of how children themselves experienced their faith in emotional terms.

. . .

Figure 15.1 Eighteenth-century British sampler, cotton on linen, The Metropolitan Museum of Art, New York, From the Collection of Mrs. Lathrop Colgate Harper, Bequest of Mabel Herbert Harper, 1957.

Note: for more information: www.metmuseum.org/art/collection/search/228004.

CHILDREN'S SAMPLERS, RELIGIOUS APHORISMS

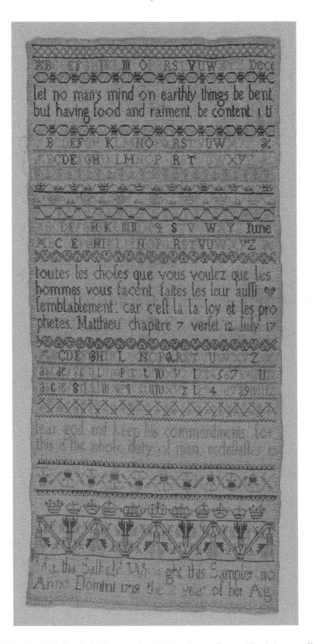

Figure 15.2 Martha Wright, British sampler 1719, silk on linen, The Metropolitan Museum of Art, New York, From the Collection of Mrs. Lathrop Colgate Harper, Bequest of Mabel Herbert Harper, 1957.

Note: the French text reads: 'So in everything, do to others what you would have them do to you, for this sums up the Law and the Prophets. Matthew chapter 7 verse 12, July 17. For more information: www.metmuseum.org/art/collection/search/227989.

RELIGION

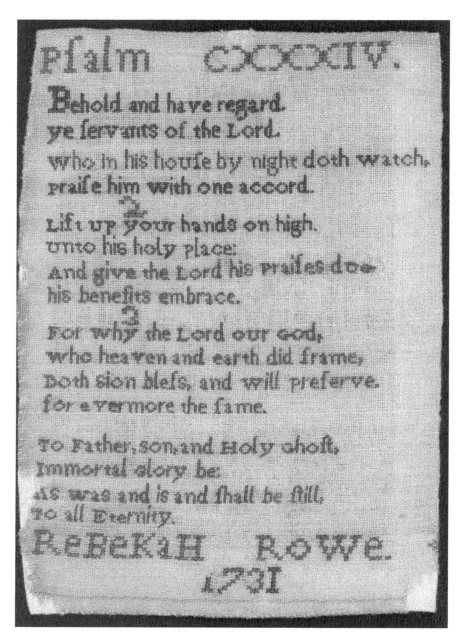

Figure 15.3 Rebekah Rowe Sampler, charity school, 1731, silk on linen, The Metropolitan Museum of Art, New York, From the Collection of Mrs. Lathrop Colgate Harper, Bequest of Mabel Herbert Harper, 1957.

Note: for more information: www.metmuseum.org/art/collection/search/228471.

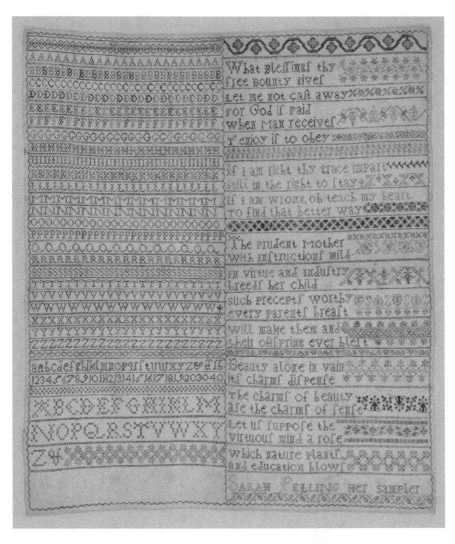

Figure 15.4 Sarah Pelling, Eighteenth-century British sampler, cotton on linen, The Metropolitan Museum of Art, New York, From the Collection of Mrs. Lathrop Colgate Harper, Bequest of Mabel Herbert Harper, 1957.

Note: for more information: www.metmuseum.org/art/collection/search/228283.

RELIGION

Figure 15.5 Eighteenth-century British sampler, wool, The Metropolitan Museum of Art, New York, From the Collection of Mrs. Lathrop Colgate Harper, Bequest of Mabel Herbert Harper, 1957.

Note: the French text reads: Sunday Prayer. Our Father who art in heaven, Hallowed be thy name. Thy kingdom come. Thy will be done on earth as it is in heaven. Give us this day our daily bread, and forgive us our trespasses, as we forgive those who trespass against us, and lead us not into temptation, but deliver us from evil. For thine is the kingdom, and the power, and the glory. Amen. The King's crown. For more information: www.metmuseum.org/art/collection/search/228493.

16

ERIK PONTOPPIDAN (1698–1764), *TRUTH UNTO GODLINESS (SANDHED TIL GUDFRYGTIGHED)*

(Copenhagen, 1737)

Erik Pontoppidan was a Danish-Norwegian Bishop in the Lutheran Church of Norway.[1] He wrote *Truth unto Godliness*, by royal order, as an explanatory catechism for the church, alongside a hymnbook. A catechism lays out the church doctrine – its main beliefs and principles – for the congregation. Pontoppidan's catechism was thus a key document in shaping the faith from the eighteenth century onwards, and particularly fuelled the Lutheran pietist movement. The text moves through the key beliefs of the church, positing them as a form of questions and answers under particular themes, and providing the relevant bible teachings that supported the answers. Such documents exist for most Christian denominations, and they often have a similar shape, if differing in details. They provide important evidence of how various faiths interpreted affections, passions and emotions through a moral lens, directing people to avoid certain feelings and behaviours and encouraging others. The excerpts below – taken from the discussion of the ten commandments and translated into English from Danish – highlight how religion was used to guide family and community relationships, and how these relationships were defined in terms of how people felt about each other.

. . .

The Fourth Commandment: Honour your father and mother, that your days may be long in the land which the Lord your God gives you

By which is meant:

We should so fear, and love God: that we may not despise nor displease our parents and superiors, but honour, serve, obey, love, and esteem them.

159.　What good is enjoined in the fourth commandment?
　　　To honour, serve, obey, and esteem our parents.

RELIGION

160. What is forbidden in the fourth commandment?
To despise and offend our parents.

161. Who are meant by father and mother in the fourth commandment?
First our natural parents, then all of those who in some way have command and counsel over us, such as government officials, guardians, husbands, priests, and schoolmasters and the like, who are all parents, each according to his estate.

162. How many estates are there?
Three, namely:

1) The government, in which kings, princes, and other authorities are parents and their subjects are their children.
2) The teachers, in which pastors and schoolmasters are parents and their students and congregations are children.
3) The household, in which fathers and mothers, husbands, wives, guardians, benefactors and honest elders should be considered as parents by children, grandchildren, stepchildren, servants, minors and other young people.

163. Why must a child, a servant and a pupil honour these parents?
Because it is the word of God and serves to their own welfare.

164. Who has put their authority over us?
God himself.
Rom 13, 1. There is no other authority without God.

165. Are we then obliged, for God's sake, to obey even an ungodly authority?
Yes, Peter, wanted the first Christians to be submissive to a Pagan authority when he said: Submit yourselves to every ordinance of man for the Lord's sake. 1. Pet 2, 13.

166. How ought subjects to deport themselves toward their superiors?

1) They should willingly obey them.
Rom 13, 5. Wherefore ye must needs be subject, not only for wrath, but also for conscience sake.
2) They must honour them.
Rom 13, 7. Render therefore to all their dues: honour to whom honour.
3) They must pray for them.
1 Tim 2, 1. I exhort therefore, that, first of all, supplications, prayers, intercessions, and giving of thanks, be made for all men, for kings, and for all that are in authority; that we may lead a quiet and peaceable life in all godliness and honesty.
4) They have to pay them taxes, duties and tithes honestly.
Matt 22, 21. Render therefore unto Caesar the things which are Caesar's; and unto God the things that are God's.

PONTOPPIDAN, *SANDHED TIL GUDFRYGTIGHED*

167. Are customs fraud and embezzlement such great sins?
Yes, certainly.

Rom 13, 6. 7. For this cause pay ye tribute also: for they are God's ministers, attending continually upon this very thing. Render therefore to all their dues: tribute to whom tribute is due; custom to whom custom; fear to whom fear; honour to whom honour.

168. May one disobey an authority or neglect their command?
Never, unless being ordered to do what is manifestly sin against God's commandments, for then one should obey God more than men. Acts. 5, 29.

169. What is the duty of superiors to their subjects?
To love them, seek their temporal and eternal welfare, keep peace and good order in punishing evil and rewarding good.

Rom 13:4 For he is the minister of God to thee for good. But if thou do that which is evil, be afraid; for he beareth not the sword in vain: for he is the minister of God, a revenger to execute wrath upon him that doeth evil.

170. By whom are teachers and preachers ordained?
By God.

2 Cor 5, 20. Now then we are ambassadors for Christ, as though God did beseech you by us: we pray you in Christ's stead, be ye reconciled to God.

171. Should congregations obey their pastors' admonitions?
Yes, certainly.

Hebr 13, 17 Obey them that have the rule over you, and submit yourselves: for they watch for your souls, as they that must give account, that they may do it with joy, and not with grief: for that is unprofitable for you.

172. Should one also follow and obey an ungodly teacher?
Not his deeds, but certainly his words if abides by the truth of scripture, which must be tested after the example in Berea.

Acts 17, 11. 1 Joh 4,1. As it says in Matt 23, 2–3. Saying the scribes and the Pharisees sit in Moses' seat: All therefore whatsoever they bid you observe, that observe and do; but do not ye after their works: for they say, and do not.

173. What do congregants owe their teachers?
To love, honour, obey, reward them, and pray for their welfare.

Gal 6, 6. Let him that is taught in the word communicate unto him that teacheth in all good things.

174. What is a teacher's duty to his students?
To teach, exhort and punish with a loving, meek and diligent heart, as well as constantly praying for them and leading them by a good example.

1 Pet 5, 2–3; 1 Cor 1, 11; 1 Cor 4, 16.
2 Tim 4, 2. Preach the word; be instant in season, out of season; reprove, rebuke, exhort with all long suffering and doctrine.

RELIGION

175. Is not a priest set to comfort all people?
No, only the penitent. For the self-assured, consolation is a poison to the soul.

Ez 3, 18. When I say unto the wicked, thou shalt surely die; and thou givest him not warning, nor speakest to warn the wicked from his wicked way, to save his life; the same wicked man shall die in his iniquity; but his blood will I require at thine hand.

176. Who are the false prophets amongst the teachers, that one should guard against?
Next to many others, which cannot be enumerated, are chiefly, in the words of the Saviour, those who make the way to heaven wide and deceive souls with the hope of salvation until they awake in Hell.

Matt 7, 14–15. Because strait is the gate, and narrow is the way, which leadeth unto life, and few there be that find it. Beware of false prophets, which come to you in sheep's clothing, but inwardly they are ravening wolves.

Isa 3, 12. O my people, they which lead thee cause thee to err, and destroy the way of thy paths.

177. What are the duties of parents and guardians towards the young?
To pray for them and care for their temporal, spiritual and eternal welfare
Eph 6, 4. bring them up in the nurture and admonition of the Lord.

178. What should parents do for disobedient children?
They must punish them in a sensible and loving way, not producing bitterness, but for their improvement.

Prov 13, 24. He that spareth his rod hateth his son: but he that loveth him chasteneth him betimes.

179. Does God then punish the parents who let their children rule over them?
Yes, we see that in Eli's example. 1. Sam 2, 31.

180. Can you punish your children too much?
Yes.

Eph 6, 4. And, ye fathers, provoke not your children to wrath

181. What is the children's duty toward their parents?
To honour, love, serve and obey them with heart, words, gestures, and deeds, even when the children are of age, wise, rich and honourable, as well as praying for them.

Sir 3, 7. Honor your father with deed and word that blessing may come upon you from him.[2]

Sir 3, 11. Dear child, help your father in old age and do not grieve him while he lives.

Sir 3, 15. He that forsaketh his father, he is like a blasphemer, and he that angereth his mother is cursed of the Lord.

PONTOPPIDAN, *SANDHED TIL GUDFRYGTIGHED*

182. Can a child marry without the will and consent of his parents?
No, because it is a cause of great sorrow to them.

183. Should one obey one's parents in what is evil and sinful?
No.
Matt 10, 37. He that loveth father or mother more than me is not worthy of me: and he that loveth son or daughter more than me is not worthy of me.

184. What is the duty of masters and mistresses towards their servants?

1) To provide any diet due as part of their contract and to pay them on time. Lev. 19:13 the wages of him that is hired shall not abide with thee all night until the morning.
2) To guide and govern them with loving patience. Eph 6, 9. And, ye masters, do the same things unto them, forbearing threatening: knowing that your Master also is in heaven; neither is there respect of persons with him.
3) To take care of their physical needs, especially in times of sickness, as well as their spirituality by teaching, exhortation, and intercession, as the chief of Capernaum did, Matt 8, 6. Gen. 18, 19.

185. What is the duty of servants towards their masters and mistresses?
They should love, honor and obey them, look to their best interests being diligent and faithful in both their absence and presence, as well as diligently praying for them.
Eph 6, 5–8. Servants, be obedient to them that are your masters according to the flesh, with fear and trembling, in singleness of your heart, as unto Christ; Not with eyeservice, as menpleasers; but as the servants of Christ, doing the will of God from the heart; With good will doing service, as to the Lord, and not to men: Knowing that whatsoever good thing any man doeth, the same shall he receive of the Lord, whether he be bond or free.

186. But what if an employer is difficult to come to terms with?
Then a Christian servant must exercise patience.
1 Pet 2, 18–19. Servants, be subject to your masters with all fear; not only to the good and gentle, but also to the froward. For this is thankworthy, if a man for conscience toward God endure grief, suffering wrongfully.

187. Can the duty of servants to be obedient be used to put them to sinful deeds?
No, by no means, for high is the commandment of a master, but higher is the commandment of God.
Acts 5, 29. We ought to obey God rather than men.

188. What does God promise obedient children and servants who keep the fourth commandment?
They will prosper and will live long in the land.

RELIGION

189. Does God then give all pious people a long and blissful life?
Yes, if he finds it useful for their salvation, otherwise not.

190. Why does he often let the wicked grow old?
Because he will give them all the more time and opportunity for repentance.

191. Does God then punish children's disobedience, just as he rewards their obedience to parents?
Yes, we have a great example in Absalom, the stubborn son of David, who was hung by his hair in an oak and pierced with three spears. 2 Sam 18, 9–15.

The sixth commandment: Thou shalt not commit adultery

By which is meant:
We should so fear and love God: as to live a chaste and pure life, saying or doing nothing lewd, each loving and honouring his own wife.

206. What is marriage?
The oldest estate and orderly condition, instituted in paradise by God himself, who wanted man and woman to be one flesh.

207. Is not this condition sinful and unholy?
No, when it is kept only according to the Word and will of God.
Hebr 13, 4. Marriage is honourable in all, and the bed undefiled.

208. To what end has God instituted marriage?

1) For the reproduction of the human race.
Gen 1, 28. Be fruitful, and multiply, and replenish the earth
2) To ward off immoral desires.
1 Cor. 7, 2. Nevertheless, to avoid fornication, let every man have his own wife, and let every woman have her own husband.
3) For mutual help, comfort and advice.
Gen. 2, 18. And the LORD God said, It is not good that the man should be alone; I will make him an help meet for him.

209. How should a husband behave towards his wife?
He should faithfully love, honour, guide, govern and provide for her, with patience bear her frailties, pray for her and seek the salvation of her soul.
Col 3, 19. Husbands, love your wives, and be not bitter against them.

210. How should a wife behave towards her husband?
She should be submissive to him in love, faith, and in her diligent care for the household, praying for him and seeking the salvation of his soul.
Gen. 3, 16. thy desire shall be to thy husband, and he shall rule over thee.
1 Cor 7, 34. she that is married careth for the things of the world, how she may please her husband. 1 Cor 7, 16. 1 Pet 3, 1.

PONTOPPIDAN, *SANDHED TIL GUDFRYGTIGHED*

211. What is the consolation of pious widows and orphans?
Our Heavenly Father's most gracious care and protection.
Psal. 68, 5–6. A father of the fatherless, and a judge of the widows, is God in his holy habitation. God setteth the solitary in families
See more: Ex 22, 22–24. Deut 27, 19. Sir. 35, 14–15. &c

212. What is the duty of pious widows?
To live honourably and devoutly.
1 Tim 5, 5–6. Now she that is a widow indeed, and desolate, trusteth in God, and continueth in supplications and prayers night and day. But she that liveth in pleasure is dead while she liveth.

213. What sin is forbidden to us in the sixth commandment?
Adultery, unchastity, incest, bestiality, defilement of the body, contempt of marriage, lusting after foreign beauty, and all kinds of impurity in thoughts, words, gestures, and deeds, both in and outside marriage.

214. What is fornication in thought?
Unclean and fleeting desires which are not hidden from God, who knows the heart.
Matt 5, 28. But I say to you that whoever looks at a woman to lust for her has already committed adultery with her in his heart.

215. What is fornication in word?
All lewd and shameless speech, lewd books, novels, shows and songs, jesting and foolish nonsense, which lead to fornication or at least goes against appropriate Christian seriousness.
Eph 4, 29. Let no corrupt communication proceed out of your mouth.
Eph 5, 3–5. But fornication, and all uncleanness, or covetousness, let it not be once named among you, as becometh saints; Neither filthiness, nor foolish talking, nor jesting, which are not convenient: but rather giving of thanks. For this ye know, that no whoremonger, nor unclean person, nor covetous man, who is an idolater, hath any inheritance in the kingdom of Christ and of God.

216. What are unchaste and impure gestures?
All external signs and occasions, which betray an outrageous heart, be it the expressions of the eyes and face, the indecent exposure of the body, indecent clothing, playing kissing, dancing, skipping and the like.
Sir. 26, 10–12. Keep a strong guard over a shameless daughter that she should not use her will when she finds leave for it. Guard against her impudent eye, and do not wonder if she sins against you. Sir. 9, 7. 11.

217. Are lewd words and gestures such a great sin?
Yes, not only are they obscene to Christians in themselves, but they are also followed by dangerous effects and serve to further arouse sinful desires, until the latter lead to immoral actions.

RELIGION

James 1, 14–15. But every man is tempted, when he is drawn away of his own lust, and enticed. Then when lust hath conceived, it bringeth forth sin: and sin, when it is finished, bringeth forth death.

218. What makes this sin abominable and punishable above others?
Because it defiles and corrupts both soul and body, which should be the temple of God, but becomes the abode of the unclean spirit.

1 Cor 6, 15–18. Know ye not that your bodies are the members of Christ? shall I then take the members of Christ, and make them the members of an harlot? God forbid. What? know ye not that he which is joined to an harlot is one body? for two, saith he, shall be one flesh. But he that is joined unto the Lord is one spirit. Flee fornication. Every sin that a man doeth is without the body; but he that committeth fornication sinneth against his own body.

219. What is commanded in the sixth commandment?
To preserve both body and soul in true chastity, whether one is married or unmarried, so that one must always be fit for fellowship with God.

Matt 5, 8. Blessed are the pure in heart: for they shall see God.

220. What means should one use to protect against unchastity?
When the spirit is willing, but the flesh is weak, one must watch and pray and beware of all that ignites lust.

221. What is it that ignites the lusts of the flesh?
Gluttony and drunkenness.

222. Are gluttony and drunkenness so dangerous and great a sin?
Yes indeed, for they exclude us from the kingdom of God, just as much as adultery, murder and theft.

Gal 5, 19–21. Now the works of the flesh are manifest, which are these; Adultery, fornication, uncleanness, lasciviousness, Idolatry, witchcraft, hatred, variance, emulations, wrath, strife, seditions, heresies, Envyings, murders, drunkenness, revellings, and such like: of the which I tell you before, as I have also told you in time past, that they which do such things shall not inherit the kingdom of God.

Luk 21, 34. And take heed to yourselves, lest at any time your hearts be overcharged with surfeiting, and drunkenness, and cares of this life, and so that day come upon you unawares.

223. But is it so dangerous from time to time to drink to intoxication, when one does not make a daily habit of it?
Yes, when done intentionally, it is always a reprehensible sin that can never endure with the grace of God and the hope of salvation.

224. Should you limit your intake even if you have a high tolerance for alcohol?
Do not eat or drink more than necessary. See 1 Pet 4, 3, where a distinction is made between excess drinking and drunkenness, and yet both are named as pagan sins.

225. What else may tempt to unchastity?
Idleness, immoral company, novels, amorous books and pictures, lascivious plays, dancing, acting, and everything that feeds the lust of the eyes, of the flesh and an intemperate life.

226. What good thoughts are able to suppress carnal temptations?
To remember the countenance and presence of the Most Holy God, the crucified Jesus in his bodily suffering, the terrible agony of the condemned in Hell, and the brief pleasure of the sin of unchastity, following the well-known verse: But whoso committeth adultery with a woman lacketh understanding: he that doeth it destroyeth his own soul. A wound and dishonour shall he get; and his reproach shall not be wiped away.[3]

227. Who has thus retained his chastity against challenge?
Joseph, when he said to Potiphar's wife: How can I do this great evil and sin against God? Gen 39, 9.

The eighth commandment: Thou shalt not bear false witness against thy neighbour

By which is meant:
We should so fear and love God: as to not falsely deceive others, betray others, slander others, defame others, but forgive them, think and speak well of them, and put the most charitable construction on all his actions.

248. What evil is forbidden in the eighth commandment?
To bear false witness against one's neighbour.

249. What is false witness?
All untruthful and unloving talk about our neighbours, in or out of court.

250. How is false testimony given in court?

1) When the prosecutor makes false accusations.
   Prov 19, 5. He that speaketh lies shall not escape.
2) When a witness confirms the lie.
   Prov 19, 5. A false witness shall not be unpunished.
3) When the defender defend lies against his conscience.
   Ex 23, 1. Thou shalt not raise a false report: put not thine hand with the wicked to be an unrighteous witness.
4) When the judge intentionally or out of ignorance determines lies to be truth and right to be wrong.
   Prov 17, 15. He that justifieth the wicked, and he that condemneth the just, even they both are abomination to the LORD. 2 Chron 19, 6–7; Eph 10, 1–2.

143

RELIGION

251. Can Christians lead trials against each other?
In important cases and in extreme emergencies, they must take refuge in the office of the judge, which is the Order of God, and complain of their distress without hatred to their adversary, but to quarrel for all small wrongs, and in every instance prove themselves to be stubborn or vengeful, is very wicked.

1 Cor 6, 7. Now therefore there is utterly a fault among you, because ye go to law one with another. Why do ye not rather take wrong? why do ye not rather suffer yourselves to be defrauded? Prov 20, 22; Matt 5, 39; Rom 12, 19.

252. How is false testimony told outside the court?
When one belies his neighbour, and falsely brings him into evil repute.

Sir. 5, 16. Be not called a whisperer, and be not taken in thy tongue, and confounded.

253. But must one not speak evil of your neighbour if it is true?
No, not unless it is already known to every man, and even then one should not take pleasure in it, as this is unloving.

254. How can one betray one's neighbour?

1) When one reveals what he has secretly confided in us.
Prov 11, 13. A talebearer revealeth secrets: but he that is of a faithful spirit concealeth the matter.
2) When one spreads his hidden faults to his detriment and the indignation of others.
Sir 19, 7–8. Rehearse not unto another that which is told unto thee, and thou shalt fare never the worse. Whether it be to friend or foe, talk not of other men's lives; and if thou canst without offence, reveal them not.

255. May one denounce a neighbour's sin to the authorities or the pastor?
Yes, when it happens out of love and care for the neighbour, and to avert sin, such as when Joseph brought the sins of his brothers before their father. See also Matt 18, 17, where Christ commands us to tell the congregation of a neighbour's sin, when a secret admonishment will not bear fruit. But when it comes from revenge or gossip, it is a sin.

256. Are there other occasions when it is sinful to speak?
Yes, all useless words are sinful.

Matt 12, 36. But I say unto you, That every idle word that men shall speak, they shall give account thereof in the day of judgment.

257. What good is commanded in the eighth commandment?
To forgive our neighbour, think and speak well of them, and put the most charitable construction on all his actions.

258. Can one then have good thoughts about all people?
When by their works they do not betray any inner evil, one must follow love in hoping for the best and not suspect anyone of evil.

1 Cor 13, 5–7. Love does not think evil, it endures all things, believes all things, hopes all things.

But when evil is manifest, do not call it good.

Isa 5, 20. Woe unto them that call evil good, and good evil.

259. Should one take a neighbour's part when others speak against him?
Yes, if one can honestly, especially when he is not present to explain himself.

Sir. 6, 6. A sweet tongue makes many friends.

1 Pet 4, 8. for charity shall cover the multitude of sins.

Notes

1 Translated by Katie Barclay. With thanks to Nina Koefoed for her advice on selecting passages and checking the translation.
2 Book of Sirach
3 Prov 6:32

17

GEORGE BROWN (C.1715–1779), *DIARY OF GEORGE BROWN, MERCHANT IN GLASGOW, 1745–53*

(Glasgow: Thomas Constable, 1856), pp. 132–143, 298–305

George Brown was a merchant in Glasgow, Scotland, who kept a spiritual diary. He was a member of the Calvinist Church of Scotland. Spiritual diaries were common amongst early modern Christians, especially Protestants, and provided a space for people to reflect on their moral behaviour and character, to recount their sins and spiritual experiences, and to draw closer to God and Christian living. Writing the diary was a form of devotional practice, where the opportunity for confession and spiritual exploration enhanced moral reformation in the individual. In this excerpt, Brown explores how his commitment to holy living is made challenging by his everyday experiences, whether falling in love, or an argument with his father. The account highlights spirituality as something felt, and where the goal of the Christian was to pursue and manage moral emotions and to downplay and avoid the sinful passions that would lead one from God. A key issue here included a hardening of heart, where the Christian did not show an appropriate degree of enthusiasm in their worship.

. . .

Sabbath, 4th May 1746. – Rose in the morning and prayed to the Lord God of the Sabbath; heard sermon forenoon and afternoon in North-west Church, by Mr. Gray preacher, on second Chapter Hebrews, sixteenth and seventeenth verses, where I heard many useful and important truths. After sermon I retired at four o'clock to prayer, under much difficulty and in much opposition from a carnal mind. Spent much of this night in meditating on the falls and miscarriages of others, and the improvement I should make of it. Prayed again to the Lord, read a portion of Scripture, and went to bed.

Monday, 5th May 1746. – Rose in the morning and prayed to the Lord, and concluded the day with the same duty.

Tuesday, May 6th, 1746. – Rose in the morning and began the day with prayer; heard sermon in Trone Church, by Mr. Thom, on first chapter Proverbs, about the twenty-fourth verse. In this and the preceeding day I have been much assaulted with a temptation that frequently has ensnared me, and led me aside, and, alas! at this time has prevailed too much against me: the temptation flowed from an extraordinary regard I had towards one mentioned formerly in my Diary, whom I was courting. Affection and love on the one hand to my friend, who, I knew, had a sincere regard for me, and, on the other hand, difficultys rising only from opposition of friends, whose chief objection was, that I was not rich enough; these two things threw me into a perplexity what part to act, – love made me incline to begin correspondence, which had been broke off for reasons formerly mentioned, and love forbad me to desire this, because it would bring the resentment of friends on her. I cannot tell the various things that tossed me on this subject, neither is there need to mention them; but I felt the sad effects of it, which were drawing my heart from God and spiritual things, creating inward disquiet and anxiety in my soul attended with a restless discontent of spirit, and indifferency about going about the dutys of a religious or temporal nature. In this melancholy state I betook myself to the Lord by prayer, and spread my complaint before Him, sought His grace might be sufficient for me, that he would make darkness lift before me, lead me in the way I should go, and teach me the part I should act; if for His glory and my good, that He would remove hindrances in the way of my marriage, and in every temptation give a way of escape. Among the many sins into which I have been lead by this affair, for which, Lord help to true penitential sorrow, it is comfortable to me to think that the world has not influenced me – that my regard to my friends excites in me an earnest concern for their eternal interests, and also for the eternal wellfare of those that are the means of opposition to my inclinations; and that my view in it was not the bettering my wordly circumstances, but that we might live both by grace, as heirs of the grace of life, living quiet and peaceable lives in godliness and honesty; to me it is matter of thankfulness, that my views in this matter have not been confined to the world, and that uprightness in principle and end, is what I have been by grace aiming at, and I hope have attained to, in some measure, in this matter. To me also it is matter of thankfulness that I have met with such kindness and regard from my friend, and that I have such evidence of their love to me; but, on the other hand, I have reason to mourn that this matter so often employs my thoughts, and steals away my affections – so frequently breaks in on me in duty, and disturbs me in my religious exercises. Attained to some fervency in prayer, and went to bed.

Wednesday, 7th May 1746. – Rose in the morning and prayed to the Lord. When I think on the exercise of my soul to-day, how many sins state me in the face! Sett them so in order before me, as I may thereby be excited to sincere repentance for them, and to faith in the blood of the Redeemer. Ended the day as usual with reading a portion of Scripture and prayer.

Sabbath, 18th May 1746. – This day I have been very much indisposed for the dutys of a Sabbath, being strongly assaulted with a temptation of which I have

RELIGION

made frequent mention, and which for some time past seems to have been gathering strength, and now comes with redoubled force upon me; this temptation makes me weary in duty, makes retirement a burden to me, makes me indifferent and formal in prayer. It has made me frequently to neglect the reading of God's word, and is the occasion of the frequent interruptions in my Diary, for every thing within me looks so dark and dismal that I care not to think on them, and far less to write them down. Many a time I feel an inclination after deliverance, sorrow of mind that it is thus with me, and a wishing and longing that the Lord would again return unto me, and would deal bountifully with me. Many at time I have been inclined to the use of means, and have felt my soul pushed as it were to prayer as a mean of relief from trouble and victory over temptation, which I did obey, but alas! found my heart as dead for the most part as ever; indeed, a few warm breathings, to my uptaking, from the bottom of my heart would break forth, and these would be succeeded by a deadness and inactivity of spirit that cannot be described, being better felt. The temptation is concerning my settlement in the world. Sure I am have greatly offended God in this matter, and grievously provoked the Lord to depart from me, and leave my soul a prey to the wild beasts of the forest, to many inordinate worldly passions, desires, and inclinations, which fill my soul with tormenting and distracting thoughts, many of these desires being contrary and opposite the one unto the other. In reviewing my Diary, I find I have made many resolutions and promises to wrestle, strive against, and resist this temptation, which all have been fruitless and vain, never having been able to put them in practice, so as to get victory over the temptation. O how weak am I, and how inexcusable in this weakness, as it is guilty, wilfull weakness. O Lord, help me to holy mourning and contrition of soul for sin the procuring cause of my present distressed condition, and enable to groaning under the just tokens of they displeasure gone forth against me, and give experience of the healing virtue of the blood of sprinkling healing my soul that has sinned against thee. Here I must remark one intake among many of the free and unmerited, undeserved loving-kindness and tender mercy of the Lord towards me, in that, notwithstanding of my dreadfully aggravated guilt, He did not cease to be a reprover unto me, carryng home frequently on my mind alarming impressions of death and a future judgement, particularly for some nights by past, my soul, – conscious of the guilt of the past day, especially of mocking God in my secret duty, by drawing near to Him with the mouth, while the heart was far from Him – has been pierced thro' with awfull thoughts of God, as He who is my witness, and shortly will be my judge. When I have just arose from prayers, and gone to my bed, such thoughts as these have occurred to me, and I have said thus to my soul, "now my conscience testifys to me that I have been but mocking God this night in my secret prayers, now I am sensible I am not in such a condition and frame I would wish to be in, when death comes; what if this very night that summonds of death be put into my hand, and before the next morning I be sisted before the tribunal of the great God whom I have this night mocked and offended; how shall I then stand in judgement, and how can I hope with confidence to lift my guilty face before God!" Thus I was afraid of the terrors of the Lord; but my fear did not so affect me to spur to diligence and unweared activity in seeking the Lord with the whole heart, for still my soul was saying yet a little sleep, yet a little slumber and folding of the hands. O how great is the perverseness of my corrupted nature, which is neither influenced by the terrors or mercys of the Lord, by the promises or threatnings of the Gospell! Thus, experience teaches me that all means are vain and fruitless, unless accompanyed with the powerful efficacy of the Spirit of Jesus. O Eternal Spirit! the awakener of sleeping and secure consciences, the quickner and healer of dead and diseased souls, the reviver and restorer of languishing and wandering spirits, cause me to awake from sleep, to hear thy voice calling to me "arise from the dead;" do thou bless me with light and life, with spiritual health, strength, and joy. Thou whose office it is to take of Christ's purchase and to shew them to sinners, do thou glorify the Redeemer by communicating out of his fullnesss to me all the blessings I stand in need of, remission of sin and the comfortable sense of it, the privileges of adoption and begun sanctification, with all the benefits flowing from these, and do thou supply all my needs according to the riches of thy glory in Christ Jesus.

Tuesday, 20th May, 1746. – Through the whole of this and the preceeding day I have been labouring under a heartlessness in duty, going about it in such a dead and lifeless manner, as if I were unconcerned whether my religious exercises were acceptable in the Lord's sight or not; and here I must remark a strong temptation to undutifullness to my father which assaulted me both yesterday and to day, and which prevailed against me, so as to make me speak irreverently towards my parent. This temptation which proved ensnaring to me was this, my father had allowed me full liberty to assert his right to a third part of a seat in New Church which he thought was dubious, but which on enquiry I found he had a claim to. However, he changed his mind, and would give over any right he had to the third part of that seat to the other persons who claimed; this I was against, and had my temper twice ruffled in speaking to him about it, which occasioned me to utter so angry, bitter, and undutiful words towards him; my conscience in the evening began severely to check me for this my conduct, and I felt much pain and inward disquiet of mind on this account, whereby I was justly punished, being made my own tormentor. I saw that I was acting from a forward disposition, while my father shewed more of the Christian in his behaviour. His meekness was a sharp rebuke to my fierceness. I soon began to see the folly of my conduct in this matter, and was saying within myself thus, "Why should I give way to unreasonable anger and bitterness of spirit? should I not as a Christian be of a meek and quiet spirit, why should I not give my advice with calmness and submission to my superior, and not be offended tho' it should not be followed?" Methinks that it need not seem strange that others do not follow my advice when I think on the perverseness of my own spirit in repeated refusals of the counsels of the eternall wisdom of God. Methinks the consideration of patience of God in waiting to be gracious to sinners, and notwithstanding of their obdurate hardness, his reasoning and expostaliting with them to mind the things belonging to their peace, should excite me still to continue to give my advice with prudence and meekness to others, tho' formerly

RELIGION

they have not followed it. This spiritual indisposition of my soul, increased by repeated yielding to this temptation already mentioned, is the more affecting to me, as it is an evidence to me that I am not in a suitable frame for the partaking of the Sacrament of the Supper which I have in view next Lord's day at Kirkintilloch to do. O Lord God, from whom comes the preparation of the heart, grant to me amidst all difficultys needfull grace to wait on thee in this ordinance, and may I find it good so to do. Give humiliation of soul on account of a body of sin and death; give faith in the Redeemer's blood, and love to an unseen Saviour; give sincerity and truth in the inward parts; give a feeling of heart *** give access to thy throne of mercy thro' a Redeemer to whom be glory and praise. Amen.

. . .

Sabbath, January 18th, 1747. – "And what the exceeding greatness of His power to usward who believe, according to the working of His mighty power, which He wrought in Christ, when He raised Him from the dead." On which words I heard Mr. McLaurin this day preach, taking occasion from them, to show the great importance of seeking earnestly right apprehensions, and real experience of the greatness of the power of divine grace on the soul, as a power that was necessary to restore and promote the image of God in the soul, necessary to make means effectual, necessary to break the power of corruption, to make resolutions effectual, and to strengthen our impressions of the greatness of the objects of faith. A power, which gratitude to God for the great things He has done to purchase it, lays under the strongest obligation to seek after which the whole heart. A power, with dependence on which prayers will be hypocritical; the want of dependence on which encourages and animates the soul with hope in midst of all fears and doubts arising from corruption, weaknesses, temptation, and many hinderances. Finally, a power that ought to be sought after with the greatest sense of need, the deepest impressions of unworthiness, with suitable regards to the mediation of Christ, the purchaser and procurer, with praise and thankfullness for the free offers of it. And a power, the peculiar effects whereof I should endeavour, in dependence on it, to seek earnestly and particularly the experience of, on my own soul.

When I arose this morning, I found my body a little indisposed, but that was not the worst, – my heart was not fixed or stayed in God, and things spiritual. In the forenoon I heard Mr. McLaurin lecture on sixth chapter first Timothy. Observed some things which gave me a check and rebuke for an immoderate concern about the conveniencys and superfluitys of life, while I have food to eat, and raiment to put on. Conscience told me I was the man! That this was an evil I had lately addicted to; my conscience told me that love of riches, and desire of increasing my worldly substance, was an evil prevalent with me, whereby I had fallen into temptation, a snare, and many foolish and hurtfull lusts, and whereby I had pierced myself thro' with many sorrows, and an evil with the opposition made to my ** sometimes contributed to increase tho', at the same time I must own, to the praise of God's grace, that an opposition founded on wordly motives had been a mean of showing me, more than ever, the vanity of the world, and worldly riches and honours.

150

In the afternoon, I was helped for some time to some suitable measure of attention to the things spoken to me by His servant, tho' short of what formerly I have experienced; but towards the close of the sermon my mind began to waver, and my thoughts to wander. Frequently during this evening, when engaged in spiritual dutys, my deceitfull heart would start aside, and suddenly, as it were, spring into the world; particularly when I was just thinking to go to God, and pray for these things I had been hearing thro' the day, and had begun so to do, my heart took a wandering, that I could not get my mind fixed to the duty, – then I arose. How strong a proof of the strength of corruption, and my own weakness, when the smallest temptation will disturb my peace, make me stumble and fall! When this was the case, I went and wrote doun what my exercise was thro' what was past of this Sabbath day, as I have now shortly and imperfectly narrated it. After this I went to prayer again, in hopes of success and help, then joined in family worship, prayed again, then read a part of a practical book, afterwards read a portion of Scripture, and concluded the work of the day with prayer.

This night I was also reviewing the conduct of providence towards me the last week, on which I observed that it is of great importance and advantage not to be anxiously carefull about any temporal god, but, in dependence on grace, to be labouring to know and do what is present duty, looking to the Lord for a blessing, and leaving events to Him. I think I have seen much of the hand of providence in ordering my worldly affairs in a way otherwise than I designed or thought of, and in a way that was more to my advantage. The experience of the goodness of God this way makes me hope for further proofs of it, in the after part of my life. I think I have been much of the hand of providence in making my keenest attempts and endeavours in pursuing my worldly calling, fruitless, or in some measure unsuccessfull; while on the other hand He has blessed with success these endeavours and that diligence in my worldly business that was consistent with fervency in the service of God, and was [. . .] with anxious hurtfull cares, thus shewing that it is the blessing of the Lord that only maketh rich. Further, I observed, that in following one's worldly business, there is great need of grace, to teach and enable to do justice, live righteously, and speak the truth in the heart, so as to have a conscience void of offence towards God and man. Unjustice, fraud, unrighteousness, dissimulation and lying, are evils flowing from an inordinate love of the world, and to which there are ensnaring and bewitching temptations in following people's wordly business, and into which the soul may be led in lesser or higher degrees of guilt, unless constantly watching and guarding. Let my conversation be without covetousness, being content with such things as I have! Again, I observed that all human friendship is changeable and uncertain – one may be in favour and esteem at one time, and, thro' prejudice or misrepresentation, be in disesteem and discredit at another time. But O how precious is the friendship and love of God, which is unchangeable and everlasting! There is no misrepresenting of things to Him, because He sees all things; fellow-creatures may be friends to-day, and enemies to-morrow, but the Lord if the everlasting friend of His people! O that my ways were pleasing to the Lord! then He can, and would make enemies to be at peace with me.

RELIGION

Wednesday, 21st January, 1747. – "I pray that thou shouldst keep them from the evil of the world." On this and the preceding two days, the world has been very troublesome to me, occasioning differencies between my and my neighbours. How often is the love of wealth the root of many foolish jars and contentions! When under these ensnaring worldly temptations, I felt an inward strugle and perplexity of soul, sometimes inclining to one thing and then to another; sometimes the love of peace inclined me to part even with my right, for peace sake; at other times I thought I was bound to do justice to myself as well as others, and while I wronged not others, it was my duty not to wrong myself. While in this doubting condition, I found it hard to determine what was duty, tho' still I thought I would have most peace in my mind if I yielded, and did not keep so strict justice and law in the matter. Lord, let me, while in the world, be kept from the evil of the world, and grant, that thro' grace, escaping the corruptions of the world thro' lust, I may be made a partaker of the divine nature!

18

NICOLAUS LUDWIG VON ZIZENDORF UND POTTENDORF (1700–1760), *HYMNS COMPOSED FOR THE USE OF THE BRETHREN* (1749), A SELECTION

Nicolas Zizendorf was from a noble family in Lower Austria and Bishop in the Moravian Church, a Protestant denomination. He was an important figure in the eighteenth-century Moravian revival, particularly in promoting the growth of the faith through supporting missionaries across the globe. He produced a number of writings that became important teachings for the church, including a large number of hymns. Below are some of his hymns translated in the eighteenth century into English. The translations were quite literal, and sometimes poor, and as a result, they added to the 'oddness', and perhaps the mystique, of this religious group for British readers. Both in English and German however, the faith put significant emphasis on the worship of Jesus's body, and especially the wounds produced by the passion – the holes in his hands and feet, the piercing of his side and the thorn marks on his forehead. This followed their significance in the Catholic and pre-reformation faith. They are good examples of how hymns, typically sung by the congregation or in family groups, were used to express and encourage love of God and an appreciation of his suffering, something that was meant to bring people closer to salvation. Hymns are interesting as repetitive and ritual devotional practices, that helped produce emotion in singers; these examples are also interesting as evidence of how this religious community was thought of by outsiders. Zinzendorf's visit to Britain is mentioned in source 7 and Moravian missionary work in source 13.

. . .

Hymn 24

O Holy Ghost, a Mother thou,
  Most suitably art named;
O Spirit who, the Scriptures thro',
  Hast *Jesus'* Praise proclaimed.
O Spirit, whose whole Diocese
  In *Jesu's* Rings appeareth;

RELIGION

For thy maternal Heart she prays,
    Which Heart for all things careth.
Thy Wounds, Lord *Jesus*, and the Wreath
    That pierc'd thy sacred Forehead,
And all thy Sufferings unto Death,
    Shine from the *Moravian* Handmaid.

Hymn 33

    Chicken blessed,[1]
    And caressed,
Little Bee on *Jesu's* Breast,
    From the Hurry,
    And the Flurry,
Of the Earth thou'rt now at rest.
From our Care in lower Regions,
Thou art taken to the Legions,
Who 'bove human Griefs are rais'd,
There thou'rt kept, the Lamb be praid'd![2]
    Chicken blessed!
    Be caressed,
    Thou that sleep'st on *Jesu's* Breast.

Hymn 42

God's Side-hole, hear my Prayer,
    Accept my Meditation:
On thee I cast my Care
    With Child-like Adoration.
While Days and Ages pass, and endless periods roll,
An everlasting Blaze shall sparkle from that Hole.

Hymn 43

Have endless Thanks, ye Wounds so dear,
And thou, O Side, pierc'd by the Spear,
    For all your Penance bloody.
I am redeem'd on Cross's stem,
Thro' the Blood of my dearest Lamb.
    O Blood in Soul and Body,
      Stream now,
      Quite thro'.
Penetrate me through, and heat me,
Make me holy, happy, cheerful, light and oily.
And had my Lamb not laid on me some Labour,
    I should certainly mind nothing else but eating:

HYMNS FOR THE USE OF THE BRETHREN

I could by the dear Wounds so red,
My Office and my Brethrens Need
   Be easily forgetting.
Since I, dearly, love to sit near,
Every Scar dear,
     Them revising,
     On his Body herbalizing.
And when I from the Pulpit speak,
The Wounds my general Heads to make,
   And special too most meetly;
And in a Congregation Room,
Upon the Wound-holes still I come;
  These make the Hours pass sweetly.
     Spears Wound,
     Chief Ground,
     Which I tender,
     To each Sinner!
     Templum Pacis,[3]
     Thou mak'st Churches, *ex Cloacis*.[4]

Hymn 46

His dear Apostle (as believ'd in general)
     Did as to Day agree,
     Out of their Nest to flee.
     Twelve Birds in Crosses Air,
     Who they Arch-healds are,
     Thou Wound-holes Church so dear!
     They fled so prettily,
     In every Country:
     God bless their Journey!

  But whither did they go?
  For there is none does know.
  Two or three are all,
  (Who *Thomas, Thomas!* Bawl,
  A wretched Company,)
  Who Witnesses can be.
  And, O, I wish they were
  St. *Thomas'* Hearts so dear,
  And did both feel and hide,
  Deep in the Lamb's-side.

  Since one no Knowledge hath
  Of the Apostles Path,
  Or whether on this Day,

Or on another they
Good Gentlemen did part,
Thro' every Land to dart:
I too a Matter know.
Just seven Years ago,
We such a Parting bore,
Out of our Choir and Door,
To *Moor* and *Tescarore*.[5]

Hymn 57

Lovely Side hole, dearest Side-hole,
  Sweetest Side-hole made for me,
O my most beloved Side-hole,
  I wish to be lost in thee.
  O my dearest Side-hole,
  Thou art to my Bride Soul.
  The most dear and loveliest Place:
  Pleura's Space!
  Soul and Body in thee pass!

Hymn 61

My dearest, most beloved Lamb,
I who in tenderest Union am
To all they Cross's Air-birds bound,
Smell to and kiss each Corpse's Wound,
  Yet at the Side-hole's Part,
  There pants and throbs my Heart.
    That dearest Side-hole!
Be prais'd, O God, for this Spear's Slit!
I thank thee, Soldier, too for it,
I've lick'd this Rock's Salt round,
Where can such Relish else be found!
In this Point, at this Season,
The Side-hole has stole my Reason.

  Yet, you dear Hearts, I've more to sing,
I am a little, happy Thing:
And own this Side-hole's Print of his
Elections only Reason is.
This tells me the *Mamma*,
Mother of *Joshua*,
The very Instant with this Thrust,
Hallelujah, then out I burst.

We praise the Side-hole.
Does not the Babe, that little Thing,
Gladly around its Mammy cling?
Therefore I cling so round the Side.
  *The Holy Ghost.

Ye Wounds, you all I greatly prize,
But yet this one attracts my Eyes,
I kiss you all most inwardly,
And also Cross's-air-birdly.
  Yet one to me is,
  Arrheta Sentio –
Here are my Meals, both first and last,
I eat and drink a full Repast,
  'Till all my own Existence
  Is in one Side's Consistence.

Hymn 64

My short Aspiration this is,
  My Side-hole Good-Friday-ly:
In there, says my Doctrine's *Thesis*,
  Flesh and Soul go bodily.
  And my Song, (*Quam suave*,)[6]
  Little Side-hole, *Ave?*[7]
  And my Essence, Sinner poor,
  Whom the Side bore;
  The Lamb forms me such all o'er.

Hymn 75

Mary! he calls: a Greeting this?
  Her sparkling Eyes she raises:
My Lord, she cries, (her Tongue loose is)
  I must here give thee Kisses.
Nay, saith the Lamb, don't kiss me here,
But go and tell my Brethren dear,
  That thou thyself hast seen me.
She can obedient be, she goes:
  But I could not have moved.
As creeps the Snail into its House,
  So in the Side beloved,
I wou'd have slid quite hastily;
He should not so get rid of me,
  No Reason would persuade me.

RELIGION

Hymn 83

Tho' I can't see him bodily,
Yet still I see him really
　　Stand in another *foro*.
With Eyes which me my dear Lamb gave,
Since I a spiritual Body have,
　　His inhians devoro
　　　Deum meum,[8]
　　　My Creator,
　　　Mediator,
　　Who loves Glances,
　　Shew'd in Death's Circumstances.

Hymn 89

So sideward looking constantly,
So Side-hole homesick-feelingly,
Lamb's Heart to creep thro' so intent,
So smelling for the Lamb's Sweat's Scent,
　　On the magnetick Side:
So quivering with Love's Ague sweet,
　　Like thi' Infant Leaping:
So drawing Breath in Corpse's Air,
So spouting forth Wound's Moisture clear,
So from Grave's Vapours in a Dew,
So panting the Son's Sign to view –
　　So Lamblike happily,
　　So Dovelike, and so childlikely,
　　With Sinner-shame so inly red,
　　So like a Sinner, playful, glad,
　　While in the Heart does hum,
　　Efflavit animum:[9]
　　Thro' Cross's Joy to weep so prone,
　　So quite in Breast-plate Scholar's Tone,
　　　Like *John* the Fav'rite: –
　　The Lamb shall keep his Bride's Soul,
　　Till she can kiss his Side's Hole.

Hymn 106

To you, ye Wounds, we pay,
A thousand Tears this Day,
That you have us presented,
With many happy Virgin Rows,
Since the Year Thirty –

Pappa! Mamma!
Your Heart's Flamelein,
Brother Lamblein,
Give the Creatures,
Virgin Hearts and Features.

Hymn 110

What does a Bird in Cross's Air,
When it flies up to the Lamb near.
Dear Hearts, look, look and see!
The little Bird finds presently,
Its Nest in the dear Cavity.
Within the Hole where Blood cast Rays,
The Bird itself entangled has:
And round the Castle of the Side,
Are Wound-Swans in the Canal wide.
Then learns the little Piper,
In the Hole to be a Dipper.
   But when the Bird in Cross's Air,
Has done some Thing that is not fair;
And is beat on the little Bill,
By the other Hearts, what doth it still?
Away to the Arm it whips,
Of the Lamb, and Mercy pipes –
This is the Cross's Air-bird's Plan,
Here they leave off, here they began:
So Lamb-like, bloody, happily,
So Turtle-dove-like, prettily.

Notes

1 Chicken here should probably have been hen, reflecting bible verses on this theme.
2 Lamb here references Christ as the Lamb of God.
3 Temple of peace.
4 From the sewer, e.g. Christ can transform even from waste.
5 E.g. 'Tuscarora,' an American Indian group.
6 How sweet!
7 Hail!
8 My God.
9 He passed away.

19

EDWARD SYNGE (1659–1741), *SOBER THOUGHTS FOR THE CURE OF MELANCHOLY, ESPECIALLY THAT WHICH IS RELIGIOUS*

(London: Thomas Trye, 1749), 5–18, 22–23

Edward Synge was an Irish Bishop in the Anglican Church of Ireland and renowned preacher. He authored over sixty volumes of sermons and religious tracts in his lifetime, and was known for his rationalist approach to the faith. This excerpt came from a text that provided advice for those suffering from spiritual melancholy, notably distinguishing between melancholy caused by sin or crisis of the faith, and that produced by bodily illness. Advice literature on a wide range of topics was a popular form of writing since the late medieval period, and was used by readers to help them improve their lives and moral behaviour. Much advice drew on a Christian moral framework, not least in discussions of health and wellbeing. Melancholy was a significant illness in the early modern European imagination, widely written about it and discussed. Synge was participating in a wide-ranging conversation on this subject, while also offering practical strategies for those living with melancholy. As a well-known minister, his contribution explicitly situates melancholy as a problem of faith and that can be resolved through religious exercises. It provides useful insights both into how melancholy was perceived during this period, and how such emotional disorders were interpreted and managed through a religious lens.

. . .

By *Melancholy* I mean such a Disposition of the *Mind*, as renders it sorrowful, dejected, and dissatisfied, and consequently uneasy.

Melancholy, where it prevails, is a great Affliction and Trouble to the Person who labours under it: And, therefore, it must be of Service to Mankind to find out the Way of preventing or curing it.

Some Persons think to drive away all *Melancholy*, by giving themselves up to what we call Diversions; such as Hunting, Stage-plays, Balls, Dances, Musick, or

SOBER THOUGHTS FOR THE CURE OF MELANCHOLY

any Thing that may, for the present, raise their Spirits (as they express it) and stir them up to Mirth.

That some Diversion, moderately used, are both innocent and healthful, is granted. But if a Man allows himself in such as are unbecoming a good Christian; or if he spends so much of his Time in those that are most innocent, as to suffer himself thereby to be diverted from doing that Good in the World, of which God has made him very capable, and therefore most certainly requires it from him when, by Sickness or Old Age, he comes to lose the Relish of these Diversions, and begins to reflect how foolishly and unprofitably, or it maybe wickedly, he has spent so great a Part of his previous Time (of which he must give an Account to the righteous Judge of the World) he will certainly find his *Melancholy*, his Sorrow and Anguish of Mind to be much increased; and would give ten thousand Worlds, if he had them, for so much Time as might enable him to repair the Loss of what he has thus squandered away.

Mirth or Diversion then (however innocent) is not the proper Remedy to prevent or cure *Melancholy*.

It is a known Maxim, that, if the Cause be taken away, the Effect will cease. In order therefore to prevent or cure *Melancholy*, let us consider what are the Causes of it, and how they are to be removed.

When a Man is *melancholy*, and knows no Reason why he is so, it is justly to be presumed that the Original Cause of his Disorder is not in his Mind (however that may be affected by the Disorder itself) but in his Body. Some very good Men there are, who are diligent and industrious in the Performance of every Part of their Duty; whose Conscience does not accuse them of any Thing beyond the common Frailties of Mankind, of which also they repent and beg God's Pardon as often as they find themselves guilty of them, and yet they are very much oppressed by *Melancholy*. Ask such a Man, what is the Cause of this Trouble in his Mind, and upon the strictest Examination of his whole Life, he is able to assign no Reason for it. He has sincerely repented of all his Sins, and has made ample Reparation to every Man whom he thinks he has any Way wronged; and stedfastly resolves to live virtuously and religiously during the remaining Part of his Days. His Reason is convinced that this is all that a good and merciful God (who gave his Son to die for us) requires from frail Man: And yet Imagination works so strongly in him as to lay him under dreadful Apprehensions, that his Sins are not forgiven. *Melancholy* in such Men is known to arise from an Indisposition of Body. Rational Arguments ought sometimes to be applied to such a Man's Understanding (of which by and by) but Diet, Exercise, and proper bodily Medicines are known, by frequent Experience, to be in such Cases, necessary.

Often, when the body is not thus indisposed yet great *Melancholy* seizes Men, arising from some Apprehensions that have taken Possession of the Mind: For which I see no other Remedy but rational Arguments and Discourse, by which they may be brought to have right Notions of Things and to think and do what is proper for removing disorder.

Many have been very *melancholy* from an Apprehension that they are not, or possibly may not be, of the Number of God's *Elect*.

RELIGION

From some obscure Passages of the Holy Scripture, misinterpreted by some learned Men, they have formed an Opinion that god, from all Eternity has absolutely predestinated a certain Number of Men and Women (called his *Elect* or *Chosen*) to eternal Salvation. These they conclude are certainly to be saved, and all others to be everlastingly damned; and the Fear that they are not of the Number of the *Elect*, is a continual Load upon their Spirits, and deprives them of all Comfort.

The Way to cure this *Melancholy* is to bring such Men to a right Apprehension of God's Manner of dealing with us his rational Creatures; and thereby to let them plainly see that He has put every Man's Salvation in his own Power.

No Text of Scripture ought to be interpreted in direct Opposition to any Self-evident Truth: Nor ought any obscure Text to be interpreted in Opposition or Contradiction to other Texts that are manifestly plain. Now the clearest Reason and the most manifest Tenour of the Holy Scriptures, taken in Conjunction, do most evidently assures us of the following Truths:

That God, who is the supreme Judge, will certainly always do that which is right:

> That, however absolute his Authority may be over his Creatures, and, however He may afflict us for our own Good, if we make the right Use of Afflictions; yet He will not inflict any Thing, by Way of *Punishment*, upon any Man, except it be for some Fault whereby the Man himself has justly deserved it:
>
> That He never created any Man with a *Design* to make him eternally and unavoidably miserable; from whence it follows, that He will not eternally damn any of *Adam's* Posterity, barely and only for the Sin of their first Parent.

Add to all this, that the Holy Scriptures gives us Assurance that *Christ* died for all Men, without Exception; that God has promised, for his Sake, to pardon the Sins of true Penitents; and that he requires nothing from any Man, but what is possible (and indeed easy with a willing Mind) for him to Perform.

These and such like Truths are as clear as if they had been written with a Sunbeam whereas all the Passages of Scripture, which are brought to uphold the Doctrine of absolute Predestination and Reprobation, are allowed to be obscure, hard to be understood, and capable of another Interpretation.

Let then such Persons, as I am now speaking of, honestly and sincerely do all that is in their Power (and more it cannot be supposed that God will require from them) first, to know what the Will of God is and then to perform it accordingly; and it will soon appear to be a groundless Fear, That a good and gracious God will, by any absolute Decree, exclude them from Salvation.

Others there are, who are sensible that their Sins are very great and many, of which they have not truly and sincerely repented; and therefore they look upon themselves to be obnoxious to the Displeasure of God, and to eternal Damnation.

SOBER THOUGHTS FOR THE CURE OF MELANCHOLY

Where this is really the Case, and as long as a Man continues in these sad Circumstances it is no Wonder that he should be exceeding *melancholy*. For *it is a fearful Thing to fall into the Hands of the living God.*

The only Remedy for this *Melancholy* is true, sincere, and timely Repentance. Let not such a Man deceive himself by imagining that God will pardon him, because he is sorrowful for his Sins (which he cannot but be, if he is afraid of Damnation) or because he makes fruitless Resolutions against them; or because, when he comes to lie upon a Death-bed, he bewails them, and earnestly begs Forgiveness of them: For to such imperfect Performances as these God has no where made any such Promise. True Repentance is nothing else but a real, universal, and lasting Amendment of Life; to which, and to which alone, God has promised the Forgiveness of all past Sins. Let a Man thus amend his Life, and that whilst he has a Life to live; let him, to his Power, repair all the Scandal he has given, and make all the Amends he can to every one whom he has oppressed or any way injured; and let him continue in this good Course during the whole Remainder of his Days; and then, and then only, he will find such Comfort in the Promises of God, made and often repeated to penitent Sinners, as will free him from all *melancholy* Thoughts, and put his Mind at perfect Ease.

But some there are who, though they sincerely forsake their Sins, and diligently endeavour to live in the Practice of their whole Duty are yet in great Fear that their Repentance is defective, and consequently their Pardon not obtained; and that for this Reason, because they think they are not sorrowful enough for their Sins. They find their Minds affected with Joy or Grief at the Good or Evil that befalls them in this World, but are sensible of no such Transports either at the Remembrance of their Sins, whereby they have offended God, or in the Performance of those Duties whereby they endeavour to please Him. Without *godly Sorrow* there can be no true Repentance; and without *Joy in the Lord* no duty can be acceptable to Him: And because they find this *Sorrow* and this *Joy* so faint and feeble within themselves, therefore they think that they are not accepted of God; and this makes them very *melancholy*.

I shall first speak of *godly Sorrow*; and the Application to *joy in the Lord* will be very plain.

There is a manifest Difference between a *rational Sorrow* and a *passionate Sorrow*.

When a Man's Judgment is convinced of the Evil of his Sins, and the Displeasure he has thereby given to Almighty God; insomuch that he heartily wishes he had never committed them, would willingly recal them, if it were in his Power, and stedfastly resolves never more to be guilty of them; this I call a *rational Sorrow*. And without such a *Sorrow* as this for Sin, it is manifest that no Man can repent of it.

Upon this *rational Sorrow*, sometimes, but not always, there arises in the Mind a strong *Emotion* of Grief and Trouble, which often even forces Sighs from the Heart, and Tears from the Eyes; and this may well be called a *passionate Sorrow*.

If a Sinner sets himself seriously to consider the heinous Nature of his Sins, with all the evil Consequences of them, as every Man may and ought to do, he cannot but disapprove of them, and entertain in his Mind that *rational Sorrow* for

RELIGION

them which I have but now described. *Rational Sorrow* for Sin is always therefore our Duty.

But a *passionate Sorrow* for Sin is not always in our Power, as depending upon the Temper and Disposition of the Man; and for this Reason is not always a Duty; however commendable upon many Occasions it may be.

True Repentance (as I have said) is nothing else but a real, universal, and lasting Amendment of Life: And if the *rational Sorrow*, which a Man has conceived for his Sins, has brought him to such an Amendment of his Life, it is true *godly Sorrow* and consequently acceptable to God. *Godly Sorrow worketh Repentance*, says St. *Paul*.

After the same Manner we are to form a right Notion of *Joy in the Lord.* There is a *rational Joy*, when *Reason* is convinced and satisfied in the Performance of Duty; and there is a *Passionate* [or affectionate] *Joy*, when the Affections are brought with Pleasure into it. *Rational Joy*, or Satisfaction of Mind, is always the Effect of virtuous Practice, joined with sober and serious Consideration; which, through the Grace of God, is in every Man's Power, and therefore may be looked on as a Duty: But to bring our Affections in a lively Manner into this same *Joy*, although every good Man always desires it, yet the best of Men have declared, that they are not always, nor it may be very often, able to effect it.

Another Cause of *Melancholy*, in many good Men, is that they think they do not love God as well as they ought to do: They feel no Transports in their Love to God and therefore fear that it is cool and defective.

But such Men should consider that there is a *rational Love* of God, which, the Holy Scripture informs us, consists intirely in a fixed and steddy Resolution of *keeping all his Commandments.* Where this *Resolution* is, and is carefully held to, there the Love of God is true and since, although the *Affections* seem not be much moved or raised by it. If my Child (for example) is always diligent in doing whatever is pleasing and acceptable to me, he shews that he truly loves me, although he does not fondle or caress me.

Another Thing that some complain of is, that they cannot often keep wicked, and sometimes blasphemous Thoughts, out of their Minds; which is a great Grief and Uneasiness to them.

Indeed, to desire, design, or approve of any Thing that is contrary to God's Commands, is an Act of the Will, and therefore a Sin, because it is in our Power to avoid it. But barely to think of any Words or Actions, however wicked, and this without any Approbation of them, is what sometimes we cannot avoid; and therefore has nothing sinful in it. If I hear a Man swear, curse or blaspheme, or if I see him commit Murder, it is impossible for me not to think of what I thus hear or see: But if I am so far from approving of any of these Things, that, on the contrary, I look upon them with the utmost Disapprobation and Abhorrence; I commit no Manner of Sin in thus thinking of them. Our Actions, Words, Desires, Designs, and Approbations, are in our own Power; and therefore we are certainly accountable for them. But, whether we will or no, Thoughts will often arise in our Minds, sometimes from external Objects, and sometimes from the inward Motions of the

SOBER THOUGHTS FOR THE CURE OF MELANCHOLY

Mind itself; and if we take all the Care we can so to curb and regulate them, as they have no evil Influence upon the Will, which through the Grace of God is within our Power, they cannot involve us in any Guilt; and therefore, however they may often be troublesome, ought not to make us *melancholy*.

Many well-disposed Persons are much grieved, for that, in the midst of their most solemn Devotions to God, idle and impertinent, and sometimes evil Thoughts arise in their Minds, and divert that Attention, which they are sensible they ought constantly to give to what they are about, upon all such Occasions: And this, as they apprehend, is to *draw nigh to God with their Lips, when their Hearts are far from him.*

Prepare your Hearts unto the Lord, to serve him. Keep thy Foot (that is, be watchful over thyself) *when thou goest in to the House of the Lord*; into the Church, thy Closet, or any Place where thou proposest to offer up they Devotions to God. He who neglects to do this (which I fear is the Case of many) offers great Contempt to the Divine Majesty.

But when we have taken the best Care we can to keep ourselves attentive in our Prayers and Devotions, foolish Thoughts will sometimes suddenly and unavoidably arise in our Minds: Concerning which I must say the same as I have but now done of wicked Thoughts upon other Occasions. Such Thoughts are like Flies, which in hot Weather are very troublesome to us. We must strive to drive them away as well as we can; but sometimes it is impossible wholly to get rid of them; and that which is impossible God will not require from us.

A Man's *Heart* is then only said to be *far from God*, when he is careless or negligent in the Performance of his Duty. And if, after our greatest Care and Diligence, some Frailties and Weakness stick to us against which we constantly and earnestly strive, but cannot wholly overcome; our good and gracious God will not lay them to our Charge. *He knows our Frame, He remembers we are but Dust*; and therefore *as a Father pitieth his Children, even so hath the Lord Compassion upon those that fear him*; who are not stubbornly disobedient, but to their Power strive to serve Him.

Some there are who earnestly endeavour to perform every Part of their Duty, and yet are very *melancholy*, because they apprehend that they have not true Faith. *Without Faith it is impossible to please God*; and where there is not a firm Belief of those Truths, which God has made known to Mankind, there can be no true Faith. Now, because they Men find in themselves some speculative Doubts or Hesitations, arising from Weakness of Judgement, concerning the Truth of Religion, or some of the great Articles of it; they are under great Fear that their Faith is not true, at least not as firm as they think it ought to be; and consequently that they neither do nor can *please God*: Which has been a very afflicting Consideration to some *melancholy* Persons.

. . .

To sum up all in a few Words; Mirth, Pastimes, and Diversions, even those which in themselves are innocent, although for the present, they may be some Ease or

RELIGION

Relief to *Melancholy*, yet they will not cure it, or hinder it from returning again, perhaps, with more Violence than before. If *Melancholy*, either in the Whole or in Part, arises from the Constitution of Body, proper Diet, Exercise, and Medicines ought to be made use of: But as far as it is seated in the Mind, it is only to be removed by rational Arguments and Considerations, which alone can work upon the Understanding. Let a Man sincerely repent of all his Sins, and be watchful to amend his Life, and perform his Duty in every Instance: Let him *exercise himself always to have a Conscience void of Offence towards God and towards Men*; and then, and only then, whatever befalls him, in this uncertain Life he will find true Peace with God, and solid Joy and Comfort in his own Mind. *Our Rejoicing is this, the Testimony of our Conscience, that in Simplicity and godly Sincerity, not with fleshly Wisdom, but, by the Grace of God, we have had our Conversation in the World.* 2 Cor.i.12.

Why are thou cast down, O my Soul? And why are thou disquieted within me? Hope thou in God; for I shall yet praise Him, who is the Health of my Countenance, and my God; Psal. Clii II. The same Thing has before been said, v. 5. and is again repeated, *Psal. Xliii. 5.* for which Reason it ought the more to be taken Notice of.

20

JOSÉ MARÍA GENOVESE (1681–1757), *THE SACRED HEART OF THE MOST HOLY PATRIARCH SAINT JOSEPH, VENERATED FOR EVERY DAY OF THE WEEK (EL SAGRADO CORAZON DEL SANTISSIMO PATRIARCHA, SR SAN JOSEPH, VENERADO POR TODOS LOS DIAS DE LA SEMANA)*

(Mexico City, 1751), 38–50, 76–91

José María Genovese was a Jesuit priest.[1] He was born in Palermo, Sicily, but went to Mexico as a missionary in 1715. Before he left for Mexico, he had a vision of the Blessed Virgin Mary, who told him to paint her representation as it would be a source of joy to the world. He took this to Mexico, where it was placed in the Church of Leon, Guanajuato, and later became the site of a significant devotion. This excerpt comes from a series of meditations on the heart of St Joseph written by Genovese. Meditations were common in the Catholic faith and were designed as a series of spiritual exercises that an individual could work through, usually over several days or weeks, to perfect their soul and ready themselves for salvation. Cults of the hearts of Mary and Jesus Christ were popular in Europe, not least amongst Jesuits. A cult of the heart of St Joseph was more controversial, but expanded rapidly in the eighteenth-century Spanish empire, especially encouraged by Jesuits like Genovese. This text, written in Spanish and translated into English, was a key writing in nurturing this cult and taught people to view Joseph as a model for Christian living and an access point to God. As a source for the history of emotions, it provides evidence not only of the emotional language of devotion, but the tools that Catholics used to entrain their emotions as part of spiritual practice.

. . .

RELIGION

Third meditation for Tuesday. The Heart of Saint Joseph, a greater paragon of Purity and Chastity than the Angels.

Point 1. Consider that the Chastity and Purity of the Angels arise from these three noble prerogatives. The first: that they are strong, and invincible, because even if they were assaulted, and fought in combat, they would never be defeated by their enemies, and would never yield to them. The second: that they are free and totally remote from all assault, and the challenge of their enemies, because being of Holy Angelic Spirit and having no body and flesh, they are incapable of temptation and lusts of the flesh. The third: that it is plain, because they are common in spirit with God, that they are by their very nature Holy, and they have a great enthusiasm, and love of all purity, whose fragrance is their sweetest, and unspeakable, delight, and for that reason they love, and favor pure souls, and chastity, and have extreme horror and abhorrence of all impurity. These three illustrious prerogatives of Purity and Chastity held by this spotless Saint are therefore greater than those of Angels and more than that of Seraphins, because in these Sublime Spirits it is natural, and having no body, they are incapable of any temptation to impurity, but Saint Joseph is virtuous and overflowing in the grace of Heaven. The Purity of this Renowned Patriarch was of the greatest strength and invincible, because he fortified his Chastity with the walls of the vow of perpetual Virginity, a promise made to God at the age of twelve, as the Venerable María de Ágreda[2] assures us, and with vigilance he fled all possible dangers, even passing them quickly, and surrounded himself with a fence of profound humility and self-doubt, continuously contemplating the things of heaven, and working with diligence, always fleeing from idleness; he also defended his purity through guarding his senses, acting with the most honest decency, mortifying his body through harsh treatment, and with abstinence and the parsimony of a poor meal. And so he was always the strongest and impregnable in his Purity; for although he had been attacked by his enemies, he never yielded, but always attained a glorious victory over them. You must be vexed, and weep, if you have ever vilely yielded to the enemies of your chastity; and from this Glorious Saint you must learn the way to strengthen your heart, so your chastity is strong and impregnable.

Second point. Consider that the Purity of the Angels is very remote and free from all challenge; because they are pure spirits, nor do they have a body and flesh. And this privilege is granted to this spotless spouse of Maria, because from his childhood, and as the Venerable María de Ágreda affirms, from the seven months of his conception, in him the concupiscence of the flesh found itself enchained, and thus in all his life he never suffered temptations of the flesh, never had any movement of a sensual nature, and never had images or representations, or thoughts of obscene things, whether when awake, or in dreams. His spotless heart, like the clearest crystal, was never tarnished with even the slightest breath of unclean imagination. It was an unfading lily, that throughout life always remained uncontaminated, always blossoming, always fragrant, and never even slightly tainted for the smallest amount of time by a dishonourable spirit; and thus the purity of his Spotless Heart exceeded that of the Seraphin themselves; because having body and flesh, he shone with the light of his angelic cleanliness. Esteem this so exalted gift of Purity, with which the Heart of this Chaste Saint was adorned, who was so unique, and above all humans, suited to be a Worthy Husband of the Immaculate Mother of God: and give humble thanks to the Divine Goodness having it granted, and seek by the exercise of discretion over your senses, and with the most cautious modesty of your actions, and words, to close the door to the enemies of your purity, and with a careful vigilance deny them the entrance to your soul, if they ever attack you; and supplicate to this Spotless Saint, who deigns to be the Defender and guard of your chastity.

Third point. Consider that the other prerogative of Angelic Purity is that it is part of their nature, and that is why the Angels have a great inclination to this virtue, they love it in others, and they delight in joining in their beauty and sweetness, and abhor and have great horror for any atom of impurity. Although not natural to the Spotless Heart of Saint Joseph because he was not pure Spirit, but he had a body and flesh, nevertheless he obtained through grace the effects of this prerogative; and thus he had a natural inclination to live chastely, and rejoiced, and received a great consolation in living thus; and having an incredible affection for this virtue, he loved and admired his Spotless Wife, whose virginal Purity instilled in his Heart a heavenly gentleness and sweetness; as to the contrary, he had utter hatred, and abhorrence of the least shadow of filthiness or lewdness. Hear me! Not all: *Capiunt verbum istud*,[3] because they have smelled their own putrid Soul, and cannot perceive the sweeter smell of this virtue, and their eyes are mired with dirt so they cannot look at its beauty. Pray to this Chaste Saint to wipe your eyes, and to heal the scent of your soul, so that you can see the beauty, and perceive the sweetness of this Angelic virtue, so that you can esteem it, and love it, and with all care, and diligence, gradually come to procure it.

Colloquium

O Pure Heart of my Excellent Saint, I greet you and adore you, I praise you and esteem you more than Angelic Purity, and I humbly thank the Divine Goodness for having adorned you with it, so that you were a worthy Spouse of the Immaculate Mother of God. O, and how tormented, and ashamed I am, looking at my heart so filthy, and so stained, and continually battling feelings of lust. Ah! I have not known the value of this Angelic virtue, nor been renewed in the light of its heavenly beauty! O mine Holy One, open the eyes of my soul, so that I esteem its beauty, and instil in my soul an endearing love, and appreciation for this divine virtue, so that at the cost even of life, my mind and body remain always pure and uncontaminated; so firmly I set forth and determine, confident in your protection, and patronage, to perform it until death. Amen.

The rest common above, fol 20.[4]

RELIGION

Fruit, which is to be taken from this meditation

1 To have a great love and appreciation of this heavenly virtue, which is a jewel of Paradise, and a pearl of such inestimable value, that with it is bought the benevolence, and the espousal of the King of Glory, and of the Queen of the Angels, and they merit your friendship, gifts, and gentle usage.

2 To always encircle the lily of chastity, with the thorns of a continuous mortification of the senses, suppressing the sight and touch of pernicious objects, and even the decent parts of your own body uncovered; with abstinence from fine meats, and parsimony in food and drink; with harshness and austerity of the body, and with comeliness and honesty in speech and all actions, and in clothes and apparel. And to keep it always in bloom with the irrigation of a true humility, and self-doubt, knowing that there is always a danger of losing it, if not guarded by the Lord; and because of that draw always on his Divine Majesty with zeal and confidence; especially when tempted.

3 Be always on guard so as to prevent impure images from entering your imagination and thoughts; then when they approach, close the door to them, occupying the mind with holy thoughts, or of death, or of the Passion of the Lord, or of Glory, or of Hell.

4 Flee from the company and conversation of frivolous and loose people, and from all occasions that stain even slightly holy chastity.

5 Keep the heart pure, without having too much affection for any person, even if it is honest and spiritual; for from this honest and spiritual affection, if it is inordinate, the door opens, and it shifts to the sensual and impudent.

6 Take as your Guards, Defenders and Protectors of your own chastity, Holy Mary and her Holy Husband, and when you are attacked by feelings of lust, and by the Devil, then you will cry out to these Defenders, saying: I am, My Lady and my Holy Lord Saint Joseph, besieged by my enemies, help me, and defend the Jewel, which is under your protection.

...

Sixth Meditation for Friday. The Heart of Saint Joseph, arsenal of crosses, and of thorns, and mirror of patience and resignation.

Point one. Consider that as the Pure Heart of the Blessed Virgin was for her whole life pierced with excruciating suffering, so it was necessary that the Heart of her Heavenly Spouse, in order to be a perfect copy of the Heart of Mary, be afflicted and tormented by many and very serious sorrows and hardships. And who can describe the intimate pain, that penetrated his Heart, like a sharp sword, when he saw his Divine Spouse was pregnant, and had doubt about the cause, not knowing the Mystery? This pain was so great, and this cross so heavy, that the same Saint, appearing to the Venerable Marina de Escobar[5] (a) called it the most grievous and unbelievable, because of the supreme love that he had for Our Lady. How great too were the afflictions of his Most Holy Heart, when in Bethlehem, seeking board and lodging, he was dismissed with contempt and disdain, not only by family, friends and acquaintances, but the common lodgings and inns? And how much increased were the torments of his Most Pious Heart, when he was forced by necessity to lodge in an unclean cave, dirty, and entirely unfurnished, which served as a stable for the beasts, and which had to lodge the Mother of God, and Queen of the Angels, and be the birthing place of the Human Word, King and Lord of the Universe? And what a double-edged knife did not penetrate the loving Heart of this Most Holy Patriarch, when he heard from Saint Simeon of the Passion, and Death of the Divine Child and the piercing of the Heart of his Most Pure Mother?

Tuam ipse animam pertransibit gladius.[6] Loved, this Renowned Saint, with an unspeakable love that Divine Child, and his Most Holy Mother, who was also his most loving wife; what penetrating sorrow, then, did not break his Heart upon hearing the certain prediction of the most bitter Passion and Death of that Divine Child, and in feeling compassion for his Most Pious Mother? The pain of the Most Loving Heart of Saint Joseph was indescribable, and it continued throughout his life, because of the great knowledge that the Lord of the Holy Scriptures communicated to him, and of the Prophecies, he knew everything that the Redemptor would experience: thus the same Saint told the Venerable Marina de Escobar (b) with the addition of these words: "The Cross, that he (the Savior) had in mind from the moment of his Conception, I also had in mind; and this transferred to me strength of soul, and having in my unworthy arms our Lord, many times I happened to, considering what he was going to suffer, shed many tears on his Holy garments; and other times, holding him in my arms in times of cold weather warmed his sacred hands with the breath of my mouth." Add to these pains the hardships and labour, inseparable companions of great poverty, and of having to sustain a family with the sweat of his brow, which afflicted the Purest Heart of this Great Saint. Ah! The one who aims for the way of the world is very deceived, sowing all of the vile, and fleeting flowers of treats, delights, and pleasures, wandering from Holiness, and Heaven. The paths, which lead to perfection and to Glory, are all full of thorns and populated with crosses; for this is necessary for those who aspire to walk in Holiness, and to Glory.

Second point. Consider that it was not these single thorns that wounded the Most Holy Heart of this Glorious Father: others had, and most sharply, deeply penetrated it. These were: the message, and command, that were intimated from Heaven, so that with his Holy Wife and the Divine Child, he fled to Egypt to avoid the persecution of Herod, and undertook such a long journey of two hundred leagues, for the detour they made, as stated by V.M. Ágreda, (c) and with so much poverty, with so many dangers, and in winter time, and always on foot through deserted and unpopulated lands; were living for so many years in such a barbarous country, and among a nation so wicked and sacrilegious, and seeing the abominable cults, adorations and sacrifices made to idols, failing to recognise the true God, who was among them; the taunts, insults, and bad treatments, suffered by the Holy Virgin from that evil and wicked people. These were the sharpest thorns, which grievously and incredibly lacerated the loving Heart of this Pure Husband of Mary, as the Saint himself said to the Venerable Marina de Escobar: (d) thorns were also, and felt very acutely by his most sweet Heart, the labour, the needs, the fatigue, that he suffered returning from Egypt to the land of Israel, and the cares, fears, and sudden passions, which hurt him, when he heard that in Judea reigned Archelao, son of Herod, fearing that the God Child would fall into his tyrannical hands. But the most penetrating thorn, that like a dagger pierced his Heart, and would have put his life in danger, if God had not given him comfort, which he revealed to V.M. Ágreda, (e) was the pain, and excessive affliction, that he suffered in the Loss of the God Child in Jerusalem: because for three continuous days he was looking for him among his relatives, and knew with unspeakable pain, and with extreme fatigue, and weariness, forgetting to eat, and care for himself, the true and delicate love that he had for the Child Jesus. Such were the thorns, which came and wounded his Heart, joining together with the fever diseases and intense headaches, that for almost eight years before his death, this Most Fortunate Saint tolerated, as we are assured by V.M. Ágreda. (f) These were the offerings, the accolades, and the most precious gifts with which God favored this Great Saint, whom he loved above all the sons of men, so that we might at once persuade ourselves, that the crosses of our labours, and thorns of adversity are the richest gifts, and the most priceless jewels, that Heaven will distribute to its chosen ones.

Third point. Consider the undefeated forbearance and the affectionate resignation to the Divine will of the Heart of Saint Joseph in so many labours, pains and crosses. His virtue was so perfect, that a word of anger or impatience never came out of his mouth, and he was so heroic and eminent, that he reached the peak of perfection; thus the Blessed Virgin said to Saint Brigid, (g) and the V.M. Ágreda expresses it to us in these words, "That neither due to the weight and severity of his infirmities and sorrows, nor for the rest of his labours, did he complain or sigh, nor ask for relief in them, nor when suffering frailty or need, but all was tolerated by the Great Patriarch with incomparable patience and greatness of courage." (h) So much love, and esteem of suffering and the cross, which he endured in life, for it was the will and pleasure of his Divine Majesty, would be unbelievable, if the Holy Patriarch himself had not appeared to the Venerable Marina de Escobar with a Cross on his chest so resplendent and uncanny, that the Servant of God could not take her eyes off him, nor run away, he affirmed, saying "Know you, that this cross, which I suffered silently, was all my treasure, all my greatness, all my beatitude, and I esteem them, and I esteem them more, for they are so pleasant in Divine eyes, those being of the Spouse of the Virgin Mary." (i) O exalted Heart, O incomparable Heart, which loved and cherished the cross to such a high degree, and suffered to be so pleasing to God, with no less than the most super-eminent dignity, and happy to be the spouse of the Mother of God, and Father in authority, and affection of the Human Word! O inestimable value of suffering, and of the Cross! O! and how long will we be so blind, and foolish to always run away from the labour, and hardships, that are so pleasing to God, and to our greatest good?

Ah! Yes, if we love the cross, and the thorns, then God, because he loves us, sent them to us and we suffer them with love, humility, and resignation, just to be pleasing to his most Sweet Heart: because the benefits are incomprehensible, and greatness to which they will raise us up: and if your natural inclination resists, let us go to this Most Glorious Saint, so that with his intercession we may receive from the Divine Goodness so much Strength, and virtue of encouragement, that we will want to carry the cross, and the labours with great joy, and happiness.

Colloquium

O Most Excellent Heart of my Lord Saint Joseph, who with such unspeakable strength and love suffered the sharp thorns, that in this life always hurt you and pierced you, because you knew that they were pleasing to God, and his Most Holy Will, who was the centre of all your affections and desires. Ah! And until when will I live deceived, always fleeing the cross, and suffering, these being the richest gifts, and the most precious donations, distributed by Divine Goodness to its most dear souls? Illuminate, I beg you, O Most Glorious Saint, my understanding, so that I may know the inestimable value of the Cross, and fortify my heart, so that I love it ardently, and enjoy being nailed to it with my Most Loving Redeemer, and God; and so that, judged unworthy, common as I am, of a favour so great, admire his Divine Goodness, who deigned to deal kindly with this great sinner. Do it, my Holy One, with your prayers, for the love that you have for the Human God, and for you Holy Spouse, so that I come to resemble in this life my Crucified Lord, and merit to be alike in Glory. Amen.

The rest as above, fol.20.

Fruit, what to get out of this meditation

1   To have a high appreciation of the cross, and of suffering for the love of God, because in this life there is nothing more precious, or of greater value; for in suffering for God, there is his Divine pleasure, his benevolence, and love, and the prize of eternal happiness in Heaven, and a state most sublime and eminent.

2   Suffer with love and resignation in the Divine will any cross, and labour, that from any part comes to us, because it always comes to us from God, who sends it to us, because he loves us. And in this are three degrees. In the first are those faithful, who suffer the cross with patience and goodwill, without complaining or giving signs of impatience, conforming to the Divine will, and giving thanks to God for the cross, which he sends them. In the second are those who with great peace and serenity of mind and joy of heart suffer it to please and satisfy the Divine Heart, tolerating it for his love and for the great reward which comes from it. In the third are those who not only love and enjoy suffering and the cross, but knowing that suffering for God is a very high and sublime thing, and the greatest offering and gift that God grants

RELIGION

to his chosen ones, they humble themselves, and they consider themselves unworthy of it, and they honour the Divine Goodness, that, despite their being so vile and abominable, so highly favours them, and confused they do not know what to do to thank their Divine Majesty for such a sublime favour. *Aemulamini charismata meliora*:[7] seeking with Divine grace to rise to the peak of this perfection.

Notes

1 Translated by Katie Barclay, with thanks to François Soyer.
2 Mary of Jesus of Ágreda (1602–1665).
3 Can accept this.
4 Folio 20 laid out the standard prayer to be said here.
5 Marina de Escobar (1554–1633).
6 Of your own soul a sword shall pierce.
7 Covet earnestly the best gifts, I Corinthians 12:31

21

ELIZABETH CAIRNS (1685–1741), *MEMOIRS OF ELIZABETH CAIRNS*

(Glasgow: John Brown, 1762), pp. 45–53, 61–63, 65

Elizabeth Cairns was a working-class Scottish Calvinist, who variously worked as a shepherd, servant, and schoolteacher. She is known for her mysticism and visionary encounters, and lay preaching. Cairns wrote a memoir, where she reflected on her spiritual journey through different stage of her life. The account is not unlike a spiritual diary, in its reflection on her moral self, sins and passions, but written with the benefit of hindsight, and with the goal of encouraging others in their religious life. Not unlike Brown's (source 17) or Stenberg's (source 22) writings, we see her explore the practice of the faith as an experience of emotion and emotional management. The excerpt below explores a period in her early twenties where she is tempted by Satan, an encounter that she describes as a form of melancholy, intercepted with moments of joy when she has encounters with God. The devil was a known figure in Calvinist Scotland before the mid-eighteenth century, especially associated with immoral or unchristian emotions, such as lust or despair. Notably such personal confessions of temptation, and their associated emotions, and the ultimate victory over them were also considered useful for readers as a form of advice and encouragement.

. . .

On the day following I was pleading with God in prayer, that he would remove the darkness from my soul, and lift on me the light of his countenance again, and as I continued pleading, my soul was like to turn desperate, and I opened my mouth thus unreasonably to God, and said, take away my life, ere thou take away the light of thy countenance; and immediately the vail was drawn aside, and I got a sight of his glory. But O this pleasant blink lasted but for a moment, and my darkness did immediately return. And on the day following, that word was brought to me with power, Psal. xxxi 15. *My times are wholly in thy hand:* this I applied to myself, and said, my times are also wholly in my good. So I went on for several days pleading and hoping, that my enjoyments would return again: but alas! I was disappointed.

   After this, there was one who was reported of for an experienced Christian, with whom I endeavoured to be acquaint; and after converse with her, I imparted some of my mind to her, and told her of my sweet life I had enjoyed through the last year, and what a sudden deprival I had met with. She told me that I must part with that life, or I must go out of the world, as also she told me, of a life of faith a believer lived by, in this world, and that sensible manifestations were reserved for eternity. And by a similitude she taught me, that Christ did with his young converts, as a woman doth with her child, when it is young, she carries it in her arms, and leads it by the hands, but when it comes to more strength, she lets it walk alone and take a fall, and rise again, and yet her love is still the same: so doth Christ with his people in their first entry into his way, he manifests much of his love to them, but when they come to more experience, he withdraws sense from them that they may be taught to walk by faith, but yet his love is still the same to them: as also she told me, I must not think always to enjoy the blinks of divine light, and love, but I must come down from the mount of manifestations, and take part of the dark steps of the wilderness, as the cloud of witnesses, that had done before me, had done.

O! this was good advice, but alas I knew not how to take it. In my former life I had been smitten by ministers, and Christians, and nearest relations had been the instruments of my tryal, yet when all streams were much dryed up, my relief came still from the foundation himself, and if I parted with that life he called sense, I knew not how to live.

Thus I lived for the time of two months, reasoning with myself, how to live this life of faith; but still my darkness did remain, and the beloved of my soul had hid his face from me, and my condition was so ill, that one night in prayer, I began to cast away my hopes, and in the same night that word was sent to me with such a rebuke, that ever since. I durst not raze my state, however low my condition was, the word is in Deut xxxii. 6. *Do you thus requite the Lord, O foolish people and unwise.* This I did apply to myself as a just rebuke for my bad requital of all the kindnesses I had met with from a gracious and kind Lord: so immediately my soul grasped, as it were, and took hold of God, as my covenanted God, and I resolved in the strength of his grace never to quite grips of my interest in him, although my condition should never be so low.

After this, Satan began with his temptations, representing himself to my fancy, in several shapes, and I was daily tormented with the fears of his appearance. And one day as I was praying for the destruction of his kingdom, I thought he said unto me, Forbear me, and I will forbear you. Short time after this, I fell under straitening in prayer, and my former liberty and freedom was with held upon this, Satan upbraided me, that I had yielded to him. Another day I was praying, that God would be with some friends, that were absent from me, as also with myself, and suddenly that was darted in upon me, that God could not be every where present.

This temptation came with such power, that it struck me silent: O! this was bitter to me, that he should thus tempt me to *atheism*, and this imbittered it the more to me, that God did with-hold his wonted help; for formerly, when Satan had thrown in his fiery darts at me, I would have found present relief, with a power sent me, by which I could have drawn the sword of the Spirit, the word of God and so have resisted him; but, alas! Now the sword is blunted in my hand, and I have no power to manage it: Satan also continued representing himself to my fancy, in several shapes, and in the duty of prayer he set more furiously on me, so that I could not continue any time; but when I was helped to draw the screen of the covenant about me, and when I was allowed to pour out my soul to a reconciled God, in a Mediator, and to view my Redeemer as a conqueror over Satan, and all his emissaries. One night in prayer, he made a visible approach, so that I was forced to fly out of the place: yet the Lord mercifully appeared for me relief, and sent that word with power on my soul, *Fear not, for I am with thee to deliver thee*, Isa. xli. 10 And while I was thus molested with his temptations, and felt the members of the body of death arising against me, and my glorious Redeemer with-holding the sense of his love from me, this brought me into a great strait, how to live in the world: and when I was thus sitting down disconsolate, that word came to me with power and life, *I will guide thee with my counsel while here, and afterwards receive thee to glory*, as in Psal. lxxiii. 24. After this, the devil went away and left me for a season with these sort of temptations, that had continued three quarter of a year. All this passed in the twentieth year of my life, being the first year of this dark cloud.

The next two years, I shall join them both together, for it proceeded from evil to worse with me; and these two years, there was not only a with-holding of the blinks of divine light, in the sensible down-pourings of the Spirit, and of the smiles of divine love, but there was also a deprival of the exercise of all grace, as to my sense and feeling; as also a deadness, and powerlessness overspread my soul, so that there was no duty I could perform, as I had done, and there was nothing left me, but the views of my interest in the covenant, and some hopes, that the Lord would return again, and if not in time, yet sure at the end of time, I should be put in the possession, and full enjoyment of my glorious Redeemer to all eternity.

I am persuaded, if this had not been allowed me, I had gone distracted; for formerly, I would have wondered, when I heard the people of God, complaining of a wandering heart in time of duty, and of vain thoughts in time of hearing sermon: but now alas! I found those to my sad experience, although formerly I could have heard a sermon, and prayed without a vain thought, but now I found it a great difficulty to bring my heart to duty, and to keep it there, so I went from duty to duty where formerly I was wont to enjoy the gracious presence of Christ: but alas! *my Beloved was gone, I sought him, but I could not find him; called him but he gave me no answer*, as in Song v. 6. Thus I went on lamenting and bewailing my sad loss, but alas! I got no out-gate. O! the bitterness of soul I then did endure, both under the power of prevailing sin, a tempting devil, and a hiding God, with-holding grace to oppose and batter them down. Much more past in these two years, that I forbear to mention.

Thus past these three sad years of my life. Now three years of this dark cloud are over; but alas! the fourth year was darker than them all, for now I was not only deprived of the blinks of divine light, and of the sensible smiles of my Beloved; but also of the sensible exercise of all grace, and all duties, I had been exercised in: and this was not all, but the chain of the devil was let out, and all the troops of infernal spirits, and swarms of lusts, members of the body of death, did gather themselves together against me. This did holy sovereignty see meet to permit for ends known to himself. Here I stood ript naked of all my armour, as to my sense, and exposed to the open field of temptation, where I endured the thunder-bolts, and fiery darts of the devil; yet, notwithstanding of all these, I was allowed to hold fast my grips of an interest in the covenant.

One day as I sat down to read my Bible, the tempter bade me cast it away; it was not only once or twice, he so did but for many days he continued calling me to cast it away, and I was so far deprived of my armour, that I could do no more to resist him, but hold my Bible with both my hands, and weep over it.

Another day as I was lamenting my weary life, when compared with the life I lived formerly, the tempter came with that temptation. Curse the day wherein thou was born, and I could say no more against him but this, O! shall that which was Job's sin, be my duty? Thus I went for several days, thinking still my mouth would open, and curse my day; but I declare to bless the Lord, who preserved me, for I do not remember that ever I opened my mouth, or yet gave the least consent to this temptation; this was still presented to me, O! shall that which was Job's sin, be my duty? Yet the tempter continued, from day to day, so that the poison of his arrows was like to drink up my spirits, and I thought it was with me, as it was with those people, Deut. xxviii. 67. *In the morning thou shall say, Would God it were even; and at even thou shall say, Would God it were morning, for the fear of thine heart wherewith thou shalt fear, and for the sight of thine eyes which thou shalt see.* But that which was worse than all this, my glorious Redeemer did still hide his face from me, and the Spirit of prayer was withdrawn, and the sword of the Spirit, the word of God, was turned to be a dead letter; yet when I was in this sad condition, my soul clave to God, and said, *Although thou shouldst kill me, yet will I trust in these*, Job xiii. 15. Thus I was allowed to hold fast my interest in God, as my covenanted God, notwithstanding all that was come on me.

After this, the tempter came with that temptation, and said, Murder thyself for thou needst not fear, they eternal interest is secured. This temptation he continued for many days.

One day I was praying alone in a secret place, and he set violently upon me, and presented to me both conveniency and instruments to murder myself; upon this I was forced to fly out of the place. Another day, I was going some space of way myself alone, and in the way there was a ditch of water, where he set violently on me to drown myself, busking his temptation with this, Thou needest not fear, thou wilt immediately go to heaven, and the world will never know what is become of thee. O! now I was like to go distracted, for I could give no resentment; but I was kept from yielding to him, and helped by an unknown support of an almighty God, to resist the temptation in all its appearances.

When I was in this sad condition, and like to lose my reason, I was one day on my knees before God in prayer, and, as I thought, both hell and heaven were realized to my mind, and saw, as it were, the devil mocking at me, and ready to pull me in to him; yet, in the mean time of this extremity, glorious Christ appeared for my relief, who hath the chain in his own hand, that holds the devil, so that he could not win at me; yet being under great agony of mind, through the violence of long and great temptations, I uttered unadvised and unbecoming words before the Lord; but blessed ever be his name, he took me not at my word, as justly he might have done, but being full of pity, he forgave my sin, and did not destroy me because of my foolishness. So it pleased a gracious and merciful God, to restrain the devil, and deliver me from his temptations for a season.

. . .

So immediately after this, I felt a power on my soul, that brought those graces to a lively exercise, *viz* Faith and repentance; for there was a full sight of my sinful miscarriages laid before me, with all those particularly aggravations, upon which my heart was melted down before God, and I felt the out-going of my soul to renew its acceptance of Christ, as held forth in the promise of the gospel, with an eye to the infinite value of the blood of sprinkling, to take away sin. And while I was thus exercised, that word came with such power, efficacy and light into my mind, as in 1 John i. 7. *The blood of Jesus Christ his Son cleanseth us from all sin.* So, as thereby the guilt was removed from my conscience, for I believed that God had pardoned me, and that sweet word, (*Who is a God like unto thee, that pardoneth iniquity, and passeth by the transgressions of the remnant of his heritage, he retaineth not his anger for ever, because he delighteth in mercy,* Micah vii. 8.) was sent for my further confirmation that he had pardoned me, the vision (so to speak) being doubled. O! here, I cannot but admire the wonderful condescension of sovereignty, in answering me thus both in pardoning me and telling me that he had done it: O! here did I see grace glorified, in pardoning one of the chief of sinners. Now I could reason with the tempter, and say, although I was among the chief of sinners, yet I am come to the chief of Saviours, *who is able to save to the uttermost, all that come to God by him,* Heb. vii. 25.

After this I went on rejoicing, like the birds, after a long stormy winter, when the spring begins, they sing although the summer be not yet come: thus my soul, after the long winter of desertion and storms of temptation, began to rejoice in what God had done for me, although my condition at this time was as far different from what it was in my nineteenth year, as the light and heat of the sun in the spring differs from its light and heat, in the time of summer.

Thus, I went on rejoicing for several weeks, but yet, alas! my sun was still as in a cloud, according to the first part of the similitude, mentioned as above; for, although God had removed the dark cloud, and set a reviving to my soul, so that duties became more pleasant and refreshing to me, yet there was a with-holding of the sensible down-pourings of his Spirit, and of the soul-transforming blinks of divine light and love, I had formerly enjoyed.

O! here, I did greatly mistake the way the believer was to live in this world, having forgotten the said advice I got from my dear Christian friend, formerly mentioned in the first year of the dark cloud, she having told me, That the believer was to live by faith while here and sense was reserved for eternity. But she being taken away by death, I had now no human help to go to, to whom I could impart

RELIGION

my mind; and as for the way of faith's bringing food from the promises, through the channel of gospel ordinances, I was much acquainted with it at this time.

After this, I tried the ordinances, and so laboured to bring every thing home, with application to myself, sometimes I heard man's misery by the fall, and the evil of sin holden out, as also the necessity of regeneration, and of closing with Christ: also I heard sin reproved, calls to duty, and Christ commended, and the souls that closed with him, and had gotten a sight of their interest in him, and of the pardon of all their sins, to be the happiest souls in all the world. And, upon reflections on all this, I could not deny but I was one of those souls the gospel called happy: yet alas! this answered not my case, for neither sense of interest in Christ, nor yet pardon of sin could satisfy me, while he was absent from my soul, with the sense of his love and the light of his countenance: so I went on still lamenting my sad loss.

. . .

Upon this, I went to God with these words in my mouth, and said, If my sins be such, as thou wilt mark with a perpetual stroke, let it be on my body, and not on my soul: O give to me the light of thy countenance, and do with my body what thou pleases. O poor and foolish wretch that I was, who would thus take upon me to prescribe to the Almighty; yet in this he took me, as it were, at my word.

Few days thereafter, the Lord gave to me the light of his countenance, and with it he sent the rod upon my body, which was both undesirable as to its nature, and dangerous to its effects: upon this were several words sent until me with power, such as, *Who is a God like unto thee, wonderful in counsel, great in power, terrible in working, and doing wonders:* those words remained with me, until I saw them all made out; and I was made with submission to say, the cup that infinite wisdom and love, had mixed, why should I refuse to drink it? So I went on for the space of two months rejoicing in what God allowed of the light of his countenance, though the rod was made more and more heavy.

22

PEHR STENBERG (1758–1824),
DIARY OF PEHR STENBERG:
1758–1784

Umea University

Pehr Stenberg was a minister in the Swedish Lutheran church.[1] He was the son of farmers near Umeå, and went to university before being ordained. He kept a diary, in the form of an autobiography, for over forty years; it runs to almost 5,000 handwritten pages in Swedish. As an autobiography, the text is less immediate than a diary, and instead picks key events that provided opportunity, for him or others, to learn moral lessons, or to draw closer to God. The text therefore is not a true spiritual diary, where the writer wrestles with his faith, but rather reflects back on previous actions and lessons. Stenberg offers himself as an exemplar for other Christians, who could learn from his mistakes and live better lives. The excerpt below, translated from English, shows Stenberg reflecting on key moments in his youth, where his religious values and pastoral potential were solidified. It provides a useful account of the practice of the faith was experienced as and through emotion, but also of the everyday practices and feelings of trying to live morally as a young man.

. . .

Chapter VII. Closer knowledge of myself; Christmas holidays

[October 1774] In the hall outside was a Sofa bed that I had to share with my comrade's Uncle's servant Jonas, who at first appearance looked rather foolish. The first two nights I lay beside him, I noticed how his whole body sometimes stirred, like an earthquake, which, however, quickly ceased; but often reoccurred. I was very curious as to what was wrong with him. By carefully listening, I noticed that he was reading and praying, and every time he called God or Jesus' name, so his whole body was in motion. Here my heart received a hard blow, for it gave me reason to think about the condition of my soul. Ach! I thought, how stands it with you! Shall now he, who not so much as associated with the word of God, surpass me, who so much have read and been in fellowship with the Lord's words.

181

RELIGION

Morning and evening, I have prayed on my knees along with my comrades in the Master's chamber, but when have I ever prayed with such devotion? When have I known such a devout movement of the heart and soul? Never; on the contrary, my mouth has many times recited prayers that my tongue has been conditioned to utter without me having the slightest reflection thereon; they have gone in one ear and out the other. Yes, my thoughts have often been so scattered that I have not even heard what and which prayers the other read. Lying there, it now came to my mind with what pleasure and emotion I read God's word in my childhood, and how I sometimes then in my bed prayed with devotion to my God. Now I realized how great a sin I committed in disappointing God with my prayers. And now played all my past wrongdoing and great sins in my memory, which sufficiently clearly made me aware I had deserved God's wrath and condemnation. "Jonas," I said then, "be good and read a little louder that I too can hear." He did so. And now spoke only my heart, but my mouth was mostly silent and from my eyes flowed rivers of tears. My sins, both secret and apparent, I confessed with remorse before God, and prayed earnestly that he from his covering grace for Christ's sake will forgive me them all. During my worship and prayer, I became such that I barely knew myself. I cannot describe or express the sweet state, which I happened upon, but I can say, that it was now my greatest pleasure to pray and praise God, where I often heretofore found much languor thereto. Oh does not from this clearly shine God's hidden ways with the people; for what could not well be achieved and executed from all the Learned Master's admonitions, could now be performed by a foolish servant's clear example. O! How highly necessary is it then for true Christians, yes an unconditional obligation, to let their light shine before men, that they may see their good deeds and glorify their Father who is in heaven.[2] And each and every one should seek the kingdom of God to multiply as far as their own pound allows.[3] Yes, Lord God teach me to advance you, and deprive and root out of me and out of my heart the depraved human fear that will prevent me from widely proclaiming Your wonders as I should. Praise be great Triune God, who at this moment awakened me out of my slumber and made me part of your mercy and took away my sins.

[November 1774] This autumn, the state-surgeon Lithorin[4] set up his electricity machine to try through the power of electricity to cure a paralyzed man from Tegsnäset. When one evening Aunt Burman went there to look, I followed too. First, the Apothecary Freijer, Alderman Möller and others took puffs, and when one got the puff so did all the others who held together. At last, I also wanted to take an Electricity puff and placed myself in between the others holding each other's hands. For me, it felt quite harsh and sore over the chest and in the arms where I was most ill when I had the smallpox. They wanted me to take with them several puffs, but since I felt it so painful, I passed.

I then became somewhat familiar with his Son.

[December 1774] Already this past winter one of our comrades had given up, namely Olof Lindal went from us and travelled home to the parish of Normalings, and would there read for his father's Adjunct Olof Renhorn, and this fall Erik

DIARY OF PETER STENBERG

Lund decreased our number and travelled to Hernösand to continue his studies. This he did more out of pride than necessity; for surely the Master could teach him everything he needed and could grasp, but he thought it too difficult to stand under the Master's obedience. As soon as the Master was out he spoke so steely and sarcastically, but the Master's presence forced him to nevertheless be humble; because of this, the Master, when he heard that Lund was leaving his education so suddenly, sought to sympathise with him, saying that he knew him as so modest that he would not have chosen to stop his schooling without previously mentioning it, let along not consulting with him on such an important matter; the Master placed the blame on the parents. But I, and as I believe also my other comrades who knew him better, thought completely differently. As shipbuilder Ekenberg came this fall with his wife and children to Umeå, the Master accepted his sons, Carl, Erik and Gustaf, as students in their place, so that we were still as many.

One week before Christmas I got leave from school to go home to my parents, where I mostly amused myself catching salmon on hooks. Saturday or Christmas Eve I went, along with my Father and Mother, on the road to Nordmaling parish to Christmas dinner at Uncle Anders Ersson's house in Håknäs Village, as the farmhand was there for so long as he was trading about a homestead. On the road we happened to be in the company of other Christmas guests, so that it was not tiresome. And when we came to the first village in Nordmalings Parish, which was called Ängersjön, we went to the house of a spry elderly woman, who did not look beautiful, but had after her own special art brewed a magnificent beer, of which we drank a good dose. This art my mother learned from her the next winter, when the old woman was with us and sold soap that she had also made herself. From here we travelled after some rest, and came to another village from which no more remained of the road than ¾ mile, but after the description we got in Ängersjön, we turned off the public highway on a road which was a ¼ mile shorter than the right one. We went a good way, but came in the end to a fork in the road. Here we stood and did not know which way to go. My father had once previously been in Håknäs and knew from this that the village was on the other side of the river: we therefore took the road that lay to the right. After a little progress we came again to a fork, and for the same reason stayed to the right, but came to the end in a rather stubby meadow, where the road became only a few barns. We were forced therefore to turn around again until we came to the other road and just as we had put a piece of him behind our back came another fork, and for the aforementioned reason we turned to the right, but the journey was hampered a second time when the road ended at the precipice of a riverbank, whose height seemed to us so much more horrible as a roaring rapids flowed in there. This was a place from which they had dragged sawn timber. After going so far astray we were already beginning to despair if we ever would find a way out, but even in our anxiety we were still happy there at this time, so that not even an old busybody met on the road could have blamed us for taking a good drop before we travelled from the city like last time. We re-ignited our courage again as soon as we in due course became aware of the Village where we were to travel on the

RELIGION

other side of the river; wherefore we now took the last road to the left, until we happily approached the doors of my uncle and aunt, who we found in health and who tolerably well received us. Thus we lost as much time on our short cut, as we were going to win. On Christmas day, we travelled to their Church, which was a ¼ mile from there, and got to see a beautiful Church and hear good Priests, but miserable singers. After the festive feast, we wished Uncle and Aunt farewell and went home, which journey ends happily.

[January 1775] Eleven days after New Year, my Brother Erick and I went to a meadow a short distance from the village to get hay. When we arrived home past nine o'clock and I entered our cottage, what a spectacle did not then appear before our eyes. There lay our nearest neighbour's wife dead on the floor a little away from the stove; her husband was sitting on the bench with his hand under his cheek. Her 70 year old and limping father paced the floor, wringing his hands and crying terribly. Her maid as well as my mother laboured, crying and using every measure to get life into her, thinking her only unconscious, but in vain. I had to tell them she had gone.

Anders Ersson in Håknäs, with whom we visited on the then newly past Christmas feast, came to us the day before to inquire if there was a homestead in our village available to buy. He brought with him an old, skinny horse. When it got dark, our nearest neighbour Anders Larsson came to us, who also had a somewhat old, though not lean but steady horse. These two began to agree with each other on a horse swap; it came so far that they would try each other's horses, wherefore we all followed to Anders Larsson's farm, which went quite well. On arrival at the latter's place, Uncle says 'Let us now step in here to further agree, then you may wish to consult your wife about it, perhaps she will disagree'. 'No', he swears, 'it is completely unnecessary'. We then all went home to our house again, where the exchange after a short time was confirmed. But in the morning, as soon as Anders Larsson's wife learned about the previously-mentioned deal, she became quite dissatisfied, especially after she got to see the horse. She therefore came to us, and after she had greeted us good morning, she turned to Uncle saying: 'Now I am here to seek a return on the horse exchange, as my husband has done this without my knowledge, and the horse is all too pitiful for me ever to be content with him. At the same time, her old Father came into us. Uncle answers, 'All were willing; I am thus satisfied. I have fairly exchanged horses with your husband, and I am not to blame for this happening to you unwittingly, for I told him several times that he should take care of your interest therein'. My Mother then fetched her a chair, saying: 'Please sit down'. She answered, 'I thank you; I have not now time to sit'. These were her last words; for scarcely had my mother turned from her than she fell, dropped down by my mother's side, stone dead on the floor. There was though one great mercy in this misfortune that her own father was himself personally present at this deplorable sight, for otherwise my parents and Uncle could have suffered severe inconveniences for the suspicion of violent assault against her, if My Parents in that event had not been able to prove their innocence.

At the end of my Christmas leave, I was going to as usual attend the St Knut's Day Celebrations before my departure to the City. On this occasion, through each

184

DIARY OF PETER STENBERG

contributing some malt, we had brewed ourselves some good beer. We did not have brandy as it was a banned item at this time. At the gathering, each took a good portion of the beer, which I did not neglect though with moderation, so that I nonetheless became a little touched. Our party was held at the house of the farmer's Petter Zakri's son, who himself was unmarried. After a little while I walked with my youngest Brother Andreas to the next spruce farm belonging to Johan Jonsons. On the road, he says, 'I desire to go to Anders Olof's son to buy beer; he has good beer, which costs so and so much a quart'. 'Do not go there', I replied, 'it is so wanton to go to the pub and squander away money, you have drunk enough before, and if you want more get some at the playhouse farm'. Finally, I persuaded him to follow me back to the playhouse. After a while I was missing my brothers Anders and Erik: Jealous for their welfare, I thought, are they now somewhere practicing their vices? I hastened therefore out to search for them. And was told that they would be with Nils Pers' son. I hurried there, but how appalled I became when I was not even in the hall but heard a horrible noise inside. I went in and saw them both sitting on a long chair next to each other. My younger brother Anders shrieked and roared with a full throat, then he sat and then he stood, and all that he got out of it was to overturn his tankard. He wanted to fight, to whip up a half dozen boys was then not much for him. In a word, he bore himself like a beast and every word he spoke cut me to the heart. But Erik on the other hand spoke well with quite a loud voice that he too had drunk beer, but he sought in every way with meekness to still his brother's excess; he bid him be quiet, and not shout so much; he represented to him how shameful it was to feed himself like the greatest drunken dog and to behave like Turks and infidels; he pushed him down on the chair when he wanted to get up and become too extreme, but it was all in vain, for the more he enjoined and sought to persuade him the worse he became. I now came to his aid, but both of our efforts were fruitless. Nothing gave me more pain than that Nils Pers' son and his wife should be witnesses to this. Therefore I tried to get him out of there, and finally after much persuasion he gave in to us. In the yard, I told him distinctly how ill he had behaved: 'is it not shameful', I said, 'and do you not think it dishonourable when you behave so that we all must be ashamed for your sake, when around the whole town and parish you become proclaimed as a sot'. But he heard nothing, continuing still with his extravagance. And as I was, as I have said, not clearheaded, so I was much more sensible and could therefore not prevent myself from bursting out in the bitterest weeping. But now all his boldness instantly disappeared; when he saw me crying, he became silent and did not say a word. We all then went again to the playhouse, seeking the ordinary cheer, but my brother Anders sat down in a corner completely quiet and still and wanted neither to dance or anything else, yea he appeared entirely sorrowful. I sought well to hearten him, saying: 'do not now grieve over this, without dancing and having cheer, for you are allowed to do so as long as it is with moderation, so that you do not progress to such an extreme as before'. In the end, he left us all and our party, and went home and settled to sleep. And ever since then, I have never seen him so drunk as this time. And therefore I can never regret that I then wept, when it was the only means of impressing on him an eternal disgust for drunkenness and such behaviour as he then used.

Notes

1 Translated by Katie Barclay, with thanks to Kaarle Wirta for his help.
2 Matt 5:16.
3 Matt 25: 14–30.
4 Martin Lithorin (1759–1807).

Part 4

POLITICS AND LAW

Part 4

Politics and law

Eighteenth-century European political economy was influenced by Enlightenment ideas about the sensible body and human nature. Philosophers debated the nature of the social contract, and the traits and characteristics common to humans that shaped its operation. These ideas influenced new models of law and order, including punishment, and were driven by anthropological investigations and encounters with people around the world. The capacity to experience emotion, and the impacts of such feeling, shaped new models of governance and new imaginings of the nation-state, often explored during this period in philosophical and legal texts that advocated for reform. Emotion could also be deployed as a mode of persuasion to enable political and legal effects, such as in sermons and speeches, and observations of the body underpinned diplomatic engagements and political relationships, especially as Europeans moved across the globe.

23

REUBEN THWAITES, ED. (1853–1913), *THE JESUIT RELATIONS AND ALLIED DOCUMENTS: TRAVELS AND EXPLORATIONS OF THE JESUIT MISSIONARIES IN NEW FRANCE, 1610–1791: VOL. 67 LOWER CANADA, ABENAKIS, LOUISIANA 1716–1727*

(Cleveland: Burrows Brothers, 1900),
pp. 231–247

Sébastien Rale (1657–1724), known here as Father Rasles, was a French Jesuit priest and missionary to North America, where he worked amongst the Abenakis. He was killed during 'Dummer's War', a series of battles fought between the British at New England and the Wabanaki Confederacy, allied with New France, over the location of the border. Father Rales was a central figure in these conflicts, considered by the English to be involved in mobilising the Abenakis for the French, and they placed a bounty on his head. For the French, he was a martyr who died for his faith and mission work; for the English, he was an incendiary. The account below was written by Pierre de la Chasse (1670–1749), the superior of the Jesuit Missions in New France, and an important political liaison for the French with the Abenakis. The letter was designed to promote the death of Rale as a martyrdom, both for Rale's sake as a Jesuit missionary and as a propaganda tool during the war with the British. Taking the form of a personal letter between members of the same faith provides the account with a greater appearance of veracity than another form of writing. The letter deploys emotion for rhetorical effect, and describes Rale's emotions to affirm his sanctity, offering evidence of how character was read through gesture and emotional displays.

. . .

Letter from Father de la Chasse, Superior-General of the Missions in New France, to Father * * *, of the same Society.

Quebec, October 29, 1724.

MY Reverend Father,

The peace of Our Lord

In the deep grief that we are experiencing from the loss of one of our oldest Missionaries, it is a grateful consolation to us that he should have been the victim of his own love, and of his zeal to maintain the Faith in the hearts of his Neophytes. From other letters you have already learned the origin of the war which broke out between the English and the Savages: with the former, a desire to extend their rule; with the latter, a horror of all subjection, and an attachment to their Religion – these caused, in the beginning, the misunderstandings which in the end were followed by an open rupture.

Father Rasles, the Missionary of the *Abnakis*, had become very odious to the English. As they were convinced that his endeavors to confirm the Savages in the Faith constituted the greatest obstacle to their plan of usurping the territory of the Savages, they put a price on his head; and more than once they had attempted to abduct him, or to take his life. At last they have succeeded in gratifying their passion of hatred, and in ridding themselves of the apostolic man; but, at the same time, they have procured for him a glorious death, which was ever the object of his desire, – for we know that long ago he aspired to the happiness of sacrificing his life for his flock. I will describe to you in few words the circumstances of that event.

After many acts of hostility had been committed on both sides by the two Nations, a little army of Englishmen and their Savage allies, numbering eleven hundred men, unexpectedly came to attack the Village of *Nanrantsouak*. The dense thickets with which that Village is surrounded helped them to conceal their movements; and as, besides, it was not enclosed with palisades, the Savages were taken by surprise, and became aware of the enemy's approach only by a volley from their muskets, which riddled all the cabins. At that time there were only fifty warriors in the Village. At the first noise of the muskets, they tumultuously seized their weapons, and went out of their cabins to oppose the enemy. Their design was not rashly to meet the onset of so many combatants, but to further the flight of the women and the children, and give them time to gain the other side of the river, which was not yet occupied by the English.

Father Rasles, warned by the clamor and the tumult of the danger which was menacing his Neophytes, promptly left his house and fearlessly appeared before the enemy. He expected by his presence either to stop their first efforts, or, at least, to draw their attention to himself alone, and at the expense of his life to procure the safety of his flock.

As soon as they perceived the Missionary, a general shout was raised which was followed by a storm of musket-shots that was poured upon him. He dropped dead at the foot of a large cross that he had erected in the midst of the Village, in order to announce the public profession that was made therein of adoring a crucified God. Seven Savages who were around him, and were exposing their lives to guard that of their father, were killed by his side.

The death of the Shepherd dismayed the flock; the Savages took to flight and crossed the river, part of them by fording, and part by swimming. They were exposed to all the fury of their enemies, until the moment when they retreated into the woods which are on the other side of the river. There they were gathered, to the number of a hundred and fifty. From more than two thousand gunshots that had been fired at them only thirty persons were killed, including the women and children; and fourteen were wounded. The English did not attempt to pursue the fugitives; they were content with pillaging and burning the Village; they set fire to the Church, after a base profanation of the sacred vessels and of the adorable Body of Jesus Christ.

The precipitate retreat of the enemy permitted the return of the Nanrantsouak-ians to the Village. The very next day they visited the wreck of their cabins, while the women, on their part, sought for roots and plants suitable for treating the wounded. Their first care was to weep over the body of their holy Missionary; they found it pierced by hundreds of bullets, the scalp torn off, the skull broken by blows from a hatchet, the mouth and the eyes filled with mud, the bones of the legs broken, and all the members mutilated. This sort of inhumanity, practiced on a body deprived of feeling and of life, can scarcely be attributed to any one but to the Savage allies of the English.

After these devout Christians had washed and kissed many times the honored remains of their father, they buried him in the very place where, the night before, he had celebrated the holy Sacrifice of the Mass, – that is, in the place where the altar had stood before the burning of the Church. By such a precious death did the apostolic man finish, on the 23rd of August in this year, a course of thirty-seven years spent in the arduous labors of this Mission. He was in the sixty-seventh year of his life. His fastings and his continual hard work had, at the last, weakened his constitution; he had walked with some difficulty for about nineteen years, owing to the effects of a fall by which he broke, at the same time, the right hip and the left leg. Then it happened, since the callus was growing wrong at the place of fracture, that it became necessary to break the left leg again. At the time when it was most violently struck, he bore that painful operation with an extraordinary firmness and an admirable tranquillity. Our Physician, who was present, appeared so astonished at this that he could not refrain from saying: *Ah! my Father, let at least a few groans escape; you have so much cause for them!*

Father Rasles joined to the talents which make an excellent Missionary, the virtues which the evangelical Ministry demands in order that it be exercised to any profit among our Savages. He had robust health; and I do not know that, excepting the accident of which I have just spoken, he had ever had the least indisposition.

POLITICS AND LAW

We were surprised at his facility and his perseverance in learning the different Savage tongues; there was not one upon this continent of which he had not some smattering. Besides the *Abnakis* language, which he had spoken longest, he also knew the Huron, the Outaouais, and the Illinois; and he had used them to advantage in the different Missions where they were spoken. From the time of his arrival in Canada his character had ever been consistent; he was always firm and resolute, severe with himself, but tender and compassionate toward others.

Three years ago, by order of Monsieur our Governor, I made a tour of Acadia. In conversing with Father Rasles, I represented to him that in case war should be declared against the Savages, he would run a risk of his life; that, as his Village was only fifteen leagues from the English forts, he would be exposed to their first forays; that his preservation was necessary to his flock; and that he must take measures for the safety of his life. *My measures are taken*, he replied in a firm voice; *God has confided to me this flock, and I shall follow its fate, only too happy to be sacrificed for it*. He often repeated the same thing to his Neophytes, that he might strengthen their constancy in the Faith. *We have realized but too well*, they themselves said to me, *that that dear Father spoke to us out of the abundance of his heart; we saw him face death with a tranquil and serene countenance, and expose himself unassisted to the fury of the enemy, – hindering their first attempts, so that we might have time to escape from the danger and preserve our lives*.

As a price had been set on his head, and various attempts had been made to abduct him, the Savages last spring proposed to take him farther into the interior, toward Quebec, where he would be secure from the dangers with which his life was menaced. *What idea, then, have you of me?* he replied with an air of indignation, *do you take me for a base deserter? Alas! what would become of your Faith if I should abandon you? Your salvation is dearer to me than my life*.

He was indefatigable in the exercises of his devotion; unceasingly occupied in exhorting the Savages to virtue, his only thought was to make them fervent Christians. His impassioned and pathetic manner of preaching made a deep impression upon their hearts. Some Loup families, who have very recently come from Orange, told me with tears in their eyes that they were indebted to him for their conversion to Christianity; and that the instructions which he had given them when they received Baptism from him, about 30 years ago, could not be effaced from their minds, – his words were so efficacious, and left so deep traces in the hearts of those who heard him.

He was not content with instructing the Savages almost every day in the Church; he often visited them in their cabins. His familiar conversations charmed them; he knew how to blend with them a holy cheerfulness which is much more pleasing to the Savages than a serious and melancholy manner. He had also the art of winning them to do whatever he wished; he was among them like a master in the midst of his pupils.

Notwithstanding the continual occupations of his ministry, he never omitted the sacred exercises which are observed in our houses. He rose and made his Prayer

194

at the prescribed hour. He never neglected the eight days of annual retreat; he enjoined upon himself to make it in the first days of Lent, which is the time when the Savior entered the desert. *If a person do not fix a time in the year for these sacred exercises,* said he to me one day, *occupations succeed each other, and, after many delays he runs the risk of not finding leisure to perform them.*

Religious poverty appeared in his whole person, in his furniture, in his living, in his garments. In a spirit of mortification he forbade himself the use of wine, even when he was among Frenchmen; his ordinary food was porridge made of Indian cornmeal. During certain winters in which sometimes the Savages lacked everything, he was reduced to living on acorns; far from complaining at that time, he never seemed more content. For the last three years of his life, the war having prevented the Savages from free scope in hunting and from sowing their lands, their want became extreme; and the Missionary was in frightful need. Care was taken to send him from Quebec the necessary provisions for his subsistence. *I am ashamed,* he wrote to me, *of the care that you take of me; a Missionary born to suffer ought not to be so well treated.*

He did not permit any one to lend him a helping hand in his most ordinary needs; he always waited upon himself. He cultivated his own garden, he made ready his own firewood, his cabin, and his sagamité; he mended his torn garments, seeking in a spirit of poverty to make them last as long a time as was possible. The cassock which he had on when he was killed seemed so worn out and in such poor condition to those who had seized it, that they did not deign to take it for their own use as they had at first designed. They threw it again upon his body, and it was sent to us at Quebec.

In the same degree that he treated himself harshly, was he compassionate and charitable toward others. He had nothing of his own, and all that he received he immediately distributed to his poor Neophytes. Consequently, the greater part of them showed at his death signs of deeper grief than if they had lost their nearest relatives.

He took extraordinary pains in decorating and beautifying his Church, believing that this outward pomp which strikes the senses quickens the devotion of the barbarians, and inspires them with a most profound veneration for our holy Mysteries. As he knew a little of painting, and as he was quite skillful in the use of the lathe, the Church was decorated with many works which he himself had wrought.

You may well believe, my Reverend Father, that his virtues, of which new France has been for so many years witness, had won for him the respect and affection of Frenchmen and Savages.

He is, in consequence, universally regretted. No one doubts that he was sacrificed through hatred to his ministry and to his zeal in establishing the true Faith in the hearts of the Savages. This is the opinion of Monsieur de Bellemont, Superior of the Seminary of saint Sulpice at Montreal. When I asked from him the customary suffrages for the deceased, because of our interchange of prayers, he replied to me, using the well-known words of saint Augustine, that it was doing injustice to a Martyr to pray for him, – *Injuriam facit Martyri qui orat pro eo.*[1]

May it please the Lord that his blood, shed for such a righteous cause, may fertilize these unbelieving lands which have been so often watered with the blood of the Gospel workers who have preceded us; that it may render them fruitful in devout Christians, and that the zeal of Apostolic men yet to come maybe stimulated to gather the abundant harvest that is being presented to them by so many peoples still buried in the shadow of death!

In the meantime, as it belongs only to the Church to declare the saints, I commend him to your holy Sacrifices and to those of all our Fathers. I hope that you will not forget in them him who is, with much respect, etc.

Note

1 Injury makes a martyr, not those who pray for him.

24

CESARE BONESANA DI BECCARIA (1738–1794), *AN ESSAY ON CRIMES AND PUNISHMENTS*

Trans. Edward D. Ingraham, 2nd ed.
(Philadelphia: Philip H. Nicklin, 1764/1819),
pp. 47, 93–108

Cesare Beccaria was an Italian jurist and politician from an aristocratic family. He is considered a significant Enlightenment thinker, particularly for his *Essay on Crimes and Punishments*. The treatise argues for the need for reform in the penal system, particularly arguing against arbitrary power, torture and the overuse of capital punishment. Drawing on the concepts of social contract and utility, he argues that punishment should be designed to promote the former and to serve the public good. It was remarkably influential, translated into many languages – the version here in English – and shaped penal reform under Catherine the Great in Russia (see source 24) and in the new American republic. As can be seen in the excerpts below, the text revolves around eighteenth-century ideas of the sensate body, where pain and pleasure are key motivating factors for human action, the important role of the imagination in emotional life, and punishment as something that should be shaped to accord with the human's sympathetic nature. It provides insight into how Enlightenment thinkers used ideas about the human and the body to justify new forms of political order and governance.

. . .

Chap. XII: Of the intent of punishments

FROM the foregoing considerations it is evident that the intent of punishments is not to torment a sensible being, nor to undo a crime already committed. Is it possible that torments and useless cruelty, the instrument of furious fanaticism or the impotency of tyrants, can be authorised by a political body, which, so far from being influenced by passion, should be the cool moderator of the passions of individuals? Can the groans of a tortured wretch recal the time past, or reverse the crime he has committed?

POLITICS AND LAW

The end of punishment, therefore, is no other than to prevent the criminal from doing further injury to society, and to prevent others from committing the like offence. Such punishments, therefore, and such a mode of inflicting them, ought to be chosen, as will make the strongest and most lasting impressions on the minds of others, with the least torment to the body of the criminal.

Chap. XXVII: Of the mildness of punishments

THE course of my ideas has carried me away from my subject, to the elucidation of which I now return. Crimes are more effectually prevented by the certainty than the severity of punishment. Hence in a magistrate the necessity of vigilance, and in a judge of implacability, which, that it may become an useful virtue, should be joined to a mild legislation. The certainty of a small punishment will make a stronger impression than the fear of one more severe, if attended with the hopes of escaping; for it is the nature of mankind to be terrified at the approach of the smallest inevitable evil, whilst hope, the best gift of Heaven, hath the power of dispelling the apprehension of a greater, especially if supported by examples of impunity, which weakness or avarice too frequently afford.

If punishments be very severe, men are naturally led to the perpetration of other crimes, to avoid the punishment due to the first. The countries and times most notorious for severity of punishments were always those in which the most bloody and inhuman actions and the most atrocious crimes were committed; for the hand of the legislator and the assassin were directed by the same spirit of ferocity, which on the throne dictated laws of iron to slaves and savages, and in private instigated the subject to sacrifice one tyrant to make room for another.

In proportion as punishments become more cruel, the minds of men, as a fluid rises to the same height with that which surrounds it, grow hardened and insensible; and the force of the passions still continuing, in the space of an hundred years the *wheel* terrifies no more than formerly the *prison*. That a punishment may produce the effect required; it is sufficient that the *evil* it occasions should exceed the *good* expected from the crime, including in the calculation the certainty of the punishment, and the privation of the expected advantage. All severity beyond this is superfluous, and therefore tyrannical.

Men regulate their conduct by the repeated impression of evils they know, and not by those with which they are unacquainted. Let us, for example, suppose two nations, in one of which the greatest punishment is *perpetual slavery*, and in the other the *wheel*: I say, that both will inspire the same degree of terror, and that their can be no reasons for increasing the punishments of the first, which are not equally valid for augmenting those of the second to more lasting and more ingenious modes of tormenting, and so on to the most exquisite refinements of a science too well known to tyrants.

There are yet two other consequences of cruel punishments, which counteract the purpose of their institution, which was, to prevent crimes. The *first* arises from the impossibility of establishing an exact proportion between the crime and punishment; for though ingenious cruelty hath greatly multiplyed the variety of torments, yet the human frame can suffer only to a certain degree, beyond which it is impossible to proceed, be the enormity of the crime ever so great. The *second* consequence is impunity. Human nature is limited no less in evil than in good. Excessive barbarity can never be more than temporary, it being impossible that it should be supported by a permanent system of legislation; for if the laws be too cruel, they must be altered, or anarchy and impunity will succeed.

Is it possible without shuddering with horror, to read in history of the barbarous and useless torments that were cooly invented and executed by men who were called sages? Who does not tremble at the thoughts of thousands of wretches, whom their misery, either caused or tolerated by the laws, which favoured the few and outraged the many, had forced in despair to return to a state of nature, or accused of impossible crimes, the fabric of ignorance and superstition, or guilty only of having been faithful to their own principles; who, I say, can, without horror, think of their being torn to pieces, with slow and studied barbarity, by men endowed with the same passions and the same feelings? A delightful spectacle to a fanatic multitude!

Chap. XXVIIL: Of the punishment of death

THE useless profusion of punishments, which has never made men better, induces me to inquire, whether the punishment of *death* be really just or useful in a well governed state? What *right*, I ask, have men to cut the throats of their fellow-creatures? Certainly not that on which the sovereignty and laws are founded. The laws, as I have said before, are only the sum of the smallest portions of the private liberty of each individual, and represent the general will, which is the aggregate of that of each individual. Did any one ever give to others the right of taking away his life? Is it possible that, in the smallest portions of the liberty of each, sacrificed to the good of the public, can be contained the greatest of all good, life? If it were so, how shall it be reconciled to the maxim which tells us, that a man has no right to kill himself, which he certainly must have, if he could give it away to another?

But the punishment of death is not authorised by any right; for I have demonstrated that no such right exists. It is therefore a war of a whole nation against a citizen, whose destruction they consider as necessary or useful to the general good. But if I can further demonstrate that it is neither necessary nor useful, I shall have gained the cause of humanity.

The death of a citizen cannot be necessary but in one case: when, though deprived of his liberty, he has such power and connections as may endanger the security of the nation; when his existence may produce a dangerous revolution in the established form of government. But, even in this case, it can only be necessary when a nation is on the verge of recovering or losing its liberty, or in times of absolute anarchy, when the disorders themselves hold the place of laws: but in a reign of tranquillity, in a form of government approved by the united wishes of the nation, in a state well fortified from enemies without and supported by strength within, and opinion, perhaps more efficacious, where all power is lodged in the hands of a true sovereign, where riches can purchase pleasures and not authority, then, can be no necessity for taking away the life of a subject.

If the experience of all ages be not sufficient to prove, that the punishment of death has never prevented determined men from injuring society, if the example of the Romans, if twenty years reign of Elizabeth, empress of Russia, in which she gave the fathers of their country an example more illustrious than many conquests bought with blood; if, I say, all this be not sufficient to persuade mankind, who always suspect the voice of reason, and who choose rather to be led by authority, let us consult human nature in proof of my assertion.

It is not the intenseness of the pain that has the greatest effect on the mind, but its continuance; for our sensibility is more easily and more powerfully affected by weak but repeated impressions, than by a violent but momentary impulse. The power of habit is universal over every sensible being. As it is by that we learn to speak, to walk, and to satisfy our necessities, so the ideas of morality are stamped on our minds by repeated impressions. The death of a criminal is a terrible but momentary spectacle, and therefore a less efficacious method of deterring others than the continued example of a man deprived of his liberty, condemned, as a beast of burden, to repair, by his labour, the injur; he has done to society, *If I commit such a crime*, says the spectator to himself, *I shall be reduced to that miserable condition for the rest of my life*. A much more powerful preventive than the fear of death which men always behold in distant obscurity.

The terrors of death make so slight an impression, that it has not force enough to withstand the forgetfulness natural to mankind, even in the most essential things, especially when assisted by the passions. Violent impressions surprise us, but their effect is momentary; they are fit to produce those revolutions which instantly transform a common man into a Lacedaemonian or a Persian; but in a free and quiet government they ought to be rather frequent than strong.

The execution of a criminal is to the multitude a spectacle which in some excites compassion mixed with indignation. These sentiments occupy the mind much more than that salutary terror which the laws endeavour to inspire; but, in the contemplation of continued suffering, terror is the only, or at least predominant sensation. The severity of a punishment should be just sufficient to excite compassion in the spectators, as it is intended more for them than for the criminal.

A punishment, to be just, should have only that degree of severity which is sufficient to deter others. Now there is no man who, upon the least reflection, would put in competition the total and perpetual loss of his liberty, with the greatest advantages he could possibly obtain in consequence of a crime. Perpetual slavery, then, has in it all that is necessary to deter the most hardened and determined, as much as the punishment of death. I say it has more. There are many who can look upon death with intrepidity and firmness, some through fanaticism, and others through vanity, which attends us even to the grave; others from a desperate resolution, either to get rid of their misery, or cease to live: but fanaticism and vanity forsake the criminal in slavery, in chains and fetters, in an iron cage, and despair seems rather the beginning than the end of their misery. The mind, by collecting itself and uniting all its force, can, for a moment, repel assailing grief; but its most vigorous efforts are insufficient to resist perpetual wretchedness.

In all nations, where death is used as a punishment, every example supposes a new crime committed; whereas, in perpetual slavery, every criminal affords a frequent and lasting example; and if it be necessary that men should often be witnesses of the power of the laws, criminals should often be put to death: but this supposes a frequency of crimes; and from hence this punishment will cease to have its effect, so that it must be useful and useless at the same time.

I shall be told that perpetual slavery is as painful a punishment as death, and therefore as cruel. I answer, that if all the miserable moments in the life of a slave were collected into one point, it would be a more cruel punishment than any other; but these are scattered through his whole life, whilst the pain of death exerts all its force in a moment. There is also another advantage in the punishment of slavery, which is, that it is more terrible to the spectator than to the sufferer himself; for the spectator considers the sum of all his wretched moments whilst the sufferer, by the misery of the present, is prevented from thinking of the future. All evils are increased by the imagination, and the sufferer finds resources and consolations of which the spectators are ignorant, who judge by their own sensibility of what passes in a mind by habit grown callous to misfortune.

Let us, for a moment, attend to the reasoning of a robber or assassin, who is deterred from violating the laws by the gibbet or the wheel. I am sensible, that to develop the sentiments of one's own heart is an art which education only can teach; but although a villain may not be able to give a clear account of his principles, they nevertheless influence his conduct. He reasons thus: "What are these laws that I am bound to respect, which make so great a difference between me and the rich man? He refuses me the farthing I ask of him, and excuses himself by bidding me have recourse to labour, with which he is unacquainted.

Who made these laws? The rich and the great, who never deigned to visit the miserable hut of the poor, who have never seen him dividing a piece of mouldy bread, amidst the cries of his famished children and the tears of his wife. Let us break those ties, fatal to the greatest part of mankind, and only useful to a few indolent tyrants. Let us attack injustice at its source. I will return to my natural state of independence, I shall live free and happy on the fruits of my courage and industry. A day of pain and repentance may come, but it will be short; and for an hour of grief I shall enjoy years of pleasure and liberty. King of a small number as determined as myself, I will correct the mistakes of fortune, and I shall see those tyrants grow pale and tremble at the sight of him, whom, with insulting pride, they would not suffer to rank with their dogs and horses."

Religion then presents itself to the mind of this lawless villain, and, promising him almost a certainty of eternal happiness upon the easy terms of repentance, contributes much to lessen the horror of the last scene of the tragedy.

But he who foresees that he must pass a great number of years, even his whole life, in pain and slavery, a slave to those laws by which he was protected, in sight

201

POLITICS AND LAW

of his fellow-citizens, with whom he lives in freedom and society, makes an useful comparison between those evils, the uncertainty of his success, and the shortness of the time in which he shall enjoy the fruits of his transgression. The example of those wretches, continually before his eyes, makes a much greater impression on him than a punishment, which instead of correcting, makes him more obdurate.

The punishment of death is pernicious to society, from the example of barbarity it affords. If the passions, or the necessity of war, have taught men to shed the blood of their fellow creatures, the laws, which are intended to moderate the ferocity of mankind, should not increase it by examples of barbarity, the more horrible as this punishment is usually attended with formal pageantry. Is it not absurd, that the laws, which detest and punish homicide, should, in order to prevent murder, publicly commit murder them selves? What are the true and most useful laws? Those compacts and conditions which all would propose and observe in those moments when private interest is silent, or combined with that of the public. What are the natural sentiments of every person concerning the punishment of death? We may read them in the contempt and indignation with which every one looks on the executioner, who is nevertheless an innocent executor of the public will, a good citizen, who contributes to the advantage of society, the instrument of the general security within, as good soldiers are without. What then is the origin of this contradiction? Why is this sentiment of mankind indelible to the scandal of reason? It is, that, in a secret corner, of the mind, in which the original impressions of nature are still preserved, men discover a sentiment which tells them, that their lives are not lawfully in the power of any one, but of that necessity only which with its iron sceptre rules the universe.

What must men think, when they see wise magistrates and grave ministers of justice, with indifference and tranquillity, dragging a criminal to death, and whilst a wretch trembles with agony, expecting the fatal stroke, the judge, who has condemned him, with the coldest insensibility, and perhaps with no small gratification from the exertion of his authority, quits his tribunal, to enjoy the comforts and pleasures of life? They will say, "Ah! those cruel formalities of justice are a cloak to tyranny, they are a secret language, a solemn veil, intended to conceal the sword by which we are sacrificed to the insatiable idol of despotism. Murder, which they would represent to us an horrible crime, we see practised by them without repugnance or remorse. Let us follow their example. A violent death appeared terrible in their descriptions, but we see that it is the affair of a moment. It will be still less terrible to him who, not expecting it, escapes almost all the pain." Such is the fatal though absurd reasonings of men who are disposed to commit crimes, on whom the abuse of religion has more influence than religion itself.

If it be objected, that almost all nations in all ages have punished certain crimes with death, I answer, that the force of these examples vanishes when opposed to truth, against which prescription is urged in vain. The history of mankind is an immense sea of errors, in which a few obscure truths may here and there be found.

But human sacrifices have also been common in almost all nations. That some societies only either few in number, or for a very short time, abstained from the

202

AN ESSAY ON CRIMES AND PUNISHMENTS

punishment of death, is rather favourable to my argument; for such is the fate of great truths, that their duration is only as a flash of lightning in the long and dark night of error. The happy time is not yet arrived, when truth, as falsehood has been hitherto, shall be the portion of the greatest number.

I am sensible that the voice of one philosopher is too weak to be heard amidst the clamours of a multitude, blindly influenced by custom; but there is a small number of sages scattered on the face of the earth, who will echo to me from the bottom of their hearts; and if these truths should happily force their way to the thrones of princes be it known to them, that they come attended with the secret wishes of all mankind; and tell the sovereign who deigns them a gracious reception, that his fame shall outshine the glory of conquerors, and that equitable posterity will exalt his peaceful trophies above those of a Titus, an Antoninus, or a Trajan.

How happy were mankind if laws were now to be first formed! now that we see on the thrones of Europe benevolent monarchs, friends to the virtues of peace, to the arts and sciences, fathers of their people, though crowned, yet citizens; the increase of whose authority augments the happiness of their subjects, by destroying that intermediate despotism which intercepts the prayers of the people to the throne. If these humane princes have suffered the old laws to subsist, it is doubtless because the are deterred by the numberless obstacles which oppose the subversion of errors established by the sanction of many ages; and therefore every wise citizen will wish for the increase of their authority.

25

ADAM FERGUSON (1723–1816), *AN ESSAY ON THE HISTORY OF CIVIL SOCIETY*

(Dublin: Boulter Grierson, 1767), pp. 85–98

Adam Ferguson was a Scottish philosopher and historian, and the son of a minister. He wrote several works on political economy and ethics, often drawing on classical works and travel literature to reflect on a human nature where 'fellow feeling' was the key human characteristic. His *Essay on the History of Civil Society* offers a history of the human race and the development of political systems, as well as their downfall. In the sections below, he argues that the happiness of the nation is produced through its system of government, but that the latter needs to be adapted to the characteristics of the people. The book reflects a growing concern in Enlightenment philosophy with the idea that 'happiness' could be produced through secular human activities and systems of governance, not just aspired to as a spiritual benefit, and that humans could be defined as 'nations' or groupings based on their characteristics or identities and that such groupings could have collective emotions.

. . .

Sect. IX: Of national felicity

MAN is, by nature, the member of a community; and when considered in this capacity, the individual appears to be no longer made for himself. He must forego his happiness and his freedom, where these interfere with the good of society. He is only part of a whole; and the praise we think due to his virtue, is but a branch of that more general commendation we bestow on the member of a body, on the part of a fabric, or engine, for being well fitted to occupy its place, and to produce its effect.

If this follow from the relation of a part to its whole, and if the public good be the principal object with individuals, it is likewise true, that the happiness of individuals is the great end of civil society: for, in what sense can a public enjoy any good, if its members, considered apart, be unhappy?

The interests of society, however, and of its members, are easily reconciled. If the individual owe every degree of consideration to the public, he receives, in paying that very consideration, the greatest happiness of which his nature is capable; and the greatest blessing the public can bestow on its members, is to keep them attached to itself. That is the most happy state, which is most beloved by its subjects; and they are the most happy men, whose hearts are engaged to a community, in which they find every object of generosity and zeal, and a scope to the exercise of every talent, and of every virtuous disposition.

After we have thus found general maxims, the greater part of our trouble remains, their just application to particular cases. Nations are different in respect to their extent, numbers of people, and wealth; in respect to the arts they practise, and the accommodations they have procured. These circumstances may not only affect the manners of men; they even, in our esteem, come into competition with the article of manners itself; are supposed to constitute a national felicity, independent of virtue; and give a title, upon which we indulge our own vanity, and that of other nations, as we do that of private men, on the score of their fortunes and honours.

But if this way of measuring happiness, when applied to private men, be ruinous and false, it is so no less when applied to nations. Wealth, commerce, extent of territory, and the knowledge of arts, are, when properly employed, the means of preservation, and the foundations of power. If they fail in part, the nation is weakened; if they were entirely with-held, the race would perish: Their tendency is to maintain numbers of men, but not to constitute happiness. They will accordingly maintain the wretched as well as the happy. They answer one purpose, but are not therefore sufficient for all; and are of little significance, when only employed to maintain a timid, dejected, and servile people.

Great and powerful states are able to overcome and subdue the weak; polished and commercial nations have more wealth, and practise a greater variety of arts, than the rude: But the happiness of men, in all cases alike, consists in the blessings of a candid, an active, and strenuous mind. And if we consider the state of society merely as that into which mankind are led by their propensities, as a state to be valued from its effect in preserving the species, in ripening their talents, and exciting their virtues, we need not enlarge our communities, in order to enjoy these advantages. We frequently obtain them in the most remarkable degree, where nations remain independent, and are of a small extent.

To increase the numbers of mankind, may be admitted as a great and important object: But to extend the limits of any particular state, is not, perhaps, the way to obtain it; while we desire that our fellow-creatures should multiply, it does not follow, that the whole should, if possible, be united under one head. We are apt to admire the empire of the Romans, as a model of national greatness and splendour: But the greatness we admire in this case, was ruinous to the virtue and the happiness of mankind; it was found to be inconsistent with all the advantages which that conquering people had formerly enjoyed in the articles of government and manners.

The emulation of nations proceeds from their division. A cluster of states, like a company of men, find the exercise of their reason, and the test of their virtues,

205

in the affairs they transact, upon a foot of equality, and of separate interest. The measures taken for safety, including great part of the national policy, are relative in every state to what is apprehended from abroad. Athens was necessary to Sparta in the exercise of her virtue, as steel is to flint in the production of fire; and if the cities of Greece had been united under one head, we should never have heard of Epaminondas or Thrasybulus, of Lycurgus or Solon.

When we reason in behalf of our species, therefore, although we may lament the abuses which sometimes arise from independence, and opposition of interest; yet, whilst any degrees of virtue remain with mankind, we cannot wish to crowd, under one establishment, numbers of men who may serve to constitute several; or to commit affairs to the conduct of one senate, one legislative or executive power, which, upon a distinct and separate footing, might furnish an exercise of ability, and a theatre of glory to many.

This may be a subject upon which no determinate rule can be given; but the admiration of boundless dominion is a ruinous error; and in no instance, perhaps, is the real interest of mankind more entirely mistaken.

The measure of enlargement to be wished for in any particular state, is often to be taken from the condition of its neighbours. Where a number of states are contiguous, they should be near an equality, in order that they may be mutually objects of respect and consideration, and in order that they may possess that independence in which the political life of a nation consists.

When the kingdoms of Spain were united, when the great fiefs in France were annexed to the crown, it was no longer expedient for the nations of Great Britain to continue disjoined.

The small republics of Greece, indeed, by their subdivisions, and the balance of their power, found almost in every village the object of nations. Every little district was a nursery of excellent men, and what is now the wretched corner of a great empire, was the field on which mankind have reaped their principal honours. But in modern Europe, republics of a similar extent are like shrubs, under the shade of a taller wood, choaked by the neighbourhood of more powerful states. In their case, a certain disproportion of force frustrates, in a great measure, the advantage of separation. They are like the trader in Poland, who is the more despicable, and the less secure, that he is neither master nor slave.

Independent communities, in the mean time, however weak, are averse to a coalition, not only where it comes with an air of imposition, or unequal treaty, but even where it implies no more than the admission of new members to an equal share of consideration with the old. The citizen has no interest in the annexation of kingdoms; he must find his importance diminished, as the state is enlarged: But ambitious men, under the enlargement of territory, find a more plentiful harvest of power, and of wealth, while government itself is an easier task. Hence the ruinous progress of empire; and hence free nations, under the shew of acquiring dominion, suffer themselves, in the end, to be yoked with the slaves they had conquered.

Our desire to augment the force of a nation is the only pretext for enlarging its territory; but this measure, when pursued to extremes, seldom fails to frustrate itself.

Notwithstanding the advantage of numbers, and superior resources in war, the strength of a nation is derived from the character, not from the wealth, nor from the multitude of its people. If the treasure of a state can hire numbers of men, erect ramparts, and furnish the implements of war; the possessions of the fearful are easily seized; a timorous multitude falls into rout of itself; ramparts may be scaled where they are not defended by valour; and arms are of consequence only in the hands of the brave. The band to which Agesilaus pointed as the wall of his city, made a defence for their country more permanent, and more effectual, than the rock and the cement with which other cities were fortified.

We should owe little to that statesman who were to contrive a defence that might supersede the external uses of virtue. It is wisely ordered for man, as a rational being, that the employment of reason is necessary to his preservation; it is fortunate for him, in the pursuit of distinction, that his personal consideration depends on his character; and it is fortunate for nations, that, in order to be powerful and safe, they must strive to maintain the courage, and cultivate the virtues, of their people. By the use of such means, they at once gain their external ends, and are happy.

Peace and unanimity are commonly considered as the principal foundations of public felicity; yet the rivalship of separate communities, and the agitations of a free people, are the principles of political life, and the school of men. How shall we reconcile these jarring and opposite tenets? It is, perhaps, not necessary to reconcile them. The pacific may do what they can to allay the animosities, and to reconcile the opinions, of men; and it will be happy if they can succeed in repressing their crimes, and in calming the worst of their passions. Nothing, in the mean time, but corruption or slavery can suppress the debates that subsist among men of integrity, who bear an equal part in the administration of state.

A perfect agreement in matters of opinion is not to be obtained in the most select company; and if it were, what would become of society? "The Spartan legislator," says Plutarch, "appears to have sown the seeds of variance and dissention among his countrymen: he meant that good citizens should be led to dispute; he considered emulation as the brand by which their virtues were kindled; and seemed to apprehend, that a complaisance, by which men submit their opinions without examination, is a principal source of corruption."

Forms of government are supposed to decide of the happiness or misery of mankind. But forms of government must be varied, in order to suit the extent, the way of subsistence, the character, and the manners of different nations. In some cases, the multitude may be suffered to govern themselves; in others they must be severely restrained. The inhabitants of a village, in some primitive age, may have been safely intrusted to the conduct of reason, and to the suggestion of their innocent views; but the tenants of Newgate can scarcely be trusted, with chains locked

POLITICS AND LAW

to their bodies, and bars of iron fixed to their legs. How is it possible, therefore, to find any single form of government that would suit mankind in every condition?

We proceed, however, in the following section, to point out the distinctions, and to explain the language which occurs in this place, on the head of different models for subordination and government.

Sect. X: The same subject continued

IT is a common observation, That mankind were originally equal. They have indeed by nature equal rights to their preservation, and to the use of their talents; but they are fitted for different stations; and when they are classed by a rule taken from this circumstance, they suffer no injustice on the side of their natural rights. It is obvious, that some mode of subordination is as necessary to men as society itself; and this, not only to attain the ends of government, but to comply with an order established by nature.

Prior to any political institution whatever, men are qualified by a great diversity of talents, by a different tone of the soul, and ardour of the passions, to act a variety of parts. Bring them together, each will find his place. They censure or applaud in a body; they consult and deliberate in more select parties; they take or give an ascendant as individuals; and numbers are by this means fitted to act in company, and to preserve their communities, before any formal distribution of office is made.

We are formed to act in this manner; and if we have any doubts with relation to the rights of government in general, we owe our perplexity more to the subtilties of the speculative, than to any uncertainty in the feelings of the heart. Involved in the resolutions of our company, we move with the crowd before we have determined the rule by which its will is collected. We follow a leader, before we have settled the ground of his pretensions, or adjusted the form of his election: and it is not till after mankind have committed many errors in the capacities of magistrate and subject, that they think of making government itself a subject of rules.

If, therefore, in considering the variety of forms under which societies subsist, the casuist is pleased to inquire, What title one man, or any number of men, have to controul his actions? he may be answered, None at all, provided that his actions have no effect to the prejudice of his fellow-creatures; but if they have, the rights of defence, and the obligation to repress the commission of wrongs, belong to collective bodies, as well as to individuals. Many rude nations, having no formal tribunals for the judgment of crimes, assemble, when alarmed by any flagrant offence, and take their measures with the criminal as they would with an enemy.

But will this consideration, which confirms the title to sovereignty, where it is exercised by the society in its collective capacity, or by those to whom the powers of the whole are committed, likewise support the claim to dominion, wherever it is casually lodged, or even where it is only maintained by force?

This question may be sufficiently answered, by observing, that a right to do justice, and to do good, is competent to every individual, or order of men; and that the exercise of this right has no limits but in the defect of power. Whoever, therefore, has power, may employ it to this extent; and no previous convention is required to justify his conduct. But a right to do wrong, or to commit injustice, is an abuse of language, and a contradiction in terms. It is no more competent to the collective body of a people, than it is to any single usurper. When we admit such a prerogative in the case of any sovereign, we can only mean to express the extent of his power, and the force with which he is enabled to execute his pleasure. Such a prerogative is assumed by the leader of banditti at the head of his gang, or by a despotic prince at the head of his troops. When the sword is presented by either, the traveller or the inhabitant may submit from a sense of necessity or fear; but he lies under no obligation from a motive of duty or justice.

The multiplicity of forms, in the mean time, which different societies offer to our view, is almost infinite. The classes into which they distribute their members, the manner in which they establish the legislative and executive powers, the imperceptible circumstances by which they are led to have different customs, and to confer on their governors unequal measures of power and authority, give rise to perpetual distinctions between constitutions the most nearly resembling each other, and give to human affairs a variety in detail, which, in its full extent, no understanding can comprehend, and no memory retain.

In order to have a general and comprehensive knowledge of the whole, we must be determined on this, as on every other subject, to overlook many particulars and singularities, distinguishing different governments; to fix our attention on certain points, in which many agree; and thereby establish a few general heads, under which the subject may be distinctly considered. When we have marked the characteristics which form the general points of co-incidence; when we have pursued them to their consequences in the several modes of legislation, execution, and judicature, in the establishments which relate to police, commerce, religion, or domestic life; we have made an acquisition of knowledge, which, though it does not supersede the necessity of experience, may serve to direct our inquiries, and, in the midst of affairs, give an order and a method for the arrangement of particulars that occur to our observation.

When I recollect what the President Montesquieu has written, I am at a loss to tell, why I should treat of human affairs: But I too am instigated by my reflections, and my sentiments; and I may utter them more to the comprehension of ordinary capacities, because I am more on the level of ordinary men. If it be necessary to pave the way for what follows on the general history of nations, by giving some account of the heads under which various forms of government may be conveniently ranged, the reader should perhaps be referred to what has been already delivered on the subject by this profound politician and amiable moralist. In his writings will be found, not only the original of what I am now, for the sake of order, to copy from him, but likewise probably the source of many observations, which, in different places, I may, under the belief of invention, have repeated, without quoting their author.

The ancient philosophers treated of government commonly under three heads; the Democratic, the Aristocratic, and the Despotic. Their attention was chiefly occupied with the varieties of republican government, and they paid little regard to a very important distinction, which Mr. Montesquieu[1] has made, between despotism and monarchy. He too has considered government as reducible to three general forms; and, "to understand the nature of each," he observes, "it is sufficient to recal ideas which are familiar with men of the least reflection, who admit three definitions, or rather three facts: That a republic is a state in which the people in a collective body, or a part of the people, possess the sovereign power: That monarchy is that in which one man governs, according to fixed and determinate laws: And a despotism is that in which one man, without law, or rule of administration, by the mere impulse of will or caprice, decides, and carries every thing before him."

Republics admit of a very material distinction, which is pointed out in the general definition; that between democracy and aristocracy. In the first, supreme power remains in the hands of the collective body. Every office of magistracy, at the nomination of this sovereign, is open to every citizen; who, in the discharge of his duty, becomes the minister of the people, and accountable to them for every object of his trust.

In the second, the sovereignty is lodged in a particular class, or order of men; who, being once named, continue for life; or, by the hereditary distinctions of birth and fortune, are advanced to a station of permanent superiority. From this order, and by their nomination, all the offices of magistracy are filled; and in the different assemblies which they constitute, whatever relates to the legislation, the execution, or jurisdiction, is finally determined.

Mr. Montesquieu has pointed out the sentiments or maxims from which men must be supposed to act under these different governments.

In democracy, they must love equality; they must respect the rights of their fellow-citizens; they must unite by the common ties of affection to the state. In forming personal pretensions, they must be satisfied with that degree of consideration they can procure by their abilities fairly measured with those of an opponent; they must labour for the public without hope of profit; they must reject every attempt to create a personal dependence. Candour, force, and elevation of mind, in short, are the props of democracy; and virtue is the principle of conduct required to its preservation.

How beautiful a pre-eminence on the side of popular government! and how ardently should mankind wish for the form, if it tended to establish the principle, or were, in every instance, a sure indication of its presence!

Note

1 Charles-Louis de Secondat, Baron de La Brède et de Montesquieu (1689–1755).

26

CATHERINE II (1729–1796), *THE GRAND INSTRUCTIONS TO THE COMMISSIONERS APPOINTED TO FRAME A NEW CODE OF LAWS FOR THE RUSSIAN EMPIRE*

Trans. Michael Tatischeff
(London: T. Jeffreys, 1768), pp. 112–113,
115–118, 121–124, 125–127, 137–141

Catherine the Great was the Empress of Russia, after overthrowing her husband Peter III.[1] Born in modern-day Poland, she was a member of the German aristocracy and highly educated. Catherine was committed to modernising Russia along Enlightenment principles, manifested, amongst other things, in her penal reform. The excepts below are taken from her instructions for a new code of laws, designed to be used by lawmakers in Russia but published in many languages (including English as seen here) and so contributing to a European conversation on penal reform. The work is influenced by Beccaria's writing (source 24) and evidences the same imagining of the sensible body, the imagination, and the need for moderate punishment. Like Ferguson (source 25), she also reflects on modes of governance and how to enable the general health and happiness of her people. Here emotions can belong to individuals and so the law and punishment should adapt to human nature, but the nation, and particularly its rulers, are also held responsible for reducing suffering and enabling general felicity.

. . .

184 It is highly necessary in all Laws, *to specify exactly* the principal Rules upon which the *Credibility* of the Evidence depends, and the *Strength* of the Proof required for every Crime.

185 Every Man of good Sense, that is, whose Ideas have a Connection with each other, and whose Sensations sympathize with the Sensations of those who are like himself, is qualified to be a Witness. But the Credit due to his Evidence will be exactly *in Proportion*, as he *is interested* in declaring,

POLITICS AND LAW

or concealing the Truth. Credit must be given to Witnesses in every Case, where they have no Reason to give a false Testimony.

. . .

192 Q.3. Whether the Torture of the Rack does not violate the Rules of Equity; and whether it produces the End proposed by the Laws?

193 The Torture of the Rack is a Cruelty, established and made use of by many Nations, and is applied to the Party accused during the Course of his Trial, either to extort from him a Confession of his Guilt, or in order to clear up some Contradictions, in which he had involved himself during his Examination, or to compel him to discover his Accomplices, or in order to discover other Crimes, of which, though he is not accused, yet he may *perhaps* be guilty.

194 (1.) No Man ought to be looked upon as *guilty*, before he has received his judicial Sentence; nor can the Laws deprive him of *their* Protection, before it is proved that he has *forfeited all Right* to it. What Right therefore can Power give to any to inflict Punishment upon a Citizen at a Time, when it is yet dubious, whether he is *innocent* or *guilty*? Whether the Crime be known or unknown, it is not very difficult to gain a thorough Knowledge of the Affair by duly weighing all the Circumstances. If the Crime be known, the Criminal ought not to suffer any Punishment but what the Law ordains; consequently the Rack is quite unnecessary. If the Crime be not known, the Rack ought not to be applied to the Party accused; for this Reason, *That the Innocent ought not to be tortured*; and, in the Eye of the Law, every Person is innocent whose Crime is not yet *proved*. It is undoubtedly extremely necessary, that no Crime, after it has been proved, should remain unpunished. The Party accused on the Rack, whilst in the Agonies of Torture, is not Master enough of himself to be able to declare the Truth. Can we give more Credit to a Man, when he is light-headed in a Fever, than when he enjoys the free Use of his Reason in a State of Health? The Sensation of Pain may arise to such a Height, that, after having subdued the whole Soul, it will leave her no longer the Liberty of producing any proper Act of the Will, except that of taking the shortest instantaneous Method, in the very twinkling of an Eye, as it were, of getting rid of her Torment. In such an Extremity, even an *innocent* Person will roar out, that he is *guilty*, only to gain *some Respite* from his Tortures. Thus the very same Expedient, which is made use of to distinguish the Innocent from the Guilty, will take away the *whole Difference* between them; and the Judges will be as uncertain, whether they have an *innocent* or a *guilty* Person before them, as they were before the Beginning of this *partial* Way of Examination. The Rack, therefore, is a sure Method of condemning an *innocent* Person of a weakly Constitution, and of acquitting a *wicked Wretch*, who depends upon the Robustness of his Frame.

195 (2.) The Rack is likewise made use of to oblige the Party accused to clear up (as they term it) the Contradictions in which he has involved himself in the

GRAND INSTRUCTIONS TO THE COMMISSIONERS

Course of his Examination; as if the Dread of Punishment, the Uncertainty and Anxiety in determining what to say, and even gross Ignorance itself, common to both *Innocent* and *Guilty*, could not lead a timorous *Innocent*, and a *Delinquent*, who seeks to hide his Villanies, into Contradictions; and as if Contradictions, which are so common to Man even in a State of Ease and Tranquillity, would not increase in that Perturbation of Soul, when he is plunged entirely in Reflections, how to escape the Danger he is threatened with.

196 (3.) To make use of the Rack for discovering, whether the Party accused has not committed *other* Crimes, besides *that* which he has been *convicted* of, is a certain Expedient to *screen every Crime* from its proper Punishment: For a Judge will always be discovering new Ones. Finally, this Method of Proceeding will be founded upon the following Way of reasoning: *Thou art guilty of one Crime, therefore, perhaps, thou hast committed an Hundred others: According to the Laws, thou wilt be tortured and tormented; not only because thou art guilty, but even because thou mayest be still more guilty.*

197 (4.) Besides this, the Party accused is tortured, to oblige him to discover his Accomplices. But when we have already proved, that the Rack cannot be the proper Means for searching out the Truth, then how can it give any Assistance in discovering the Accomplices in a Crime? It is undoubtedly extremely easy for him, who accuses himself, to accuse others. Besides, is it just to torture one Man for the Crimes of others? Might not the Accomplices be discovered by examining the Witnesses, who were produced against the Criminal? by a strict Inquiry into the Proofs alledged against him, and even by the Nature of the Fact itself, and the Circumstances which happened at the Time when the Crime was committed? In short, by all the Means which serve to prove the Delinquent guilty of the Crime he had committed?

. . .

204 Q.5. *What is the proper Estimate of the Degrees of Crimes?*

205 The Intent of well-regulated Punishments, is not merely to torment a sensible Being: They are ordained for this wise End; which is, to prevent a Criminal from doing *farther* Injury to the Community for the future; and to *deter* his fellow Citizens from committing the *like* Offences. For this Reason, such Punishments, and *such a Mode* of inflicting them, ought to be selected, as will make the *deepest* and most *durable* Impression on the Minds of the People, and at the same Time with the *least* Cruelty to the Body of the Criminal.

206 Who can read, without being struck with Horror, the History of so many barbarous and useless Tortures, invented and executed without the least Remorse of Conscience, by *People* who assumed to themselves the *Name of Sages*? Who does not feel within himself a sensible Palpitation of the Heart, at the Sight of so many Thousands of unhappy Wretches, who have suffered, and still suffer: *frequently* accused of Crimes, which are *difficult, or*

213

POLITICS AND LAW

impossible to happen, proceeding often from I*gnorance*, and some-times from *Superstition*? Who can look, I say, upon the Dismembering of these People, who are executed with *slow* and *studied* Barbarity, by the *very Persons* who are *their Brethren*? Countries and Times, in which the most *cruel Punishments* were made use of, are those, in which the most *inhuman Villainies* were perpetrated.

207   That a Punishment may produce the *desired* Effect, it will be sufficient; when the *Evil* it occasions exceeds the *Good* expected from the Crime, including in the Calculation the *Excess* of the Evil *over* the Good, the undoubted *Certainty* of the Punishment, and the *Privation* of all the *Advantages* hoped for from the Crime. All Severity *exceeding* these Bounds is *useless*, and consequently *tyrannical*.

208   Wherever the Laws have been extremely severe, they have either been altered, or the Impunity of the Criminals arose from the very Severity of the Laws. The *Degrees* of Punishment ought to be referred to the present *Situation* and *Circumstances* in which every People finds itself. In *Proportion* as the *Minds* of those who live in a Community become *enlightened*, the *Sensibility* of every Individual *increases*; and if Sensibility increases amongst the Citizens, then the *Severity* of Punishments must *abate* in Proportion.

209   Q. 6. *Whether the Punishment of* Death *is really useful and necessary in a Community for the Preservation of Peace and good Order?*

210   Proofs from Fact demonstrate to us, that the frequent Use of capital Punishment never mended the Morals of a People. Therefore, if *I* prove the *Death* of a Citizen to be neither *useful* nor *necessary to Society in general*, I shall confute *those* who *rise up against* Humanity. I repeat here, *to Society in general*; because the Death of a Citizen can *only* be useful and necessary in *one* Case; which is, when, though he be *deprived* of Liberty, yet he has *such Power* by his *Connections*, as may *enable* him to raise Disturbances dangerous to the publick Peace. This Case can happen only, when a People either loses, or recovers their Liberty; or in a Time of Anarchy, when the *Disorders* themselves hold the *Place* of Laws. But in a Reign of Peace and Tranquillity, under a Government established with the united Wishes of a whole People; in a State well fortified against external Enemies, and protected within by strong Supports; that is, by its own internal Strength and virtuous Sentiments rooted in the Minds of the Citizens; and where the whole Power is lodged in the Hands of a Monarch; in such a State, there can be *no* Necessity for *taking away the Life* of a Citizen. The twenty Years Reign of the Empress *ELIZABETH PETROVNA* gives the Fathers of the People a more illustrious Example for Imitation than a Reign of the most shining Conquests.

211   It is not the *Excess* of Severity, nor the *Destruction* of the human Species, that produce a powerful Effect in the Hearts of the Citizens, but the *continued Duration* of the Punishment.

212   The Death of a Malefactor is not so efficacious a Method of deterring from Wickedness, as the *Example continually remaining* of a Man, who is deprived

214

GRAND INSTRUCTIONS TO THE COMMISSIONERS

of his Liberty for *this End*, that he might *repair*, during a Life of *Labour*, the *Injury* he has done to the Community. The Terror of Death, excited by the Imagination, may be more strong, but has not Force enough to resist that *Oblivion*, so natural to Mankind. It is a general Rule, that rapid and violent Impressions on the human Mind, *disturb* and *give Pain*, but do not operate long upon the Memory. That a Punishment, therefore, might be conformable with Justice, it ought to have such a Degree of Severity only, as might be sufficient to *deter* People from committing the Crime. Thence *I* presume to affirm, that there is no Man who, upon the least Degree of Reflection, would put the *greatest possible* Advantages he might flatter himself with from a Crime *on the one Side*, into the Balance against a Life *protracted* under a *total* Privation of Liberty, *on the other*.

. . .

217 Great Care ought to be taken not to inflict corporal and painful Punishments upon those, who are infected with the Vice of Enthusiasm, either by pretending to Inspiration, or by counterfeiting a false Appearance of Sanctity. This Vice, founded upon Pride, and puffed up by Self-conceit, will derive *Glory*, and *fresh* Nourishment from the *very* Punishment itself. There have been Instances of this in the late *secret Chancery where such Persons used to come voluntarily on particular Days, merely for the Sake of suffering Punishment.*

213 *Infamy* and *Ridicule*, are the *only* Punishments which ought to be employed against these *pretendedly* inspired, and *counterfeit* Saints. For these may *abase* their *Pride*; and wise Laws, by opposing *those* Forces with Forces of the *same Kind*, will scatter, like Dust, that Admiration of these *false Doctrines*, which may *nestle* in the *weak* Minds of the Populace.

219 *Infamy* ought not be inflicted upon a *Number* of Persons at once.

220 A Punishment ought to be *immediate, analogous* to the *Nature* of the Crime, and *known* to the Publick.

221 The *sooner* the Punishment succeeds to the Commission of a Crime, the *more useful* and *just* it will be. *Just*; because it will spare the Malefactor the torturing, and useless Anguish of Heart about the *Uncertainty* of his Destiny. Consequently the Decision of an Affair, in a Court of Judicature, ought to be finished in as little Time as possible. *I have said before, that Punishment immediately inflicted is most useful*; the Reason is, because the *smaller* the Interval of Time is, which passes between the Crime and the Punishment, the more the Crime will be esteemed as a *Motive* to the Punishment, and the Punishment as an *Effect* of the Crime. Punishment must be *certain* and *unavoidable*.

222 The most certain Curb upon Crimes, is not the *Severity* of the Punishment, but the absolute Conviction in the People, that Delinquents will be *inevitably* punished.

223 The *Certainty* even of a small, but *inevitable* Punishment, will make a *stronger* Impression on the Mind, than the *Dread* even of *capital* Punishment,

POLITICS AND LAW

connected with the Hopes of escaping it. As Punishments become *more* mild and moderate; Mercy and Pardon will be *less* necessary in Proportion, for the Laws themselves, at such a Time, are replete with the *Spirit* of Mercy.

. . .

264 *Of the Propagation of the human Species in a State.*
265 Russia is not only *greatly* deficient in the *number* of her Inhabitants; but at the same Time, extends her Dominion over *immense* Tracts of Land; which are neither peopled nor improved. And therefore, in a Country so circumstanced, *too much* Encouragement can never be given to the *Propagation* of the human Species.
266 The Peasants generally have twelve, fifteen, and even twenty Children by one Marriage; but it rarely happens, that one Fourth of these ever attains to the *Age* of Maturity. There must therefore be some Fault, either in their Nourriture, in their Way of Living, or Method of Education, which occasions this *prodigious* Loss, and disappoints the *Hopes* of the Empire. How flourishing would the State of this Empire be, if we could but ward off, or prevent this fatal Evil by proper Regulations!
267 You must add too to *this*, that two Hundred Years are now elapsed, since a *Disease* unknown to our Ancestors was imported from America, and *hurried* on the Destruction of the human Race. This Disease spreads *wide* its *mournful* and *destructive* Effects in *many* of our Provinces. The utmost Care ought to be taken of the Health of the Citizens. It would be highly prudent, therefore, to stop the Progress of this Disease by the Laws.
268 Those of Moses may serve here for an Example. Levitic. chap. xiii.
269 It seems too, that the Method of exacting their Revenues, *newly* invented by the Lords, diminishes both the *Inhabitants*, and the *Spirit of Agriculture* in Russia. Almost all the Villages are *heavily* taxed. The Lords, who seldom or never *reside* in their Villages, lay an Impost on every Head of one, two, and even five Rubles, without the least Regard to the *Means* by which their Peasants may be able to *raise* this Money.
270 It is highly necessary that the Law should prescribe a Rule to the Lords, for a more judicious Method of raising their Revenues; and oblige them to levy *such* a Tax, as *tends least* to separate the Peasant from his House and Family; this would be the Means by which Agriculture would become more extensive, and Population be more increased in the Empire.
271 Even now some Husbandmen do not see their Houses for fifteen Years together, and yet pay the Tax annually to their respective Lords; which they procure in Towns at a vast Distance from their Families, and wander over the whole Empire for that Purpose.
272 The more happily a People live under a Government, the more easily the Number of the Inhabitants increases.
273 Countries, which abound with Meadow and Pasture Lands, are generally *very thinly* peopled; the Reason is, that *few* can find Employment in those

GRAND INSTRUCTIONS TO THE COMMISSIONERS

Places: But arable Lands are much *more* populous; because they *furnish* Employment for a *much greater* Number of People.

274 Wherever the Inhabitants can enjoy the Conveniences of Life, there Population will certainly increase.

275 *But a Country, which is so overwhelmed with Taxes, that the People, with all their Care and Industry can with the utmost Difficultys and Means for procuring a bare Subsistance, will, in length of Time, be deserted by its Inhabitants,*

276 Where a People is poor for no other Reason, but because they live under oppressive Laws, and esteem their Lands not so much a *Fund* for their Maintainance, as a *Pretence* for their Oppression; in such places, the Inhabitants cannot increase. They have not the Means of Subsistance sufficient for themselves, how then can they think of yielding a Part of it to their Offspring? They are not able to take Care of *themselves*, even in their *own* Illness; how then can they bring up and look after *Creatures*, which are in a State of *continual* Illness, that is, *Infancy*? They bury their Money in the Earth, and are afraid to let it circulate; and they fear to appear rich, because their Wealth might expose them to Persecution and Oppression.

277 The Ease of asserting, and the Incapacity for thoroughly examining an Affair, have induced many to affirm, *That the poorer the Subjects live, the more numerous their Families will be; and the heavier the Taxes are, the more readily they will find the Means of paying them.* These are two Sophisms, which ever did, and ever will bring Destruction upon Monarchies.

278 The Evil is almost incurable, when the Depopulation of the Country has been of long standing, from some internal Defect in the Constitution, and a bad Administration. The People drop off there by an imperceptible and almost habitual Malady. Born in Languor and Misery, under the Oppression, or false Maxims adopted by Government, they see themselves destroyed frequently, without perceiving the Causes of their Destruction.

279 In order to re-establish a State stripped in such a Manner of its Inhabitants, it will be in vain to expect Assistance from the Children, which may be born in future. This Hope is totally over: People in their Desart have neither Courage nor Industry. Lands, which might feed a whole People, can scarce yield Food for a single Family. The common People in those Parts have no *Share* even in that, which is the Cause of their Misery; that is, the Lands which lie fallow and uncultivated, with which the Country abounds; either some of the principal Citizens, or the Sovereign, insensibly ingross the *whole Extent* of these desert Countries. The ruined Families have *left* their Oppressors the *whole* for *Pastures*, and the laborious Man has nothing.

Note

1 Thanks to Deborah Simonton for suggesting this source.

27

PATRICK HENRY (1736–1799), *SHALL LIBERTY OR EMPIRE BE SOUGHT?* A SPEECH GIVEN ON 5 JUNE 1788 AT THE VIRGINIA CONVENTION TO RATIFY THE CONSTITUTION OF THE UNITED STATES

Patrick Henry was an American planter, politician and 'founding father' of the United States of America. He was a known orator, who gave several speeches in support of American independence and in debates around the form that the new constitution should take. Effective oratory required not only skilled rhetoric but the capacity to perform well and capture the attention and interest of audiences. This could be a physical feat in an era before the voice could be enhanced through microphones. At the Virginia Convention, where the US constitution was eventually ratified, Henry led the opposition to endorsing the constitution in the proposed form. As he argued in the speech below, the constitution gave too much power to the federal government, and especially to the new role of President; he thought that this was too like monarchy and that power should primarily be vested in the states. The Convention was well attended by the public and the press, and the speeches given there were quickly circulated for the public in pamphlets and newspapers. The speech below highlights how emotional language can be used as part of persuasive discourse, but also how rhythm, style, and argument itself, can be used to shape the emotions of listeners, and later, readers.

. . .

THIS, sir, is the language of democracy – that a majority of the community have a right to alter government when found to be oppressive. But how different is the genius of your new Constitution from this! How different from the sentiments of freemen that a contemptible minority can prevent the good of the majority! If, then, gentlemen standing on this ground are come to that point, that they are willing to bind themselves and their posterity to be oppressed, I am amazed and inexpressibly astonished. If this be the opinion of the majority, I must submit; but

SHALL LIBERTY OR EMPIRE BE SOUGHT?

to me, sir, it appears perilous and destructive. I can not help thinking so. Perhaps it may be the result of my age. These may be feelings natural to a man of my years, when the American spirit has left him, and his mental powers, like the members of the body, are decayed. If, sir, amendments are left to the twentieth, or tenth part of the people of America, your liberty is gone for ever.

We have heard that there is a great deal of bribery practised in the House of Commons of England, and that many of the members raise themselves to preferments by selling the rights of the whole of the people. But, sir, the tenth part of that body can not continue oppressions on the rest of the people. English liberty is, in this case, on a firmer foundation than American liberty. It will be easily contrived to procure the opposition of the one-tenth of the people to any alteration, however judicious. The honorable gentleman who presides told us that, to prevent abuses in our government, we will assemble in convention, recall our delegated powers, and punish our servants for abusing the trust reposed in them. Oh, sir! we should have fine times, indeed, if, to punish tyrants, it were only sufficient to assemble the people! Your arms, wherewith you could defend yourselves, are gone; and you have no longer an aristocratical, no longer a democratical spirit. Did you ever read of any revolution in a nation, brought about by the punishment of those in power, inflicted by those who had no power at all? You read of a riot act in a country which is called one of the freest in the world, where a few neighbors can not assemble without the risk of being shot by a hired soldiery, the engines of despotism. We may see such an act in America.

A standing army we shall have, also, to execute the execrable commands of tyranny; and how are you to punish them? Will you order them to be punished? Who shall obey these orders? Will your mace-bearer be a match for a disciplined regiment? In what situation are we to be? The clause before you gives a power of direct taxation, unbounded and unlimited – an exclusive power of legislation, in all cases whatsoever, for ten miles square, and over all places purchased for the erection of forts, magazines, arsenals, dockyards, etc. What resistance could be made? The attempt would be madness. You will find all the strength of this country in the hands of your enemies; their garrisons will naturally be the strongest places in the country. Your militia is given up to Congress, also, in another part of this plan; they will therefore act as they think proper; all power will be in their own possession. You can not force them to receive their punishment: of what service would militia be to you, when, most probably, you will not have a single musket in the State? For, as arms are to be provided by Congress, they may or may not furnish them.

The honorable gentleman then went on to the figure we make with foreign nations; the contemptible one we make in France and Holland, which, according to the substance of the notes, he attributes to the present feeble government. An opinion has gone forth, we find, that we are contemptible people; the time has been when we were thought otherwise. Under the same despised government we commanded the respect of all Europe; wherefore are we now reckoned otherwise? The American spirit has fled from hence: it has gone to regions where it has never

219

been expected; it has gone to the people of France in search of a splendid government, a strong, energetic government. Shall we imitate the example of those nations who have gone from a simple to a splendid government? Are those nations more worthy of our imitation? What can make an adequate satisfaction to them for the loss they have suffered in attaining such a government – for the loss of their liberty? If we admit this consolidated government, it will be because we like a great, splendid one. Some way or other we must be a great and mighty empire; we must have an army, and a navy, and a number of things. When the American spirit was in its youth, the language of America was different; liberty, sir, was then the primary object.

We are descended from a people whose government was founded on liberty; our glorious forefathers of Great Britain made liberty the foundation of everything. That country is become a great, mighty, and splendid nation; not because their government is strong and energetic, but, sir, because liberty is its direct end and foundation. We drew the spirit of liberty from our British ancestors; by that spirit we have triumphed over every difficulty. But now, sir, the American spirit, assisted by the ropes and chains of consolidation, is about to convert this country into a powerful and mighty empire. If you make the citizens of this country agree to become the subjects of one great consolidated empire of America, your government will not have sufficient energy to keep them together. Such a government is incompatible with the genius of republicanism. There will be no checks, no real balances, in this government. What can avail your specious, imaginary balances, your rope-dancing, chain-rattling, ridiculous ideal checks and contrivances? But, sir, "we are not feared by foreigners; we do not make nations tremble." Would this constitute happiness or secure liberty? I trust, sir, our political hemisphere will ever direct their operations to the security of those objects.

Consider our situation, sir; go to the poor man and ask him what he does. He will inform you that he enjoys the fruits of his labor, under his own fig tree, with his wife and children around him, in peace and security. Go to every other member of society; you will find the same tranquil ease and content; you will find no alarms or disturbances. Why, then, tell us of danger, to terrify us into an adoption of this new form of government? And yet who knows the dangers that this new system may produce? They are out of sight of the common people; they can not foresee latent consequences. I dread the operation of it on the middling and lower classes of people; it is for them I fear the adoption of this system. I fear I tire the patience of the committee, but I beg to be indulged with a few more observations.

When I thus profess myself an advocate for the liberty of the people, I shall be told I am a designing man, that I am to be a great man, that I am to be a demagog; and many similar illiberal insinuations will be thrown out; but, sir, conscious rectitude outweighs those things with me. I see great jeopardy in this new government. I see none from our present one. I hope some gentleman or other will bring forth, in full array, those dangers, if there be any, that we may see and touch them. I have said that I thought this a consolidated government; I will now prove it. Will the great rights of the people be secured by this government? Suppose it should prove oppressive, how can it be altered? Our Bill of Rights declares that "a majority of the community hath an indubitable, unalienable, and indefeasible right to reform, alter, or abolish it, in such manner as shall be judged most conducive to the public weal."

The voice of tradition, I trust, will inform posterity of our struggles for freedom. If our descendants be worthy the name of Americans they will preserve and hand down to their latest posterity the transactions of the present times; and tho I confess my exclamations are not worthy the hearing, they will see that I have done my utmost to preserve their liberty, for I never will give up the power of direct taxation but for a scourge. I am willing to give it conditionally – that is, after non-compliance with requisitions. I will do more, sir, and what I hope will convince the most skeptical man that I am a lover of the American Union; that, in case Virginia shall not make punctual payment, the control of our customhouses and the whole regulation of trade shall be given to Congress, and that Virginia shall depend on Congress even for passports, till Virginia shall have paid the last farthing and furnished the last soldier.

Nay, sir, there is another alternative to which I would consent; even that they should strike us out of the Union and take away from us all federal privileges till we comply with federal requisitions; but let it depend upon our own pleasure to pay our money in the most easy manner for our people. Were all the States, more terrible than the mother country, to join against us, I hope Virginia could defend herself; but, sir, the dissolution of the Union is most abhorrent to my mind. The first thing I have at heart is American liberty; the second thing is American union; and I hope the people of Virginia will endeavor to preserve that union. The increasing population of the Southern States is far greater than that of New England; consequently, in a short time, they will be far more numerous than the people of that country. Consider this and you will find this State more particularly interested to support American liberty and not bind our posterity by an improvident relinquishment of our rights. I would give the best security for a punctual compliance with requisitions; but I beseech gentlemen, at all hazards, not to give up this unlimited power of taxation. The honorable gentleman has told us that these powers given to Congress are accompanied by a judiciary which will correct all. On examination you will find this very judiciary oppressively constructed, your jury trial destroyed, and the judges dependent on Congress.

This Constitution is said to have beautiful features; but when I come to examine these features, sir, they appear to me horribly frightful. Among other deformities, it has an awful squinting; it squints toward monarchy, and does not this raise indignation in the breast of every true American? Your president may easily become king. Your Senate is so imperfectly constructed that your dearest rights may be sacrificed to what may be a small minority; and a very small minority may continue for ever unchangeably this government, altho horridly defective. Where are your checks in this government? Your strongholds will be in the hands of your enemies. It is on a supposition that your American governors shall be honest that all the good qualities of this government are founded; but its defective and imperfect construction puts it in their power to perpetrate the worst of mischiefs should they be bad men; and, sir, would not all the world, blame our distracted folly in resting our rights upon the contingency of our rulers being good or bad? Show me that age and country where the rights and liberties of the people were placed on the sole chance of their rulers being good men without a consequent loss of liberty! I say that the loss of that dearest privilege has ever followed, with absolute certainty, every such mad attempt.

If your American chief be a man of ambition and abilities, how easy is it for him to render himself absolute! The army is in his hands, and if he be a man of address, it will be attached to him, and it will be the subject of long meditation with him to seize the first auspicious moment to accomplish his design, and, sir, will the American spirit solely relieve you when this happens? I would rather infinitely – and I am sure most of this Convention are of the same opinion – have a king, lords, and commons, than a government so replete with such insupportable evils. If we make a king we may prescribe the rules by which he shall rule his people, and interpose such checks as shall prevent him from infringing them; but the president, in the field, at the head of his army, can prescribe the terms on which he shall reign master, so far that it will puzzle any American ever to get his neck from under the galling yoke. I can not with patience think of this idea. If ever he violate the laws, one of two things will happen: he will come at the head of the army to carry everything before him, or he will give bail, or do what Mr. Chief Justice will order him. If he be guilty, will not the recollection of his crimes teach him to make one bold push for the American throne? Will not the immense difference between being master of everything an being ignominiously tried and punished powerfully excite him to make this bold push? But, sir, where is the existing force to punish him? Can he not, at the head of his army, beat down every opposition? Away with your president! we shall have a king: the army will salute him monarch; your militia will leave you, and assist in making him king, and fight against you: and what have you to oppose this force? What will then become of you and your rights? Will not absolute despotism ensue?

28

ANDREW GREENFIELD (1750–1788), *THE CAUSE AND CURE OF NATIONAL DISTRESS: A SERMON*

(Edinburgh: William Creech, 1779)

Andrew Greenfield was a Scottish minister, chaplain to the Countess Dowager of Moray, and rector of Moira Presbyterian Church in Northern Ireland. He wrote a number of poems and sermons. The following sermon was written during the American Revolutionary War, between the thirteen original colonies in North America and Great Britain. For many Christians, the success of the nation was closely tied to providence – God's will – and so during times of national distress or success, the community were encouraged to pray, fast or otherwise enact penitence for their sins. In this sermon, Greenfield suggests that Britain's lack of military success reflected that God had turned away from a sinful nation – sins that he identifies in their pursuit of pleasure and the spirit of faction (political partisanship). Like other Enlightenment texts, Greenfield explores ideas of national happiness and public welfare, but also how individual sins, interpreted in emotional terms, contributed to national distress. Sermons are important sources for the history of emotions as they were a key source of education and moral improvement for the ordinary people who listened to them, and sometimes bought them in cheap pamphlet form. As forms of rhetoric – designed to persuade and engage the passions – they also evidence writerly techniques used to move the emotions of audiences of the period.

. . .

Psalm IV. 6: There by many that say, who will shew us any good? Lord lift thou up the light of thy countenance upon us!

Who will shew us any good? Is a question which hath been asked, with unwearied anxiety, by all ranks of men, in every age of the world. Formed with a propensity to seek for happiness wherever they suppose it may be found, they are eager in following this natural inclination of the heart. But it is mournful to observe how

223

POLITICS AND LAW

widely they wander form the right path; and how many pursue airy phantoms for substantial felicity. "God made man upright; but he hath sought out many inventions." The pleasures, the profits, the praises of the world, are the charms that entice him from his duty, and entangle him in a thousand snares. While the desire of happiness remains in its original force, the method of attaining it is unfortunately mistaken, from the native degeneracy or acquired perversity of the mind.

But, if this inquiry after good be so common in *all* situations, it is particularly urgent in seasons of distress. Then the soul is not only impelled to it by the general wish for enjoyment, but is impatient to be relieved from the burthen of its sufferings. In this case, like the other, the means are frequently mistaken. Some engage in a hurry of business to divert their attention – others repair the losses of fortune by force or fraud. Some fly to pleasures, to soothe them to forgetfulness – other to drunkenness, to drown their cares. Many seek a desperate relief to their sorrows by rash accusation of Providence – all are anxious to obtain a happy issue out of their afflictions: And "Who will shew us any good?" is asked by those who will not hearken to salutary counsel.

But, if this disposition be so common in *private* calamity, it is still more remarkable in times of *national* distress. When the public welfare is supposed to be in danger; when the sacred and civil rights of a people are threatened with violence, it is natural for every one to inquire with earnestness, what means are ready, what resources in our power to avert the stroke? What hope of preserving the eminence, or even the existence of the state? In the days of David, "there were many who said, Who will shew us any good?" when an unnatural son had drawn the sword against an indulgent father, and spread the flame of rebellion through the tribes of Israel. In *our* days, when a similar scene is exhibited; when the sons of a great empire, grown up under the wings of her protection are attempting to pierce the heart of their parent, and have pointed against her the weapons of her antient enemies, together with their own, we cannot wonder that the same question is echoed by thousands, and rings the alarm of danger to the remotest corners of the kingdom.

But, while the attention is roused to the perils of our situation, and so many are asking, "Who will shew us any good?" have we no reason to apprehend, that, in *this* case also, the way of attaining it is overlooked, and the true answer to the inquiry treated with contempt?

The cause of national calamity lies deeper than is generally considered. It is not the mere result of counsels in the senate, or contentions in the field, but the prevalence of public depravity and corruption. The wisdom of God, in whose hands is the supreme direction of all events, hath established a connection between the virtue and welfare, the wickedness and misery of nations, and bestows or withdraws the blessings of his goodness according to their general deserts. "The Lord is with you," saith his prophet, "while ye be with him; and if ye seek him, he will be found of you; but if ye forsake him, he will forsake you." Accordingly, when "he is grieved with a sinful generation," and his justice visits their offences, one nation is made "the rod of his wrath" to another, and sometimes the instrument of ruin, if the measure of its iniquities be full.

224

Whoever traces the history of the empires which have once been conspicuous in the world, will find that their fall was preceded by dissolute manners, which weakened and wasted the constitution of the state. This naturally prepared them for the fatal stroke, and provoked the Almighty to let it fall by his ministers of judgment.

How far *our* condition is similar of that of the nations whose honours have been laid in the dust, it may be deemed presumptuous to determine: Yet, in an hour like this, when much is felt and more is apprehended, and when the piety of our superiors hath directed us to deprecate the wrath of Heaven, it cannot be unseasonable to consider the leading characters of the times, and condemn "the sins that do more easily beset us."

Is it not then evident to the slightest observation, that the LOVE OF PLEASURE, and the SPIRIT OF FACTION, two mortal enemies to public welfare, have erected their standards in these kingdoms, and are followed by a train too numerous to be thought of without a melancholy presage of "wrath to come?"

1. The love of pleasure enervates the mind, unfits it for manly exertion or useful employment and disposes it to frivolous or to profligate pursuits. It appears in a verity of alluring forms; and under these like a painted sepulchre, it hides corruption.

What numbers doth it prompt to a life of incessant dissipation; to fly from themselves, as their greatest enemies, to the giddy circles of fashionable folly; to waste, in a course of trifles, their precious and irrevocable time, to improve and adorn the body, while the mind is a neglected wilderness; and to be careful about every thing but that which is of most concern? I speak not against innocent recreation or amusement, but against those *habits* which engross the heart, and render crouds of those who *call* themselves Christians, "lovers of pleasure more than lovers of God."

But this love of pleasure not only points to objects that are merely vain, but frequently to such as are vicious. It excites the love of gain to gratify its wishes, and of gaming as the shortest ways to such gratification. Of this it may be truly asserted, in the striking words of the apostle, "That it leads into temptation and a snare, and into many foolish and hurtful lusts, which drown men in destruction and perdition." Yet the evident effects prevent not the contagion from spreading wide. For the slaves of Mammon will consider till they feel how little real pleasure can be fund in the precarious plunder which tomorrow may snatch away, in the violent convulsions of mind to which they are continually subject and in the gradual corruption of the tender and benevolent, the upright and honourable sentiments of the heart, in the deep and unpitied ruin into which they daily plunge others and themselves.

But the love of pleasure sometimes takes a different direction, inflaming the sensual appetites, and impelling them to every kind of destructive gratification.

Gluttony is insatiable in quest of fresh luxuries, and ransacks every quarter of the globe for the most exquisite means of shortening, by a variety of diseases, a shameful and unprofitable life. The simplicity of nature, and the pleasures of temperance, (terms hardly understood in the fashionable world) give way to the complicated arts of poisoning, which vanity vies with appetite to introduce, and of which it is almost a virtue to be ignorant.

But if such arts and such revellings are inconsistent not only with the welfare of individuals, but of the public, and with the practice of religion which is founded on self-denial, how greatly more so is the vice of drunkenness, since the means of indulgence are most easily obtained, and the effects of it so extensively pernicious? Health, fortune, character, reason, religion, are the costly sacrifices offered to a lust, "which is not only sensual but devilish." It may well be accounted the mercy of God, if even misfortunes can reclaim its votaries, by cutting off the channels which have been feeding their intemperance.

Finally, The love of pleasure fills up the measure of its guilt, by opening the floodgates of debauchery. The stream of pollution runs down from the higher to the lower ranks of life, overflowing the bounds of decency as well as virtue. Purity is an ornament which many would blush to wear, and make haste to trample under foot. Innocence falls a victim to a base and brutal appetite, or to the miserable vanity of doing mischief. All of that is distracting to human nature; the peace of families murdered – the bonds of amity dissolved – the most solemn covenant broken – the offspring of infamy neglected or destroyed – the bloom of youth, and the hope of happiness blasted – the body torn with loathsome distempers – the conscience trembling with remorse, or feared into insensibility. – Such are the transports which the sons of *pleasure* boast of, as the perfection of enjoyment! Strange! that the most perverted imagination can suppose any *joy* in the venal company of wretches, the most profligate and irretrievable ruin of chastity; in the danger and the perjury of adulterous connections; in changing parental tenderness into silent shame or savage cruelty in the pain spreading misery to a wide extent, and bidding open defiance to the laws both of God and man!

Yet, notwithstanding the gall of bitterness so copiously poured into the cup of pleasure, with what surprise and sorrow may we see, on every side, the very dregs of it drunk up with greediness? while many are thirsting after the envied draught, restrained from tasting it by the fear of human censure, and not of divine judgment? So little is the practice of our pure and undefiled religion regarded; "For they that are Christ's, have crucified the flesh with the affections and lusts." And so loudly doth the guilt of a sinful and adulterous generation cry to heaven for the vengeance which it labours to deserve.

II. To the love of pleasure, the spirit of faction joins its influence to tarnish the honour of the nation, and expose its divided and corrupted state to the insults of its enemies, and the wrath of the Most High. The love of our country, so much in the mouth, and sometimes so little in the heart, consists in a real regard to the constitution, and in preference of the public good to private advantage. The constitution of this state is so beautiful in itself, and beneficial to the community, that no duty is more evident than to offer daily praises to providence for so important a blessing, and daily prayers for its continuance and security; while, as the same time, each individual, in his station, should exert what influence he possesses to support it unblemished and entire. Yet we see it assaulted and shaken by the

THE CAUSE AND CURE OF NATIONAL DISTRESS

violence of contending parties, who are equally ungrateful to God and regardless of themselves. Some overstraining their loyalty, wish to bend it to the side of arbitrary power; and, to compass their end, have erected many engines to scatter corruption through a venal land. Others run eagerly into an opposite extreme, and seem anxious to subvert what they profess to reverse, using the word "liberty as a cloak for maliciousness," and almost as a signal for sedition.

The fire which, in the last century, preyed on the vitals of the constitution, has been suppressed, but its not extinguished. It has lately broken out beyond the Atlantic, laying waste the wide extremity of the empire, and sparks of it are appearing in the British isles, which opportunity would blow into a flame.

But it behoves us to consider well the baneful tendency of such attempts, and discountenance all encroachments on our public happiness. It behoves us to condemn not only the open and direct attacks on the constitution, but the insidious hypocrisy of that spirit which agitates the conspicuous faction of the times, which, under the mask of patriotism, has only *private* grandeur in view, and hesitates at nothing to promote its interested designs. The aim of such a faction must ever be, to counteract the great end of society and government, by disuniting those who should join their exertions for the welfare of the whole. Its aim must ever be to depreciate and defeat the measures, however salutary, of those whose emoluments it covets, and whose honours it would transplant. Its aim must ever be to deceive or to force them into courses that are pernicious or absurd, and then accuse them for the errors and the dangers of which the accusers themselves have been the cause. If in this way it fail to accomplish their ruin, rather than be disappointed, it will hazard the ruin of the whole.[1] For the vehemence of faction increases by unexpected and astonishing degrees. Even wise and good men, when once they give way to it, cannot tell how far they may be carried, especially in a land of freedom, whose active spirit is apt to hurry persons into wild behaviour, and urge public disputes to very dangerous extremes. So requisite, in such a case, is the important admonition of the apostle: "Brethren, ye have been called unto liberty; only use not liberty for an occasion to the flesh, but by love serve one another."

How many have been deaf to this call from heaven, and forget that, in the civil as well as the spiritual state, "a kingdom divided against itself cannot stand?" Nay, civil dissensions have been widened by religious animosities. Alas! how much hath the gospel been warped from its proper tendency? How little have "peace on earth, and good will towards man," been the great objects of a Christian attention? Hath not the glory of God been even supposed to be promoted by holy wars, as if "the wrath of man could work the righteousness of God?" Hath not the prophecy of Jesus been unhappily accomplished, that "he came not to send peace on earth, but a sword?" Have not many of his followers shewn themselves more worthy, as well as more willing, to take up the crescent[2] than the cross? The variety of forms into which his religion has been thrown, has seldom taught the exercise of charity, "without which all our doings are nothing worth," but has rather "cooled the love," while it kindled the zeal of many; a "zeal not according to knowledge," but ready to break forth, not only in words, but in deeds of violence. The rule of scripture on

227

this subject has been but partially observed, "That the servants of the Lord must not strive, but be gentle to all men, in patience and meekness instructing their opponents, if God peradventure will give them repentance, to the acknowledgement of the truth." Of course, not only have the minds of those who should "love as brethren" been animated against each other, but occasion has been given to their common adversaries to "blaspheme the holy name by which we are called." For, when they "who sit in the seat of the scornful," observe that we consider not "what spirit we are of," or to what body we belong, that we shew forth the praise of the gospel with our lips, but deny the power of it in our lives, they require no better proof of the falsehood of our faith, and are confirmed in the principles of infidelity. This cause hath increased the rapidity of its progress, a cause that must afflict, and a progress that must alarm the devout and the discerning mind. For the persuasion is dangerous indeed to the community, that men are not restrained by the sanctions of religion, and are not responsible to their maker and their judge. When they renounce that fear which is the beginning of wisdom, the great barrier of virtue is broken, and a torrent of immorality rushes in, which no other principle is able to resist. When the worms of earth dare to raise themselves in defiance against the majesty of heaven, while they grovel in the impurities of their native dust, will they not be swept away by "the blasting of the breath of its displeasure?" The society then is left without means of defence, either against the violence of its members, or against the visitation of an offended God. If his long-suffering goodness will not lead to repentance, but rather prompt Presumption to say, "Where is the day of his coming?" the voice of his thunder will be heard at last, and announce his coming in an hour when he is least expected. Nay, the strong alliance between irreligion and iniquity, is of itself sufficient to work out the destruction of a state, without a visible instrument of divine vengeance. For, "from whence come wars and fightings among ourselves, but of the lusts which are uncontrouled by religion, of that love of the world which is enmity with God?" If then infidelity goes forth unabashed and unrebuked, and is received with the complacency due to the principles of goodness and the oracles of God, it will sink the nation in the depth of distress, although its power were shining forth in meridian glory.

But, alas! it hath declined from its envied eminence, and its lustre hath bee darkened by gathering clouds. The outward means of safety and prosperity are wanting which we enjoyed in the days of union and concord. Not only our "open enemies", but "our own familiar friends, who did eat of our own bread, and with whom we took sweet counsel together, even they have lift up their heel against us."

This, then, is *not* the time to give scope to licentious opinions, and the ruinous practices they promote. This, then, is not the time to provoke, by the least appearance of profanity, that all-powerful God, on whose providence the kingdoms of the earth depend evermore for preservation. But it is now that we should be zealous to reconcile his favour by a change of our hearts and reformation of our habits, and to supplicate with fervency the throne of grace to second our necessary exertions.

To whom else can we go in the hour of trouble, to dispel the clouds which threaten us with all their storms? If "there be many that now say, Who will shew

THE CAUSE AND CURE OF NATIONAL DISTRESS

us any good?" let us answer, "Lord lift thou up the light of they countenance upon us!" "Thy hand is not shortened, that it cannot save. – Thy ear is not heavy, that is cannot hear. – But our iniquities have separated between us and thee. – Our sins have turned away thy face that thou *wilt* not hear. – We have waited for light, but behold obscurity – for brightness, but we walk in darkness: – Yet still thou hast not forgotten to be gracious. – Thou wilt not shut up thy loving-kindness in displeasure. – *Thou hast* shewed us what is *good*; and what hast thou required of they servants, but to do justice, to love mercy, and to walk humbly with their God?" Cherish, we beseech thee, such holy dispositions in our hearts. – Teach us that "righteousness exalteth a nation, but that sin is the reproach and the ruin of a people." – Teach us, that the sorrows of the penitent are prevalent with thee, who turned away thy fierce anger from the repenting multitudes of Nineveh. – Teach us that the fervent prayers of the faithful are effectual with thee, who at Abraham's intercession, would have spared even Sodom and Gomorrah, had only ten righteous been found therein. – Teach us that thy blessed Son, who wept over the perversity of Jerusalem, and wished she would have known the things belonging to her peace, is *ever* ready to be the Saviour of all who fly to him as the rock of their salvation!

In him may we therefore place our trust, and not in human policy and power, unsupported by his presence, and unsanctified by his benediction. "So shall our light break forth as the morning, and our health spring forth speedily." So "shall our God be a fun and shield;" a sun to enliven our hearts and the beams of his most gracious favour, and a shield to defend us in all assaults of our enemies, through the mind of Jesus Christ, our Lord and our Redeemer. Amen.

Notes

1 Bishop Secker.
2 The banner of Mahomet.

29

JOHN HAWKESWORTH (1715–1773), *AN ACCOUNT OF THE VOYAGES UNDERTAKEN BY THE ORDER OF HIS PRESENT . . .*

3 vols (London: W. Strahan, 1783), pp. 152–158, 186–188, 231–233, 410–412

These excerpts are taken from a volume of travel diaries, published by John Hawkesworth, in 1783. The publication was commissioned by the British Admiralty who thought they were of scientific interest, but the result was controversial, with some critics arguing that some of the descriptions of other cultures was damaging to morality. The diary accounts, written by the Captains as a record of events and for scientific purposes, provide significant evidence of encounters between explorers and the original inhabitants, and sometimes invaders, of various nations across the globe. They provide insight into the emotions – the anxieties and fears – of sailors, descriptions of how Europeans read emotions on the bodies of those from very different cultures, and the emotional dynamics of negotiations for trade, friendship, science and more between various groups. Moments of encounter were significant events in the political life of nations and their success often rested on how groups interpreted gestures and expressions as evidence for positive and negative feeling. The first excerpts below are taken from Samuel Wallis's (1728–1795) voyage as Captain of the *HMS Dolphin* to 'discover the southern continent', which described his journey in the South Pacific and particularly his travel to Tahiti. The final excerpt comes from Philip Carteret's (1733–1796) journey as Captain on the *HMS Swallow*. It initially was a companion ship to the *Dolphin*, but they separated after the Strait of Magellan. The events below happened off the coast of Macassar in Indonesia, then held by the Dutch.

. . .

December 1766 [Captain Wallis's Voyage]

Wednesday 17 The natives continued abreast of the ship all night, making several great fires, and frequently shouting very loud. As soon as it was light, on Wednesday morning the 17th, we saw great numbers of them in motion, who made signs

230

for us to land. About five o'clock I made the signal for the boats belonging to the Swallow and the Prince Frederick to come on board, and in the mean time hoisted out our own. These boats being all manned and armed, I took a party of marines, and rowed towards the shore, having left orders with the master to bring the ship's broad-side to bear upon the landing place, and to keep the guns loaded with round shot. We reached the beach about six o'clock, and before we went from the boat, I made signs to the natives to retire to some distance: they immediately complied, and I then landed with the Captain of the Swallow, and several of the officers: the marines were drawn up, and the boats were brought to a grappling near the shore. I then made signs to the natives to come near, and directed them to sit down in a semicircle, which they did with great order and chearfulness. When this was done, I distributed among them several knives, scissars, buttons, beads, combs, and other toys, particularly some ribands to the women, which they received with a very becoming mixture of pleasure and respect. Having distributed my presents, I endeavoured to make them understand that I had other things which I would part with, but for which I expected somewhat in return. I shewed them some hatchets and bill-hooks, and pointed to some guanicoes, which happened to be near, and some ostriches which I saw dead among them; making signs at the same time that I wanted to eat; but they either could not, or would not understand me: for though they seemed very desirous of the hatchets and the bill-hooks, they did not give the least intimation that they would part with any provisions; no traffic therefore was carried on between us.

Each of these people, both men and women, had a horse, with a decent saddle, stirrups, and bridle. The men had wooden spurs, except one, who had a large pair of such as are worn in Spain, brass stirrups, and a Spanish cimeter, without a scabbard; but notwithstanding these distinctions, he did not appear to have any authority over the rest: the women had no spurs. The horses appeared to be well made, and nimble, and were about 14 hands high. The people had also many dogs with them, which, as well as the horses, appeared to be of a Spanish breed.

As I had two measuring rods with me, we went round and measured those that appeared to be tallest among them. One of these was six feet seven inches high, several more were six feet five, and six feet six inches; but the stature of the greater part of them was from five feet ten to six feet. Their complexion is a dark copper colour, like that of the Indians in North America; their hair is strait, and nearly as harsh as hog's bristles: it is tied back with a cotton string, but neither sex wears any head-dress. They are well made, robust, and boney; but their hands and feet are remarkably small. They are cloathed with the skins of the guanico, sewed together into pieces about six feet long, and five wide: these are wrapped round the body, and fastened with a girdle, with the hairy side inwards; some of them had also what the Spaniards have called a puncho, a square piece of cloth made of the downy hair of the guanico, through which a hole being cut for the head, the rest hangs round them about as low as the knee. The guanico is an animal that in size, make, and colour, resembles a deer, but it has a hump on its back, and no horns. These people wear also a kind of drawers, which they pull up very tight,

POLITICS AND LAW

and buskins, which reach from the mid-leg to the instep before, and behind are brought under the heel; the rest of the foot is without any covering. We observed that several of the men had a red circle painted round the left eye, and that others were painted on their arms, and on different parts of the face; the eye-lids of all the young women were painted black. They talked much, and some of them called out Ca-pi-ta-ne; but when they were spoken to in Spanish, Portuguese, French, and Dutch, they made no reply. Of their own language we could distinguish only one word, which was *chevow*; we supposed it to be a salutation, as they always pronounced it when they shook hands with us, and when, by signs, they asked us to give them any thing. When they were spoken to in English, they repeated the words after us as plainly as we could do; and they soon got by heart the words "Englishmen come on shore." Every one had a missile weapon of a singular kind, tucked into the girdle. It consisted of two round stones, covered with leather, each weighing about a pound, which were fastened to the two ends of a string about eight feet long. This is used as a sling, one stone being kept in the hand, and the other whirled round the head till it is supposed to have acquired sufficient force, and then discharged at the object. They are so expert in the management of this double-headed shot, that they will hit a mark, not bigger than a shilling, with both the stones, at the distance of fifteen yards; it is not their custom, however, to strike either the guanico or the ostrich with them in the chace, but they discharge them so that the cord comes against the legs of the ostrich, or two of the legs of the guanico, and is twisted round them by the force and swing of the balls, so that the animal being unable to run, becomes an easy prey to the hunter.

While we stayed on shore, we saw them eat some of their flesh meat raw, particularly the paunch of an ostrich, without any other preparation or cleaning than just turning it inside out, and shaking it. We observed among them several beads, such as I gave them, and two pieces of red baize, which we supposed had been left there, or in the neighbouring country, by Commodore Byron.

After I had spent about four hours with these people, I made signs to them that I was going on board, and that I would take some of them with me if they were desirous to go. As soon as I had made myself understood, above an hundred eagerly offered to visit the ship; but I did not chuse to indulge more than eight of the number. They jumped into the boats with the joy and alacrity of children going to a fair, and having no intention of mischief against us, had not the least suspicion that we intended any mischief against them. They sung several of their country songs while they were in the boat, and when they came on board did not express either the curiosity or wonder which the multiplicity of objects, to them equally strange and stupendous, that at once presented themselves, might be supposed to excite. I took them down into the cabbin, where they looked about them with an unaccountable indifference, till one of them happened to cast his eyes upon a looking-glass: this however excited no more astonishment than the prodigies which offer themselves to our imagination in a dream, when we converse with the dead, fly in the air, and walk upon the sea, without reflecting that the laws of nature are violated; but it afforded them infinite diversion: they advanced,

232

HAWKESWORTH, *AN ACCOUNT OF THE VOYAGES*

retreated, and played a thousand tricks before it, laughing violently, and talking with great emphasis to each other. I gave them some beef, pork, biscuit, and other articles of the ship's provisions: they eat, indiscriminately, whatever was offered to them, but they would drink nothing but water. From the cabbin I carried them all over the ship, but they looked at nothing with much attention, except the animals which we had on board as live stock: they examined the hogs and sheep with some curiosity, and were exceedingly delighted with the Guinea hens and turkies; they did not seem to desire any thing that they saw except our apparel, and only one of them, an old man, asked for that: we gratified him with a pair of shoes and buckles, and to each of the others I gave a canvas bag, in which I put some needles ready threaded, a few slips of cloth, a knife, a pair of scissars, some twine, a few beads, a comb, and a looking glass, with some new six pences and halfpence, through which a hole had been drilled, that was fitted with a riband to hang round the neck. We offered them some leaves of tobacco, rolled up into what are called segars, and they smoked a little, but did not seem fond of it. I showed them the great guns, but they did not appear to have any notion of their use. After I had carried them through the ship, I ordered the marines to be drawn up, and go through part of their exercise. When the first volley was fired, they were struck with astonishment and terror; the old man in particular, threw himself down upon the deck, pointed to the muskets, and then striking his breast with his hand, lay some time motionless, with his eyes shut: by this we supposed he intended to shew us that he was not unacquainted with fire-arms, and their fatal effect. The rest seeing our people merry, and finding themselves unhurt, soon resumed their cheerfulness and good humour, and heard the second and third volley fired without much emotion; but the old man continued prostrate upon the deck some time, and never recovered his spirits till the firing was over. About noon, the tide being out, I acquainted them by signs that the ship was proceeding farther, and that they must go on shore: this I soon perceived they were very unwilling to do; all however, except the old man and one more, were got into the boat without much difficulty; but these stopped at the gang-way, where the old man turned about, and went aft to the companion ladder, where he stood some time without speaking a word; he then uttered what we supposed to be a prayer; for he many times lifted up his hands and his eyes to the heavens, and spoke in a manner and tone very different from what we had observed in their conversation: his oraison seemed to be rather sung than said, so that we found it impossible to distinguish one word from another. When I again intimated that it was proper for him to go into the boat, he pointed to the sun, and then moving his hand round to the west, he paused, looked in my face, laughed, and pointed to the shore: by this it was easy to understand that he wished to stay on board till sun-set, and I took no little pains to convince him that we could not stay so long upon that part of the coast, before he could be prevailed upon to go into the boat; at length however he went over the ship's side with his companion, and when the boat put off they all began to sing, and continued their merriment till they got on shore. When they landed, great numbers of those on shore pressed eagerly to get into the boat; but the officer on board, having positive orders to bring none of them off, prevented them, though not without great difficulty, and apparently to their extream mortification and disappointment.

When the boat returned on board, I sent her off again with the master, to sound the shoal that runs off from the point: he found it about three miles broad from north to south, and that to avoid it, it was necessary to keep four miles off the Cape, in twelve or thirteen fathom water.

...

April 1767.

Thursday 2. On Thursday, the second of April, the master of the Swallow, who had been sent out to seek for anchoring places, returned, and reported that he had found three on the north shore, which were very good; one about four miles to the eastward of Cape Providence, another under the east side of Cape Tamer, and the third about four miles to the eastward of it; but he said that he found no place to anchor in under Cape Providence, the ground being rocky.

This day two canoes came on board, with four men and three young children in each. The men were somewhat more decently dressed than those that we had seen before, but the children were stark naked. They were somewhat fairer than the men, who seemed to pay a very tender attention to them, especially in lifting them in and out of the canoes. To these young visitors I gave necklaces and bracelets, with which they seemed mightily pleased. It happened that while some of these people were on board, and the rest waiting in their canoes by the ship's side, the boat was sent on shore for wood and water. The Indians who were in the canoes, kept their eyes fixed upon the boat while she was manning, and the moment she put off from the ship, they called out with great vociferation to those that were on board, who seemed to be much alarmed, and hastily handing down the children, leaped into their canoes, without uttering a word. None of us could guess at the cause of this sudden emotion, but we saw the men in the canoes pull after the boat with all their might, hallooing and shouting with great appearance of perturbation and distress. The boat outrowed them, and when she came near the shore, the people on board discovered some women gathering muscles among the rocks. This at once explained the mystery; the poor Indians were afraid that the strangers, either by force or favour, should violate the prerogative of a husband, of which they seemed to be more jealous than the natives of some other countries, who in their appearance are less savage and sordid. Our people, to make them easy, immediately lay upon their oars, and suffered the canoes to pass them. The Indians; however, still continued to call out to their women, till they took the alarm and ran out of sight, and as soon as they got to land, drew their canoes upon the beach, and followed them with the utmost expedition.

June 1767

Saturday 27. The next morning I sent the boats on shore, with a guard, to fill some more casks with water, and soon after the people were on shore, the same old man

HAWKESWORTH, *AN ACCOUNT OF THE VOYAGES*

who had come over the river to them the first day, came again to the farther side of it, where he made a long speech, and then crossed the water. When he came up to the waterers, the officer shewed him the stones that were piled up like cannon balls upon the shore, and had been brought thither since our first landing, and some of the bags that had been taken out of the canoes which I had ordered to be destroyed, filled with stones, and endeavoured to make him understand that the Indians had been the aggressors, and that the mischief we had done them was in our own defence. The old man seemed to apprehend his meaning, but not to admit it: he immediately made a speech to the people, pointing to the stones, slings, and bags, with great emotion, and sometimes his looks, gestures, and voice were so furious as to be frightful. His passions, however, subsided by degrees, and the officer, who to his great regret could not understand one word of all that he had said, endeavoured to convince him, by all the signs he could devise, that we wished to live in friendship with them, and were disposed to shew them every mark of kindness in our power. He then shook hands with him, and embraced him, giving him at the same time several such trinkets as he thought would be most acceptable. He contrived also to make the old man understand that we wished to traffic for provisions, that the Indians should not come down in great numbers, and that they should keep on one side of the river and we on the other. After this the old man went away with great appearance of satisfaction, and before noon a trade was established, which furnished us with hogs, fowls, and fruit in great abundance, so that all the ship's company, whether sick or well, had as much as they could use.

. . .

December 1767 [Captain Carteret's Voyage]

Wednesday 16. The next morning, at break of day, I sent the Lieutenant to the town, with a letter to the Governor, in which I acquainted him with the reason of my coming thither, and requested the liberty of the port to procure refreshments for my ship's company, who were in a dying condition, and shelter for the vessel against the approaching storms, till the return of a fit season for sailing to the westward. I ordered that this letter should, without good reason to the contrary, be delivered into the Governor's own hand; but when my officer got to the wharf of the town, neither he nor any other person in the boat was suffered to land. Upon his refusal to deliver the letter to a messenger, the Governor was made acquainted with it, and two officers, called the shebander and the fiscal, were sent down to him, who, as a reason why he could not deliver the letter to the Governor himself, pretended that he was sick, and said, that they came by his express order to fetch it; upon this the letter was at length delivered to them, and they went away. While they were gone, the officer and men were kept on board the boat, exposed to the burning heart of the sun, which was almost vertical at noon, and none of the country boats were suffered to come near enough to sell them any refreshment. In the mean time, our people observed a great hurry and bustle on shore, and all the sloops and vessels that were proper for war were fitted out with the utmost

POLITICS AND LAW

expedition: we should, however, I believe, have been an overmatch for their whole sea force, if all our people had been well. In the mean time I intended to have gone and anchored close to the town, but now the boat was absent, our united strength was not sufficient to weigh the anchor though a small one. After waiting five hours in the boat, the Lieutenant was told that the Governor had ordered two gentlemen to wait upon me with an answer to my letter. Soon after he had returned, and made this report, the two gentlemen came on board, and we afterwards learnt that one of them was an ensign of the garrison, named Le Cerf, and the other Mr Douglas, a writer of the Dutch East India Company: they delivered me the Governor's letter, but it proved to be written in Dutch, a language which not a single person on board could understand: the two gentlemen who brought it, however, both spoke French, and one of them interpreted the contents to me in that language. The purport of it was, "that I should instantly depart from the port, without coming any nearer to the town; that I should not anchor on any part of the coast, or permit any of my people to land in any place that was under his jurisdiction." Before I made any reply to this letter, I shewed the gentlemen who brought it the number of my sick: at the sight of so many unhappy wretches, who were dying of languor and disease, they seemed to be much affected; and I then urged again the pressing necessity I was under of procuring refreshment, to which they had been witnesses, the cruelty and injustice of refusing to supply me, which was not only contrary to treaty, as we were in a King's ship, but to the laws of Nature as we were human beings: they seemed to admit the force of this reasoning, but they had a short and final answer ready, "that they had absolute and indispensible orders from their masters, not to suffer any ship, of whatever nation, to stay at this port, and that these orders they must implicitly obey." To this I replied, that persons in our situation had nothing worse to fear than what they suffered, and that therefore if they did not immediately allow me the liberty of the port, to purchase refreshments, and procure shelter, I would, as soon as the wind would permit, in defiance of all their menaces, and all their force, go and anchor close to the town; that if at last I should find myself unable to compel them to comply with requisitions, the reasonableness of which could not be controverted, I would run the ship aground under their walls, and, after selling our lives as dearly as we could, bring upon them the disgrace of having reduced a friend and ally to so dreadful an extremity. At this they seemed to be alarmed, as our situation alone was sufficient to convince them that I was in earnest, and urged me with great emotion to remain where I was, at least till I had heard again from the Governor: to this, after some altercation, I consented, upon condition that I heard from the Governor before the sea-breeze set in the next day.

Thursday 17. We passed all the remainder of this day, and all the night, in a state of anxiety, not unmixed with indignation, that greatly aggravated our distress; . . .

Part 5

SCIENCE AND PHILOSOPHY

Part 5

Science and philosophy

Emotion was a central topic within the writings of eighteenth-century European scientists and philosophers. They were especially interested in defining and explaining human nature, where human self-love and sociable nature were key concepts. These ideas were underpinned by anthropologies and driven by encounters across the globe and new medical sciences that highlighted vitalism and nerves as more critical to the sensible and sensate body than the humoural model, which it slowly replaced. As sources for the history of emotion, scientific and philosophical writings highlight current understandings of the body, human nature and how our capacity to relate and be human relied on the exchange of emotion – sympathy – across bodies. At the same time, emotion required management if people were to operate smoothly and healthily in society, and a number of writers provided explicit advice to encourage particular forms of emotion management and virtuous action.

30

JAMES BLONDEL (1666–1734), *THE POWER OF THE MOTHER'S IMAGINATION OVER THE FOETUS*

(London: John Brotherton, 1729),
pp. 1–5, 13–18

James Blondel was a French physician, working in London in the 1720s. In this pamphlet, written in English, he addressed a popular early modern belief that the power of the imagination could shape the foetus in the mother's body. According to this idea, frights, shocks or other strong emotions during pregnancy could imprint on the child. Blondel contested this, exploring alternative explanations. Inspired by the Mary Toft controversy where a woman claimed she had given birth to rabbits, the pamphlet was written as part of an exchange with the physician Daniel Turner (1667–1740) on the maternal imagination, and is an example of how scientists, like other scholars, often used the medium of the press to engage in scientific debates and to publicise their ideas. At times, such accounts could become heated and notorious, and they could be useful for developing a professional reputation. In his pamphlet, Blondel provides many examples of strong emotional experiences and their potential results (or lack thereof). It provides an important example of how emotions were understood to operate in the early modern period, and how such models were being reinvented during the scientific revolution.

. . .

Chap. I: The state of the question

Deformities, which some children bring into the World, being always frightful, and the Occasion of great Surprise, and Concern in tender Parents; my Design in this Treatise is to enquire into their true Cause, and to examine how far the common Opinion, which lays the Fault upon the Mother's *Imagination*, may be allowed to be true, and how far it seems to be false.

If, in the Management of the Controversy, I do differ from the Judgment of others, I hope the Reader will be so kind as to excuse me; since I declare sincerely, I don't do it to be singular, and by a Spirit of Contradiction, but in Charity, Justice

SCIENCE AND PHILOSOPHY

and Equity; and with no other View, than to ease the Minds of those, who do wrongfully fancy themselves guilty of what, I believe, they are entirely innocent.

Imagination in pregnant Women, so far as it relates to the *Foetus*, and is the Subject of this Dispute, is a Modification of the Mother's Thoughts upon certain outward Objects, which are commonly referred to these few Heads.

1 A strong Longing for something in particular, in which Desire the Mother is either gratified, or disappointed. 2. A sudden Surprise. 3. The Sight and Abhorrence of an ugly and frightful Object. 4. The Pleasure of Looking on, and Contemplating, even for a long Time, a Picture, or whatsoever is delightful to the Fancy. 5. Fear, and Consternation, and great Apprehension of Dangers. 6. And lastly, An Excess of Anger, of Grief, or of Joy.

I This being premised, several Questions do naturally present themselves to be examined. The first is, in what Sense can the Mother do an Injury to the *Foetus* in *Utero*?

I answer, that the Child may receive some Hurt by Means of its Mother, this being laid down as a general Rule, that Prosperity of the *Foetus* does depend on the Welfare of the Mother; and that, whatever is detrimental to her is directly, or indirectly, prejudicial to the other.

It suffers not only by distempers of the Parents, but also be several Accidents, as great Falls, Bruises, and Blows the Mother receives, by her laborious Work, by odd and constrained Positions of her Body; by the Irregularity of her Diet, and of her Actions; by immoderate Dancing, Running, Jumping, Riding, Excess of Laughing, frequent and violent Sneezing, and all other Agitations of the Body.

The Child may also suffer by the Affections of the Mother's Mind. For the Disappointment of what she desires is sufficient to make her uneasy, and pine away; deprive her of Sleep and Quiet, and even of Food, and consequently the Child runs the Risk, for Want of due and wholesome Nourishment, to grow feeble and weak, and at last to lose its Life. Upon that Account, 'tis very necessary to gratify the Longing of pregnant Women, if it be possible and safe.

Frightful and Ugly Objects, which are shocking even to *Men* of Courage, are to be carefully removed from the Sight of pregnant Women, as being apt to disturb their Minds, and to fill them with Horror, Fear, and Apprehension.

Anger is a Passion that puts the whole Fabrick of the Body out of Frame. Cholerick Persons in their *Furor* have been seised with Fits of Apoplexy: In those People, the Agitations of the Mind, and of the Body, seem now and then, to threaten an entire Ruin, as it appears by their Clamours and Foaming at the Mouth, the Colour and Swelling of their Eyes, the violent Palpitation of the Heart, and a Sort of an universal Convulsion. In that Case, 'tis much to be feared, that the Blood, flowing with great Vehemence towards the *Uterus*, may separate the *Placenta*, and cause an Abortion.

Surprise is very dangerous: I appeal to Persons who have been frightened, if they did not feel their Heart fluttering, a general *Tremor*, and the Bowels, as it

THE POWER OF THE MOTHER'S IMAGINATION

were, drawn inwards, and their Back opened in two. The Cause is the violent and convulsive Motion of the *Diaphragm*, and of the Muscles of the *Abdomen*, which, like a strong Bar, strike upon the *Viscera*. Now, where's the Wonder, that, such a Force pressing upon the *Uterus*, which is also in Convulsion, should knead the tender Child, and cause Dislocations, Fractures, Mutilations, Hernias, Ecchymoses, &c?

II   The next Questions are, Whether the strong Attention of the Mother's Mind to a *determinate* Object can cause a *determinate*, or a *specific* Impression upon the Body of the Child, without any Force, or Violence from abroad?

And lastly, Whether in the Fit of *Imagination*, CHIRAPSY, or the Application of the Mother's Hand to any particular Place of Her Body, through accidental, and not premeditated, can work *sympathetically* upon the like Part of the Body of *Foetus*, and be of any dangerous Consequence?

Most People are for the Affirmative of these two Questions. They believe that the *Imagination* of a pregnant Woman is able to imprint upon the Child the Representation of the Object, which the Mother has in View; as for Instance, that the strong Desire of *Peaches*, or *Cherries* not being satisfied does cause the Colour and Shape of a *Peach*, or of a *Cherry* upon the *Foetus*; that the mere Longing for *Muscles* is sufficient to *transubstantiate* the true and original Head of the Child into a *Shell-Fish*: The the frightful Sight of a lame Man, without any concomitant Injury from abroad, will mutilate the Hand of the *Embryo*, &c.

The Motion of the Hand is also a Circumstance, which is very seldom, or never omitted in giving an Account of *monstrous* Births, that *Gesticulation*, being thought to be essential, and of great Virtue and Efficacy; as if *Imagination* made Use of it, for a Signal to her *Dragoons* to take free Quarters no where else but in the Place which she points at.

Father *Malebranche*, a high *Imaginationist*, has made a notable Discovery in that *Terra incognita*, which is not to be slighted; for he's very positive, that the Exercise of the Hand, being managed in a prudent Way, may, in Part, be a Sort of Preservative against the Worst of the Accidents, or like a *Damm*, to turn aside and divert the violent Streams of the turbulent Spirits to a safer Part in the Child's Body, where they'll have full Liberty of *Prancing* without any great Inconvenience. I'll give the Receipt in another Place for the Benefit of the Publick.

I own, *Mercurialis*, IIb.2. *de morb. Mulier*, says that this is an *idle* Notion [*Nugae*] and that, if any Part is marked rather than another, 'tis from its Disposition, or by Chance: But in that Particular he does entirely differ from all others. And indeed the Power of *Imagination*, and the Virtue of *Chirapsy*, seem, in that System, to be inseparable, both of them being equally supported by the same Tradition, the same Witnesses, and the same Assurance in their Depositions: So that there's no Medium, they must stand or fall both together.

But these Opinions in my Judgment, are so full of Absurdities, that I'm inclin'd to take them for vulgar Errors, which have insensibly crept into the World, and

243

SCIENCE AND PHILOSOPHY

are now generally received, without any Examination, though they be contrary to EXPERIENCE, REASON and ANATOMY, all which I'll endeavour to shew in the following Chapters.

. . . .

Chap. III: More proofs, that experience is against the current opinion

BUT to put this Controversy in a true Light, 'tis very necessary to examine all possible Cases relating to the Mother's *Imagination*.

1 There is sometimes *Imagination*, and yet afterwards neither Marks nor Deformities follow.
2 There are *Marks*, &c. without any precedent *Imagination*.
3 There are *Marks*, &c. pretended to be Subsequent to, and the Effect of the Mother's *Imagination*.

Now, in all these three different cases experience is against the Imaginationists: *imagination, and no specific marks*

Imagination is not so malignant to the *Foetus*, as 'tis commonly reported, or else the Race of Men should insensibly degenerate into a Generation of *Monsters*. How many Women are disturbed, during their Pregnancy, by strange Desires, odd Passions, and Frights, and yet *Experience* shews that the Children come into the World well shaped, and without the least Token of the Mother's *Fancy*; except when there has been some outwards Force or Violence on the *Uterus*, and the Body of the *Foetus*.

A Gentlewoman, of very good Credit, who had an Aversion against Cats, has assured me, that one Evening, being read to go to Bed, a large Cat rushed unexpectedly into her Chamber through the Casement, and flew directly to her Body, from which, with some Difficulty, it was removed by Servants: And yet, notwithstanding this great Fright, she was, in two or three Months Time, safely delivered of a beautiful Son, who had not the least Shew of Smellers or Claws, nor of any Thing resembling that Animal. But 'tis very remarkable, that afterwards, instead of being afraid of Cats, the Child loved to handle, and even to torment them, as if he took Pleasure to revenge the Insult his Mother had suffered.

I could give a long Catalogue of pregnant Women, who had been frightened by dismal Objects, or other dreadful Accidents, or disappointed in their Desires; and yet those Misfortunes did not appear, upon the Birth of the Children, to have been visibly of such an ill Consequence to them, as to mark their Bodies.

I am only satisfy'd to take Notice of MARY QUEEN OF SCOTS. Every Body knows, that her Majesty being at Supper in her Closet, some Persons entered her Apartment Sword in Hand, and in a very rude and disrespectful Manner, and stabbed *David Rixio* her Secretary; who, thinking to save his Life, did immediately seize the Queen about the waste, crying for Mercy, at the same Time that the Executioners were repeating the Blows. It is impossible to express the Heighth of Fright and Consternation that Princess was put to, during that bloody Tragedy, the Table, Candles, Meat and Dishes being overthrown, and the Place filled with the Shrieks and Groans of the unhappy Sufferer, and the *Queen's* loud Exclamations; and yet, when the *Royal Prince*, King JAMES *the First* was born, not one single Scratch was found about his Body, nor any Similitude of Wounds; tho' I am apt to believe, that *Imagination* is no Respecter of Persons, and was not afraid, if she meddled with that Royal Babe, to be indicted for High Treason.

I own, that it is reported of that King, that he could not bear the Sight of a *Naked Sword*; but was he not as much disordered at the Report of a Gun, as if *David Rixto* had been shot? Can't we find about us many People who the same Weakness, and yet their Mothers were never affrighted in their Pregnancy. I have been assured that Persons of very great Courage, have in the Beginning of an Engagement betrayed some Concern in their Looks, and that even they have been subject to certain Accidents, which are in reality more owing to the Debility and Relaxation of certain *Sphincters*, than to Want of Valour and Resolution.

To account for the Aversion King *James* had to a naked Sword, there's no Necessity to have Recourse to *Imagination*.

If Babes are accidentally frighted, and fall into Convulsion Fits, which afflict them afterwards during the whole Course of their Lives, 'tis often a Secret which is carefully confined within the Nursery.

His Majesty King *James* the First has the Misfortune to be train'd up to *Fear* from his Infancy. His Attendants were his Mother's bitter Enemies, who, no doubt, in their Conversations, repeated continually the dreadful Stories of *David Rixio's* miserable Death, and of the barbarous *Murder* of the Lord *Darnly*, the King's Father, and that in the Hearing of the Infant; and probably with Threatnings and Aggravations, and with heavy Reflections upon the Queen his Mother. Don't we know, that Children, even, when they can hardly speak, give great Attention to the Discourse Nurses are too apt to make upon Spirits, Apparitions, and Witches, and that they retain an odd Impression of Fear so long as they live. The King's Governess, and his Tutor a learned *Pedant*, used him very roughly and with Haughtiness, *My Lady Marr*, says Sir *James Melvil* in his Memoirs, *held the King in great* Awe, *and so did Mr* George Buchanan – *he was a Stoician, and did not look before him.* Money was coined in his Name, with a Sword or Digger erect, in the Middle of those frightful Words, *Pro Me Merco, Si non in me*, which was as much as to hang continually the Point of a Sword over his Head. His Minority was attended with Great Troubles and eminent Dangers, from the ill Designs of the Earl of *Bothwell*; and at last his Majesty had the Affliction, to hear of the barbarous Execution of his Mother. All which unhappy Circumstances were enough to make him hate the very Name of Fighting. After all I am apt to believe, that his pacific Temper had given Occasions to say more of him than was literally true.

Let it be how it will, to attribute the King's fearful Inclination, to his Mother's *Imagination*, is but a Conjecture, and a Supposition; but what is certain, that he was born without any Bruise or Wounds, which is sufficient to demonstrate the *Impotency* of *Imagination*, even when it is in its full Strength.

Marks and Deformaties without any preceeding imagination

A long *Experience*, which can never be brought into Question, shews, that some Children are born with *Marks* and *Deformities*, and yet the Mothers never had any Surprize, nor Longing, nor any other Accident, to be the Occasion of those *Marks*, &c.

I have seen a young Man, who had the *Integuments*, immediately above the *Sternum*, so thin, that the Blood-Vessels were, in a Manner, perfectly bare, and, by their several Turnings and Complications, did represent a Bunch of *Grapes*. His Mother being then alive, I desired him to inquire, if she had longed for that Fruit, or whether she could give a Reason for such an extraordinary Conformation; but I was answered in the Negative.

I remember to have been sent for to a Female Infant, who had, in Fifteen or Twenty different Places of her Body, large Spots, which by their Shape and Colour appeared like painted *Black-Cherries*. If they were prest downwards with the Finger they would give Way, but return immediately to their former State; which made me judge, that they were nothing else, but a Dilation of the Blood Vessels. I was not mistaken; for in a due Time the Skin being grown thicker, and the Vessels having acquired a greater Strength, the *Marks* are now more solid, and seem to be like *Straw-berries*, having a Mixture of Red and White Strokes, somewhat raised above the Skin. The Mother assured me, that she never had any Disorder during her Pregnancy, nor any Desire of Black or Red *Cherries*.

I say, the same of a Child, who had upon his Thigh a Discolouration, which the Nurses were pleased to call a *Peach*, and yet the Mother could give no Manner of Account how that came upon the Body of her Son.

But for fear Dr. *Turner* should say, that these Stories are of my own Invention, I refer him to Dr. *Jacobus Bircherodius's* Letter to *Thomas Bartholin*, the Substance of which is, that in 1662, a Child was born in a village of *Fionia*, entirely perfect in all the Parts of her Body, except the Head, on the back Part of which grew a large Excrescence *hanging* upon the Neck, in Imitation of the *Head-cloaths* the Gentlewomen of *Denmark*, used to wear at that Time; upon the Question put to the Mother, whether she had any such Thing in her Mind during her Pregnancy, she did solemnly declare, *that she had never seen in her whole Life any such Dress, nor had the Representation of it in her Thoughts, when she was with Child.* There are several such Cases in the said Letter, upon the same Subject.

31

JEWISH LOVE POTION, FROM A MEDICAL RECIPE BOOK, ITALY, 18–19TH C

British Library or 10268, f.10r

Love potions and incantations were popular across Europe and persisted across the eighteenth century, found amongst other medical recipes in personal books and collections. Love potions could encourage people to fall in love, act as aphrodisiacs to enable sexual function, or conversely help to banish unwanted feelings. The recipes varied over time and place but the idea that chemical solutions to love could be useful remains persistent. They highlight the complex place of love as passion to be desired and sometimes resisted amongst groups who often married for less romantic reasons. The recipe below is from the Hebrew tradition and appears in recipes books between the sixteenth and eighteenth centuries across Europe in very similar form. This version appeared in an Italian personal notebook. The solution was designed to be taken before the wedding night, following the ceremony itself. The recipes themselves generally do not contain significant discussions of love or emotions, but they highlight how even for ordinary people, with less access to philosophical and scientific discussions, emotions were topics of concern and management. They may also provide evidence of how emotions were conceptualised to work in particular cultures.

. . .

עם שניהם הברכה כתוב שם עשיית לאחר מהחופה כשיבאו – וכלה חתן בין אהבה להרבות
לאיש האשה ושם לאשה האיש שם עליו שכתוב העלה לאכול ותן סלוויאה עלי 'ב על דבש

To increase love between bridegroom and bride – when they come from the huppah[1] after saying the blessing, write their names in honey onto two sage leaves and give the leaf with the man's name on it to the woman and the woman's name to the man.

Note

1 The huppah is the canopy which Jewish people stand under when getting married.

32

MARTIN ENGELBRECHT (1685–1756), AFTER C. LE BRUN, COLLECTION OF ETCHINGS OF EMOTIONS

Martin Engelbrecht was a German engraver, and Charles le Brun (1618–1690) was a French painter and head of the French Academy of Art. As a painter, Le Brun was interested in capturing emotional expression within portraits and paintings; he wrote a treatise, *Méthode pour apprendre à dessiner les passions* [*Methods for Learning to Draw the Passions*] (1698), on this topic that was published after his death. It included a number of images of faces expressing particular emotions, that could be used as examples to replicate when painting the passions. These images were copied several times over the subsequent centuries due to the general agreement of their accuracy, including by Engelbrecht who made a series of engravings. The images operated on the assumption that the expression of emotion was universal across humans, and if it could be accurately captured, that people could read it in paintings and interpret the message. They are useful for the history of emotions as they were widely praised as capturing genuine emotional expression, and so give an indication of how people portrayed emotion through their bodies, and they indicate ideas about what counts as an emotion and how it should be represented.

. . .

Figure 32.1 M. Engelbrecht (1685–1756), Augsburg, after C. Le Brun, *A Bearded Man expressing Scorn*, engraving, 1732, Wellcome Collection. CC BY.

Note: for more details: https://wellcomecollection.org/works/km87unqy.

SCIENCE AND PHILOSOPHY

Figure 32.2 M. Engelbrecht (1685–1756), Augsburg, after C. Le Brun, *A Female Face expressing Admiration Tinged with Astonishment,* engraving, 1732, Wellcome Collection. CC BY.

Note: for more details: https://wellcomecollection.org/works/szaqazau.

Figure 32.3 M. Engelbrecht (1685–1756), Augsburg, after C. Le Brun, *A Laughing Face*, engraving, 1732, Wellcome Collection. CC BY.

Note: for more details: https://wellcomecollection.org/works/a4hsa9yc.

Figure 32.4 M. Engelbrecht (1685–1756), Augsburg, after C. Le Brun, *Head of a Man with Hair Raised, expressing Despair*, engraving, 1732, Wellcome Collection. CC BY.

Note: for more details: https://wellcomecollection.org/works/b6qr66sw.

Figure 32.5 M. Engelbrecht (1685–1756), Augsburg, after C. Le Brun, *The Face of a Man expressing Horror,* engraving, 1732, Wellcome Collection. CC BY.

Note: for more details: https://wellcomecollection.org/works/bt7sxq8q.

Figure 32.6 M. Engelbrecht (1685–1756), Augsburg, after C. Le Brun, *A Man Glowering, expressing Hatred or Jealousy,* engraving, 1732, Wellcome Collection. CC BY.

Note: for more details: https://wellcomecollection.org/works/dr64etdn.

Figure 32.7 M. Engelbrecht (1685–1756), Augsburg, after C. Le Brun, *Face of a Bearded Man expressing Anger,* engraving, 1732, Wellcome Collection. CC BY.

Note: for more details: https://wellcomecollection.org/works/f2jw7eu6.

33

JOHANN GEORG ZIMMERMAN (1728–1795), *SOLITUDE*

(London: T. Maiden, [1758] 1799), pp. 215–228

Johan Georg Zimmerman was a Swiss philosophical writer and physician, who wrote widely on a range of topics. His works were remarkably popular, translated from German into many languages including this version of *Solitude* in English. As a result, he was in high-demand in the Enlightenment courts of the period as a physician and advisor. *Solitude* engages in a debate of the period amongst philosophers and similar writers about whether the moral emotions are best nurtured in society or seclusion. Later writers like Rousseau (source 4) and Madame de Genlis (source 14) argued for the benefits of retirement, especially when rearing children. Conversely Zimmerman highlights that solitude can allow passions to grow without control, heightening tensions between individuals, unlike in cities where people can be distracted or encouraged to moderate feeling. Like other Enlightenment thinkers, such debates reflect on the sociability of the human and the production of the social contract, and provide evidence of how the period envisioned emotions as emerging through environment and socialisation.

. . .

Chapter VI: The influence of solitude on the passions

THE PASSIONS lose in Solitude a certain portion of that regulating weight by which in Society they are guided and controlled; The counteracting effects produced by variety, the restraints imposed by the obligations of civility, and the checks which arise from the calls of humanity, occur much less frequently in Retirement than amidst the multifarious transactions of a busy world. The desires and sensibilities of the heart having no real objects on which their vibrations can pendulate, are stimulated and increased by the powers of imagination. All the propensities of the soul, indeed, experience a degree of restlessness and vehemence greater than they ever feel while diverted by the pleasures, subdued by the surrounding distresses, and engaged by the business of active and social life.

The calm which seems to accompany the mind in its retreat is deceitful; the passions are secretly at work within the heart; the imagination is continually heaping fuel on the latent fire, and at length the labouring desire bursts forth, and glows with volcanic heat and fury. The temporary inactivity and inertness which Retirement seems to impose, may check, but cannot subdue the energies of spirit. The high pride and lofty ideas of great and independent minds may be, for a while, lulled into repose; but the moment the feelings of such a character are awakened by indignity or outrage, its anger springs like an elastic body drawn from its centre, and pierces with vigorous severity the object that provoked it. The perils of Solitude, indeed, always encrease in proportion as the sensibilities, imaginations, and passions of its votaries are quick, excursive, and violent. The man may be the inmate of a cottage, but the same passions and inclinations still lodge within his heart: *his* mansion may be changed, but *their* residence is the same; and though they appear to be silent and undisturbed, they are secretly influencing all the propensities of his heart. Whatever be the cause of his retirement, whether it be a sense of undeserved misfortune, the ingratitude of supposed friends, the pangs of despised love, or the disappointment of ambition, memory prevents the wound from healing, and stings the soul with indignation and resentment. The image of departed pleasures haunts the mind, and robs it of its wished tranquillity. The ruling passion still subsists; it fixes itself more strongly on the fancy; moves with greater agitation; and becomes, in retirement, in proportion as it is inclined to VICE or VIRTUE, either a horrid and tormenting *spectre*, inflicting apprehension and dismay, or a delightful and supporting *angel*, irradiating the countenance with smiles of joy, and filling the heart with peace and gladness.

> Blest is the man, as far as earth can bless,
> Whose measur'd PASSIONS reach no wild excess;
> Who, urged by Nature's voice, her gifts enjoys,
> Nor other means than Nature's force employs.
> While warm with youth the sprightly current flows,
> Each vivid sense with vigorous rapture glows;
> And when he droops beneath the hand of age,
> No vicious habit stings with fruitless rage;
> Gradual his strength and gay sensations cease,
> While joys tumultuous sink in silent peace.

The extraordinary power which the PASSIONS assume, and the improper channel in which they are apt to flow in retired situations, is conspicuous from the greater acrimony with which they are in general tainted in small villages than in large towns. It is true, indeed, that they do not always explode in such situations with the open and daring violence which they exhibit in the metropolis; but lie buried as it were, and mouldering in the bosom with a more malignant flame. To those who only observe the listlessness and languor which distinguish the characters of those who reside in small provincial towns, the slow and uniform rotation of amusements which fills up the leisure of their lives; the confused wildness of their cares; the poor subterfuges to which they are continually resorting, in order to avoid the clouds of discontent that impend in angry darkness, over their heads; the lagging current of their drooping spirits; the miserable poverty of their intellectual powers; the eagerness with which they strive to raise a card party; the transports they enjoy on the prospect of any new diversion or occasional exhibition; the haste with which they run toward any sudden, unexpected noise that interrupts the deep silence of their situation; and the patient industry with which, from day to day, they watch each other's conduct, and circulate reports of every action of each other's lives, will scarcely imagine that any virulence of passion can disturb the bosoms of persons who live in so quiet and seemingly composed a state. But the unoccupied time and barren minds of such characters cause the faintest emotions, and most common desires, to act with all the violence of high and untamed passions. The lowest diversions, a cock fighting, or a pony race, make the bosom of a country 'squire beat with the highest rapture; while the inability to attend the monthly ball fills the minds of his wife and daughter with the keenest anguish. Circumstances, which scarcely make any impression on those who reside in the metropolis, plunge every description of residents in a country village into all the extravagances of joy, or the dejection of sorrow; from the peer to the peasant, from the duchess to the dairy maid, all is rapture and convulsion. Competition is carried on for the humble honors and petty interests of a sequestered town, or miserable hamlet, with as much heat and rancor, as it is for the highest dignities and greatest emoluments of the state. Upon many occasions, indeed, ambition, envy, revenge, and all the disorderly and malignant passions, are felt and exercised with a greater degree of violence and obstinacy amidst the little contentions of claybuilt cottages, than ever prevailed amidst the highest commotions of courts. PLUTARCH relates that when CÆSER, after his appointment to the government of *Spain*, came to a little town, as he was passing the Alps, his friends, by way of mirth, took occasion to say, "Can there here be any disputes for offices, any contentions for precedency, or such envy and ambition as we behold among the great in all the transactions of imperial ROME?" The idea betrayed their ignorance of human nature; while the celebrated reply of their great commander, that *He would rather be the first man in this little town, than the second even in the imperial city*, spoke the language, not of an individual, but of the species; and instructed them that there is no place, however insignificant, in which the same passions do not proportionately prevail. The humble competitors for village honors, however low and subordinate they may be, feel as great anxiety for pre-eminence, as much jealousy of rivals, and as violent envy against superiors, as agitate the bosoms of the most ambitious statesmen in contending for the highest prize of glory, of riches, or of power. The manner, perhaps, in which these inferior candidates exert their passions may be less artful, and the objects of them less noble, but they are certainly not less virulent. "Having," says EUPHELIA, who had quitted *London*, to enjoy the quietude and happiness of a rural village, "been driven by the mere necessity of escaping from absolute inactivity, to make myself more acquainted with the affairs and happiness of this place, I am now no longer a stranger to *rural conversation* and employments; but am far from discerning in them more innocence or wisdom than in the sentiments or conduct of those with whom I have passed more cheerful and more fashionable hours. It is common to reproach the tea table and the park, with giving opportunities and encouragement to scandal I cannot wholly clear them from the charge, but must, however, observe, in favor of the modish prattlers, that if not by principle, we are at least by accident, less guilty of defamation than the country ladies. For, having greater numbers to observe and censure, we are commonly content to charge them only with their own faults or follies, and seldom give way to malevolence, but such as arises from injury or affront, real or imaginary, offered to ourselves. But in those distant provinces, where the same families inhabit the same houses from age to age, they transmit and recount the faults of a whole succession. I have been informed how every estate in the neighbourhood was originally got, and find, if I may credit the accounts given me, that there is not a single acre in the hands of the right owner. I have been told of intrigues between beaus and toasts, that have been now three centuries in their quiet graves; and am often entertained with traditional scandal on persons of whose names there would have been no remembrance, had they not committed somewhat that might disgrace their descendants. If once there happens a quarrel between the principal persons of two families, the malignity is continued without end; and it is common for old maids to fall out about some election in which their grandfathers were competitors. Thus malice and hatred descend here with an inheritance; and it is necessary to be well versed in history, that the various factions of the country may be understood. You cannot expect to be on good terms with families who are resolved to love nothing in common; and in selecting your intimates, you are, perhaps, to consider which party you most favor in the Barons' Wars."

Resentments and enmities burn with a much more furious flame among the thinly-scattered inhabitants of a petty village, than amidst the ever varying concourse of a great metropolis. The objects by which the passions are set on fire are hidden from our view by the tumults which prevail in a crowded city, and the bosom willingly loses the pains which such emotions excite when the causes which occasioned them are forgot: but in country villages, the thorns by which the feelings have been hurt are continually before our eyes, and preserve on every approach toward them, a remembrance of the injuries sustained. An extreme devout and highly religious lady, who resided in a retired hamlet in *Swisserland*, once told me, in a conversation on this subject, that she had completely suppressed all indignation against the envy, the hatred, and the malice of her surrounding neighbours; for that she found they were so deeply dyed in sin, that a rational remonstrance was lost upon them; and that the only vexation she felt from a sense of their wretchedness arose from the idea that her soul would at the last day be obliged to keep company with such incorrigible wretches.

The inhabitants of the country, indeed, both of the lower and middling classes, cannot be expected to possess characters of a very respectable kind, when we look at the conduct of those who set them the example. A country magistrate, who has certainly great opportunities of forming the manners and morals of the

SCIENCE AND PHILOSOPHY

district over which he presides, is in general puffed up with high and extravagant conceptions of the superiority of his wisdom, and the extent of his power; and raising his idea of the greatness of his character in an inverse proportion to his notions of the insignificance and littleness of those around him, he sits enthroned with fancied pre-eminence, the disdainful tyrant, rather than the kind protector of his neighbours. Deprived of all liberal and instructive society, confined in their knowledge both of men and things, the slaves of prejudice and the pupils of folly; with contracted hearts and degraded faculties the inhabitants of a country village feel all the base and ignoble passions, sordid rapacity, mean envy, and insulting ostentation more forcibly than they are felt either in the enlarged society of the metropolis, or even in the confined circle of the monastery.

The social virtues, indeed, are almost totally excluded from cloisters, as well as from every other kind of solitary institution: for when the habits, interests, and pleasures of the species are pent up by any means within a narrow compass, mutual jealousies and exasperations must prevail; every trifling immunity, petty privilege, and paltry distinction, becomes an object of the most violent contention; and increasing animosities at length reach to such a degree of virulence, that the pious flock is converted into a herd of famished wolves, eager to worry and devour each other.

The laws of every convent strictly enjoin the holy sisterhood to live in Christian charity and sincere affection with each other. I have, however, when attending these fair recluses in my professional character, observed many of them with wrinkles, that seemed rather the effect of angry perturbation, than of peaceful age, with aspects formed rather by envy, hatred, malice, and all uncharitableness, than by mild benevolence and singleness of heart. But I should do injustice if I did not declare, that I have seen some few who were strangers to such unworthy passions; whose countenances were unindented by their effects: and whose beauty and comeliness still shone in their native lustre and simplicity. It was, indeed, painful to reflect upon the sufferings which these lovely innocents must endure, until the thoughts of their lost hopes, defeated happiness, and unmerited wrongs, should have changed the milky kindness of their virtuous dispositions into the gall-like bitterness of vexation and despair; until the brightness of their charming features should be darkened by the clouds of discontent, which their continued imprisonment would create; and until their cheerful and easy tempers should be perverted by the corrosions of those vindictive passions which the jealous furies, with whom they were immured, and to whom they formed so striking a contrast, must in time so cruelly inflict. These lovely mourners, on entering the walls of a convent, are obliged to submit to the tyranny of an envious superior, or the jealousy of the older inmates, whose angry passions arise in proportion as they perceive others less miserable than themselves; and retiring, at the stated periods, from their joint persecution, they find that the gloomy solitude to which they have flown, only tends to aggravate and widen the wound it was expected to cure. It is, indeed, almost impossible for any female, however amiable, to preserve in the joyless gloom of conventual Solitude the cheering sympathies of nature. A retrospect of her past life most probably exhibits to her tortured fancy, superstition stinging with scorpion like severity her pious mind; love sacrificed on the altar of family pride; or fortune ruined by the avarice of a perfidious guardian; while the future presents to her view the dreary prospect of an eternal and melancholy separation from all the enjoyments of society, and a continual exposure to the petulance and ill humour of the dissatisfied sisterhood. What disposition, however mild and gentle by nature, can preserve itself amidst such confluent dangers? How is it possible to prevent the most amiable tenderness of heart, the most lively and sensible mind from becoming, under such circumstances, a prey to the bitterness of affliction and malevolence? Those who have had an opportunity to observe the operation of the passions on the habits, humours, and dispositions of recluse females, have perceived with horror the cruel and unrelenting fury with which they goad the soul, and with what an imperious and irresistible voice they command obedience to their inclination.

The passion of Love, in particular, acts with much greater force upon the mind that endeavours to escape from its effects by retirement, than it does when it is either resisted or indulged.

---------------- Who is free from LOVE?
All space he actuates, like almighty Jove!
He haunts us waking, haunts us in our dreams;
With vigorous flight bursts thro' the cottage windows.
If we seek shelter from his persecution
In the remotest corner of a forest,
We there elude not his pursuit; for there
With eagle wing he overtakes his prey.

Retirement, under such circumstances, is a childish expedient; it is expecting to achieve that, by means of a fearful flight, which it is frequently too much for the courage and the constancy of heroes to subdue. Retirement is the very nest and harbour of this powerful passion. How many abandon the gay and jovial circles of the world, renounce even the most calm and satisfactory delights of friendship, and quit, without a sigh, the most delicious and highest seasoned pleasures of Society, to seek in Retirement the superior joys of Love! a passion in whose high and tender delights the insolence of power, the treachery of friendship, and the most vindictive malice, is immediately forgot. It is a passion, when pure, that can never experience the least decay; no course of time, no change of place, no alteration of circumstances, can erase or lessen the ideas of that bliss which it has once imprinted on the heart. Its characters are indelible. Solitude, in its most charming state, and surrounded by its amplest, powers, affords no resource against its anxieties, its jealous fears, its tender alarms, its soft sorrows, or its inspiringly tumultuous joys. The bosom that is once deeply wounded by the barbed dart of real love, seldom recovers its tranquillity, but enjoys, if happy, the highest of

SCIENCE AND PHILOSOPHY

human delights; and if miserable, the deepest of human torments. But, although the love-sick shepherd fills the lonely vallies, and the verdant groves, with the softest sighs, or severest sorrows, and the cells of the monasteries and convents resound with heavy groans and deep-toned curses against the malignity of this passion, SOLITUDE may perhaps, for a while suspend, if it cannot extinguish its fury. Of the truth of this observation, the history of those unfortunate, but real lovers, ABELARD and ELOISA, furnishes a memorable instance.

34

ADAM SMITH (1723–1790), *THE THEORY OF MORAL SENTIMENTS*

3rd ed. (London: A. Millar, 1767), pp. 1–15

Adam Smith was a Scottish philosopher and key figure of the Scottish Enlightenment, particularly known for his works on political economy. His first work, *The Theory of Moral Sentiments* explores how humanity's sociability shaped their moral action, and the various factors involved in this process. Smith places a particular emphasis on sympathy, whereby we partake in the feelings of other. This capacity can be dangerous, as a person might be overwhelmed by another's feeling and so lose their sense of an independent self, but it can also encourage sociable behaviour, as we attend to other's feelings and so behave ethically in response. He assumes a sensible body, where our emotions are shaped by our senses, experiences and imagination, and which is underpinned by a core self-love, a product of our human nature. Like other Enlightenment texts of the period, it gives insight into how the body, emotions and the society they underpin were being conceptualised by scientists and philosophers.

. . .

Chap. I: *Of* sympathy

How selfish soever man may be supposed, there are evidently some principles in his nature, which interest him in the fortune of others, and render their happiness necessary to him, though he derives nothing from it except the pleasure of seeing it. Of this kind is pity or compassion, the emotion which we feel for the misery of others, when we either see it, or are made to conceive it in a very lively manner. That we often derive sorrow from the sorrow of others, is a matter of fact too obvious to require any instances to prove it; for this sentiment, like all the other original passions of human nature, is by no means confined to the virtuous and humane, though they perhaps may feel it with the most exquisite sensibility. The greatest ruffian, the most hardened violator of the laws of society, is not altogether without it.

As we have no immediate experience of what other men feel, we can form no idea of the manner in which they are affected, but by conceiving what we ourselves should feel in the like situation. Though our brother is upon the rack, as

SCIENCE AND PHILOSOPHY

long as we ourselves are at our ease, our senses will never inform us of what he suffers. They never did, and never can, carry us beyond our own person, and it is by the imagination only that we can form any conception of what are his sensations. Neither can that faculty help us to this any other way, than by representing to us what would be our own, if we were in his case. It is the impressions of our own senses only, not those of his, which our imaginations copy. By the imagination we place ourselves in his situation, we conceive ourselves enduring all the same torments, we enter as it were into his body, and become in some measure the same person with him, and thence form some idea of his sensations, and even feel something which, though weaker in degree, is not altogether unlike them. His agonies, when they are thus brought home to ourselves, when we have thus adopted and made them our own, begin at last to affect us, and we then tremble and shudder at the thought of what he feels. For as to be in pain or distress of any kind excites the most excessive sorrow, so to conceive or to imagine that we are in it, excites some degree of the same emotion, in proportion to the vivacity or dulness of the conception.

That this is the source of our fellow-feeling for the misery of others, that it is by changing places in fancy with the sufferer, that we come either to conceive or to be affected by what he feels, may be demonstrated by many obvious observations, if it should not be thought sufficiently evident of itself. When we see a stroke aimed and just ready to fall upon the leg or arm of another person, we naturally shrink and draw back our own leg or our own arm; and when it does fall, we feel it in some measure, and are hurt by it as well as the sufferer. The mob, when they are gazing at a dancer on the slack rope, naturally writhe and twist and balance their own bodies, as they see him do, and as they feel that they themselves must do if in his situation. Persons of delicate fibres and a weak constitution of body complain, that in looking on the sores and ulcers which are exposed by beggars in the streets, they are apt to feel an itching or uneasy sensation in the correspondent part of their own bodies. The horror which they conceive at the misery of those wretches affects that particular part in themselves more than any other; because that horror arises from conceiving what they themselves would suffer, if they really were the wretches whom they are looking upon, and if that particular part in themselves was actually affected in the same miserable manner. The very force of this conception is sufficient, in their feeble frames, to produce that itching or uneasy sensation complained of. Men of the most robust make, observe that in looking upon sore eyes they often feel a very sensible soreness in their own, which proceeds from the same reason; that organ being in the strongest man more delicate, than any other part of the body is in the weakest.

Neither is it those circumstances only, which create pain or sorrow, that call forth our fellow-feeling. Whatever is the passion which arises from any object in the person principally concerned, an analogous emotion springs up, at the thought of his situation, in the breast of every attentive spectator. Our joy for the deliverance of those heroes of tragedy or romance who interest us, is as sincere as our grief for their distress, and our fellow-feeling with their misery is not more real than that with their happiness. We enter into their gratitude towards those faithful friends who did not desert them in their difficulties; and we heartily go along with their resentment against those perfidious traitors who injured, abandoned, or deceived them. In every passion of which the mind of man is susceptible, the emotions of the by-stander always correspond to that, by bringing the case home to himself, he imagines should be the sentiments of the sufferer.

Pity and compassion are words appropriated to signify our fellow-feeling with the sorrow of others. Sympathy, though its meaning was, perhaps, originally the same, may now, however, without much impropriety, be made use of to denote our fellow-feeling with any passion whatever.

Upon some occasions sympathy may seen to arise merely from the view of a certain emotion in another person. The passions, upon some occasions, may seem to be transfused from one man to another, instantaneously and antecedent to any knowledge of what excited them in the person principally concerned. Grief and joy, for example, strongly expressed in the look and gestures of any one, at once affect the spectator with some degree of a like painful or agreeable emotion. A smiling face is, to every body that sees it, a cheerful object; as a sorrowful countenance, on the other hand, is a melancholy one.

This, however, does not hold universally, or with regard to every passion. There are some passions of which the expressions excite no sort of sympathy, but before we are acquainted with what gave occasion to them, serve rather to disgust and provoke us against them. The furious behaviour of an angry man is more likely to exasperate us against himself than against his enemies. As we are unacquainted with his provocation, we cannot bring his case home to ourselves, nor conceive any thing like the passions which it excites. But we plainly see what is the situation of those with whom he is angry, and to what violence they may be exposed from so enraged an adversary. We readily, therefore, sympathize with their fear or resentment, and are immediately disposed to take part against the man from whom they appear to be in so much danger.

If the very appearances of grief and joy inspire us with some degree of the like emotions, it is because they suggest to us the general idea of some good or bad fortune that has befallen the person in whom we observe them: and in these passions this is sufficient to have some little influence upon us. The effects of grief and joy terminate in the person who feels those emotions, of which the expressions do not, like those of resentment, suggest to us the idea of any other person for whom we are concerned, and whose interests are opposite to his. The general idea of good or bad fortune, therefore, creates some concern for the person who has met with it, but the general idea of provocation excites no sympathy with the anger of the man who has received it. Nature, it seems, teaches us to be more averse to enter into this passion, and, till informed of its cause, to be disposed rather to take part against it.

Even our sympathy with the grief or joy of another, before we are informed of the cause of either, is always extremely imperfect. General lamentations, which express nothing but the anguish of the sufferer, create rather a curiosity to inquire

265

into his situation, along with some disposition to sympathize with him, than any actual sympathy that is very sensible. The first question which we ask is, What has befallen you? Till this be answered, though we are uneasy both from the vague idea of his misfortune, and still more from torturing ourselves with conjectures about what it may be, yet our fellow-feeling is not very considerable.

Sympathy, therefore, does not arise so much from the view of the passion, as from that of the situation which excites it. We sometimes feel for another, a passion of which he himself seems to be altogether incapable; because, when we put ourselves in his case, that passion arises in our breast from the imagination, though it does not in his from the reality. We blush for the impudence and rudeness of another, though he himself appears to have no sense of the impropriety of his own behaviour; because we cannot help feeling with what confusion we ourselves should be covered, had we behaved in so absurd a manner.

Of all the calamities to which the condition of mortality exposes mankind, the loss of reason appears, to those who have the least spark of humanity, by far the most dreadful, and they behold that last stage of human wretchedness with deeper commiseration than any other. But the poor wretch, who is in it, laughs and sings perhaps, and is altogether insensible of his own misery. The anguish which humanity feels, therefore, at the sight of such an object, cannot be the reflection of any sentiment of the sufferer. The compassion of the spectator must arise altogether from the consideration of what he himself would feel if he was reduced to the same unhappy situation, and, what perhaps is impossible, was at the same time able to regard it with his present reason and judgment.

What are the pangs of a mother, when she hears the moanings of her infant that during the agony of disease cannot express what it feels? In her idea of what it suffers, she joins, to its real helplessness, her own consciousness of that helplessness, and her own terrors for the unknown consequences of its disorder; and out of all these, forms, for her own sorrow, the most complete image of misery and distress. The infant, however, feels only the uneasiness of the present instant, which can never be great. With regard to the future, it is perfectly secure, and in its thoughtlessness and want of foresight, possesses an antidote against fear and anxiety, the great tormentors of the human breast, from which reason and philosophy will, in vain, attempt to defend it, when it grows up to a man.

We sympathize even with the dead, and overlooking what is of real importance in their situation, that awful futurity which awaits them, we are chiefly affected by those circumstances which strike our senses, but can have no influence upon their happiness. It is miserable, we think, to be deprived of the light of the sun; to be shut out from life and conversation; to be laid in the cold grave, a prey to corruption and the reptiles of the earth; to be no more thought of in this world, but to be obliterated, in a little time, from the affections, and almost from the memory, of their dearest friends and relations. Surely, we imagine, we can never feel too much for those who have suffered so dreadful a calamity. The tribute of our fellow-feeling seems doubly due to them now, when they are in danger of being forgot by every body; and, by the vain honours which we pay to their memory, we endeavour, for our own misery, artificially to keep alive our melancholy remembrance of their misfortune. That our sympathy can afford them no consolation seems to be an addition to their calamity; and to think that all we can do is unavailing, and that, what alleviates all other distress, the regret, the love, and the lamentations of their friends, can yield no comfort to them, serves only to exasperate our sense of their misery. The happiness of the dead, however, most assuredly, is affected by none of these circumstances; nor is it the thought of these things which can ever disturb the profound security of their repose. The idea of that dreary and endless melancholy, which the fancy naturally ascribes to their condition, arises altogether from our joining to the change which has been produced upon them, our own consciousness of that change, from our putting ourselves in their situation, and from our lodging, if I may be allowed to say so, our own living souls in their inanimated bodies, and thence conceiving what would be our emotions in this case. It is from this very illusion of the imagination, that the foresight of our own dissolution is so terrible to us, and that the idea of those circumstances, which undoubtedly can give us no pain when we are dead, makes us miserable while we are alive. And from thence arises one of the most important principles in human nature, the dread of death, the great poison to the happiness, but the great restraint upon the injustice of mankind, which, while it afflicts and mortifies the individual, guards and protects the society.

Chap. II: Of the pleasure of mutual sympathy

BUT whatever may be the cause of sympathy, or however it may be excited, nothing pleases us more than to observe in other men a fellow-feeling with all the emotions of our own breast; nor are we ever so much shocked as by the appearance of the contrary. Those who are fond of deducing all our sentiments from certain refinements of self-love, think themselves at no loss to account, according to their own principles, both for this pleasure and this pain. Man, say they, conscious of his own weakness, and of the need which he has for the assistance of others, rejoices whenever he observes that they adopt his own passions, because he is then assured of that assistance; and grieves whenever he observes the contrary, because he is then assured of their opposition. But both the pleasure and the pain are always felt so instantaneously, and often upon such frivolous occasions, that it seems evident that neither of them can be derived from any such self-interested consideration. A man is mortified when, after having endeavoured to divert the company, he looks round and sees that nobody laughs at his jests but himself. On the contrary, the mirth of the company is highly agreeable to him, and he regards this correspondence of their sentiments with his own as the greatest applause.

Neither does his pleasure seem to arise altogether from the additional vivacity which his mirth may receive from sympathy with theirs, nor his pain from the disappointment he meets with when he misses this pleasure; though both the one and the other, no doubt, do in some measure. When we have read a book or poem so often that we can no longer find any amusement in reading it by ourselves, we

SCIENCE AND PHILOSOPHY

can still take pleasure in reading it to a companion. To him it has all the graces of novelty; we enter into the surprise and admiration which it naturally excites in him, but which it is no longer capable of exciting in us; we consider all the ideas which it presents rather in the light in which they appear to him, than in that in which they appear to ourselves, and we are amused by sympathy with his amusement which thus enlivens our own. On the contrary, we should be vexed if he did not seem to be entertained with it, and we could no longer take any pleasure in reading it to him. It is the same case here. The mirth of the company, no doubt, enlivens our own mirth, and their silence, no doubt, disappoints us. But though this may contribute both to the pleasure which we derive from the one, and to the pain which we feel from the other, it is by no means the sole cause of either; and this correspondence of the sentiments of others with our own appears to be a cause of pleasure, and the want of it a cause of pain, which cannot be accounted for in this manner. The sympathy, which my friends express with my joy, might, indeed, give me pleasure by enlivening that joy: but that which they express with my grief could give me none, if it served only to enliven that grief. Sympathy, however, enlivens joy and alleviates grief. It enlivens joy by presenting another source of satisfaction; and it alleviates grief by insinuating into the heart almost the only agreeable sensation which it is at that time capable of receiving.

It is to be observed accordingly, that we are still more anxious to communicate to our friends our disagreeable than our agreeable passions, that we derive still more satisfaction from their sympathy with the former than from that with the latter, and that we are still more shocked by the want of it.

How are the unfortunate relieved when they have found out a person to whom they can communicate the cause of their sorrow? Upon his sympathy they seem to disburthen themselves of a part of their distress: he is not improperly said to share it with them. He not only feels a sorrow of the same kind with that which they feel, but as if he had derived a part of it to himself, what he feels seems to alleviate the weight of what they feel. Yet by relating their misfortunes they in some measure renew their grief. They awaken in their memory the remembrance of those circumstances which occasioned their affliction. Their tears accordingly flow faster than before, and they are apt to abandon themselves to all the weakness of sorrow. They take pleasure, however, in all this, and, it is evident, are sensibly relieved by it; because the sweetness of his sympathy more than compensates the bitterness of that sorrow, which, in order to excite this sympathy, they had thus enlivened and renewed. The cruelest insult, on the contrary, which can be offered to the unfortunate, is to appear to make light of their calamities. To seem not to be affected with the joy of our companions is but want of politeness; but not to wear a serious countenance when they tell us their afflictions, is real and gross inhumanity.

Love is an agreeable; resentment, a disagreeable passion; and accordingly we are not half so anxious that our friends should adopt our friendships, as that they should enter into our resentments. We can forgive them though they seem to be little affected with the favours which we may have received, but lose all patience if they seem indifferent about the injuries which may have been done to us: nor are we half so angry with them for not entering into our gratitude, as for not sympathizing with our resentment. They can easily avoid being friends to our friends, but can hardly avoid being enemies to those with whom we are at variance. We seldom resent their being at enmity with the first, though upon that account we may sometimes affect to make an awkward quarrel with them; but we quarrel with them in good earnest if they live in friendship with the last. The agreeable passions of love and joy can satisfy and support the heart without any auxiliary pleasure. The bitter and painful emotions of grief and resentment more strongly require the healing consolation of sympathy.

As the person who is principally interested in any event is pleased with our sympathy, and hurt by the want of it, so we, too, seem to be pleased when we are able to sympathize with him, and to be hurt when we are unable to do so. We run not only to congratulate the successful, but to condole with the afflicted; and the pleasure which we find in the conversation of one whom in all the passions of his heart we can entirely sympathize with, seems to do more than compensate the painfulness of that sorrow with which the view of his situation affects us. On the contrary, it is always disagreeable to feel that we cannot sympathize with him, and instead of being pleased with this exemption from sympathetic pain, it hurts us to find that we cannot share his uneasiness. If we hear a person loudly lamenting his misfortunes, which, however, upon bringing the case home to ourselves, we feel, can produce no such violent effect upon us, we are shocked at his grief; and, because we cannot enter into it, call it pusillanimity and weakness. It gives us the spleen, on the other hand, to see another too happy or too much elevated, as we call it, with any little piece of good fortune. We are disobliged even with his joy; and, because we cannot go along with it, call it levity and folly. We are even put out of humour if our companion laughs louder or longer at a joke than we think it deserves; that is, than we feel that we ourselves could laugh at it.

35

JOHN LEAKE (1729–1792), *PRACTICAL OBSERVATIONS TOWARDS THE PREVENTION AND CURE OF CHRONIC DISEASES PECULIAR TO WOMEN*

7th ed. (London, Baldwin, [1777] 1792),
pp. 224–228, 229–232, 237–248, 252–253

John Leake was an English man-midwife and son of a clergyman, who worked in Portugal and England. He helped to found, and later worked as a physician, at the Westminster Lying-In Hospital, where poor women came to give birth. This gave him ample practical experience of midwifery, and Leake wrote his subsequent medical treatises, including this source, for female readers, rather than other physicians. In the excerpt below, he explores female nervous disorders, often marked by their impact on the emotions. While hysteria had a longer history, Leake's account uses contemporary nerve theory to explain emotional disorders, and reflects current thinking that links nerves and vitalism, with sensibility and imagination, in the production of emotional experience.

. . .

Section X: Of nervous disorders, hysteric affections, low spirits, and melancholy; their treatment and care

THE word *Nervous* has been so vaguely and indiscriminately applied, that it is necessary to ascertain the complaints truly such, and to distinguish them from others improperly so called.

THOSE disorders may be deemed nervous, where, from an *original* fault, or *infirm texture* of the nerves, they become disagreeably affected by such slender causes as would not produce the like sensations in others, whose nerves were in a natural state.

INSTEAD of regarding this simple distinction, almost every disorder accompanied with weak nerves, has been improperly called *nervous:* But in this general and indefinite sense, all diseases may be called so for, the nerves being the only susceptible parts of animal bodies, and every where interwoven with their solids, must suffer in proportion as they are injured by disease or external violence.

SUCH complaints being only symptoms or consequences of preceding diseases, cannot with propriety be called *nervous*, any more than a person may be said to be deeply consumptive, after a severe fit of illness which had reduced him to skin and bones.

BEFORE we proceed further, it will be necessary to explain, in a simple manner, the nature of those bodily powers which constitute the very *principles of life*.

THE human body is sustained and kept alive by three principal powers, which, like the movements of a watch, co-operate and mutually assist each other: The first is the *Brain* and *nervous system* proceeding from it, the great source of all sensation; the second is the *Heart*, with its *arteries* or blood vessels; and the third is the *stomach* and *bowels*, which prepare aliment for the body's nourishment.

In speaking of *digestion*, it was remarked, that the stomach loses its power when deprived of *nervous influence*; and we must here take notice, that the regularity and vigor of the heart's motion chiefly depend on the same cause.

As, therefore, the *brain and nerves*, the *heart and arteries*, with the *stomach and alimentary tube*, are the principal instruments of all sensation, circulation, nutrition, life and motion, and the very agents which govern and direct the whole animal machine; it will necessarily follow, that when any of them becomes disconcerted and put out of order, the vital functions of the body must then be unduly performed.

"Where one link's broken, the whole chain's destroy'd."

Such is the extraordinary sympathy and intercourse between those several organs, that, like so many little provinces, allied by mutual interest, not one of them can exercise its full power without the concurrence of the whole; for, as the heart and stomach cannot act without the assistance of the brain, or the stomach digest without receiving a due quantity of blood from the heart; so neither can the heart have sufficient force to keep up the circulation, without continual supplies from the stomach; or even the brain itself exert its influence over those organs without being duly nourished by both.

BUT, besides those parts, as well as the *action of the lungs*, there is a more latent principle of life, called *Irritability*, which does not depend upon either of the former powers, since it continues to exist in the body, after all *sensibility* and *circulation* are lost, and every vital principle, but itself totally extinguished and destroyed.

By *Irritability* is meant that property of the animal fibre, which, on being stimulated, has a power to contract and shorten, although the animal be dead; for the Heart, which is the most irritable part, may be excited into motion, even after the head has been cut off; hence we may conclude that Irritability is not only

SCIENCE AND PHILOSOPHY

independent of *sensibility* and *circulation*, but even of the soul itself; being found to exit after the brain, the seat of that *spiritual something*, has been destroyed or taken away.

. . .

EXPERIMENTS shew, that the degree of *Irritability* is in proportion to the firmness and consistence of that *mucas* or glue of which the whole bodily system is originally made up: Whatever, therefore, hardens this animal jelly, as cold, exercise, acids, and the like, diminish *Irritability*; and, on the contrary, the dissolving power of heat and moisture are found to increase it. Age, which also strengthens the fibres, relieves some diseases more effectually than medicines; as flushing in the face, nervous tremors, hysteric or epileptic fits, and scrophulous complaints about the time of maturity.

I have observed, that those of lax solids and delicate, hysterical habits, are thrown into a flurry of spirits from the most trifling causes; and that such impressions made on the female sex are often followed by pain in the bowels, a diarrhoea, or fever: in some cases, they occasion obstruction of the menses; in others, their excessive discharge, and sometimes a flooding in those who are pregnant.

The immediate cause of such effects has been attributed to an explosion or inordinate motion of the *animal spirits*. What are those *animal spirits*, or who ever saw them? It is very unfair thus to adopt words without meaning, or only denoting things which probably have no existence.

Such disorders seem to arise from *too much Irritability*, joined to *excess of nervous feeling*, which generally prevails at the same time; and, like the former, proceeds from want of sufficient firmness in that animal glue or cement which *constitutes the nervous coats*, as well as every part of the body.

Agreeable to this observation, we know, that long-continued illness, profuse evacuations, or whatever diminishes bodily strength, produces a preternatural degree of *Irritability* and *Sensibility*, though they are distinct qualities, and identically different from each other.

As old age approaches, the *mucus*, or animal glue, at last becomes so firm as to lose its former Irritability; hence, want of motion, or paralytic numbness in the body, succeeds; and at last, death itself.

This circumstance is sufficiently confirmed by observing how the muscular fibres which were very irritable in infancy, gradually became less so, as they are rendered more compact and tendinous from the effect of age. It also shews why those who have weak *stamina* in youth, grow stronger as they advance in years; likewise why they do not so suddenly become old as those of stronger habits, and why they are less subject to *acute diseases* arising from a firmer state of the fleshy fibres.

. . . .

So intimately connected are the body and mind, and such their correspondence, that impressions made on one mutually influence the other with like feelings:

JOHN LEAKE, *PRACTICAL OBSERVATIONS*

Thus, by *immoderate grief,* the digestive faculty of the stomach is impaired and by a blow on the head which injures the brain, the soul is as it were dethroned, and, losing its empire over the body, all sense and motion are instantly destroyed.

The mind or intellect, whilst confined to the body, "*that muddy vesture of decay,*" is obliged to stoop to the condition of the nerves, which are liable to alteration and depravity of feeling, from a thousand accidental and unavoidable causes. Those, as well as many other circumstances, concur to prove that the faculties of the mind chiefly depend on the bodily organs with which they co-operate, and where those are changed from their natural state, so are the mental feelings.

The stomach is often so much changed by age, that things grateful to it in the infant state, become disagreeable in more advanced life. Upon the same principle, the depraved appetite, or *preternatural longings,* of women with child, can only be accounted for: In pregnancy, a new system of vessels is formed, and a new circulation set on foot for nourishing the child; in consequence of this mechanical change, the *nervous feeling is altered,* which sometimes directs the appetite to things even disagreeable to it before.

How different is the disposition of body and mind when the vessels are empty or full, viz. after long fasting, or a plentiful meal? In the first, the pulse is weak and unequal, the complexion pale, the body languid, and the spirits irresolute and desponding; but, after eating and the use of wine, the springs of life are wound up, and the body and mind are restored to their native vigour.

The natural temper and genius of a people are most evident when they are left to act without restraint. A *Masquerade* will exemplify what I meant to suggest. – How great and evident is the change in the votaries of pleasure, before and after the midnight repast? He who, at first, with the gravity of a *Spaniard,* and phlegm of a *Dutchman,* silently wandered about like a Ghost waiting to be spoken to, is now suddenly transformed; the influence of beauty, and subtile spirit of Champaign, like the *orient liquor* of *Comus,* begin to animate the constitution. His spirits expand, his tongue is untied, he becomes nimble as *Mercury,* and more loquacious than a *Frenchman.*

Was it necessary farther to prove the sympathy between body and mind, and shew that every alteration of one, produces correspondent feelings in the other, it might be illustrated and confirmed by sensations peculiar to that change of constitution at the age of puberty, which influences the sexes in favour of each other, even to infatuation and madness.

All *sympathy,* as well as motion, entirely depends on the sensibility of the nerves; but, although they communicate motion to other parts, they are not at all irritable, and consequently destitute of motion themselves; a circumstance truly unaccountable.

The consent between the Brain and Heart is remarkable; for study or intense thinking quickens the pulse, and sudden fright will occasion palpitations, or a convulsive struggle or the heart, even sometimes to mortal suffocation. In both these cases, the first impression is made on the brain; and the heart, like a faithful compassion, suffers by sympathy but, whether the Nerves act as *tubes or vibrating*

273

cords, or serve as conductors to some subtle fluid, similar to that of *electric fire*, we are wholly ignorant; it is therefore not a little absurd in people to talk of *nervous fluid*, or animal spirits, with as much familiarity as if they had seen them put into a bottle.

NERVOUS *influence*, like attraction in the *load-stone*, or Irritability in the *sensitive plant*, may be considered as a property resulting from matter according to the peculiar modification of its parts, in itself utterly inexplicable, and of which we can know nothing from its effects.

As the blood-vessels proceed from the Heart, which is the instrument of circulation, so the Nerves, as already observed, are derived from the Brain, the great source of Sensation. We know, by feeling the pulse, that the action of the Heart gives motion to the blood; and it is no less evident, that the influence of the Brain governs and directs all perceptions of body and mind. Impressions, for example, made upon the last, by excessive grief or sudden terror, produce symptoms of great violence, or even death itself. Cold air admitted to the naked nerve of a decayed tooth, will feelingly persuade us, that the body, as well as the mind, may suffer by the mediation of the nerves.

The Brain seems therefore to the nerves, what the Heart is to the blood-vessels; for too violent a degree of action in the last, will increase circulation, and produce heat, as may be observed after violent exercise. In like manner, when the power of the Brain and nerves is violently impressed on the body or mind, their sensations will be rendered too quick and exquisite, like the motion of a watch, or fine machine, which becomes rapid and irregular when the main spring acts too strongly upon its subordinate movements.

Impressions made on the mind will often totally subdue those of the body; and on the contrary, such as are the made on the body will remove those of the mind; all which may supply an intelligent observer with useful hints in the cure of such nervous diseases as have been unsuccessfully treated by medicines.

Habitual *convulsions*, for instance, have sometimes been cured by the unexpected explosion of a gun, or the sudden outcry of *Fire* in the dead of night; the *hiccough* may be stopped by sudden surprise, and the approach of an *ague fit* has been prevented by the same cause.

But, the most extraordinary case which, perhaps, was ever produced to shew the *wonderful influence of mind over the body*, as well as the power of sympathy, is related by *Kaau Boerhaave* to the following purpose.

A girl at *Harlem* in *Holland*, on being frighted, fell into a strong convulsions, and, to the astonishment of the physicians there, those who crowded to her assistance, were immediately affected in the same manner. As the most powerful medicines were prescribed without any sort of relief, at last, the celebrated *Boerhaave* being sent for, determined to try the force of fear upon the imaginationl accordingly, he ordered a *formidable apparatus* of furnaces, with burning coals, and hooks of iron, to be placed before those who had been thus affected. He told them, that, since medicines had failed, there was no remedy but that of burning the arm of the first person affected, with a *red-hot iron*, down to the bone. In consequence of this, they were struck with exceeding *terror*, and so resisted with all their might the approach of the convulsive fit, that not one of them was seized with it afterwards.

It may be equally proper to mention another particular case of a contrary nature, to shew the *power of the body on the mind*. Dr. *Robinson*, in speaking of *hypochondriacal melancholy*, expresses himself in the following words:

> "A very worthy gentleman, on whose fidelity I may safely rely, assured me, that he knew a person who for several years had been melancholy mad, and who, in one of his frantic fits, flung himself out of a window three stories high, but accidentally pitching upon a *draw well*, he fell directly down into the water; and being taken up, was perfectly restored to the use of his senses. It was computed that he fell near thirty fathoms before he came to the surface of the water."

As we have seen that different passions, sensations, and appetites, at different periods of life, can only be accounted for from alteration of constitution, which *changes the nervous feeling*, so it will appear less surprising, that even diseases themselves, especially those of the *Brain* and *Nerves*, should sometimes be cured by the same cause; in consequence of age, or such immediate accidental impressions as those extraordinary ones already related.

In proportion as the solids of the body are more firm and strong, or lax and weak, the nerves, which are intimately interwoven with all its parts, will participate in the general habit, and become more or less endowed with sensibility.

For this reason, weakly women and children, in whom the membranous covering of the nerves is too soft, thin and delicate, are susceptible of slender impressions, from pain, or sudden fear, so as to produce paleness of the face, palpitation of the heart, convulsions, or other violent symptoms: On the contrary, robust men, and old people, whose nerves, in common with other parts, are hardened by the effects of age, become much less subject to those excessive emotions.

Tender bodies, such as the first, may be said to be *"trembling alive all o'er,"* and, like wax, to receive too deep an impression. Women, therefore, compared to men, are much more subject to nervous disorders, both from their natural delicacy of frame, and a more recluse manner of living, which deprives them of the benefits of exercise and fresh air.

Nervous disorders, thus arising from simple weakness, are always attended with a preternatural degree of *Feeling* and *Irritability*, and can only be cured by such means as *give more strength and firmness to the whole bodily system*.

The progress of age, which gradually imparts strength to the nervous threads interwoven with every part of the body, will therefore greatly assist in the cure of *nervous* and *hysterical* complaints arising from weakness.

Hence it may reasonably be concluded, the moderate *exercise*, in dry, pure air, the liberal use of *Peruvian bark*, with the iron waters of *Spa, Tunbridge* or *Islington*, and also the *cold bath*, are the principal remedies to be depended upon in this species of nervous disorders, as they are all known to strengthen the body; and, on the contrary, that *bleeding, vomits, strong purgatives*, the immoderate use of tea, or sedentary life, in warm, moist air, will be highly pernicious.

...

The stomach is more amply supplied with nerves than the womb, and therefore more susceptible; hence, in very irritable and delicate habits, it often becomes the seat of hysteric affections, from errors in diet, where the aliment offends in quantity or quality.

VIOLENT passions of the mind, as anger, or extreme jealousy, will often produce the same effect; and here it may again be remarked, that the impression is made on the nervous system in general, and not on those of the womb in particular.

However as hysterics have been observed to follow obstructed menses, it may be allowed, that they sometimes proceed from a local affection of the womb.

Hysterical and hypochondriae affections are of the same nature, for both proceed from weakness, and too much sensibility of the nervous system: The symptoms are only diversified by the difference of sex; in women, therefore this malady is called *hysteric passion*; in men, *hypochondriac melancholy*.

36

JOHANN HERDER (1744–1803), *OUTLINES OF A PHILOSOPHY OF A HISTORY OF MAN*

Trans. T. Churchill (New York: Bergman, [1784] 1800), pp. 98–103

Johan Herder was a German philosopher and theologian. He came from a poor household, but managed to attend university, studying under Immanuel Kant (1724–1804). He wrote a number of important works, including some key work on aesthetics and philology. *Outline of a Philosophy of a History of Man* offered an important account of human development, both emphasising universal human emotions, and how traits and characteristics were shaped by national and environmental contexts. Like other Enlightenment thinkers, he tied human nature into evolutionary and developmental processes, and saw human emotions as born of these experiences. Herder's work placed a similar emphasis on sociability, love and sympathy as critical to moral behaviour and society, as Smith (source 34) and Rousseau (source 4).

. . .

Chapter VI: Man is formed for humanity and religion

I WISH I could extend the signification of the word *humanity*, so as to comprise in it every thing I have thus far said on the noble conformation of man to reason and liberty, to finer senses and appetites, to the most delicate yet strong health, to the population and rule of the Earth: for man has not a more dignified word for his destination, than what expresses himself, in whom the image of the creator lives imprinted as visibly as it can be here. We need only delineate his form, to develope his noblest duties.

All the appetites of a living being may be traced to the *support of self*, and to *a participation with others*: the organic structure of man, if a superiour direction be added to it, gives to these appetites the nicest order. While a right line possesses the most stability, man has also for his protection the smallest circumference without, and the most varied velocity within. He stands on the narrowest basis, and therefore can most easily cover his limbs. His centre of gravity falls between the

SCIENCE AND PHILOSOPHY

supplest and strongest haunches, that any creature upon Earth can boast; and no brute displays in these parts the mobility and strength of man. His flattened, steely chest, and the position of his arms, give him the most extensive sphere of defence above, to protect his heart, and guard his noblest vital parts from the head to the knee. It is no fable, that men have encountered lions, and overcome them: the african, when he combines prudence and address with strength, is a match for more than one. It must be confessed, however, that man's structure is less calculated for attack than defence: in that he needs the assistance of art; in this he is by nature the most powerful creature upon Earth. Thus his very form teaches him to live in *peace*, not to addict himself to deeds of blood and rapine: and this constitutes the first characteristic of humanity.

2. Among the appetites, that have reference to others, the desire of propagating the species is the most powerful: and this in man is subordinate to the promotion of humanity. What with fourfooted beasts, even with the modest elephant, is copulation, with him, in consequence of his structure, is kissing and embracing. No brute has human lips, the delicate rim of which is the last part of the face formed in the womb: the beautiful and intelligent closing of these lips is, as it were, the last mark of the finger of love. The modest expression of ancient languages, that he knew his wife, is applicable to no brute. Ancient fables say, that the two sexes at first formed an hermaphrodite, as in flowers, but were afterwards separated. This and other expressive fictions were intended, to convey the secret meaning of the superiority of human over brutal love. That this desire in man is not subject to the control of seasons, as in brutes, though no accurate observations on the revolutions in the human body in this respect have yet been made, evidently shows, that it is not dependent on necessity, but on the incitement of love, remains under the dominion of reason, and was designedly left to voluntary temperance, like every thing pertaining to man. Thus love in man was to be *human*; and with this view Nature appointed, exclusive of his form, the later developement, duration, and state of desire, in both sexes: nay she brought it under the law of a *voluntary social alliance*, and the most friendly communion between two beings, who feel themselves united in one for life.

3. As all the tender affections, except imparting and receiving love, are satisfied with participation; Nature has formed man most of all living creatures for participating in the fate of others, having framed him as it were out of all the rest, and organized him similarly to every part of the creation in such a degree, that he can feel with each. The structure of his fibres is so fine, delicate, and elastic, his nerve are so diffused over every part of his vibrating frames that, like an image of the allsentient deity, he can put himself almost in the place of every creature, and can share it's feelings in the degree necessary to the creature, and which his own frame will bear without being disordered; nay even at the hazard of disordering it. Accordingly our machine, so far as it is a growing, flourishing tree, feels even with trees; and there are men, who cannot bear to see a young green tree cut down or destroyed. We regret it's blighted top: we lament the withering of a favourite flower. A feeling man views not the writhing of a bruised worm with indifference:

and the more perfect a creature is the nearer it's organization approaches our own, the more sympathy is excited in us by it's sufferings. He must possess rigid nerves, who can open a living creature; and watch it's convulsive movements: nothing but an insatiate thirst for fame and science can gradually deaden his organic sensibility. More delicate women cannot bear even the dissection of a dead body: they feel pain in each limb, as their eyes follow the course of the knife; and this pain is more acute. in proportion to the nobleness and sensibility of the part. To see the bowels torn out excites disgust and horrour: when the heart is pierced, the lungs divided, the brain cut to pieces, we feel the keen edge of the instrument in our own. We sympathize with the corpse of a dead friend, even in the grave: we feel the cold pit, which he feels not: and shudder when we touch his bones. The common mother, who has taken all things from herself, and feels with the most intimate sympathy for all, has thus sympathetically compounded the human frame. It's vibrating fibres, it's sympathising nerves, need not the call of Reason: they run before her, they often disobediently and forcibly oppose her. Intercourse with mad people, for whom we feel, excites madness; and the sooner, the more we apprehend it.

It is singular, that the ear should excite and strengthen compassion so much more powerfully than the eye. The sigh of a brute, the cry forced from him by bodily sufferance, bring about him all his fellows, who, as often has been observed, stand mournfully round the sufferer, and would willingly lend him assistance. Man, too, at the sight of suffering, is more apt to be impressed with fear and tremor, than with tender compassion: but no sooner does the voice of the sufferer reach him, than the spell is dissolved, and he hastens to him: he is pierced to the heart. Is it that the found converts the picture in the eye into a living being, and recalls and concentres in one point our recollection of our own and another's feelings? Or is there, as I am inclined to believe, a still deeper organic cause? Suffice it, that the fact is true, and it shows, that found and language are the principal sources of man's compassion. We sympathize less with a creature that cannot sigh; as it is destitute of lungs, more imperfect, and less resembling ourselves in it's organization. Some, who have been born deaf and dumb, have given the most horrible examples of want of compassion and sympathy with men and beasts; and instances enough may be observed among savage nations. Yet even among these the law of Nature is perceivable. Fathers, who are compelled by hunger and want to sacrifice their children, devote them to death in the womb, before they have beheld their eyes, before they have heard the sound of their voices; and many infanticides have confessed, that nothing was so painful to them, nothing took such fast hold of their memory, as the first feeble voice, the suppliant cry of their child.

4. Beautiful is the chain, by which the allsentient mother connects the reciprocal feeling of her children, and fashions it step by step. Where the creature is rude and insensible, so as scarcely to care for itself, it is not entrusted with the care of it's offspring. The feathered inhabitants of the air hatch and bring up their young with maternal love: the stupid ostrich, on the contrary, commits her eggs to the sand. 'She forgets,' says an ancient book, 'that a foot may tread upon them, or a wild beast destroy them: for God has deprived her of wisdom, and imparted to her no

SCIENCE AND PHILOSOPHY

understanding.' From one and the same organic cause, whence a creature derives more brain, it also acquires more warmth, brings forth or hatches living young, gives suck, and is susceptible of parental affection. The creature, that comes into the world alive, is as it were a plexus of it's mother's own nerves; the child brought up at it's parent's breast is a branch of the mother-plant, which she nourishes as a part of herself. – On this most intimate reciprocal feeling are founded all the tender affections in the economy of the animal, to which Nature could exalt it's species.

In the human species maternal love is of a higher kind: a branch of the humanity of the upright form. The suckling lies beneath his mother's eye on her bosom, and drinks the softest and most delicate fluid. It is a brutal custom, and even tending to deform the body, for women to suckle their children at their backs, which in some countries they are compelled to do by necessity. Parental and domestic love soften the greatest savages: even the lioness is affectionate to her young. The first society arose in the paternal habitation, being cemented by the ties of blood, of confidence, and love. Thus to destroy the wildness of men, and habituate them to domestic intercourse, it was requisite, that the infancy of the species should continue some years: Nature kept them together by tender bands, that they might not separate and forget each other like the brutes, that soon arrive at maturity. The father becomes the instructor of his son, as the mother had been of her infant; and thus a new tie of humanity is formed. Here lies the ground of a necessary *human society*, without which no man could grow up, and the species could not multiply. Man therefore is born for society: this the affection of his parents tells him; this, the years of his protracted infancy.

5. But as the sympathy of man is incapable of being universally extended, and could be but an obscure and frequently impotent conductor to him a limited, complex being, in every thing remote; his guiding mother has subjected it's numerous and lightly interwoven branches to her more unerring standard: this is the *rule of truth and justice*. Man is formed erect; and as every thing in his figure is subordinate to the head, as his two eyes see only one object, his two ears hear but one sound; as Nature in his whole exteriour has connected symmetry with unity, and placed unity in the midst, so that what is double always refers to it: so also is the great law of justice and equiponderance the internal rule of man: *what ye would not, that another should do unto you, do not to another; and do unto others, what ye would they should do unto you.* This incontestible rule is written even in the breast of the savage: for when he eats the flesh of others, he expects to be eaten in his turn. It is the rule of true and false, of the *idem et idem*, founded on the structure of all our senses, nay I might say on man's erect position itself. If we saw obliquely, or the light struck us in an oblique direction; we should have no idea of a right line. If our organization were without unity, our thoughts without judgment; our actions would fluctuate in curves devoid of rule, and human life would be destitute of reason and design. The law of truth and justice makes sincere brothers and associates; nay, when it takes place, it converts even enemies into friends. He, whom I press to my bosom, presses me also to his: he, for whom I venture my life, ventures his for me. Thus the laws of man, of nations, and of animals, are

founded on similarity of sentiment, unity of design among different persons, and equal truth in an alliance: for even animals, that live in society, obey the laws of justice; and men, who avoid their ties by force or fraud, are the most inhuman of all creatures, even if they be the kings and monarchs of the Earth. No reason, no humanity, is conceivable without strict justice and truth.

6. The elegant and erect figure of man forms him to *decorum*: for this is the lovely friend and servant of truth and justice. Decorum of body is for it to stand as it ought, as God has fashioned it: true beauty is nothing more than the pleasing form of internal perfection and health. Consider the divine image in man disfigured by negligence and false art: the beautiful hair torn off, or clotted together in a lump; the nose and ears bored through, and stretched by a weight; the neck and the other parts of the body deformed in themselves, or by the dress that covers them: who, even if the most capricious fashion were to judge, would discover here the decorum of the erect human frame? Just so it is with manners and actions; just so with customs, arts, and language. One and the same humanity pervades all these, which few nations upon Earth have hit, and hundreds have disfigured by barbarism and false art. To trace this humanity is the genuine philosophy of man, which the sage called down from Heaven, and which displays itself in social intercourse, as in national policy, in all the arts, as in every science.

Finally, religion is the highest humanity of mankind. Let no one be surprized, that I thus estimate it. If the understanding be the noblest endowment of man, it is the business of the understanding to trace the connexion between cause and effect, and to divine it where it is not apparent. The human understanding does this in every action, occupation, and art: for, even where it follows an established process, the understanding of some one must previously have settled the connexion between cause and effect, and thus introduced the art. But in the operations of Nature we properly see no cause in it's inmost springs: we know not ourselves, we perceive not how any thing is effected in us. So in all the effects around us every thing is but a dream, a conjecture, a name: yet it is a true dream, when we frequently and constantly observe the same effect connected with the same cause. This is the progress of philosophy; and the first and last philosophy has ever been religion. Even the most savage nations have practised it: for no people upon Earth have been found entirely destitute of it, any more than of a capacity for reason and the human form, language and the connubial union, or some manners and customs proper to man. Where they saw no visible author of events, they supposed an invisible one; and inquired after the causes of things, though with a glimmering light. It is true, they attended more to the phenomena, than to the essence of nature; and contemplated the tremendous and transitory, more than the pleasing and permanent: so that they seldom advanced so far, as to refer all causes to one. Still this first attempt was religion: and it is absurd to say, that *fear* invented the gods of most people. Fear, as fear, invents nothing: it merely rouses the understanding to conjecture, and to suppose something true or false. As soon therefore as man learned to use his understanding on the slightest impulse, that is to say, as soon as he beheld the

SCIENCE AND PHILOSOPHY

World in a manner different from a brute, he must have believed in more powerful invisible beings, that benefitted or injured him. These he sought to make or preserve his friends; and thus religion, true or false, right or erroneous, was introduced, the instructor of man, his comforter and guide through the dark and dangerous mazes of life.

37

LOUISE FLORENCE PÉTRONILLE TARDIEU D'ESCLAVELLES D'EPIGNY (1726–1783), *THE CONVERSATIONS OF EMILY*

2 vols (London: John Marshall, 1787),
pp. 49–71, 98–107

Louise d'Épinay was a French writer and well-known salon hostess, part of a circle of top Enlightenment thinkers including Rousseau (source 4), Diderot, and Voltaire (source 39). Her *Conversations of Emily* reflected on the education of her granddaughter, Émilie de Belsunce. Like similar educational treatises of the time by women, it provided a model for the education of young women (see also source 14), in this instance using an almost catechistic model of question and answer but in the form of a conversation. The latter format was highly popular as a form of pedagogy, as it emphasised the relationship between teacher and student, encouraged memorisation, and was thought to be easily understood. In the excerpt below, the child Emily is encouraged to adopt a cheerful disposition as a form of ethical behaviour; her melancholy and other anti-social emotions are discouraged as childish follies. If the work is similar to other Enlightenment child-rearing literature, in gently guiding the child to an awareness of their own behaviour and a desire to improve, it reinforces feeling as a duty and domain within the control of the well-socialised child. The text was translated into English from French in the eighteenth century, and includes notes from the translator on the challenges of transforming emotion words across languages. Like other philosophical writings, it evidences how the emotions were being conceptualised during the period.

. . .

MOTHER. What is the matter with you, *Emily?* You are melancholy.
EMILY. Yes, Mamma.
MOTHER. Are you not glad to see me again?
EMILY. Indeed, I am . . . but . . .
MOTHER. But what?
EMILY. I do not deserve your kindness, in conversing with me to-day.

MOTHER. Why so, child?

EMILY. Because the whole time you were absent . . . Now pray, Mamma, do not oblige me to tell you. I am so sorry for what I have done, that I dare not confess it.

MOTHER. If you be sensible of your fault, and sorry for it, I hope you will do so no more.

EMILY. I promise you I never will; and I have begged my Governess to put me in mind, should I forget it.

MOTHER. You are right. It is the true secret of amendment. The wicked only forget the evil they commit. When virtuous persons err, they call to mind their errors, to prevent a repetition of them. But tell me what good advice may guard you from future mischief.

EMILY. I will obey you, Mamma, and tell you all. It is however very hard! Well, Mamma, I have not done one single thing you ordered me! I have done nothing but play, and trifle away the whole morning, and I have learned nothing.

MOTHER. Did not your Governess endeavour to prevail on you to work?

EMILY. Oh! Yes! My poor Governess gave herself a great deal of trouble to induce me to it, but it was of no use: I do not know what I could be thinking of; I did not listen to her, and that is what gives me the most uneasiness, for it was very naughty.

MOTHER. Indeed it was. I hope at least you did not take her counsels amiss.

EMILY. Oh! no, Mamma! One may neglect good advice, but one cannot take it ill; beside, it is by your order that my Governess talks to me.

MOTHER. Well, and what is now to be done? For you know, it is not enough to be sorry for a fault, without making some reparation for it.

EMILY. To be sure, Mamma, but how? I will submit to any punishment you shall think proper to impose.

MOTHER. I am not fond of punishment.

EMILY. So my Governess says.

MOTHER. It is proper only for untractable, and servile dispositions. Are you of that number?

EMILY. I should not like to be so.

MOTHER. Is lost time regained by punishment?

EMILY. No, Mamma.

MOTHER. But as you have spent in play the time allotted for work; do you not think it just that you should employ in study the time usually passed in amusement?

EMILY. Yes, Mamma.

MOTHER. You must then read with attention. Sit down by me, and read aloud; and such words as you do not understand, ask me to explain to you.

EMILY. Mamma, I will ring, and tell my Governess to bring my book.

MOTHER. It is not worth while to disturb her. Take one from that shelf – that which you see at the end of the second lowest shelf.

EMILY. Is it this, Mamma?

THE CONVERSATIONS OF EMILY

MOTHER. Yes. Bring it to me.

EMILY. Mamma, it is Moral Tales.

MOTHER. So much the better; it will amuse us.

EMILY. Which shall I read.

MOTHER. The first.

EMILY. Oh! Mamma!

MOTHER. What now?

EMILY. It is . . . Let us read the second, Mamma?

MOTHER. Why not the first?

EMILY. Mamma, it is the *Naughty Girl* . . .

MOTHER. Well, we shall see if it bring to our recollection any of our acquaintance.

EMILY. Must I read aloud?

MOTHER. Without doubt; and pronounce distinctly.

EMILY. (*READS*) "In a provincial city, nearly as rich and populous as *Paris*, a man of quality who had quitted the army, lived with his lady. They had considerable possessions in the city, beside an estate at a small distance from it. They tenderly loved each other, and almost adored their daughter, a child of seven years old, who was the only one left of three they had had. Their whole care was centred in her education; but as her improvement was not equal to it, they left town and resided wholly at their country seat, that they might not be interrupted from attending to so difficult an undertaking. Fearful of injuring the reputation of their child, by exposing her bad disposition, they concealed the motives of their retirement. Their resolution was condemned, and divers judgments were formed thereon. It is to be supposed, said some, that their affairs are deranged, and how could it be otherwise? They lived at an excessive expence, kept open house, performed acts of benevolence, unknown to any body. Generosity is certainly a virtue; but it is likewise prudent to reckon with oneself, or you see, what must be the consequence. No, said another, their affairs are in very good order; I rather think the Count *d'Orville* is jealous of his wife. Jealous, indeed! Rejoined a third; she is so very reserved!" – Mamma, what is being jealous?

MOTHER. The fear of not being preferred to others.

EMILY. Is it pretty to be jealous?

MOTHER. I ask you. What is your opinion?

EMILY. No. I think it must be very uncomfortable.

MOTHER. I think so too.

EMILY. Then I will not be jealous.[1]

MOTHER. Go on with your reading.

EMILY. (*READS.*) "She is prudence itself. I do not dispute it, replied the first; but there must be some motive which we cannot discover for such an extraordinary proceeding. They have even said, they shall not receive any company, except a few intimate friends; and there must be some reasons for all this. But, gentlemen, said another more moderate than the rest, why should we judge so rashly, and wish to scrutinize the affairs of others? Suppose the Count and

285

SCIENCE AND PHILOSOPHY

Countess *d'Orville* renounce the great world, to watch more narrowly over the education of their daughter, what would you say to it? That is unlikely – had they such a motive they would make it known, but to quit all the charms of society for a child of seven years old. What an extravagant idea! If they provide food and cloaths for her, allow her proper masters, whip her when she thinks proper to have her own way, and give her a doll to keep her quiet, they discharge all the obligations of a parent; and those who do more, are very good indeed."

EMILY. Is that the general opinion of the world?

MOTHER. Nearly; and if the child only gave occasion for such false judgments, I cannot but think her sufficiently reprehensible.

EMILY. (*READS.*) "Those who do more, are very good indeed. Beside, I heard from a footman, who lived in the family, that the young lady is obstinate, and headstrong, so that she is undeserving their attention."

The footman was a very prating fellow.

MOTHER. That is not uncommon.

EMILY. It I had been in the Count's place, I would have made him hold his tongue.

MOTHER. How would you have done that? And by what authority could you prevent a man from saying what is true, and what he daily sees.

EMILY. But we ought not to speak ill of any one.

MOTHER. True, in regard to ourselves; but we cannot always impose silence on others. Would it not be the shortest way to behave well, that those who cannot be silent might only speak our praise? When we behave ill, we expose ourselves to slander.

EMILY. What, Mamma! When I have done wrong, do all your servants talk of it?

MOTHER. What you do right, you have nothing to fear from tell-tales; therefore always do the best you possible can, that you may not be uneasy respecting what is said of you.

EMILY. I will go on, Mamma.

(*SHE READS.*) "The Count and Countess *d'Orville* were not ignorant of all that was said of them; but satisfied with their own intentions, and in the hope of forming their daughter to virtue, they set out, not to return till they could introduce her to the world, without any prejudice to herself. The better to excite her emulation, they took with them one of their little nieces, who nearly the same age as their daughter, and whose name was *Pauline de Perseuil*. The Countess tool also an indigent woman of good family, whose manners and character she was well acquainted with, whom she promised to provide for; and made her Governess to her daughter and niece."

EMILY. What is manners, Mamma?

MOTHER. It is a word that alone expressed the result of the whole conduct of any one. We say virtuous manners, ill manners, amiable manners, &c.

EMILY. (*READS.*) "Miss d'Orville, was idle, self-willed, and obstinate; never expressed the least tenderness for her parents, and passed her whole time in amusements and a dress. No sooner was she spoken to respecting her

THE CONVERSATIONS OF EMILY

learning, or her duties, than she indulged her ill-humour; she cried, and sobbed; and not a day passed, in which she did not deserve two or three mortifying punishments."

EMILY. You see, Mamma, the historian of Miss *d'Orville* approves of punishments.

MOTHER. I am no friend to them.

EMILY. (*READS.*) "*Pauline*, on the contrary, was obliging and polite to all. She never received advice without gratitude and thanks to the person who gave it her. She made a visible progress in every accomplishment; in short, she was as much beloved and caressed, as little *d'Orville* was destested, who, jealous of the preference given to *Pauline*, had not sense to discern, that it was in her power to be equally beloved, by amending her errors, and correcting her ill humours; but she preferred laying the blame on others, to a generous acknowledgement of it in herself. Her Papa and Mamma repeatedly said to her, My Child, you will be miserable all your life. Other parents, less indulgent than we are, would have already abandoned you. It is in your own power to enjoy the lot of your cousin. You see how happy she is; and she is so, only because she is good and tractable. Miss *d'Orville* scarcely listened to what was said, and returned to her learning or her play without mending. Four years were thus spent in tears, ill-humour, and misery. Her parents finding her incorrigible, at length, treated her with great severity; and Miss *d'Orville* became so unhappy, that she began to make some reflections. Her cousin had acquired every kind of accomplishment. She had read much; learned many things; and she now began to repeat the fruit of the pains she had taken. She fully understood every conversation when admitted to company; and when alone, she experienced no listlessness because she knew how to employ her time. Music, drawing, and work, succeeded each other; one occupation gave place to another; and being never idle, she was never out of temper.

One day, as the Count and Countess were walking in the garden with their daughter and niece, it happened that Miss *d'Orville*, being as usual, in a bad humour, made an impertinent answer to her cousin. Her Papa and Mamma, after obliging her to ask her cousin's pardon, sent her to her chamber: To which she could not go without crossing the salloon. A gentleman and two ladies had remained there to finish a party at cards. Little *d'Orville*, who knew they were in the room, dared not appear before them. She sat down on the step just without the door, and did not move lest she should be perceived. In effect, those who were in the salloon, did not suspect she was so near. They were talking of her. What a difference, said one of the ladies, there is between *Pauline* and little *d'Orville*! *Pauline* is mild, affectionate, attentive, and accomplished. She is a charming character! Little *d'Orville* is headstrong, and passionate; she is unfeeling, idle, and ignorant; she loves no one, and no one loves her, nor ever will. I have advised her father twenty times, to put her in a convent for life. She is not fit to live in the world. For my part, said the other lady, she is so odious to me, that when she is present, I turn my head another way. A little disagreeable thing! Is it possible she can be insensible

287

SCIENCE AND PHILOSOPHY

to the anxiety she daily occasions to her father and mother? I have seen the Countess weep more than once with anguish at the perverse disposition of her daughter. You may reproach yourself in a degree, Baron, said she, to a gentleman who was at cards. There is a kind of inhumanity in talking and playing with her; she does not deserve it. She has not the sense to see you are making a jest of her, that you entertain yourself with her follies and her faults, and that you are very little interested in her welfare. Indeed, Madam, replied the Baron, she is neither my daughter nor my niece; and God forbid I ever should have a wife like her! She deserves no consideration. I think I would pay her board in a convent if her father would clear the house of her; but since she is here, I may at least amuse myself with her folly. Could I suppose she would ever be otherwise, I would not treat her so like a puppet."

EMILY. So! So! I am glad I know that! I know somebody who is always talking and laughing with me, whether I deserve it or not. Perhaps he takes me for a puppet.

MOTHER. I hope I may flatter myself no one looks on you with the same eyes as little *d'Orville*.

EMILY. I hope so too, Mamma; but let us see how it ends. It begins to be very interesting.

. . . .

EMILY. What do you mean by a well-disposed young lady?

MOTHER. It not only means one whose natural inclinations have a good tendency; but also one who in the warmth and effervescence of childhood, shews some signs of discernment, who observes a certain decorum, that prejudices in her favour, and makes her pay a proper attention and respect to all things joined to that sensibility, which bids fair, in a more advanced age, for the possession of reason and wisdom.

EMILY. Am I a well-disposed child?

MOTHER. I hope so.

EMILY. I have sensibility then?

MOTHER. I must have proofs of that.

EMILY. And how?

MOTHER. By convincing me that you are sensible on all occasions, of what belongs to persons, time, and place; for what is very proper at one time, may be highly improper at another; and by shewing a degree of reserve and reflection, even in your follies. It manifests itself mechanically in the most trifling circumstances; for instance, if the gentleman who has the complaisance to pass his leisure time with you, should look on you as a puppet, the book would be right, and that would very much afflict me, as it would bring Miss *d'Orville* to my remembrance.

EMILY. Fear nothing, my dear Mamma: he treats me like a child, but not like a puppet.

THE CONVERSATIONS OF EMILY

MOTHER. In that case all is well. But why do you conclude so?

EMILY. Though we are always merry when we meet, he takes a real interest in my improvement. You see he always is present at my exercises, the first day of every month, and how pleased he is when I deserve the cross:[2] one would think by his looks that he was going to wear it himself.

MOTHER. Certainly those are proofs; and I plainly see I may make myself easy respecting your concerns with him; and that I need not interfere with them.

EMILY. Beside, let me alone. I will be very careful in future of my behaviour. It will be a little irksome at first, perhaps; but no matter, provided I please you. Oh! Mamma! See what it is to chatter so! I had forgotten My governess told me to desire, when you send to Paris, to let somebody call at the mantua-maker's.

MOTHER. What a terrible misfortune it would have been, had the four elements, and all that followed, made us forget the mantua-maker.

EMILY. She has not brought home my new dress; and she promised I should have it to-day.

MOTHER. Probably it is not made. It is time enough.

EMILY. Oh! I shall be so happy when I have a new dress!

MOTHER. How can a new dress contribute to your happiness?

EMILY. I have no dislike to being fine.

MOTHER. Are you never unhappy when you are fine? Did you never cry when you had a new slip on?

EMILY. Oh! Yes! I know very well it has nothing to do with happiness.

MOTHER. Are you indulged in all you wish on days of finery?

EMILY. Not always.

MOTHER. Do either my friend or myself pay you more attention for your having a fine slip on?

EMILY. I believe not, Mamma.

MOTHER. On what occasions do we take the most notice of you, and the most readily grant what you request? And when do you experience that inward satisfaction, which makes you so pleased with yourself, with me, and every one else?

EMILY. It is, I believe, when have done everything well, off hand, without . . .

MOTHER. In that case, a new dress does not bestow happiness. For notwithstanding your finery, you cannot experience any pleasure so long as you feel self-reproach. I have frequently seen you very cheerful, and very happy, in a linen frock, and that somewhat dirty toward the end of the day.

EMILY. Yet, I assure you, Mamma, there is great pleasure in being dressed. Only ask Miss *de Lery*.

MOTHER. It is a vain pleasure, but which is of infinite consequence in the estimation of little children.

EMILY. But may one not enjoy the pleasure, and let alone the vanity? Pleasure is always good.

MOTHER. When virtuous, discreet, and rightly understood.

EMILY. How rightly understood?

MOTHER. Where it is not mistaken for happiness.

EMILY. Happiness is more grave.

MOTHER. Since we are on the subject, let us endeavour to discover the requisites of happiness.

EMILY. Pray let us, Mamma. I was going to say something; but I believe I am wrong.

MOTHER. No matter. Let me hear it. It is only by communicating your idea to me, that you can acquire a justness of thought.

EMILY. True, Mamma; but if I should talk nonsense?

MOTHER. I will tell you so.

EMILY. Mamma, I was going to say, let us find out the elements of happiness.

MOTHER. You would have spoken very properly. For it is precisely what I wish you to understand.

EMILY. Happiness is something I should like to know. No. it is not a science.

MOTHER. It is the most important of all sciences – the most essential object of study to mankind.

EMILY. Is it hard to understand?

MOTHER. Very difficult, and even impossible to the wicked, but easy to those who make use of their reason.

EMILY. I hope, Mamma, it will not be difficult.

MOTHER. I hope not: we have already seen that fine cloaths do not make people happy. Your Governess has no very fine cloaths; she is not rich: do you think she is happy?

EMILY. To be sure, Mamma; for she is always laughing and singing. I never saw her melancholy.

MOTHER. All those peasants, and servants, you have seen dancing on a *Sunday*, at the gate of the *Bois de Boulogne*, appear contented and merry. Yet they are not rich. They have nothing but what they work hard for all the week, to support themselves and families. You have frequently observed their gaiety. We may then conclude, that riches are not necessary to happiness.

EMILY. Then what makes all those poor people so cheerful?

MOTHER. What is your opinions?

EMILY. I think it is because they have done their work well, and are satisfied with themselves.

MOTHER. You are right. Now then, what must be the first element of happiness in all ages and conditions.

EMILY. It must be to do one's duty, and be satisfied with oneself; must it not, Mamma?

MOTHER. Most certainly. We may possess every exterior advantage, great riches, and good health, and yet be unhappy; and without fortune, with a delicate constitution, like mine, it is possible to be happy; for true happiness depends on ourselves.

EMILY. Yes, for it is only being good.

MOTHER. And there can be no happiness without goodness, and the observance of our duties; because we can neither be pleased with ourselves nor others.

EMILY. That is the reason wicked people are not happy, is it not, Mamma? So now, here is company!

MOTHER. I am not sorry for that; we have talked enough to-day; it is time to think of your little duties, since there can be no happiness without them.

EMILY. Mamma, I have something else to say to you respecting happiness, that I do not very well understand. You will give me leave to say it to your to-morrow, will you not?

MOTHER. Yes; you know I am always ready for conversation.

EMILY. In the mean time, I will go and learn the gospel for the day.

Notes

1 Adjectives, in the French language, being susceptible of various inflexions, which only point out the difference of the gender; and, Adjectives in the English language not admitting of such inflexions, the translator is under the necessity of omitting a few passages, in which the mother corrects the child for making use of the word *jaloux*, in the masculine, instead of the feminine *jalouse*. [*In the original*].

2 It is usual in most *French* schools, and even in private families, where there are many children, as the end of every month, to examine the exercises done during that time; and the pupil who has done best, is rewarded by wearing a cross on the left breast; which distinction the fortunate pupil continue to wear until excelled by another, at some following examination. [*In the original*].

Part 6

ART AND CULTURE

Part 6

Art and culture

Art, literature, music and similar cultural forms provide a key source for emotion, representing feeling and because they were often designed to produce emotion in audiences. This was not least the case during the eighteenth century's culture of sensibility, which prized art and literature that offered people the opportunity to explore the full range of human emotions. Literature was viewed as an important form of education and civilisation, and art allowed people to experience emotion in a safe, and ideally moral, form. Whether such experiences were always achieved was a topic of debate, and some accounts of emotion were thought to be potentially corrupting, especially for women. The Enlightenment also saw considerable interest in how various art forms, not least music, acted on the emotions; philosophers and scientists sought to chart and explain such effects and how they might be achieved. As sources for the history of emotion, they also have the advantage of providing insight into how emotion was thought to operate in a range of everyday contexts that are less likely to be captured by other records, and so open up the emotional world of the eighteenth century.

38

SCOTTISH BROADSIDE BALLADS (C.1720)

Broadsides were single sheets of printed paper that sold very cheaply in early modern Europe. Printed in their thousands, they contained news, stories and entertainment, not least ballads – song lyrics, sometime with an indication of the air. Ballads covered a wide-range of topics from bawdy and humorous songs, hymns and moral warnings, and love songs. The musical form was considered an important way of conveying news as it could be easily remembered and repeated by a non-literate population. Broadside were read by people at all social levels, and often survive in the collections of elite families, but they are considered especially important for giving historians access to the popular culture of lower order and very poor communities. Below are two Scottish ballads, seen in their use of Scottish dialect, and which explore romantic relationships. Both songs are humorous and explore topical issues of the century. The first asks how a couple might form a household with love, but without economic foundation, and involves a discussion with the bride's family. A lot of the humour of the songs relies on knowing that many Scots live 'But 'n' Ben' in two room houses, where the 'but' was the outer room and the 'ben' the interior room – but that both of these words have multiple meanings. The second explores the morality of pre-marital sex, a common topic for a community where such behaviour was sinful but commonplace. They are useful for highlighting the social considerations and concerns that surrounded love and sexual relationships for the poor.

· · ·

Dialogue Between Ald John M'clatchy, and Young Willie Ha, about the Marriage of his Daughter Maggy M'clatchy.

To an Excellent New Tune

THE Meal was dear short shine,[1]
When they were Married together:
Ann *Maggy* she was in her prime,

ART AND CULTURE

When *Willy* made Courtship till her.
Twa Pistols Charg'd be-guess,
To give the Courtier a Shot,
Ann fine came ben[2] the Lass,
Wee Swats drawn frae the Butt:[3]
He first spears at the Good-man,
Ann sine[4] at *Jean* her Mither,
Gin[5] ye'll gi'e us a bit Land,
We'll Buckle our selves together.

Old Man

My Daughter ye shall ha'e
I'll gi'e ye her he the Hann,[6]
But wee my Wife I man quat[7]
Gin I quat we my Lann;[8]
But your Tocher[9] shall be good,
I'll ne'er gang nen the meek,[10]
The Lass bin in her Snood,[11]
And *Cromy* that kens[12] the Stake;
Wee an ald Bedding o' Clea's,[13]
Was left me by my Mither,
They're geet-black o're wee fleas
You may H–dle[14] in them together.

Young-Man

A Bargain it shall be,
But ye man mend your Hann,[15]
Ann think on Modestie;
Gin ye'll no'quat wee your Lann,
We are but young ye ken,
Ann now we're gaen together,
A House is But and Ben,
Ann *Cromie* she wants her Fadder;[16]
The Bairns are coming on,
Ann they'll cry on there Mither,
We ha'e neither Pot nor Pan,
But four bair Legs together.

Old Man

Thou shall ha'e Tocher aneugh,
Ann that thou need not fear,
Twa good stilts to the Pleugh,[17]

SCOTTISH BROADSIDE BALLADS (C.1720)

Ann thou thy self man stear;
Thou'st ha'e twa good ald pocks,[18]
That was enst made of the Tweel,[19]
The teen to had the Groats,[20]
The tither to had the Meal:
Wee an ald Kist made o' wans[21]
I'll give thee to thy Coffer,
Wee eiken woddie bans,[22]
And that may had your Tocher.

Young- Man

Consider now Good-man,
I ha'e but barrow'd geer,[23]
The Beast that I Ride on,
Is *Sanny Wilson's* Meer;[24]
But as soon as I gan heem,
I'll take me to my Cutts,[25]
The Saddle is nean of my ain,
Ann these are barraw'd Boots,
The Clock is Geordie Wat's,
That gars me look so Cruss,[26]
Fy fill us a Cog o'Swats[27]
We'll mak ne ma-e toomrouss.

Old-Man

Thou art an onest Lad,
For telling me so plain,
I Married when little I had,
Of Gear that was my ain;
Good-sooth if it be se,
The Bride she man come forth,
Tho'a the gear she has,
It is but little worth;
A Briddle it shall be,
Se spear at *Jean* her Mither,
Content am I, quoth she,
Fy gar the Lass come hither;
The Bride lap in to the Bed,
Ann the Bridgroom ged till her
The Fidler crap in to the mids[28]
Ann they H – dled altogether.

F I N I S.

ART AND CULTURE

An Excellent Song
I N T I T U L E D
Fy gar rub her o're wi Strae,

An Italian Canzone (of seven hundred Years Standing) imitated in braid Scots

Gin[29] ye meet a bonny Lassie
Gie her a Kiss and let her gae,
But if she be a dirty *H*ussy,
Fy gar rub her o're wi Strae.[30]
Fy gar rub her, fy gar rub her.
Fy gar rub her o're wi Strae.
But if she be a bonny Lassie,
Give her a Kiss and let her gae.

Be sure ye dinna quat the Grip,
Of ilka Joy when ye are young,
Before auld Age your Vitals nip,
And lay ye twafald o're a Rung.
Fy gar rub her, fy gar rub her,
fy gar rub her, o're wi Strae,
But if she be a bonny Lassiie,
give her a Kiss and let her gae.

Sweet Youths a blyth and hartsom Time,
then Lads and Lasses while it's *May*
Gae pow the Gowan[31] in it's Prime,
before it wither and Decay,
Fy gar rub her, fy gar rub her,
fy gar rub her o're wi Strae.
But if she be a bonny Lassie,
give her a Kiss and let her gae.

Watch the fast Minutes of Delyte,
When *Jeany* speaks beneath her Breath
And Kisses laying a the Wyte
On you if she kepp ony Skath,[32]
Fy gar rub her, fy gar rub her
Fy gar rub her o're wi Strae,
But if she be a bony Lassie
give her a Kiss and let her gae.

Haith ye're ill bred she'll smilling say
ye'll worry me ye greedy Rook,[33]
Syn frae your Arms she'll rin away
and hide her self in some dark Nook[34]

300

SCOTTISH BROADSIDE BALLADS (C.1720)

Fy gar rub her, fy gar rub her,
fy gar rub he o're wi strae,
But if she be a bonny Lassie.
give her a Kiss and let her gae

Her Laugh will lead you to the Place,
Where lys the Happiness ye want,
And plainly tells you to your face,
Nineteen Naysays are haff a grant[35]
Fy gar rub her, fy gar rub her,
fy gar rub her o're wi Strae,
But if she be a bonny Lassie,
Give her a Kiss and let her gae,

Now to her heaving Bosom cling,
and sweetly toolie[36] for a Kiss.
Frae her fair finger whop[37] a Ring,
as Token of a future Bless.
Fy gar rub her, fy gar rub her,
fy gar rub her o're wi strae;
But if she be a bonny Lassie,
give her a Kiss and let her gae

These Bennisons I'm very sure,
are of the God's Indulgent Grant,
Then Surrly Carles,[38] 'whisht forbear,
to Plague us with your whining Cant.
Fy gar rub her, fy gar rub her,
fy gar rub her o're wi Strae,
But if she be a bonny Lassie,
Give her a Kiss and let her gae.

F I N I S.

Notes

1 Short party.
2 To come ben means to be forward in wooing, but also to come into the interior room of the house.
3 Weak beer drawn from a barrel/the outer room of the house.
4 Thereafter.
5 If.
6 Give her hand.
7 Quit/leave.
8 If I give away my land.
9 Dowry.
10 I'll not be shy, e.g. he will be generous.

ART AND CULTURE

11 A snood is a ribbon worn in the hair of unmarried women and so a symbol of maidenhood.
12 Knows/understands
13 Old bedding and clothes.
14 Huddle
15 Mend your hand means to refill your glass (appropriate for a wedding), but also to reform and work hard (mend the land is to plough).
16 Father.
17 A plough has two stilts – handles.
18 Pokes, e.g. bags.
19 Tweel is the cloth made from twilling, so he has two bags made from tweel.
20 The one to hold the groats; the other to hold the meal.
21 An old chest made of poor materials.
22 With oak twisted wood bands – a material used for making bags and harnesses for animals; but woddie is also used to refer to the marriage-bond and bans also refers to a promise or oath. In addition, woddie can be a gallow's noose, and bans can mean curse. So this line can be read in multiple ways with various implications.
23 Borrowed goods.
24 Mare, e.g. horse.
25 The piece of land being cultivated.
26 That makes me look so cross.
27 Wooden vessel of beer.
28 The fiddler crept into the middle.
29 If.
30 Make haste, rub her over with straw.
31 Spring flowers.
32 And kisses laying all the blame/ on you if she kept any skath, literally harm or damage, but meaning shame or reputation (e.g. virginity).
33 Plunderer.
34 Corner.
35 Nineteen refusals are halfway to consent.
36 To struggle playfully; in non-romantic contexts, to quarrel.
37 Whip, e.g. remove quickly.
38 Surly men; carle is often used in a derogatory manner or to suggest they are interfering.

39

VOLTAIRE [FRANÇOIS-MARIE AROUET] (1694–1778), 'POEM ON THE LISBON DISASTER; OR AN EXAMINATION OF THE AXIOM, "ALL IS WELL"'

In *Toleration and Other Essays*, trans. Joseph McCabe (New York: G.P. Putnam's Sons, 1912), pp. 255–263

Voltaire was a prolific French writer, who produced work in almost every genre. He was particularly known for his anti-clericalism and defence of civil liberties. He wrote the poem below, translated from French into English in the early twentieth century, in response to the 1755 Lisbon earthquake. The latter was a major disaster, devastating the city and killing between 10,000 and 60,000 people. The event captured the European imagination, with many debating the cause of the earthquake and some locating it as a punishment from God for sin. In this work, Voltaire argued that an event like the earthquake precluded the existence of an interventionist deity and to argue otherwise was fatalistic. Poetry was a significant genre of the eighteenth century, exploring a broad range of topics, events, experiences, and emotion. Voltaire's choice of this genre to make a religio-political intervention was not especially original, but perhaps allowed him to convey the horror of the events due to the aesthetic form. The earthquake reinvigorated an interest in the sublime, and Voltaire's poem seeks to convey that dimension of the experience through its description of suffering. As a source for the history of emotions, it captures the public emotional response to a mass disaster, but also how such feeling led to a searching and investigation for answers.

. . .

UNHAPPY mortals! Dark and mourning earth!
Affrighted gathering of human kind!
Eternal lingering of useless pain!
Come, ye philosophers, who cry, "All's well,"

ART AND CULTURE

And contemplate this ruin of a world.
Behold these shreds and cinders of your race,
This child and mother heaped in common wreck,
These scattered limbs beneath the marble shafts –
A hundred thousand whom the earth devours,
Who, torn and bloody, palpitating yet,
Entombed beneath their hospitable roofs,
In racking torment end their stricken lives.
To those expiring murmurs of distress,
To that appalling spectacle of woe,
Will ye reply: "You do but illustrate
The iron laws that chain the will of God"?
Say ye, o'er that yet quivering mass of flesh:
"God is avenged: the wage of sin is death"?
What crime, what sin, had those young hearts conceived
That lie, bleeding and torn, on mother's breast?
Did fallen Lisbon deeper drink of vice
Than London, Paris, or sunlit Madrid?
In these men dance; at Lisbon yawns the abyss.
Tranquil spectators of your brothers' wreck,
Unmoved by this repellent dance of death,
Who calmly seek the reason of such storms,
Let them but lash your own security;
Your tears will mingle freely with the flood.
When earth its horrid jaws half open shows,
My plaint is innocent, my cries are just.
Surrounded by such cruelties of fate,
By rage of evil and by snares of death,
Fronting the fierceness of the elements,
Sharing our ills, indulge me my lament.
"'T is pride," ye say – "the pride of rebel heart,
To think we might fare better than we do."
Go, tell it to the Tagus' stricken banks;
Search in the ruins of that bloody shock;
Ask of the dying in that house of grief,
Whether 't is pride that calls on heaven for help
And pity for the sufferings of men.
"All's well," ye say, "and all is necessary."
Think ye this universe had been the worse
Without this hellish gulf in Portugal?
Are ye so sure the great eternal cause,
That knows all things, and for itself creates,
Could not have placed us in this dreary clime
Without volcanoes seething 'neath our feet?

VOLTAIRE, 'POEM ON THE LISBON DISASTER'

Set you this limit to the power supreme?
Would you forbid it use its clemency?
Are not the means of the great artisan
Unlimited for shaping his designs?
The master I would not offend, yet wish
This gulf of fire and sulphur had outpoured
Its baleful flood amid the desert wastes.
God I respect, yet love the universe.
Not pride, alas, it is, but love of man,
To mourn so terrible a stroke as this.

Would it console the sad inhabitants
Of these aflame and desolated shores
To say to them: "Lay down your lives in peace;
For the world's good your homes are sacrificed;
Your ruined palaces shall others build,
For other peoples shall your walls arise;
The North grows rich on your unhappy loss;
Your ills are but a link in general law;
To God you are as those low creeping worms
That wait for you in your predestined tombs"?
What speech to hold to victims of such ruth!
Add not such cruel outrage to their pain.

Nay, press not on my agitated heart
These iron and irrevocable laws,
This rigid chain of bodies, minds, and worlds.
Dreams of the bloodless thinker are such thoughts.
God holds the chain: is not himself enchained;
By his indulgent choice is all arranged;
Implacable he's not, but free and just.
Why suffer we, then, under one so just?[1]
There is the knot your thinkers should undo.
Think ye to cure our ills denying them?
All peoples, trembling at the hand of God,
Have sought the source of evil in the world.
When the eternal law that all things moves
Doth hurl the rock by impact of the winds,
With lightning rends and fires the sturdy oak,
They have no feeling of the crashing blows;
But I, I live and feel, my wounded heart
Appeals for aid to him who fashioned it.

Children of that Almighty Power, we stretch
Our hands in grief towards our common sire.

ART AND CULTURE

The vessel, truly, is not heard to say:
"Why should I be so vile, so coarse, so frail?"
Nor speech nor thought is given unto it.
The urn that, from the potter's forming hand,
Slips and is shattered has no living heart
That yearns for bliss and shrinks from misery.
"This misery," ye say, "is others' good."
Yes; from my mouldering body shall be born
A thousand worms, when death has closed my pain.
Fine consolation this in my distress!
Grim speculators on the woes of men,
Ye double, not assuage, my misery.
In you I mark the nerveless boast of pride
That hides its ill with pretext of content.

I am a puny part of the great whole.
Yes; but all animals condemned to live,
All sentient things, born by the same stern law,
Suffer like me, and like me also die.

The vulture fastens on his timid prey,
And stabs with bloody beak the quivering limbs:
All 's well, it seems, for it. But in a while
An eagle tears the vulture into shreds;
The eagle is transfixed by shaft of man;
The man, prone in the dust of battlefield,
Mingling his blood with dying fellow-men,
Becomes in turn the food of ravenous birds.
Thus the whole world in every member groans:
All born for torment and for mutual death.
And o'er this ghastly chaos you would say
The ills of each make up the good of all!
What blessedness! And as, with quaking voice,
Mortal and pitiful, ye cry, "All 's well,"
The universe belies you, and your heart
Refutes a hundred times your mind's conceit.

All dead and living things are locked in strife.
Confess it freely – evil stalks the land,
Its secret principle unknown to us.
Can it be from the author of all good?
Are we condemned to weep by tyrant law
Of black Typhon or barbarous Ahriman?[2]
These odious monsters, whom a trembling world
Made gods, my spirit utterly rejects.

VOLTAIRE, 'POEM ON THE LISBON DISASTER'

But how conceive a God supremely good,
Who heaps his favours on the sons he loves,
Yet scatters evil with as large a hand?
What eye can pierce the depth of his designs?
From that all-perfect Being came not ill:
And came it from no other, for he's lord:
Yet it exists. O stern and numbing truth!
O wondrous mingling of diversities!
A God came down to lift our stricken race:
He visited the earth, and changed it not!
One sophist says he had not power to change;
"He had," another cries, "but willed it not:
In time he will, no doubt." And, while they prate,
The hidden thunders, belched from underground,
Fling wide the ruins of a hundred towns
Across the smiling face of Portugal.
God either smites the inborn guilt of man,
Or, arbitrary lord of space and time,
Devoid alike of pity and of wrath,
Pursues the cold designs he has conceived.
Or else this formless stuff, recalcitrant,
Bears in itself inalienable faults;
Or else God tries us, and this mortal life
Is but the passage to eternal spheres.
'T is transitory pain we suffer here,
And death its merciful deliverance.
Yet, when this dreadful passage has been made,
Who will contend he has deserved the crown?
Whatever side we take we needs must groan;
We nothing know, and everything must fear.
Nature is dumb, in vain appeal to it;
The human race demands a word of God.
'T is his alone to illustrate his work,
Console the weary, and illume the wise.
Without him man, to doubt and error doomed,
Finds not a reed that he may lean upon.
From Leibnitz learn we not by what unseen
Bonds, in this best of all imagined worlds,
Endless disorder, chaos of distress,
Must mix our little pleasures thus with pain;
Nor why the guiltless suffer all this woe
In common with the most abhorrent guilt.
'T is mockery to tell me all is well.
Like learned doctors, nothing do I know.

ART AND CULTURE

Plato has said that men did once have wings
And bodies proof against all mortal ill;
That pain and death were strangers to their world.
How have we fallen from that high estate!
Man crawls and dies: all is but born to die:
The world's the empire of destructiveness.
This frail construction of quick nerves and bones
Cannot sustain the shock of elements;
This temporary blend of blood and dust
Was put together only to dissolve;
This prompt and vivid sentiment of nerve
Was made for pain, the minister of death:
Thus in my ear does nature's message run.
Plato and Epicurus I reject,
And turn more hopefully to learned Bayle.
With even poised scale Bayle bids me doubt.
He, wise and great enough to need no creed,
Has slain all systems – combats even himself:
Like that blind conqueror of Philistines,
He sinks beneath the ruin he has wrought.[3]
What is the verdict of the vastest mind?
Silence: the book of fate is closed to us.
Man is a stranger to his own research;
He knows not whence he comes, nor whither goes.
Tormented atoms in a bed of mud,
Devoured by death, a mockery of fate.
But thinking atoms, whose far-seeing eyes,
Guided by thought, have measured the faint stars,
Our being mingles with the infinite;
Ourselves we never see, or come to know.
This world, this theatre of pride and wrong,
Swarms with sick fools who talk of happiness.
With plaints and groans they follow up the quest,
To die reluctant, or be born again.
At fitful moments in our pain-racked life
The hand of pleasure wipes away our tears;
But pleasure passes like a fleeting shade,
And leaves a legacy of pain and loss.
The past for us is but a fond regret,
The present grim, unless the future 's clear.
If thought must end in darkness of the tomb.
All will be well one day – so runs our hope.
All *now* is well, is but an idle dream.
The wise deceive me: God alone is right.

VOLTAIRE, 'POEM ON THE LISBON DISASTER'

With lowly sighing, subject in my pain,
I do not fling myself 'gainst Providence.
Once did I sing, in less lugubrious tone,
The sunny ways of pleasure's genial rule;
The times have changed, and, taught by growing age,
And sharing of the frailty of mankind,
Seeking a light amid the deepening gloom,
I can but suffer, and will not repine.

A caliph once, when his last hour had come,
This prayer addressed to him he reverenced:
"To thee, sole and all-powerful king, I bear
What thou dost lack in thy immensity –
Evil and ignorance, distress and sin."
He might have added one thing further – hope.

Notes

1 "Sub Deo justo nemo miser nisi meratur [Under a just God no one is miserable who has not deserved misery.]" – *St. Augustine*. [*In original translation*].
2 The Egyptian and Persian principles of evil. The problem is discussed in the preceding essay. – J.M [*In original translation*].
3 In a lengthy note Voltaire explains that Bayle never questioned Providence, and that the scepticism in which he follows Bayle is in regard to the source of evil. It will be seen from earlier pages, however, that Voltaire does not ascribe infinite power to his God. The words "all-perfect" and "almighty," which occur in this poem, are poetic phrases. – J.M.

40

JULIA MANDEVILLE [FRANCES BROOKE] (1724–1789), *THE HISTORY OF EMILY MONTAGUE*

(London: J. Dodsley, 1769), pp. 63–79, 89–92

Frances Brooke was an English novelist, playwright and translator, who migrated to Canada in the 1760s to join her husband, a military chaplain. She wrote Canada's first novel, an extract from which appears below. *The History of Emily Montague* is a sentimental novel, written in epistolary form. The main letter writers include Emily Montague, the heroine, Colonel William Fermor, Colonel Ed Rivers, and Arabella Fermor. The story plot is largely a love story, but the letters, often written when the characters are travelling across Canada, offer descriptions of scenery and relations between the English, French, Huron, and Iroquois in Quebec. At times, the form closely resembles the travel writings of the period, with such scenes providing opportunities for the characters to reflect on their own emotional experiences in comparative form. The book, published when Brooke returned to London, was positively received and reprinted several times. Eighteenth-century novels offered readers new experience through which they could imaginatively and emotionally engage, as part of an exercise in personal improvement. This novel is distinctive in encouraging such reflections within the context of invasion, war and colonisation.

. . .

LETTER XI

To Miss RIVERS, Clarges Street.

Quebec, Sept. 10.

I FIND, my dear, that absence and amusement are the best remedies for a beginning passion; I have passed a fortnight at the Indian village of Lorette, where the novelty of the scene, and the enquiries I have been led to make into their antient religion and manners, have been of a thousand times more service to me than all the reflection in the world would have been.

I will own to you that I staid too long at Montreal, or rather at Major Melmoth's; to be six weeks in the same house with one of the most amiable, most pleasing of women, was a trying situation to a heart full of sensibility, and of a sensibility which has been hitherto, from a variety of causes, a good deal restrained. I should have avoided the danger from the first, had it appeared to me what it really was; but I thought myself secure in the consideration of her engagements, a defence however which I found grow weaker every day.

But to my savages: other nations talk of liberty, they possess it; nothing can be more astonishing than to see a little village of about thirty or forty families, the small remains of the Hurons, almost exterminated by long and continual war with the Iroquoise, preserve their independence in the midst of an European colony consisting of seventy thousand inhabitants; yet the fact is true of the savages of Lorette; they assert and they maintain that independence with a spirit truly noble. One of our company having said something which an Indian understood as a supposition that they had been *subjects* of France, his eyes struck fire, he stop'd him abruptly, contrary to their respectful and sensible custom of never interrupting the person who speaks, "You mistake, brother," said he, "we are subjects to no prince; a savage is free all over the world." And he spoke only truth; they are not only free as a people, but every individual is perfectly so. Lord of himself, at once subject and master, a savage knows no superior, a circumstance which has a striking effect on his behaviour; unawed by rank or riches, distinctions unknown amongst his own nation, he would enter as unconcerned, would possess all his powers as freely in the palace of an oriental monarch, as in the cottage of the meanest peasant: 'tis the species, 'tis man, 'tis his equal he respects, without regarding the gaudy trappings, the accidental advantages, to which polished nations pay homage.

I have taken some pains to develop their present, as well as past, religious sentiments, because the Jesuit missionaries have boasted so much of their conversion; and find they have rather engrafted a few of the most plain and simple truths of Christianity on their ancient superstitions, than exchanged one faith for another; they are baptized, and even submit to what they themselves call the *yoke* of confession, and worship according to the outward forms of the Romish church, the drapery of which cannot but strike minds unused to splendor; but their belief is very little changed, except that the women seem to pay great reverence to the Virgin, perhaps because flattering to the sex. They anciently believed in one God, the ruler and creator of the universe, whom they called *the Great Spirit* and the *Master of Life*; in the sun as his image and representative; in a multitude of inferior spirits and demons; and in a future state of rewards and punishments, or, to use their own phrase, in *a country of souls*. They reverenced the spirits of their departed heroes, but it does not appear that they paid them any religious adoration. Their morals were more pure, their manners more simple, than those of polished nations, except in what regarded the intercourse of the sexes: the young women before marriage were indulged in great libertinism, hid however under the most reserved and decent exterior. They held adultery in abhorrence, and with the more reason as their marriages were dissolvable at pleasure. The missionaries are said to have

ART AND CULTURE

found no difficulty so great in gaining them to Christianity, as that of persuading them to marry for life: they regarded the Christian system of marriage as contrary to the laws of nature and reason; and asserted that, as the *Great Spirit* formed us to be happy, it was opposing his will, to continue together when otherwise.

The sex we have so unjustly excluded from power in Europe have a great share in the Huron government; the chief is chose by the matrons from amongst the nearest male relations, by the female line, of him he is to succeed; and is generally an aunt's or sister's son; a custom which, if we examine strictly into the principle on which it is founded, seems a little to contradict what we are told of the extreme chastity of the married ladies.

The power of the chief is extremely limited; he seems rather to advise his people as a father than command them as a master: yet, as his commands are always reasonable, and for the general good, no prince in the world is so well obeyed. They have a supreme council of ancients, into which every man enters of course at an age fixed, and another of assistants to the chief on common occasions, the members of which are like him elected by the matrons: I am pleased with this last regulation, as women are, beyond all doubt, the best judges of the merit of men; and I should be extremely pleased to see it adopted in England: canvassing for elections would then be the most agreeable thing in the world, and I am sure the ladies would give their votes on much more generous principles than we do. In the true sense of the word, *we* are the savages, who so impolitely deprive you of the common rights of citizenship, and leave you no power but that of which we cannot deprive you, the resistless power of your charms. By the way, I don't think you are obliged in conscience to obey laws you have had no share in making; your plea would certainly be at least as good as that of the Americans, about which we every day hear so much.

The Hurons have no positive laws; yet being a people not numerous, with a strong sense of honor, and in that state of equality which gives no food to the most tormenting passions of the human heart, and the council of ancients having a power to punish atrocious crimes, which power however they very seldom find occasion to use, they live together in a tranquillity and order which appears to us surprizing.

In more numerous Indian nations, I am told, every village has its chief and its councils, and is perfectly independent on the rest; but on great occasions summon a general council, to which every village sends deputies.

Their language is at once sublime and melodious; but, having much fewer ideas, it is impossible it can be so copious as those of Europe: the pronunciation of the men is guttural, but that of the women extremely soft and pleasing; without understanding one word of the language, the sound of it is very agreeable to me, their style even in speaking French is bold and metaphorical: and I am told is on important occasions extremely sublime. Even in common conversation they speak in figures, of which I have this moment an instance. A savage woman was wounded lately in defending an English family from the drunken rage of one of her nation. I asked her after her wound; "It is well," said she; "my sisters at Quebec

312

(meaning the English ladies) have been kind to me; and piastres, you know, are very healing."

They have no idea of letters, no alphabet, nor is their language reducible to rules: 'tis by painting they preserve the memory of the only events which interest them, or that they think worth recording, the conquests gained over their enemies in war.

When I speak of their paintings, I should not omit that, though extremely rude, they have a strong resemblance to the Chinese, a circumstance which struck me the more, as it is not the stile of nature. Their dances also, the most lively panto-mimes I ever saw, and especially the dance of peace, exhibit variety of attitudes resembling the figures on Chinese fans; nor have their features and complexion less likeness to the pictures we see of the Tartars, as their wandering manner of life, before they became christians, was the same.

If I thought it necessary to suppose they were not natives of the country, and that America was peopled later than the other quarters of the world, I should imagine them the descendants of Tartars; as nothing can be more easy than their passage from Asia, from which America is probably not divided; or, if it is, by a very nar-row channel. But I leave this to those who are better informed, being a subject on which I honestly confess my ignorance.

I have already observed, that they retain most of their antient superstitions. I should particularize their belief in dreams, of which folly even repeated disap-pointments cannot cure them: they have also an unlimited faith in their *powawers*, or conjurers, of whom there is one in every Indian village, who is at once physi-cian, orator, and divine, and who is consulted as an oracle on every occasion. As I happened to smile at the recital a savage was making of a prophetic dream, from which he assured us of the death of an English officer whom I knew to be alive, "You Europeans," said he, "are the most unreasonable people in the world; you laugh at our belief in dreams, and yet expect us to believe things a thousand times more incredible."

Their general character is difficult to describe; made up of contrary and even contradictory qualities, they are indolent, tranquil, quiet, humane in peace; active, restless, cruel, ferocious in war: courteous, attentive, hospitable, and even polite, when kindly treated; haughty, stern, vindictive, when they are not; and their resentment is the more to be dreaded, as they hold it a point of honor to dissemble their sense of an injury till they find an opportunity to revenge it.

They are patient of cold and heat, of hunger and thirst, even beyond all belief when necessity requires, passing whole days, and often three or four days together, without food, in the woods, when on the watch for an enemy, or even on their hunt-ing parties; yet indulging themselves in their feasts even to the most brutal degree of intemperance. They despise death, and suffer the most excruciating tortures not only without a groan, but with an air of triumph; singing their death song, derid-ing their tormentors, and threatening them with the vengeance of their surviving friends: yet hold it honorable to fly before an enemy that appears the least superior in number or force.

Deprived by their extreme ignorance, and that indolence which nothing but their ardor for war can surmount, of all the conveniencies, as well as elegant refinements of polished life; strangers to the softer passions, love being with them on the same footing as amongst their fellow-tenants of the woods, their lives appear to me rather tranquil than happy: they have fewer cares, but they have also much fewer enjoyments, than fall to our share. I am told, however, that, though insensible to love, they are not without affections; are extremely awake to friendship, and passionately fond of their children.

They are of a copper color, which is rendered more unpleasing by a quantity of coarse red on their cheeks; but the children, when born, are of a pale silver white; perhaps their indelicate custom of greasing their bodies, and their being so much exposed to the air and sun even from infancy, may cause that total change of complexion, which I know not how otherwise to account for: their hair is black and shining, the women's very long, parted at the top, and combed back, tied behind, and often twisted with a thong of leather, which they think very ornamental: the dress of both sexes is a close jacket, reaching to their knees, with spatterdashes, all of coarse blue cloth, shoes of deer-skin, embroidered with porcupine quills, and sometimes with silver spangles; and a blanket thrown across their shoulders, and fastened before with a kind of bodkin, with necklaces, and other ornaments of beads or shells.

They are in general tall, well made, and agile to the last degree; have a lively imagination, a strong memory; and, as far as their interests are concerned, are very dextrous politicians.

Their address is cold and reserved; but their treatment of strangers, and the unhappy, infinitely kind and hospitable. A very worthy priest, with whom I am acquainted at Quebec, was some years since shipwrecked in December on the island of Anticosti: after a variety of distresses, not difficult to be imagined on an island without inhabitants, during the severity of a winter even colder than that of Canada; he, with the small remains of his companions who survived such complicated distress, early in the spring, reached the main land in their boat, and wandered to a cabbin of savages; the ancient of which, having heard his story, bid him enter, and liberally supplied their wants: "Approach, brother," said he; "the unhappy have a right to our assistance; we are men, and cannot but feel for the distresses which happen to men;" a sentiment which has a strong resemblance to a celebrated one in a Greek tragedy.

You will not expect more from me on this subject, as my residence here has been short, and I can only be said to catch a few marking features flying. I am unable to give you a picture at full length.

Nothing astonishes me so much as to find their manners so little changed by their intercourse with the Europeans; they seem to have learnt nothing of us but excess in drinking.

The situation of the village is very fine, on an eminence, gently rising to a thick wood at some distance, a beautiful little serpentine river in front, on which are a bridge, a mill, and a small cascade, at such a distance as to be very pleasing

MANDEVILLE, *THE HISTORY OF EMILY MONTAGUE*

objects from their houses; and a cultivated country, intermixed with little woods lying between them and Quebec, from which they are distant only nine very short miles.

What a letter have I written! I shall quit my post of historian to your friend Miss Fermor; the ladies love writing much better than we do; and I should perhaps be only just, if I said they write better.

Adieu!
ED. RIVERS

LETTER XIV

To JOHN TEMPLE, Esq; Pall-Mall.

Quebec, Sept. 15.

BELIEVE me, Jack, you are wrong; this vagrant taste is unnatural, and does not lead to happiness; your eager pursuit of pleasure defeats itself; love gives no true delight but where the heart is attach'd, and you do not give yours time to fix. Such is our unhappy frailty, that the tenderest passion may wear out, and another succeed, but the love of change merely as change is not in nature; where it is a real taste, 'tis a depraved one. Boys are inconstant from vanity and affectation, old men from decay of passion; but men, and particularly men of sense, find their happiness only in that lively attachment of which it is impossible for more than one to be the object. Love is an intellectual pleasure, and even the senses will be weakly affected where the heart is silent.

You will find this truth confirmed even within the walls of the seraglio; amidst this crowd of rival beauties, eager to please, one happy fair generally reigns in the heart of the sultan; the rest serve only to gratify his pride and ostentation, and are regarded by him with the same indifference as the furniture of his superb palace, of which they may be said to make a part.

With your estate, you should marry; I have as many objections to the state as you can have; I mean, on the footing marriage is at present. But of this I am certain, that two persons at once delicate and sensible, united by friendship, by taste, by a conformity of sentiment, by that lively ardent tender inclination which alone deserves the name of love, will find happiness in marriage, which is in vain sought in any other kind of attachment.

You are so happy as to have the power of chusing; you are rich, and have not the temptation to a mercenary engagement. Look round you for a companion, a confidente; a tender amiable friend, with all the charms of a mistress: above all, be certain of her affection, that you engage, that you fill her whole soul. Find such a woman, my dear Temple, and you cannot make too much haste to be happy.

I have a thousand things to say to you, but am setting off immediately with Sir George Clayton, to meet the lieutenant governor at Montreal; a piece of respect

315

which I should pay with the most lively pleasure, if it did not give me the opportunity of seeing the woman in the world I most admire. I am not however going to set you the example of marrying: I am not so happy; she is engaged to the gentleman who goes up with me. Adieu!

Yours,
ED. RIVERS.

41

HENRY MCKENZIE (1745–1831), *THE MAN OF FEELING: A NOVEL*

(Philadelphia: Robert Bell, [1771] 1782),
pp. 7–10, 34–38

Henry McKenzie was a Scottish novelist and lawyer. His most famous work was the sentimental novel, *The Man of Feeling*, which followed the travels of the protagonist Harvey. On his journeys, Harvey met a broad range of people from different walks of life, notably including some poor and downfallen characters, who told him their life stories. Their tales were always sublime or tragic and Harvey – the man of feeling – was invariably moved, often weeping in sympathy. The novel was remarkably well-received when it was first published during the height of the culture of sensibility. It fell out of fashion in the nineteenth century, as this model of masculinity became viewed as unmanly and ridiculous. As a text that was very much of its historical moment, it provides important insights into how the portrayal and expression of emotion, and responses to such representations, change over time.

. . .

Chapter XIV: He sets out on his journey – the beggar and his dog

He had taken leave of his aunt on the eve of his intended departure; but the good lady's affection for her nephew interrupted her sleep, and early as it was next morning when Harley came downstairs to set out, he found her in the parlour with a tear on her cheek, and her caudle-cup in her hand. She knew enough of physic to prescribe against going abroad of a morning with an empty stomach. She gave her blessing with the draught; her instructions she had delivered the night before. They consisted mostly of negatives, for London, in her idea, was so replete with temptations that it needed the whole armour of her friendly cautions to repel their attacks.

Peter stood at the door. We have mentioned this faithful fellow formerly: Harley's father had taken him up an orphan, and saved him from being cast on the parish; and he had ever since remained in the service of him and of his son. Harley shook him by the hand as he passed, smiling, as if he had said, "I will not weep." He sprung hastily into the chaise that waited for him; Peter folded up the step. "My dear master," said he, shaking the solitary lock that hung on either side of his head, "I have been told as how London is a sad place." He was choked with the thought, and his benediction could not be heard: – but it shall be heard, honest Peter! where these tears will add to its energy.

In a few hours Harley reached the inn where he proposed breakfasting, but the fulness of his heart would not suffer him to eat a morsel. He walked out on the road, and gaining a little height, stood gazing on that quarter he had left. He looked for his wonted prospect, his fields, his woods, and his hills: they were lost in the distant clouds! He pencilled them on the clouds, and bade them farewell with a sigh!

He sat down on a large stone to take out a little pebble from his shoe, when he saw, at some distance, a beggar approaching him. He had on a loose sort of coat, mended with different-coloured rags, amongst which the blue and the russet were the predominant. He had a short knotty stick in his hand, and on the top of it was stuck a ram's horn; his knees (though he was no pilgrim) had worn the stuff of his breeches; he wore no shoes, and his stockings had entirely lost that part of them which should have covered his feet and ankles; in his face, however, was the plump appearance of good humour; he walked a good round pace, and a crook-legged dog trotted at his heels.

"Our delicacies," said Harley to himself, "are fantastic; they are not in nature! that beggar walks over the sharpest of these stones barefooted, whilst I have lost the most delightful dream in the world, from the smallest of them happening to get into my shoe." The beggar had by this time come up, and, pulling off a piece of hat, asked charity of Harley; the dog began to beg too: – it was impossible to resist both; and, in truth, the want of shoes and stockings had made both unnecessary, for Harley had destined sixpence for him before. The beggar, on receiving it, poured forth blessings without number; and, with a sort of smile on his countenance, said to Harley "that if he wanted to have his fortune told" – Harley turned his eye briskly on the beggar: it was an unpromising look for the subject of a prediction, and silenced the prophet immediately. "I would much rather learn," said Harley, "what it is in your power to tell me: your trade must be an entertaining one; sit down on this stone, and let me know something of your profession; I have often thought of turning fortune-teller for a week or two myself."

"Master," replied the beggar, "I like your frankness much; God knows I had the humour of plain-dealing in me from a child, but there is no doing with it in this world; we must live as we can, and lying is, as you call it, my profession, but I was in some sort forced to the trade, for I dealt once in telling truth.

"I was a labourer, sir, and gained as much as to make me live: I never laid by indeed: for I was reckoned a piece of a wag, and your wags, I take it, are seldom rich, Mr. Harley." "So," said Harley, "you seem to know me." "Ay, there are few folks in the country that I don't know something of: how should I tell fortunes else?" "True; but to go on with your story: you were a labourer, you say, and a

318

THE MAN OF FEELING: A NOVEL

wag; your industry, I suppose, you left with your old trade, but your humour you preserve to be of use to you in your new."

"What signifies sadness, sir? a man grows lean on't: but I was brought to my idleness by degrees; first I could not work, and it went against my stomach to work ever after. I was seized with a jail fever at the time of the assizes being in the county where I lived; for I was always curious to get acquainted with the felons, because they are commonly fellows of much mirth and little thought, qualities I had ever an esteem for. In the height of this fever, Mr. Harley, the house where I lay took fire, and burnt to the ground; I was carried out in that condition, and lay all the rest of my illness in a barn. I got the better of my disease, however, but I was so weak that I spit blood whenever I attempted to work. I had no relation living that I knew of, and I never kept a friend above a week, when I was able to joke; I seldom remained above six months in a parish, so that I might have died before I had found a settlement in any: thus I was forced to beg my bread, and a sorry trade I found it, Mr. Harley. I told all my misfortunes truly, but they were seldom believed; and the few who gave me a halfpenny as they passed did it with a shake of the head, and an injunction not to trouble them with a long story. In short, I found that people don't care to give alms without some security for their money; a wooden leg or a withered arm is a sort of draught upon heaven for those who choose to have their money placed to account there; so I changed my plan, and, instead of telling my own misfortunes, began to prophesy happiness to others. This I found by much the better way: folks will always listen when the tale is their own, and of many who say they do not believe in fortune-telling, I have known few on whom it had not a very sensible effect.

I pick up the names of their acquaintance; amours and little squabbles are easily gleaned among servants and neighbours; and indeed people themselves are the best intelligencers in the world for our purpose: they dare not puzzle us for their own sakes, for every one is anxious to hear what they wish to believe, and they who repeat it, to laugh at it when they have done, are generally more serious than their hearers are apt to imagine.

With a tolerable good memory, and some share of cunning, with the help of walking sometimes a nights over heaths and church-yards, with this, and showing the tricks of that there dog, whom I stole from the serjeant of a marching regiment (and by the way, he can steal too upon occasion), I make shift to pick up a livelihood.

My trade, indeed, is none of the honestest; yet people are not much cheated neither who give a few half-pence for a prospect of happiness, which I have heard some persons say is all a man can arrive at in this world. – But I must bid you good day, sir, for I have three miles to walk before noon, to inform some boarding-school young ladies whether their husbands are to be peers of the realm or captains in the army: a question which I promised to answer them by that time."

Harley had drawn a shilling from his pocket; but virtue bade him consider on whom he was going to bestow it. – Virtue held back his arm; – but a milder form, a younger sister of virtue's, not so severe as virtue, nor so serious as pity, smiled

319

ART AND CULTURE

upon him; his fingers lost their compression; – nor did Virtue offer to catch the money as it fell. It had no sooner reached the ground than the watchful cur (a trick he had been taught) snapped it up, and, contrary to the most approved method of stewardship, delivered it immediately into the hands of his master.

. . .

Chapter XXIX: The distresses of a father

HARLEY kneeled also at the side of the unfortunate daughter. "Allow me, sir," said he, "to entreat your pardon for one whose offences have been already so signally punished. I know, I feel, that those tears, wrung from the heart of a father, are more dreadful to her than all the punishments your sword could have inflicted: accept the contrition of a child whom heaven has restored to you." "Is she not lost," answered he, "irrecoverably lost? Damnation! a common prostitute to the meanest ruffian!" –

"Calmly, my dear sir," said Harley, "did you know by what complicated misfortunes she had fallen to that miserable state in which you now behold her, I should have no need of words to excite your compassion. Think, sir, of what once she was. Would you abandon her to the insults of an unfeeling world, deny her opportunity of penitence, and cut off the little comfort that still remains for your afflictions and her own!"

"Speak," said he, addressing himself to his daughter; "speak; I will hear thee." The desperation that supported her was lost; she fell to the ground, and bathed his feet with her tears.

Harley undertook her cause: he related the treacheries to which she had fallen a sacrifice, and again solicited the forgiveness of her father. He looked on her for some time in silence; the pride of a soldier's honour checked for a while the yearnings of his heart; but nature at last prevailed, he fell on her neck and mingled his tears with hers. Harley, who discovered from the dress of the stranger that he was just arrived from a journey, begged that they would both remove to his lodgings, till he could procure others for them. Atkins looked at him with some marks of surprise. His daughter now first recovered the power of speech.

"Wretch as I am," said she, "yet there is some gratitude due to the preserver of your child. See him now before you. To him I owe my life, or at least the comfort of imploring your forgiveness before I die."

"Pardon me, young gentleman," said Atkins, "I fear my passion wronged you."

"Never, never, sir," said Harley "if it had, your reconciliation to your daughter were an atonement a thousand fold." He then repeated his request that he might be allowed to conduct them to his lodgings, to which Mr. Atkins at last consented.

He took his daughter's arm. "Come, my Emily," said he, "we can never, never recover that happiness we have lost! but time may teach us to remember our misfortunes with patience."

When they arrived at the house where Harley lodged, he was informed that the first floor was then vacant, and that the gentleman and his daughter might be accommodated there. While he was upon his enquiry, Miss Atkins informed her father more particularly what she owed to his benevolence. When he turned into the room where they were Atkins ran and embraced him; – begged him again to forgive the offence he had given him, and made the warmest protestations of gratitude for his favours. We would attempt to describe the joy which Harley felt on this occasion, did it not occur to us that one half of the world could not understand it though we did, and the other half will, by this time, have understood it without any description at all.

Miss Atkins now retired to her chamber, to take some rest from the violence of the emotions she had suffered. When she was gone, her father, addressing himself to Harley, said, "You have a right, sir, to be informed of the present situation of one who owes so much to your compassion for his misfortunes. My daughter I find has informed you what that was at the fatal period when they began. Her distresses you have heard, you have pitied as they deserved; with mine, perhaps, I cannot so easily make you acquainted with. You have a feeling heart, Mr. Harley; I bless it that it has saved my child; but you never were a father, a father torn by that most dreadful of calamities, the dishonour of a child he doated on! You have been already informed of some of the circumstances of her elopement.

I was then from home, called by the death of a relation, who, though he would never advance me a shilling on the utmost exigency in his life-time, left me all the gleanings of his frugality at his death. I would not write this intelligence to my daughter, because I intended to be the bearer myself; and as soon as my business would allow me, I set out on my return, winged with all the haste of paternal affection. I fondly built those schemes of future happiness, which present prosperity is ever busy to suggest: my Emily was concerned in them all.

As I approached our little dwelling my heart throbbed with the anticipation of joy and welcome. I imagined the cheering fire, the blissful contentment of a frugal meal, made luxurious by a daughter's smile, I painted to myself her surprise at the tidings of our new-acquired riches, our fond disputes about the disposal of them.

The road was shortened by the dreams of happiness I enjoyed, and it began to be dark as I reached the house: I alighted from my horse, and walked softly upstairs to the room we commonly sat in. I was somewhat disappointed at not finding my daughter there. I rung the bell; her maid appeared, and shewed no small signs of wonder at the summons. She blessed herself as she entered the room: I smiled at her surprise. "Where is Miss Emily, sir?" said she. "Emily!" "Yes, sir; she has been gone hence some days, upon receipt of those letters you sent her." "Letters!" said I. "Yes, sir, so she told me, and went off in all haste that very night."

I stood aghast as she spoke, but was able so far to recollect myself, as to put on the affectation of calmness, and telling her there was certainly some mistake in the affair, desired her to leave me.

When she was gone, I threw myself into a chair, in that state of uncertainty which is, of all others, the most dreadful. The gay visions I had delighted myself with, vanished in an instant: I was tortured with tracing back the same circle of doubt and disappointment. My head grew dizzy as I thought. I called the servant again, and asked her a hundred questions, to no purpose; there was not room even for conjecture.

Something at last arose in my mind, which we call Hope, without knowing what it is. I wished myself deluded by it; but it could not prevail over my returning fears. I rose and walked through the room. My Emily's spinnet stood at the end of it, open, with a book of music folded down at some of my favourite lessons. I touched the keys; there was a vibration in the sound that froze my blood; I looked around, and methought the family pictures on the walls gazed on me with compassion in their faces. I sat down again with an attempt at more composure; I started at every creaking of the door, and my ears rung with imaginary noises!

I had not remained long in this situation, when the arrival of a friend, who had accidentally heard of my return, put an end to my doubts, by the recital of my daughter's dishonour. He told me he had his information from a young gentleman, to whom Winbrooke had boasted of having seduced her.

I started from my seat, with broken curses on my lips, and without knowing whither I should pursue them, ordered my servant to load my pistols and saddle my horses. My friend, however, with great difficulty, persuaded me to compose myself for that night, promising to accompany me on the morrow, to Sir George Winbrooke's in quest of his son.

The morrow came, after a night spent in a state little distant from madness. We went as early as decency would allow to Sir George's; he received me with politeness, and indeed compassion; protested his abhorrence of his son's conduct, and told me that he had set out some days before for London, on which place he had procured a draft for a large sum, on pretence of finishing his travels; but that he had not heard from him since his departure.

I did not wait for any more, either of information or comfort, but, against the united remonstrances of Sir George and my friend, set out instantly for London, with a frantic uncertainty of purpose; but there, all manner of search was in vain. I could trace neither of them any farther than the inn where they first put up on their arrival; and after some days fruitless inquiry, returned home destitute of every little hope that had hitherto supported me. The journies I had made, the restless nights I had spent, above all, the perturbation of my mind, had the effect which might naturally be expected; a very dangerous fever was the consequence.

From this, however, contrary to the expectation of my physicians, I recovered. It was now that I first felt something like calmness of mind: probably from being reduced to a state which could not produce the exertions of anguish or despair. A stupid melancholy settled on my soul; I could endure to live with an apathy of life; at times I forgot my resentment, and wept at the remembrance of my child.

Such has been the tenor of my days since that fatal moment when these misfortunes began, till yesterday, that I received a letter from a friend in town, acquainting me of her present situation. Could such tales as mine, Mr. Harley, be sometimes suggested to the daughters of levity, did they but know with what anxiety the heart of a parent flutters round the child he loves, they would be less apt to construe into harshness that delicate concern for their conduct, which they often complain of as

THE MAN OF FEELING: A NOVEL

laying restraint upon things, to the young, the gay, and the thoughtless, seemingly harmless and indifferent. Alas! I fondly imagined that I needed not even these common cautions! my Emily was the joy of my age, and the pride of my soul! – Those things are now no more! they are lost for ever! Her death I could have borne! but the death of her honour has added obloquy and shame to that sorrow which bends my grey hairs to the dust!"

As he spoke these last words, his voice trembled in his throat; it was now lost in his tears! He sat with his face half turned from Harley, as if he would have hid the sorrow which he felt. Harley was in the same attitude himself; he durst not meet his eye with a tear; but gathering his stifled breath, "Let me entreat you, sir," said he, "to hope better things. The world is ever tyrannical; it warps our sorrows to edge them with keener affliction: let us not be slaves to the names it affixes to motive or to action. I know an ingenuous mind cannot help feeling when they sting: but there are considerations by which it may be overcome; its fantastic ideas vanish as they rise; they teach us to look beyond it."

42

JOHANN WOLFGANG VON GOETHE (1749–1832), *THE SORROWS OF WERTER: A GERMAN STORY*

Tans. John Gifford (London: Harrison, [1774] 1789), pp. 34, 35–36, 38, 43, 63–64

Johann Wolfgang von Goethe was a German statesman and writer in a range of genres. His epistolary novel, *The Sorrows of Werter*, tells the story of Werter, his unrequited love for Charlotte, and his eventual suicide. It is considered part of the proto-Romantic 'Sturm and Drang' movement, which placed emphasis on the self and the expression of strong, even sublime emotions. The novel was remarkably successful, translated into many languages, including this eighteenth-century English edition. Perhaps as interesting as the tale itself – which is replete with emotional expression – is the public response to the novel. It was blamed for a spate of suicides in the years following, and inspired a wide-range of artistic responses, including prints of scenes from the book, parodies, and material goods, including Meissen porcelain (see source 10) and perfume. A group of young men, suffering from 'Werter Fever' dressed and did their hair to look like the protagonist. Eventually both the book and the fashion style was banned in several countries, as authorities sought to control the craze. The book is therefore interesting both for its use of emotion in the production of the story and for its emotional impact on the public.

...

LETTER XV

July 6.

CHARLOTTE is still with her dying friend; still the same attentive, benevolent creature; whose looks, wherever they stray, can soothe the anguish of grief, and dispense the balm of consolation. She walked out yesterday with her two little sisters, Marianne and Amelia: I was apprized of it, and went to meet them; we had a most delightful walk. On our return we stopped at my favourite fountain, which became a thousand times dearer to my heart as Charlotte was sitting on the little wall that surrounds it. I looked around me, and recalled to my mind the hours I had passed by it's side, when my heart was alone and unoccupied. 'Dear spring!' said I, 'it is long since I enjoyed the bracing freshness of your cooling stream; since then, how often have I passed, with hasty steps, your grass-grown margin, without casting even a transient look upon you!' I looked down and saw Amelia coming up the steps in great haste, with a glass of water in her hand. I then turned my eyes on Charlotte, and my soul was struck with a just sense of her value. Amelia, however, appeared with her glass, which Marianne wanted to take from her. 'No, no,' said the dear child, with the utmost sweetness of expression, 'my dear Charlotte must drink first.' I was so transported with joy at this affectionate exclamation, that I could find no other means of expressing my rapture than by taking the child in my arms, and kissing her with such eagerness, that she began to cry. 'For shame!' said Charlotte. 'Come here, my dear;' taking her by the hand, and leading her down the steps; 'make haste and wash yourself in that clear water, and then you'll be quite well again.' With what attention I observed the poor child as she was washing her cheeks with her little hands, in the firm belief that the miraculous spring would cleanse her from all pollution, and prevent a long beard from appearing on her face! Though Charlotte told her that she had washed it enough, she still continued, as if she thought that it was better to wash it too much than too little. I confess to you, my friend, that I never attended a christening with greater respect; and, when Charlotte came up the steps, I could willingly have prostrated myself before her, as before a prophet who had just expiated the sins of a people.

In the evening, I could not refrain, in the joy of my heart, from relating this little adventure to a person who, because he has wit, I was willing to believe was possessed of common sense. How grossly was I mistaken! He told me that Charlotte had acted very imprudently; that it was wrong to inspire children with such ridiculous ideas, which gave birth to an infinity of superstitious errors, that it would be difficult to eradicate. I then recollected that, about a week before, one of his own children had been christened; and therefore pursued my remarks no farther. I felt, however, an internal conviction of this important truth – That we should deal with children as God deals with us: he makes our chief happiness consist in suffering our minds to be amused by the pleasing uncertainty of flattering opinions.

· · ·

LETTER XVIII

July 13.

NO, I am not mistaken – I read in her eyes the interest I have in her heart. Yes, I feel, and every impulse of my bosom confirms the flattering idea, that she – Dare I pronounce a word so pregnant with inexpressible bliss! Yes, I Feel that she loves me. Is it the presumption of vanity, or the consciousness of truth? I know not a man who possesses sufficient influence over the heart of Charlotte, to afford me the smallest uneasiness. And yet, when she speaks of her intended husband with all the warmth and tenderness of a settled affection, I find myself in the same situation as a man who is degraded from his rank, deprived of his power, and compelled to deliver up his sword.

LETTER XIX

July 16.

HOW my heart palpitates, and the raging blood boil in my veins, when by chance I touch her hand! When my feet accidentally come in contact with hers, I retreat with precipitation as from a fire; but a secret and irresistible power again impels me forward. Such is the delirium that has taken possession of all my senses. Alas! the simple innocence and perfect freedom of her mind prevent her from feeling the torments which these privations, apparently so trifling, make me experience.

When she places her hand upon mine, and in the eagerness of conversation draws sufficiently near to me for her balmy breath to reach my lips, the sudden effect of lightning on the human frame is not more potent. This celestial bliss, my friend, this ingenuous confidence, should I never dare to – You understand me. No, my heart is not so corrupted. It is weak indeed, very weak! But may not that be deemed corruption? I consider her as a superior being. Every desire vanishes in her presence. When I am near her, I feel as if my soul were expanded beyond it's usual limits; as if my body were purified from all the grosser sensations of it's mortal state. There is an air which she plays on the harpsichord with all the energy of an angel; it is her favourite air; and is so simple and expressive, that, the moment me begins it, all my cares and sorrows are at an end. The charming simplicity of this tune affects me so sensibly, that I can easily give credit to all the magick wonders said to be performed by the musick of the ancients. Aware of the power it has over my senses, she has recourse to it whenever she observes the deep gloom of despair seated on my brow; in a moment the dismal cloud is dispelled, and my soul is restored to tranquillity.

LETTER XX

July 18.

WHAT is the whole world to our hearts, my friend, without love! It is a magick lantern without light! No sooner is it illuminated, than your wall is covered with the whimsical figures it contains. And if love was only capable of affording such transient shadows, still would they constitute our happiness, so long as the pleasing phantoms could occupy our minds. I was prevented, by company that I could not avoid, from seeing Charlotte to-day: I therefore sent my boy to enquire after her health, merely that I might have some one near me who had lately been in her presence. With what impatience did I wait his return! with what joy did I receive him! I could willingly have smothered him with kisses, if I had not been prevented by shame.

The famous stone of Bologna, when exposed to the sun, is said to attract it's rays; and so to retain them, that it can itself reflect a considerable light for some time after it is removed into the dark. The boy was the same to me; the idea that Charlotte's eyes had dwelt on his features, tendered them so dear, so precious to my soul, that I would not at that moment have parted with him for a thousand crowns; I was so delighted with him! Do not laugh at me, my friend; for, be assured that nothing can be deemed an illusion which contributes to our happiness.

. . .

LETTER XXVII

Aug. 10

WERE I not a madman, I might lead the most pleasant and comfortable life that a mortal could wish for, in my present situation. Seldom is such a fortunate combination of circumstances to be found so truly adapted to constitute the happiness of man. But, alas! I feel too sensibly, that happiness depends solely on the mind! To be considered as forming a part of the most amiable family in the world; to be beloved by the father as a son, by the children as a father, and by Charlotte too: and the worthy Albert, who does not interrupt my peace by any ill-timed effusions of fondness; who professes the most sincere and cordial friendship, and prefers me to every body but Charlotte herself! – You would be delighted to hear us converse together as we walk, when Charlotte is the subject of our discourse. Nothing can be more truly ridiculous than our situation; and yet it often brings tears into my eyes.

When he talks to me of Charlotte's worthy mother; when he gives me a description of her last moments, and the affecting scene that occurred previous to her dissolution, when she resigned her house and family to her daughter; when he tells me how that amiable girl immediately changed her childish occupations for the more serious employments of a mother, every subsequent hour of her life being distinguished by some proof of her friendship, or some production of her industry, and yet still preserving her native chearfulness and vivacity – I walk by his side, gather flowers by the way, and arrange them with great care in the form of a nosegay – then I throw them into the first brook, and stop to observe how they gradually sink to the bottom.

I know not whether I told you, in my last letter, that Albert means to establish his residence here. He has good interest at court; and has therefore obtained the promise of a place that will bring him in a comfortable income. I never met with a man who paid closer attention to business.

. . .

LETTER XXXII

Aug. 22.

SOME fatality attends me! All my active faculties are doomed to linger in rest-less indolence. I cannot remain idle, yet am wholly unable to do anything. The powers of my mind are become torpid; I am insensible to the beauties of nature, and books inspire me with disgust. How often do I wish I were a mechanick, that when I awake in the morning, I might have some object in view to occupy my thoughts for the day, and some hope for the morrow! How I envy Albert, when I see him entrenched up to the ears in papers and parchment! I am then induced to believe that, in his place, I should be happy: and so thoroughly am I impressed with this idea, that I have been frequently tempted to write to the minister for the place which you have assured me I might obtain. Indeed, I think he could not refuse me, as he has long professed an esteem for me, and has even told me that I ought to procure some employment. At times I feel myself inclined to pursue his advice; but, when I recollect the table of the Horse, who, tired of his liberty, suffered himself to be bridled and saddled, I am at a loss how to act. To be candid, my dear friend: Do not you think that the same restless disposition which makes me wish to change my situation, would equally pursue me in every station of life?

. . .

LETTER LXXII

Dec. 4.

I Can support this state no longer. To-day I was sitting by Charlotte. She was play-ing different tunes on her harpsichord, with an expression which it is impossible to describe. Her little sister was dressing her doll upon my knee. The tears came into my eyes. I stooped down, and perceived her wedding-ring. My tears flowed down my cheeks. She immediately began to play that divine air which has so often soothed my distracted soul. At first, it afforded me consolation; but it soon recalled to my mind the times that are past, the transitory moments of bliss I have experienced, and the long intervals of unavailing sorrow: and then I walked hastily up and down the room. But, every note increasing my grief – 'For Heaven's sake, Charlotte!' I emphatically exclaimed, 'for Heaven's sake, desist!' She immediately stopped; and, looking at me with a most expressive smile, said – 'Werter, you must be ill, indeed, since you are disgusted with your favourite food ! Pray go, and try to compose yourself.' I tore myself from her; and – Great God! thou seest my misery, and will put an end to it!

LETTER LXXIII

Dec. 6.

HOW often her image pursues me! Walking or sleeping, she is perpetually before me! Soon as I retire to rest, and close my weary eye-lids, I find her black eyes imprinted on my brain. I cannot express what I feel! – But those fire-darting orbs are ever present to my sight, and absorb all my faculties! What is man, that boasted demigod? Does not his very strength forsake him when he stands in the greatest need of it? And whether he soar on the wings of pleasure, or seek to sink into the abyss of grief, is he not equally obliged to stop in the midst of his career? And when he wishes to plunge into the ocean of infinity, is he not forcibly impelled to return to those cold sentiments that urge him to support a miserable existence?

LETTER LXXIV

Dec. 8.

MY dear friend, I feel, as those unfortunate beings must have felt who were formerly supposed to be possessed by devils! I am often in this situation. It is not agony; it is not passion: it is a secret rage, that excites an inward agitation, and threatens me with instant suffocation. Wretch that I am! I wander amid the dark and dreary scenes which this unfriendly season exhibits!

I went out last night. I had heard, in the evening, that the river, and all the neighbouring brooks, had overflown their banks; and that, from Walheim to this place, my favourite valley was entirely covered with water. It was past eleven when I sallied forth to view the dreadful scene! By the faint glimmering of the moon, I saw the impetuous waves rushing over the summit of the rock, and rolling, with a horrid noise over the fields and meadows, breaking down the trees and hedges in their rapid course. The whole valley was one continued sea, agitated by furious winds: and, when the pale orb of Night peeped from behind a sable cloud, it's light, reflected in the torrent, added fresh horror to the scene. It was then my tortured soul longed to take it's flight to heaven. I stood on the brink of the precipice with extended arms, casting an eager look upon the flood beneath; anxious, by plunging headlong down, to end my torments. Alas! my feet were rooted to the earth; I had not power to terminate my sorrows. My glass is not yet run. O, my friend! how chearfully would I have resigned the boasted dignity of man, to be incorporated with the impetuous blast, to rend the clouds, and disturb the surface of the deep! – And shall we never quit our earthly prison, to enjoy this sublime pleasure!

How mournfully did I cast my eyes towards a favourite spot, where I had often sat with Charlotte, beneath a willow's friendly shade, after a summer's walk! That, too, was overflown; and the extreme branches of my favourite tree were scarcely visible above the water. The steward's house, and all the surrounding fields, which I had so often traversed, then occurred to my mind. I trembled lest they should have been destroyed by the violence of the storm. Past happy scenes beamed a transitory gleam of comfort on my heart; like the wretched captive who dreams of fields, and flocks, and fragrant flowers. I was – But I do not blame myself, for I have courage to die. I should have – At present, I am like a decrepid old woman who picks sticks from the hedges, and begs her bread from door to door, to prolong, for a few sad moments, her feeble and wretched existence!

LETTER LXXV

Dec. 17.

WHAT does this mean, my dear friend? I am frightened at myself! Is not my love for her pure and holy as the chaste ardour of the cloistered nun? Has my heart ever formed a wish that it need blush to own? To attest this truth by oaths were needless. But now – such dreams! They are surely right who ascribe those nightly wanderings of the mind to some external power.

Last night – I tremble as I tell you – I held her in my arms, pressed her to my bosom, and imprinted a thousand burning kisses on her trembling lips; while our eyes beamed with the most lively expressions of pleasure. Gracious Heaven! can the happiness I now experience in recalling these transports to my mind, be deemed a crime? – Oh, Charlotte! Charlotte! my fate is now decided! – my senses are disordered! – my eyes are filled with tears! – my peace of mind is gone for ever! – I have nothing now to wish for – nothing to hope! 'Twere better to depart!

43

CHARLES AVISON (1709–1770), *AN ESSAY ON MUSICAL EXPRESSION*

(London: Lockyer Davis, 1775), pp. 1–18

Charles Avison was an English composer and church organist. As well as writing music, he produced some work of musical criticism, including his best known work excerpted below. Histories and philosophies of music were popular during the eighteenth century, where music was often closely linked to the development of human language and evolutionary development. It was generally thought that music was a basic human behaviour, a form of communication that worked by altering the emotions. In this sense, philosophies of music often saw its effects as related to the human capacity for sympathy. Music theory sought to develop these basic ideas through exploring what notes and harmonies produced particular emotional effects; some wished to be able to produce a regular science of music's impact on the body. Despite efforts, this was little consensus on this topic. This particular source provides Avison's interpretation on this question, highlighting both how music was conceptualised, at least amongst the elite, during the period, and the close connection between music and emotion.

. . .

On the force and effects of music

AS the public inclination for Music seems every day advancing, it may not be amiss, at this time, to offer a few observations on that delightful art; such observations, I mean, as may be chiefly applicable to the present times; such as may tend to correct any errors that have arisen, either in the composition, or the practice of music.

If we view this art in its foundations, we shall find, that by the constitution of man it is of mighty efficacy in working both on his imagination and his passions. The force of *harmony*, or *melody* alone, is wonderful on the imagination. *A full chord* struck, or a beautiful succession of *single sounds* produced, is no less ravishing to the ear, than just symmetry or exquisite colours to the eye.

The capacity of receiving, pleasure from these musical sounds, is, in fact, a peculiar and internal sense; but of a much more refined nature than the external senses: for in the pleasures arising from our internal sense of harmony, there is no prior uneasiness necessary, in order to our tasting them in their full perfection; neither is the enjoyment of them attended either with languor or disgust. It is their peculiar and essential property, to divest the soul of every unquiet passion, to pour in upon the mind a silent and serene joy beyond the power of words to express, and to fix the heart in a rational, benevolent, and happy tranquillity. But, though this be the natural effect of *melody* or *harmony* on the imagination, when simply considered; yet when to these is added the force of *Musical Expression*, the effect is greatly increased; for then they assume the power of exciting all the most agreeable passions of the soul. The force of sound in alarming; the passions is prodigious. Thus, the noise of thunder, the shouts of war, the uproar of an enraged ocean, strike us with terror: so again, there are certain sounds natural to joy, others to grief or despondency, others to tenderness and love; and by hearing *these*, we naturally sympathize with those who either *enjoy* or *suffer*. Thus music, either by imitating these various sounds in due subordination to the laws of *air* and *harmony*, or by any other method of association, bringing the objects of our passions before us (especially when those objects are determined, and made as it were visibly and intimately present to the imagination by the help of words) does naturally raise a variety of passions in the human breast, similar to the sounds which are expressed: and thus, by the musician's art, we are often carried into the fury of a battle or a tempest, we are by turns elated with joy, or sunk in pleasing sorrow, rouzed to courage, or quelled by grateful terrors, melted into pity, tenderness, and love, or transported to the regions of bliss, in an extacy of divine praise.

But beyond this, I think we may venture to assert, that it is the peculiar quality of Music to raise the *sociable and happy passions*, and to *subdue* the *contrary ones*. I know it has been generally believed and affirmed, that its power extends alike to every affection of the mind. But I would offer it to the consideration of the public, whether this is not a general and fundamental error. I would appeal to any man, whether ever he found himself urged to acts of selfishness, cruelty, treachery, revenge, or malevolence, by the power of musical sounds? or is he ever found jealousy, suspicion, or ingratitude engendered in his breast, either from HARMONY or DISCORD? I believe no instance of this nature can be alledged with truth. It must be owned, indeed, that the force of music may urge the *passions* to an excess, or it may fix them on false and improper objects, and may thus be pernicious in its effects: but still the passions which it raises, though they maybe *misled* or *excessive*, are of the benevolent and social kind, and in their intent at least are disinterested and noble.[1] As I take this to be the truth of the case, so it seems to me no difficult matter to assign a sufficient reason for it: we have already seen that it is the natural effect of air or harmony to throw the mind into a pleasurable state: and when it hath obtained this state, it will of course exert those powers, and be susceptible of those passions, which are the most natural and agreeable to it. Now these are altogether of the benevolent species; inasmuch as we know that the contrary assertions, such as anger, revenge, jealousy, and hatred, are always attended with anxiety and pain: whereas all the various modifications of love, whether human or divine, are but so many kinds of immediate happiness. From this view of things there sore it necessarily follows, that every species of musical sound must tend to dispel the malevolent passions, because they are *painful*; and nourish those which are benevolent, because they are *pleasing*.

The most general and striking instance of the power of Music, perhaps, that we know of, is that related of the *Arcadians* by POLYBIUS, in the fourth book of his history; which, as it expressly coincides with the subject in question, I shall venture to give the reader entire. This judicious historian, speaking of the cruelties exercised upon the *Cynœthians* by the *Ætolians*, and the little compassion that their neighbours had shewn them; after having described the calamities of this people, abhorred by all *Greece*, adds the following remarks:

"As the *Arcadians* are esteemed by the *Greeks* not only for the gentleness of their manners, their beneficence and humanity towards strangers, but also for their piety to the gods; it may not be amiss to examine, in few words, with regard to the ferocity of the *Cynœthians*, how it is possible, being incontestable *Arcadians* from their origin, they are become so much distinguished by their cruelty, and all manner of crimes, from the other *Greeks* of this time. I believe, it can only be imputed to their having been the first and sole people of all the *Arcadians*, who were estranged from the laudable institutions of their ancestors, sounded upon the natural wants of all those who inhabit Arcadia.

The study of Music (I mean that which is worthy the name) has its utility everywhere; but it is absolutely necessary among the *Arcadians*. For we must not adopt the sentiment of *Ephorus*, who, in the beginning of his writings, advances this proposition unworthy of him: *that Music is introduced amongst men, as a kind of inchantment, only to deceive and mislead them.* Neither should we imagine that it is without reason, that the ancient people of *Crete* and *Lacedæmon* have preferred the use of soft Music in war, to that of the trumpet; or, that the *Arcadians* in establishing their republic, although in other respects extremely austere in their manner of living, have shewn to Music so high a regard, that they not only teach this art to their children, but even compel their youth to a study of it to the age of thirty. These facts are notoriously known. It is also known, that the *Arcadians* are almost the only people, among whom their youth, in obedience to the laws, habituate themselves from their infancy, to sing *hymns* and *pœns*, as is usual among them, to the honour of the gods and heroes of their country. They are likewise taught the airs of *Philoxenus* and *Timotheus*; after which, every year, during the feasts of *Bacchus*, this youth are divided into two bands, the one confiding of boys, the other of their young men, who, to the music of flutes, dance in their theatres with great emulation, celebrating those games which take their names from each troop. Even in their assemblies and parties of pleasure, the *Arcadians* divert themselves less in conversation, or relating of stories, than in singing by turns, and inviting each other reciprocally to this exercise. It is no disgrace with them, to own their ignorance of other arts: but they cannot deny their ability in singing, because, at all events, they are necessitated to acquire this talent; nor, in confessing their skill,

ART AND CULTURE

can they exempt themselves from giving proofs of it, as that would be deemed amongst them a particular infamy. Besides this, at the care and expence of the public, their youth are trained in dancing and military exercises, which they perform to the music of flutes; and every year give proof of their abilities in the presence of their fellow-citizens.

Now it seems to me, that the first legislators, in forming such kind of establishments, have not had any design of introducing luxury and effeminacy; but that they have chiefly had in view the way of living among the *Arcadians*, which their manual and toilsome exercises rendered extremely laborious and severe; and the austere manners of this people, to which the coldness and severity of the air in almost every part of *Arcadia* did greatly contribute.

For it is natural to partake of the quality of this element. Thence it is, that different people, in proportion to the distance which separates them, differ from each other, not only in their exterior form and colour, but also in their customs and employments. The legislators, therefore, willing to soften and temper this ferocity and ruggedness of the *Arcadians*, made all those regulations which I have here mentioned; and instituted, besides these, various assemblies and sacrifices, as well for the men, as for the women; and also dances for their children of both sexes. In a word, they contrived all kinds of expedients to soften and aswage by this culture of their manners, the natural rudeness and barbarity of the *Arcadians*.

But the *Cynæthians*, who inhabit the most rude and savage parts of *Arcadia*, having neglected all those helps, of which on that account, they had so much the more occasion; and being, on the contrary, subject to mutual divisions and contests, they are, at length, become so fierce and barbarous, that there is not a city in *Greece*, where such frequent and enormous crimes are committed, as in that of *Cynætha*.

An instance of the unhappy state of this people, and of the aversion of all the *Arcadians* to their form of government, is the treatment that was shewn to their deputies which they sent to the *Lacedemonians* after the horrible massacre in *Cynætha*. In all the towns of *Arcadia* which these deputies entered, immediate notice was given by an herald, that they should instantly depart. But the inhabitants of *Mantinea*, after the departure of these envoys, went so far, as to purify themselves by expiatory sacrifices, and to carry the victims round the city and its territories, to purify both the one and the other.

We have related all these things; first, that other cities may be prevented from censuring in general the customs of the *Arcadians*; or, lest some of the people of *Arcadia* themselves, upon false prejudices, that the study of Music is permitted them only as a superficial amusement, should be prevailed upon to neglect this part of their discipline: in the second place, to engage the *Cynæthians*, if the gods should permit, to humanize and soften their tempers, by an application to the liberal arts, and especially to Music. For this is the only means, by which, they can ever be dispossessed of that ferocity which they have contracted."[2]

Still farther to confirm what is here advanced on the power of Music in raising the social and nobler passions only, I will transcribe a passage from the celebrated *Baron de* MONTESQUIEU.

AN ESSAY ON MUSICAL EXPRESSION

This learned and sensible writer, animadverting on the severe institutions of the Ancients in regard to manners, having referred to several authorities among the *Greeks* on this head, particularly to the relation of POLYBIUS above quoted, proceeds thus. – "In the Greek republics the magistrates were extremely embarrassed. They would not have the citizens apply themselves to trade, to agriculture, or to the arts; and yet they would not have them idle. They found, therefore, employment for them in gymnastic and military exercises; and none else were allowed by their institution. Hence the *Greeks* must be considered as a society of wrestlers and boxers. Now these exercises having a natural tendency to render people hardy and fierce, there was a necessity for tempering them with others that might soften their manners. For this purpose, Music, which influences the mind by means of corporeal organs. was extremely proper. It is a kind of medium between the bodily exercises that render men fierce and hardy, and speculative sciences that render them unsociable and sour. It cannot be said that Music inspired virtue, for this would be inconceivable: but it prevented the effects of a savage institution, and inabled the soul to have such a share in the education, as it could never have had without the assistance of harmony.

Let us suppose among ourselves a society of men, so passionately fond of hunting, as to make it their sole employment; these people would doubtless contrast a kind of rusticity and fierceness. But if they happened to receive a taste for Music, we should quickly perceive a sensible difference in their customs and manners. In short, the exercises used by the Greeks excited only one kind of passions, *viz.* fierceness, anger, and cruelty. But Music excites them all; it is able to inspire the soul with a sense of pity, lenity, tenderness, and love. Our moral writers, who declaim so vehemently against the stage, sufficiently demonstrate the power of Music over the soul.

If the society above-mentioned were to have no other Music than that of drums and the sound of the trumpet, would it not be more difficult to accomplish this end, than by the more melting tones of softer harmony? The Antients were therefore in the right, when under particular circumstances they preferred one mode to another in regard to manners.

But some will ask, why should Music be pitched upon preferable to any other entertainment? It is, because of all sensible pleasures there is none that less corrupts the soul".[3]

The fact the baron speaks of, seems to confirm what is here said on the power of Music: for we see that Music was applied by the *Greeks* to awaken the nobler passions only, such as pity, lenity, tenderness, and love. But should a state apply Music to give a roughness of manners, or inspire the contrary passions of hard-heartedness, anger, and cruelty, it would certainly miss its aim; notwithstanding that the baron seems to suppose the contrary. For he hath not alleged any instance, or any kind of proof in support of his supposition. It is true, as he observes in the second paragraph, that the sound of drums or trumpets would have a different effect from the more melting tones of softer harmony: yet still, the passions raised by these martial sounds are of the social kind: they may excite courage and contempt of death, but never hatred or cruelty.

335

ART AND CULTURE

Notes

1 Lest the two passions above-mentioned, of *terror* and *grief,* should be thought an exception to this rule, it may not be improper to remark as to the first, that the *terror* raised by *Musical Expression* is always of that grateful kind, which arises from an impression of something terrible to the imagination, but which is immediately dissipated, by a subsequent conviction that the danger is entirely imaginary: of the same kind is the terror raised in us, when we stand near the edge of a precipice, or in sight of a tempestuous ocean, or are present at a tragical representation on the stage: in all these cases, as in that of musical expression, the sense of our *security* mixes itself with the terrible impressions, and melts them into a very sensible delight. As to the second instance, that of grief, it will be sufficient to observe, that as it always has something of the social kind for its foundation, so it is often attended with a kind of sensation, which may with truth be called *pleasing. [In the original]*.

2 See *Dissertation où l'on fait voir, que les merveilleux effets, attribuez à la musique des Anciens; ne prouvent point qu'elle fût aussi parfaite que la nôtre. Par M.* BURETTE. *Memoires de Literature, tirez des registres de l'Academie Royale des Inseriptions & Belles Lettres, Tom. septieme*; whence the above fragment of POLYBIUS is translated.

In the fifth, seventh, and eleventh vols. of the *Holland* edition of this collection, the reader will find several entertaining and curious tracts on the subject of Music. *[In the original]*.

3 Spirit of Laws, vol. I. p. 56. *[In the original]*.

44

VITTORIO ALFIERI
(1749–1803), 'MYRRHA', (1786)

In *The Tragedies of Vittorio Alfieri: Complete,*
ed. Edgar Bowrig, 2 vols (London: George Bell,
[1782] 1876), pp. 317–328

Vittorio Alfieri was an Italian dramatist and poet, famous for his tragic plays. Myrrha, excerpted below in English translation, was based on the mythical figure of the same name. The latter was the mother of Adonis, born after she tricked her father into sexual intercourse. Alfieri was moved to tell her story after reading of it in Ovid and bursting into tears. In Alfieri's play, Myrrha intended in marriage to Pereus, but falling in love with her father, refuses to progress the match. Much of the play revolves around her father Cinyras, mother Cecris, and old nurse Eurycleia, trying to understand Myrrha's behaviour. The play ends with the deaths of Myrrha and Perseus. Reflecting the concern with emotional expression found in art and literature of the eighteenth century, the tragedy flourished as form. It was considered particularly suitable as a genre to explore the extremities of human behaviour – such as incest and suicide – and the feelings that would be raised in such contexts. Through attending plays, the public could share in that sublime emotional experience, and Alfieri considered the theatre to be critical to producing a patriotic public sphere. The excerpt below evidences a sentimental account of complex familial feeling, and how it could be deployed to produce sublime and tragic responses in an audience.

. . .

Act I.

Scene I.

Cecris, Eurycleia.

Ce. Come, faithful Eurycleia: now the dawn
Scarce glimmers; and to me so soon as this
My royal consort is not wont to come.
Now, thou canst tell me all that thou dost know
Of our afflicted daughter. Even now

Thy troubled face, and thy half-stifled sighs,
Announce to me . . .

Eu. O queen! . . . Unhappy Myrrha
Drags on a life far worse than any death.
I dare not to the monarch represent
Her dreadful state: the troubles of a maiden
Ill could a father understand; thou canst,
A mother. Hence to thee I come; and pray
That thou wilt hear me.

Ce. It is true, that I
For a long time have seen the lustre languish
Of her rare beauty: obstinate and mute,
A mortal melancholy dims in her
That fascinating look: and, could she weep! . . .
But, when with me, she's silent; and her eyes
With tears are pregnant, though for ever dry.
In vain do I embrace her; and in vain
Request, entreat her, to divulge her grief:
Her sorrow she denies; while day by day
I see her by her grief consumed.

Eu. A daughter
To you is she by blood; to me, by love;
Thou knowest that I brought her up: and I
Exist in her alone; and almost half
Of the fourth lustre is already spent,
Since ev'ry day I've clasp'd her to my breast
In my fond arms . . . And now, can it be true,
That e'en to me, to whom she was accustom'd
From earliest childhood to divulge each thought,
That e'en to me she now appears reserved?
And if I speak to her of her distress,
To me too she denies it, and insists,
And seems displeased with me . . . But yet she oft,
Spite of herself, bursts into tears before me.

Ce. Such sadness, in a bosom still so young.
At first I deem'd to be the consequence
Of the irresolution which she felt,
In the oft-urged selection of a spouse.
The most illustrious, pow'rful potentates
Of Greece and Asia, all in rivalry
From the wide-spreading rumor of her beauty,
To Cyprus flock'd: and, as respected us,
She was the perfect mistress of her choice.
These various impulses, unknown, discordant,

338

VITTORIO ALFIERI, 'MYRRHA'

Might in a youthful bosom well excite
No slight disturbance. She his valor praised
In one; his courteous manners in another:
This with a larger kingdom was endow'd;
In that were majesty and comeliness
Blended consummately: and he who caught
Her eyes the most, she fear'd perchance the least
Might gratify her father. Thoroughly
I, as a mother and a woman, know
What conflicts, in the young unpractised hearts
Of timid virgins, might be well excited
By such uncertainty. But, when by Pereus,
Heir of Epirus, ev'ry doubt seem'd banish'd;
To whom, for pow'r, nobility, and youth,
Valor, and comeliness, and sense, not one
Could be compared; then, when the lofty choice
Of Myrrha gave such pleasure to us all;
When she, on this account, ought to exult
With self-congratulation; we behold
The storm more furiously arise within her,
And more insufferable agonies
Consume her ev'ry day! . . . At such a sight,
I feel my heart as if asunder torn.

Eu. Ah, had she never made that fatal choice!
From that day forth, her anguish has increased:
This very night, the last one that precedes
Her lofty nuptial rites, (O Heav'ns!) I fear'd
That it had been to her the last of life. –
Motionless, silent, lay I in bed,
From hers not far remote; and, still intent
On all her movements, made pretence to sleep:
But I for months and months have now beheld her
In such a martyrdom, that all repose
Flies from my aged limbs. I for thy daughter
The comfort of benignant Sleep invoked
Most silently within myself; for o'er her
For many, many nights he has not spread
His downy wings. Her sobs and sighs at first
Were almost smothered; they were few; were broken:
Then (hearing me no longer) they increased
To such ungovernable agony,
That, at the last, against her will, they changed
To bitter tears, to sobs, to piercing sreams.
Amid her lamentations, from her lips

ART AND CULTURE

One word alone escaped: "Death! . . . death!"; and oft,
In broken accents, she repeated it.
I started from my couch; and hastily
I ran to her: and scarce had she beheld me,
When, in the midst, she suddenly repress'd
Each tear, each sigh, each word; and, recomposed
In royal stateliness, as if almost
Incensed with me, in accents calm she cried:
"Why comest thou to me? What wouldst thou with me?" . . .
I could not answer her; I wept, embraced her,
Then wept again . . . At length my speech return'd.
O! how did I implore her, how conjure her,
To tell me her affliction, which, at last,
Thus in her bosom pent, would, with her life,
My life destroy! . . . Thou surely, though a mother,
Couldst not have spoken to her with more fond,
And more persuasive love. – She well doth know
How much I love her; and, at my discourse,
Once more the torrents from her eyes gush'd forth,
And she embraced me, and with tenderness
To my fond importunities replied.
But still, inflexibly reserved, she said
That ev'ry maiden, when the nuptial day
Approaches, is oppress'd with transient grief;
And she commanded me to hide it from you.
But so deep-rooted is her malady,
So fearful are its inward ravages,
That I run tremblingly to thee; and beg
That, by thy means, these rites may be delay'd:
To death the maiden goes, be sure of this.
Thou art a mother; I say nothing more.

Ce. . . . Ah! . . . choked by weeping, . . . scarcely . . . can I speak. –
Whence can this malady arise, ah, whence? . . .
No other martyrdom, at her young age,
Is there, except the martyrdom of love.
But, if she is inflamed by love for Pereus,
Whom of her own accord she chose, say, whence,
When on the point of gaining him, this grief?
And, if another flame feed on her heart,
Wherefore hath she herself selected Pereus
Among so many others?

Eu. . . . Her fierce grief
Doth not, I swear to thee, arise from love.
She always was observed by me; nor could she,

VITTORIO ALFIERI, 'MYRRHA'

Without my seeing it, resign her heart
To have any passion. And she would, be sure,
Have told it me; her mother as to years,
But, in our love, a sister. Her deportment,
Her countenance, her sighs, her very silence,
Ah! all convince me that she loves not Pereus.
She, if not joyous, was, before she chose him,
Tranquil at least: and thou know'st well how she
Delay'd her choice. But yet, assuredly
No other man pleased her, ere she saw Pereus:
'Tis true, she seem'd to give to him the pref'rence,
Because it was, or so at least she deem'd it,
Her duty to choose one. She loves him not;
To me it seems so: yet, what other suitor,
Compared with noble Pereus, can she love?
I know her to possess a lofty heart;
A heart in which a flame, that is not lofty,
Could never enter. This I safely swear:
The man that she could love, of royal blood
Must be: or else she would not be his lover.
Now, who of these have ye admitted here,
Whom at her will she could not with her hand
Make happy? Then her grief is not from love.
Love, though it feeds itself with tears and sighs,
Yet still it leaves I know not what of hope,
That vivifies the centre of the heart;
But not a ray of hope is gleaming on her:
Incurable her wound; alas, too surely! . . .
Ah, could the death, that she invokes for ever,
Be granted first to me! I should, at least,
Not see her thus by a slow fire consumed! . . .

Ce. Thou dost distract me . . . To these marriage rites
Never will I consent, if they are destined
To take from us our only daughter . . . Go;
Return to her; and do not say to her
That thou hast spoken with me. I myself,
Soon as the tears are from my eyes dispersed,
And my face recomposed, will thither come.

Eu. Ah! quickly come. I will return to her;
I am impatient once more to behold her.
O Heav'ns ! who knows if she has not once more
Been with these frantic paroxysms seized,
While I have thus at length with thee conversed?
Alas! what pity do I feel for thee,

341

ART AND CULTURE

Unhappy mother! . . . I fly hence; but thou,
Ah, linger not! . . . The less that thou delayest,
The more good wilt thou do . . .

Ce. How much delay
Costs me, thou mayst conceive: but I will not
Call her at such an unaccustom'd hour,
Nor go to her, much less present myself
With troubled countenance. It is not fit
To strike her either with distress, or fear:
So modest, timid, pliable is she,
That no means with that noble disposition
Can be too gentle. Quickly go; in me
Repose, as I in thee alone repose.

Scene II.

Cecris.

Ce. What can it be? A year has well-nigh pass'd,
Since I was first tormented by her grief;
And yet no trace whence Myrrha's sorrow springs
Can I discern! Perchance the gods themselves,
Envious of our prosperity, would snatch
From us so rare a daughter, the sole comfort,
Sole hope of both her parents? O ye gods,
'Twere better never to have giv'n her to us!
Venus! thou sublime divinity
Of this to thee devoted, sacred isle,
Perchance her too great beauty moves thy envy?
And hence perchance thou, equally with her,
Reducest me to this distracted state?
Ah! yes, thou wilt that I should thus atone
In tears of blood, for my inordinate,
Presumptuous transports of a loving mother . . .

Scene III.

Cinyras, Cecris.

Cin. Weep not, lady. I have briefly heard
The painful narrative; to this disclosure
Constrain'd I Eurycleia. Ah! believe me,
Sooner a thousand times would I expire,
Than with our idolized and only daughter
Adopt coercive means. Who could have thought
That by this marriage, which was once her choice,

VITTORIO ALFIERI, 'MYRRHA'

She could be brought to such extremity?
But, let it be dissolved. My life, my realm,
And e'en my glory are as nothing worth,
If I see not our only daughter happy.

Ce. Yet, Myrrha ne'er was fickle. We beheld her
In understanding far surpass her years;
Discreet in ev'ry wish; and constant, eager
Our smallest wishes to anticipate.
She knows full well, that in her noble choice
We deem'd ourselves most fortunate: she cannot,
No, never, hence repent of it.

Cin. But yet,
If she in heart repent of it? – O lady,
Hear her: and all a mother's gentle pleadings
Do thou adopt with her; do thou at length
Compel her to unfold her heart to thee,
While there is time for this. And I meanwhile
Will mine unfold to thee; and I assure thee,
Nay, e'en I swear, that, of my heart's first thoughts,
My daughter is the object. It is true,
Epirus' king I wish'd to make my friend:
And the young Pereus, his distinguish'd son,
Adds, to the future hope of a rich kingdom,
Other advantages, in my esteem
More precious far. A gentle character.
A heart no less compassionate than lofty,
Doth he evince. Besides, he seems tome
By Myrrha's beauties fervently inflamed. –
I never could select a worthier consort
To make my daughter happy; and no doubts
Of these pledged marriage rites torment his heart;
His father's indignation and his own,
If we renounced our covenanted faith,
Would be most just; and their rage might to us
Be even terrible: in this behold
Many and potent reasons in the eyes
Of ev'ry other prince; but none in mine.
Nature made me a father; chance, a king.
Those which are deem'd by others of my rank
Reasons of state, to which they are accustom'd
To make all natural affections yield,
In my paternal bosom would not weigh
Against one single sigh of my dear daughter.
I, by her happiness alone, can be

ART AND CULTURE

Myself made happy. Go; say this to her;
Assure her, also, that she need not fear
Displeasing me, in telling me the truth:
Nought let her fear, except the making us,
Through her own means, unhappy. I meanwhile,
By questions artfully proposed, will learn
From Pereus if he deem his love return'd;
And thus will I prepare him for the issue,
No less afflicting to himself than me.
But yet, the time is brief for doing this,
If fate decree that we retract our purpose.

Ce.   Thou speakest well: I fly to her. It brings
Great solace to me, in our grief, to see
That one accordant will, one love, is ours.

Act II.

Scene I.

Cinyras, Pereus.

Pe.   Behold me here, obedient to thy wishes.
I hope, O king, the hour is not far distant,
When with the loving epithet of father
I may accost thee . . .

Cin.   Listen to me, Pereus. –
If thou well know thyself, thou canst not fail
To be convinced what happiness a father
Who loves his only daughter must experience
At having thee as son-in-law. 'Tis certain,
Had I myself been destined to select
A spouse for Myrrha, I had chosen thee
Among the many and illustrious rivals
Who, with thyself, contended for her hand.
Thence, thou thyself mayst judge how doubly dear
Thou wert to me, when by herself elected.
Thou, in the judgment of impartial men,
In all pretensions wert unparagon'd;
But, in my judgment, more than for thy blood,
And thy paternal kingdom, thou both wert,
And art, the first for other qualities
Intrinsically thine, whence thou wouldst be,
E'en if a private man, eternally
Greater than any king . . .

Pe.   Ah father! . . . (I

VITTORIO ALFIERI, 'MYRRHA'

E'en now exult to call thee by this name)
Father, my greatest, nay, my only prize,
Consists in pleasing thee. I have presumed
To interrupt thee; pardon me: but I
Cannot, before I merit them, receive
From thee so many praises. To my heart
Thy speech will be a high encouragement,
To make me that which thou believ'st me now,
Or wishest me to be. Thy son-in-law,
And Myrrha's consort, largely should I be
With ev'ry lofty quality endow'd:
And I accept from three the augery
Of virtue.

Cin. Ah! thou speakest as thou art.
And, since thou art such, I shall dare to speak
To thee as to a son. – I clearly see
Thou lovest Myrrha with a genuine love;
And I should wrong thee most unworthily,
Could I e'en doubt of this. But, . . . tell me now;. . .
If my request is not too indiscreet, . . .
Art thou as much beloved?

Pe. . . . I ought to hide
Nothing from thee. Ah! Myrrha would, methinks,
Love me again, and yet it seems she cannot.
I cherish'd once a hope of her regard;
And yet I hope to gain it; or, at least,
My flatt'ring wishes still prolong the dream.
'Tis true, that, most inexplicably, she
Persists in her reserve. Thou, Cinyras,
Although thou be a father, still retainest
Thy youthful vigour, and remember'st love:
Know then, that evermore with trembling steps,
And as if by compulsion, she accosts me;
Over her face a deadly pallor steals;
Her lovely eyes are never turn'd towards me;
A few irresolute and broken words
She falters out, involved in mortal coldness;
Her eyes, eternally suffused with tears,
She fixes on the ground; in speechless grief.
Her soul is buried; a pale sickliness
Dims, not annihilates, her charms divine: –
Behold her state. Yet, of connubial rites
She speaks; and now thou wouldst pronounce that she
Desired those rites; now, she herself assigns

ART AND CULTURE

The day for them, and now, she puts it off
If I enquire the reason of her sadness,
Her lip denies it; but her countenance,
Of agony expressive, and of death,
Proclaims her great, incurable despair.
Me she assures, and each returning day
Repeats, that she would have me as her spouse;
She says not that she loves me; lofty, noble,
She knows not how to feign. I wish and fear
To hear from her the truth: I check my tears;
I burn, I languish, and I dare not speak.
Now from her faith, reluctantly bestow'd,
Would I myself release her; now again
I fain would die, since to resign her quite
I have no pow'r; yet, unpossess'd her heart,
Her person would I not possess . . . Alas! . . .
Whether I live or die, I scarcely know. –
Thus, both oppress'd, and though, with diff'rent griefs,
Both with affliction equally weigh'd down,
We have at last the fatal day attain'd,
The say which she herself irrevocably
Hath chosen for our marriage . . . Ah, were I
The only victim, of such deep distress!

Cin.   As much as she, dost thou excite my pity . . .
Thy frank and fervid eloquence bespeaks
A soul humane and lofty: such a soul
Did I ascribe to thee; hence to thyself
I will not less ingenuously speak. –
I tremble for my child. I share with thee
A lover's grief; ah, prince! do thou too share
A father's grief with me. Ah, if she were
Unhappy by my means! . . . 'Tis true, she chose thee;
'Tis true that none constrain'd her. but, if fear,
Or maiden modesty . . . In short, if Myrrha
Now should repent her promise wrongfully? . . .

Pe.   No more; I understand thee. To a lover,
Who loves as I do, canst thou represent
The cherish'd object wretched for his sake?
Could I, though innocently, deem myself
The origin of all her wretchedness,
And not expire with grief? Ah! Myrrha, now
Pronounce on me, and on my destiny,
A final sentence: fearlessly pronounce it,
If Pereus' love be irksome; yet for this

346

VITTORIO ALFIERI, 'MYRRHA'

Never shall I regret that I have loved thee.
O, could I make her joyful by my tears! . . .
To me 'twould be a blessing e'en to die,
So that she might be happy.

Cin. Pereus, who
Can hear thee without weeping? . . . No, a heart
More faithful, more impassion'd than thine own,
There cannot be. Ah! as thou hast to me,
Couldst thou disclose it also to my daughter:
She could not hear thee, and refuse to open
To thee with equal confidence her own.
I do not think that she repents her choice;
(Who, knowing thee, could do this?) but perchance
Thou mayst solicit from her heart the source
Of her conceal'd distress. – Behold, she comes;
I had already summon'd her. With her
I leave thee; to the interview of lovers,
Fathers are' ever a restraint. Now, prince,
Fully reveal to her thy lofty heart,
A heart by which all others must be sway'd.

45

SERIES OF PAINTINGS/ PRINTS ON THEME OF 'THE LOVE LETTER'

The lover letter was a key genre of the eighteenth century. Writing manuals provided examples for lovers to copy, novels used the epistolary form to tell love stories, and individual men and women wrote them to each other, as part of courtship rituals undergoing transformation to reflect a growing emphasis on personal choice and love in marriage. Love letters were expected to produce a response in the beloved and were often accompanied by tears or kept close to the body as a symbol of the other. The cultural significance of the love letter in the European imagination ensured that a number of artists represented scenes of people either writing or receiving love letters. These pictures contributed to social commentary around romantic love. That such feeling could be transgressive was evidenced in figures 45.1 and 45.3, where the letter is received under conditions of secrecy; figure 45.2, where it is the subject of gossip between women, is similarly indicative of the love letter as a matter for private, rather than public, concern. The coy glance given by the recipient of the love letter in figure 45.5 is similarly suggestive that decorum might have been breached. Some prints indicate the dangers of secrecy in the exchange of love letters. Figure 45.4 highlights the risk to woman indicating that the love letter had been a form of deceit. The caption reads 'Too plain the lines so faithless prove/ The perjur'd Swain that scorns her Love/ And prove too plain a Sister's Art/ That won the Idol of her Heart'. As sources for the history of emotions that are drawn from across Europe, these prints are evidence of a shared European culture of love, while the representations of these women's bodies and gestures can provide some information about how emotion was displayed on the body – and in these cases, that emotion is not always love! Sometimes the scenes represented directly related to accounts in well-known literature of the period.

Figure 45.1 Jean-Honoré Fragonar (1732–1806), French, *The Love Letter*, oil on canvas, 1770s, The Metropolitan Museum of Art, New York, The Jules Bache Collection, 1949.

Note: for more details see: www.metmuseum.org/art/collection/search/436322.

Figure 45.2 François Boucher (1703–1770), French, *The Love Letter*, oil on canvas, 1750, Courtesy National Gallery of Art, Washington.

Note: For more details see: https://images.nga.gov/en/search/do_quick_search.html?q=%221960.6.3%22.

Figure 45.3 Nicolas Delaunay (1739–1792), Swedish, after Nicolas Lavreince, *Le Billet doux*, etching and engraving, 1778, Courtesy National Gallery of Art, Washington.

Note: for more details see: www.nga.gov/collection/art-object-page.3029.html.

Figure 45.4 E. J. Dumée (active 1790), British, after George Morland (1763–1804), *The Discovery*, engraving, published by John Raphael Smith, 1788, Yale Centre for British Art.

Note: for more details see: https://collections.britishart.yale.edu/vufind/Record/3622148.

Figure 45.5 Thomas Rowlandson (1756–1827), *The Love Letter*, watercolour, c.1790, Yale Centre for British Art.

Note: for more details see: https://collections.britishart.yale.edu/vufind/Record/1670746.